LUXURY® YACHTS
OF THE WORLD

Volume 3
2010

Front Cover, Spine & Back Cover Photographs
M/Y 'Slipstream' courtesy of CMN Yachts
Photographs by: Guillaume Plisson

1st Edition:
September 2009

Published under licence by:
European Seas Limited
88 Christchurch Road, Ringwood, Hampshire. BH24 1DR. UK.
T: +44 (0)1425 472919
F: +44 (0)1425 474368
E: info@luxuryyachtsoftheworld.com
W: www.luxuryyachtsoftheworld.com

Editor: Peter J. Bryant
Features Editor: Janet Bryant

The editor and publisher would like to express their sincere thanks
to all the contributors who have helped us to publish this book.

ISBN13: 978-0-9553757-3-6

The most luxurious yachts in the world belong to the most exclusive club in the world...

Burgess Owner's Club.

BURG

Getting Away
from it all
by OceanStyle

NAVI, Riva Venere 75, for charter

OCEAN

enjoy the journey with us...

UK

28-29 RICHMOND PLACE BRIGHTON BN2 9NA
TELEPHONE   +44 (0)1273 571 722
EMAIL   BRIGHTON@YPIGROUP.COM

FRANCE

RESIDENCE DE LA MER
6 AVENUE DE LA LIBERATION 06600, ANTIBES
TELEPHONE   +33 (0)493 340 100
EMAIL   ANTIBES@YPIGROUP.COM

MONACO

"LE VICTORIA"
13 BOULEVARD PRINCESSE CHARLOTTE
MC 98000, MONACO
TELEPHONE   +337 99 99 97 97
EMAIL   MONACO@YPIGROUP.COM

YPI BROKERAGE

"LE VICTORIA"
13 BOULEVARD PRINCESSE CHARLOTTE
MC 98000, MONACO
TELEPHONE   +377 99 99 97 97
EMAIL   BROKERAGE@YPIGROUP.COM

YPI CHARTER

RESIDENCE DE LA MER
6 AVENUE DE LA LIBERATION
06600, ANTIBES, FRANCE
TELEPHONE   +33 (0)493 340 100
EMAIL   CHARTER@YPIGROUP.COM

YPI MANAGEMENT

28-29 RICHMOND PLACE BRIGHTON BN2 9NA
UNITED KINGDOM
TELEPHONE   +44 (0)1273 571 722
EMAIL   MANAGEMENT@YPIGROUP.COM

YPI CREW

7 RUE HONORE FERRARE
06600, ANTIBES, FRANCE
TELEPHONE   +33 (0)492 904 610
EMAIL   CREW@YPIGROUP.COM

Photograph: Paul Coleshill/rawphoto.co.uk

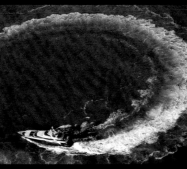

YACHTING PARTNERS

HARGRAVE
CUSTOM YACHTS

Hargrave 100 RPH
'King Baby'

Hargrave 114 RPH
'Sea Legend'

Hargrave 125 RPH
'Cocktails'

Hargrave 84 RPH
'On A Roll'

Squadron 65. The new addition to our family.

INTRODUCTION

Luxury yachts are now built on a global scale with the sheer scope and variety of designs quite astounding. Throughout the year we spend a significant amount of time travelling and researching content for this annual book, with one of the great rewards being the finding of projects, where, due to an owner's vision of a perfect yacht and the painstaking work of the designer and builder, the image actually becomes a reality.

The owner's vision is what drives the luxury yacht industry and it is my privilege to see these yachts as they are built and subsequently launched. One such yacht is featured on the front cover yacht of 'Luxury Yachts Of The World' this year. The 60m motor yacht 'Slipstream' has been built for a highly experienced yachtsman who wanted to create the perfect yacht. Visiting the yacht's builder, CMN Yachts, in Cherbourg, France, the attention to detail onboard was obvious even though several weeks before her launch, she was covered from head to toe in protective material to ensure she was perfect when unveiled. Mile upon mile of cables and piping brought the yacht to life, but it was only due to the skill of such an experienced builder in CMN and the designer, Andrew Winch, that the 'mechanics' of the yacht remained totally unseen when the yacht was subsequently launched. At her launch, her owner creatively described 'Slipstream' when he stated: "More than a yacht – a piece of Art." Indeed she is and she is certainly the perfect yacht to grace the cover of this, the third annual volume of 'Luxury Yachts Of The World'.

Owner's visions are also driving the technology behind building and refitting eco-friendly yachts. Featured in the charter section, the sailing yacht 'Ethereal' was built to highly stringent ecologically sound practices, using the latest modern technology to ensure her carbon footprint on the world is kept to the absolute minimum. Similarly, the wonderfully futuristic Picchiotti-Vitruvius yachts have been designed to minimise drag through the water and maximise the ocean cruising range and low fuel consumption these explorer yachts will need when seeking out the four corners of the world. The concern about the environment is also a concern to owners when they have their yachts refitted and we are delighted to include a special feature by Marina Barcelona '92, one of the world's top refit yards, on how, by following strict codes of practice, they reduce the environmental impact of refits.

In this volume of 'Luxury Yachts Of The World' we have reluctantly omitted the yacht industry directory due to the huge number of yachts we felt we just had to present this year. In reality, we could have featured many more wonderful yachts, but at 4kgs in weight, felt the book was big enough!

Whether you are a yacht owner, a potential yacht owner, or like me, just an avid fan of these wonderful creations, I very much hope you enjoy reading and viewing the wonderful images in this book, and I look forward to bringing you many more examples next year, in Volume 4 of 'Luxury Yachts Of The World.'

Peter J. Bryant
Editor
Luxury Yachts Of The World

'THE SNAPPER'
A SUNSEEKER 37 METRE YACHT

PERLE BLEUE, 2007
124'8 FEET

JEMASA, 2006
164 FEET

FLAMINGO DAZE, 2004
151'6 FEET

MY. TRUST, 2008
147'6 FEET

more space

more stability

more space

The **CURVELLE 33X9** has four decks and a nine meter beam. Which is one extra deck and two meters more beam than a comparable monohull.

As a result the internal and external space for guests, is about 50% more than a traditional 33m and comparable with a 40m > 42m performance monohull.

more stability

It is better to stand on two legs than one. Even at anchor…

It is a well known fact that catamarans are far more stable than monohulls.

more value

Due to clever design and logistics, we have been able to slash the cost by half, without any compromise on quality and safety.

Introductory pricing starts €1m per 1/8 fractional share or €8m for the whole yacht in case of just one owner.

more value

more speed

more flexibility

more speed

The **CURVELLE 33X9** Cruises equally well at a performance speed of 25 knots or at a trans Atlantic – economy pace of 10 knots – and any speed in between.

The most efficient fuel consumption per nautical mile is at about 20 knots and the fuel savings are around 30%.

more flexibility

The 6 double guest cabins with 6 bathrooms on the main deck, can be easily configured into 3 suites, each with his and hers bathrooms…

Whether you cruise with 3 VIP couples; a large group of grand children; or your golfing buddies; the flexible layout can be customised in a few moments by the crew…

www.curvelle.com
videos • specs • brochures • layouts

212 Piccadilly London WIJ 9HG UK
info@curvelle.com • +44 20 7917 2976

…expect more

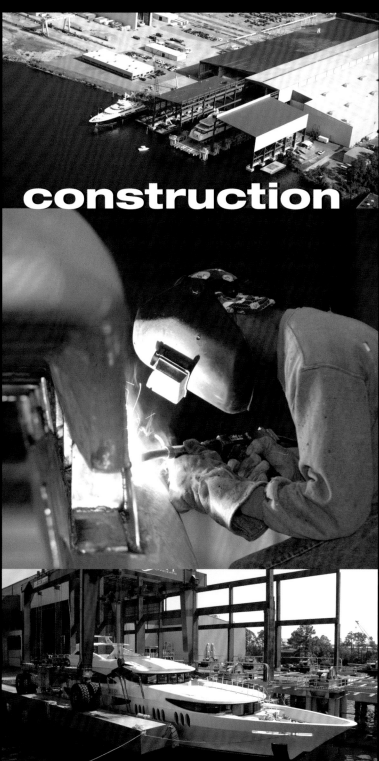

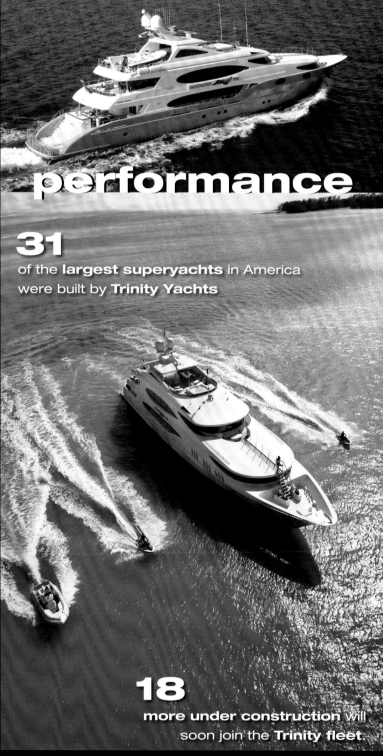

CONTENTS

17   **INTRODUCTION**

55   **SPECIAL FEATURES**

56   New Yachts
68   The Creation Of A Masterpiece
74   All The Pleasure -
     A Fraction Of The Commitment
82   Yacht Insurance Is A Topic
     For The Boss
88   Luxury Yacht Management
     And The ISM Code
94   Merging Interior & Technical Refits
100 Environmentally Friendly Refits
106 Zero Speed™ And Beyond

127 **FEATURED YACHTS**

144 Fairline
158 Oyster Marine
166 Drettmann Group
180 Princess Yachts
192 Wally Power
198 Sunboats Luxury Catamarans
206 Horizon Group
222 Sunseeker 30 Metre Yacht
228 Wally Sail
234 Cyrus Yachts
244 Hargrave Custom Yachts
260 Burger Boat Company
270 Palmer Johnson
284 CRN Shipyard
296 Moonen Shipyards
306 Sanlorenzo
316 IAG Yachts
324 Peri Yachts
338 FIPA Group
348 ISA Yachts
358 Vitters Shipyard

370 Hakvoort Shipyard
386 Soraya Yachts
394 Perini Navi
404 Picchiotti-Vitruvius Explorer Series
410 Aegean Yacht - S/Y 'Galileo'
418 Trinity Yachts
432 CMN Yachts 'Slipstream'
440 Abeking & Rasmussen
450 Lürssen Yachts
460 Oceanco
470 Platinum Yachts

481 **CHARTER & BROKERAGE**

486 What Is A Good Deal
     In Yachting Today
492 A Cruise Aboard 'Nero'
498 A Cruise Aboard 'Linda Lou'
504 A Hellenic Adventure
510 M/Y 'Amnesia'
512 M/Y 'Cloud 9'
514 M/Y 'Natori'
516 S/Y 'Ethereal'
518 M/Y 'Anjilis'
520 M/Y 'Xanadu'
522 M/Y 'Odessa'
524 M/Y 'Kogo'
526 M/Y 'Lady Sheridan'
528 S/Y 'Maltese Falcon'
530 M/Y 'Siren'
532 M/Y 'Elandess II'
534 M/Y 'Va Bene'
536 M/Y 'Boadicea'
538 M/Y 'Nero'
540 M/Y 'Indian Empress'
542 M/Y 'Slipstream'
544 M/Y 'Meamina'
546 M/Y 'Ability'
548 ISA 120

550 M/Y 'La Dea'
552 M/Y 'Momentum'
554 M/Y 'Murcielago'
556 M/Y 'Navi'
558 M/Y 'Dream'
560 M/Y 'Princess Mariana'
562 M/Y 'Latinou'
564 M/Y 'South'
566 M/Y 'Grace E'
568 M/Y 'Tribu'
570 M/Y 'Inevitable'
572 M/Y 'Cyan'
574 M/Y 'Let It Be'
576 M/Y 'Lady Ann Magee'
578 M/Y 'Leonora'
580 AB 116
582 S/Y 'Aventura'
584 M/Y 'Gladius'
586 M/Y 'Ocean Seven'
588 S/Y 'Kokomo'
590 S/Y 'Margaret Ann'
592 S/Y 'Nelson'
594 S/Y 'Red Dragon'
596 S/Y 'Ganesha'
598 S/Y 'Ludynosa G'
600 S/Y 'Moonbird'
602 S/Y 'Nostromo'
604 M/Y 'One More Toy'
606 M/Y 'Katharine'
608 M/Y 'Starship'
610 M/Y 'Domani'
612 M/Y 'Hokulani'
614 M/Y 'Big City'
616 M/Y 'Victoria Del Mar'
618 Newcastle 5500

620 **ADVERTISER INDEX**

620 **PHOTOGRAPHERS**

THE ALL NEW PERI 41M TRI-DECK **PERI 41t**

PERI YACHTS
TURKEY

PERI YACHTS MAIN OFFICE
BAGDAT CADDESI ONCU SOKAK
BUYUKHANLI KONUTLARI B2/10
SUADIYE 34740 ISTANBUL TURKEY
T +90 (216) 464 7030
F +90 (216) 464 7020
INFO@PERIYACHTS.COM

PERI YACHTS SHIPYARD
ANTALYA SERBEST BOLGESI
F ADASI (FREE TRADE ZONE)
07070 ANTALYA TURKEY
T +90 (242) 259 3653
F +90 (242) 259 3654

PERI YACHTS
FRANCE

PERI YACHTS FRANCE
14 AVENUE FREDERIC MISTRAL
PORT ROYAL
06600 ANTIBES
T +33 (0) 493 340 340
F +33 (0) 493 340 923
PERIFRANCE@PERIYACHTS.COM

Please visit our website www.periyachts.com for our distributers list

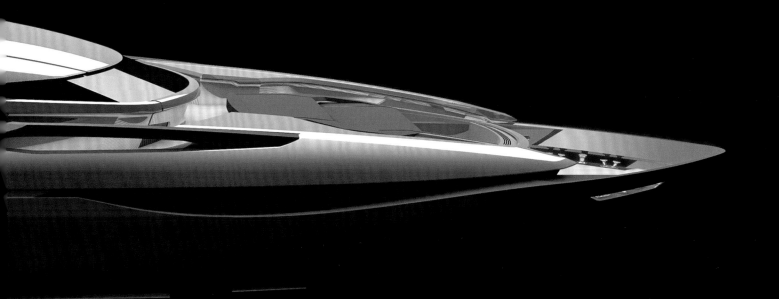

YOU BREAK BOUNDARIES; SO DO WE

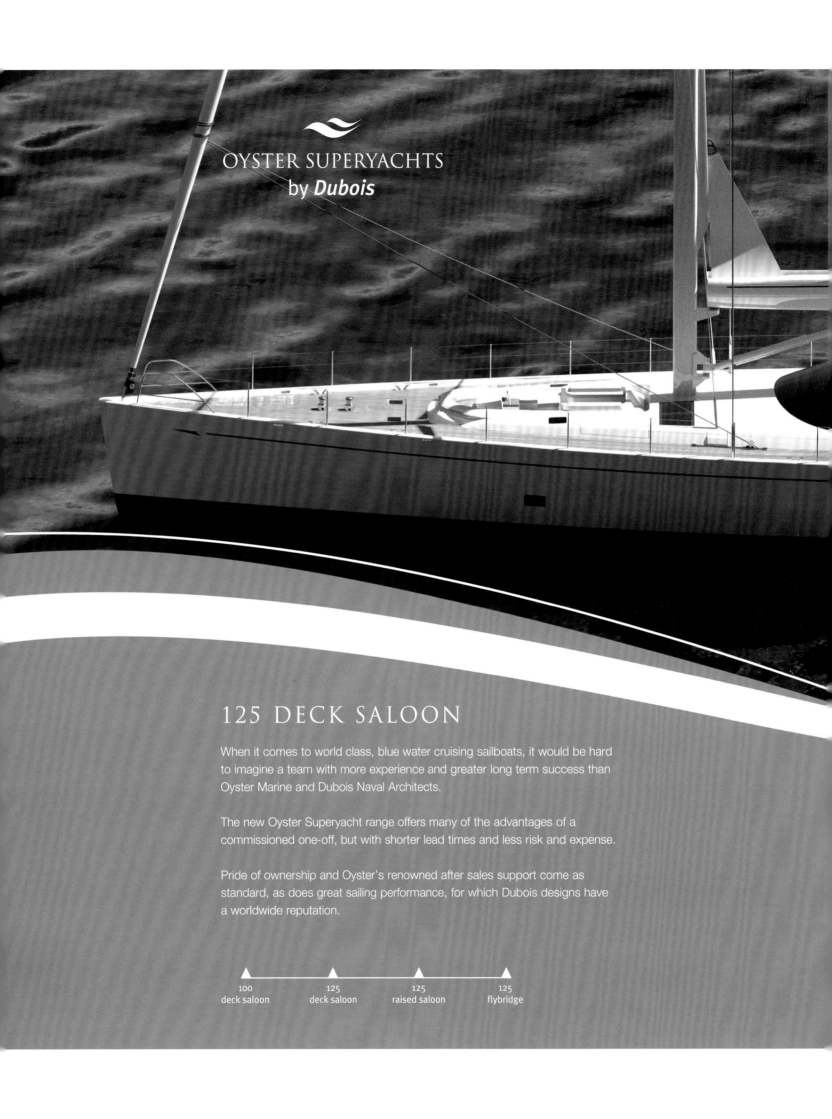

OYSTER SUPERYACHTS
by *Dubois*

125 DECK SALOON

When it comes to world class, blue water cruising sailboats, it would be hard to imagine a team with more experience and greater long term success than Oyster Marine and Dubois Naval Architects.

The new Oyster Superyacht range offers many of the advantages of a commissioned one-off, but with shorter lead times and less risk and expense.

Pride of ownership and Oyster's renowned after sales support come as standard, as does great sailing performance, for which Dubois designs have a worldwide reputation.

100	125	125	125
deck saloon	deck saloon	raised saloon	flybridge

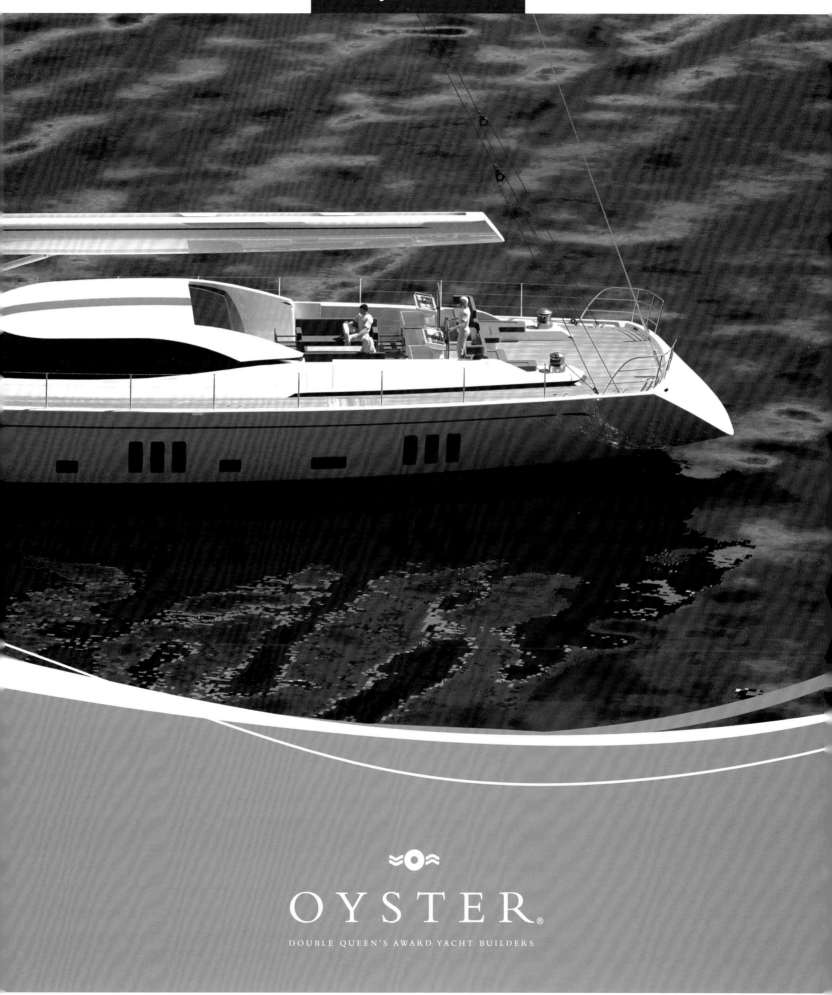

SOME OF OUR
HIGHLIGHTS...

DISCOVER THE MOST GLAMOROUS WAY
OF GETTING FROM A TO SEA.

It's rare these days to see such a sublime combination of teak, steel and canvas at the harbour's edge. Indeed, you need to look right back to the '30s, to the age of the J-Class Yachts, for a comparable sight.

ROLLS
RR
ROYCE

It means that when you drive down to the marina in your new Rolls-Royce Phantom Drophead Coupé, you and your friends will experience the exhilaration of the open sea the second you open the throttle.

Rolls-Royce Motor Cars Limited, The Drive, Westhampnett, Chichester, PO18 0SH
Tel +44 (0)1243 384 000
www.rolls-roycemotorcars.com

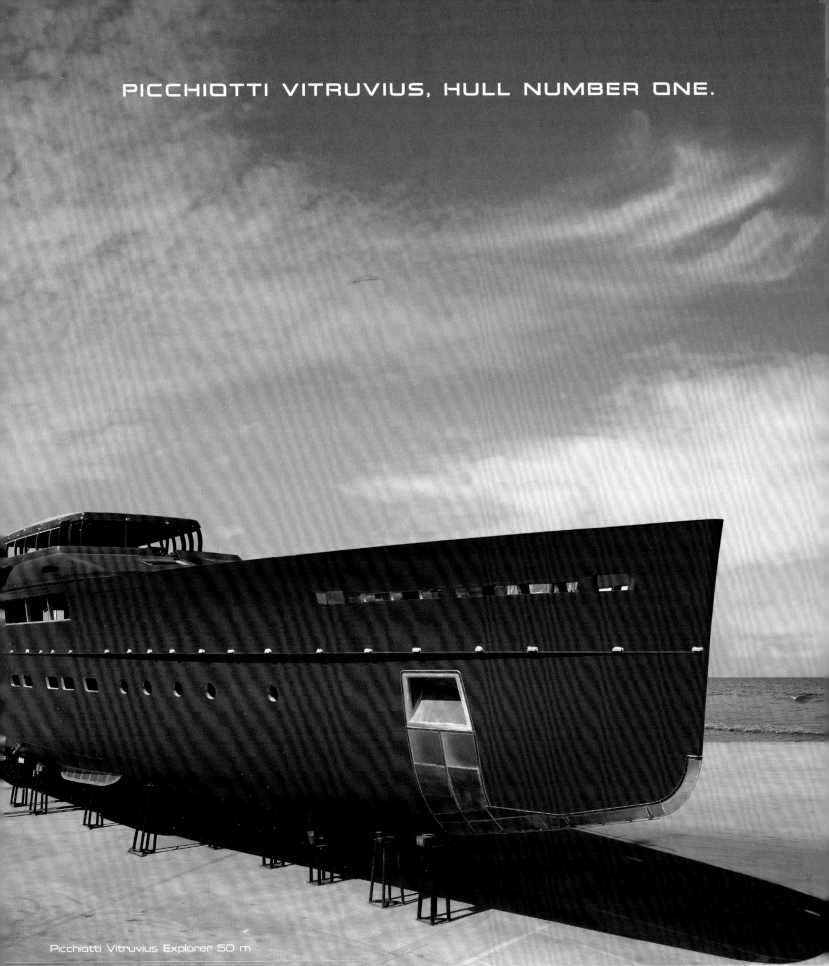

PICCHIOTTI VITRUVIUS, HULL NUMBER ONE.

Picchiotti Vitruvius Explorer 50 m

Racing sloop P2 38 m

SPEED   STYLE   BRIAND   PERINI

PERINI NAVI - PICCHIOTTI - PERINI NAVI USA - PERINI ISTANBUL - YILDIZ - CANTIERI NAVALI BECONCINI

Photography: Ed Holt - Albert Brunsting

NIRVANA, PRIX DU DESIGN MONACO 2008

VITTERS
S H I P Y A R D

CUSTOM SAILING AND POWER YACHTS

Vitters Shipyard B.V. - Stouweweg 33 - 8064 PD Zwartsluis - The Netherlands
tel. +31 (0)38 38 67 145 - fax. +31 (0)38 38 68 433 - info@vitters.com

SLIPSTREAM

SIGNED BY...

ABU DHABI MAR Group

«OUR LATEST REFERENCE»
—— 60m Slipstream ——

CMN
YACHTS

PARIS | CHERBOURG | CANNES | ABU DHABI

WWW.CMNLINE60.COM

ULYSSE NARDIN

SINCE 1846 · LE LOCLE - SUISSE

MAXI MARINE DIVER - 266-33-3A/92

SELF-WINDING. CHRONOMETER CERTIFIED.

WATER-RESISTANT TO 200 M. 18 CT ROSE GOLD.

RUBBER STRAP WITH ROSE GOLD ELEMENTS.

REDEFINING LUXURY AT SEA

Dubai

YACHT BUILDING, CONVERSION, REPAIR,

P.O. Box 17215   Tel +971 4 8833323 / 8833007   www.platinumyachts.ae
Jebel Ali · UAE   Fax +971 4 8833686 / 8833132   E-mail info@platinumyachts.ae

PLATINUM YACHTS

INTERIOR DESIGN AND YACHT MANAGEMENT.

Drydocks World

a **Dubai World** company

IAG Yachts Ltd. Pingsha Yacht ludustry Park-Zhuhai. 519055 China
Ph. +86 756 7720720 Fax. +86 756 7725511 E-mail: info@iagyachts. com

Discover the **IAG127' PRIMADONNA**

Your yacht is our passion

www. iagyachts. com

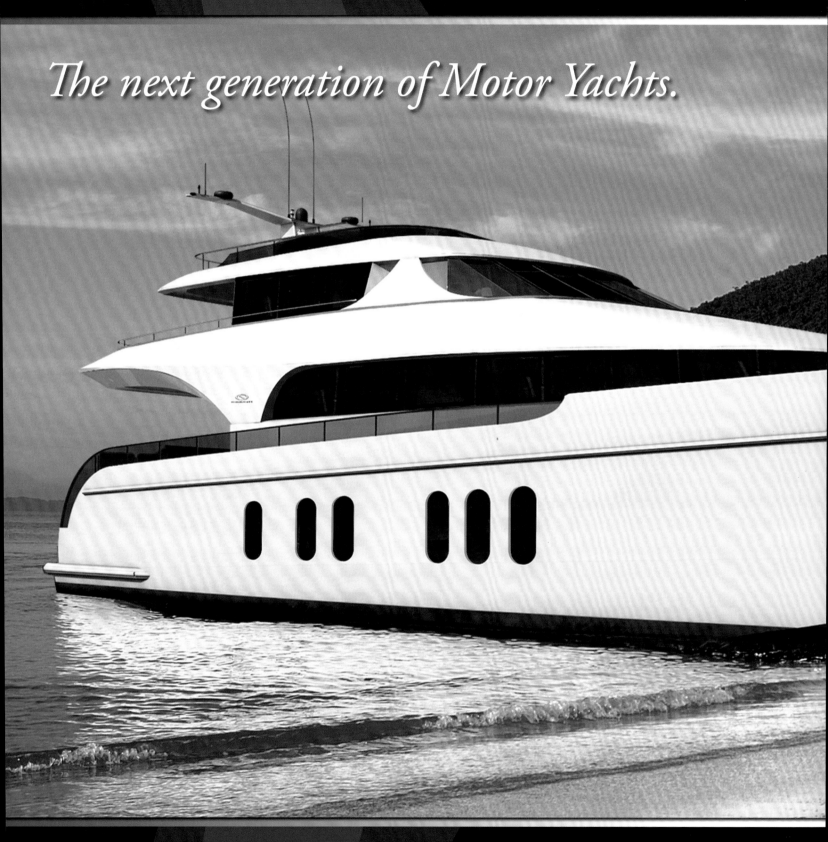

Sunboats Premium

The next generation of Motor Yachts.

M/Y Catamarans

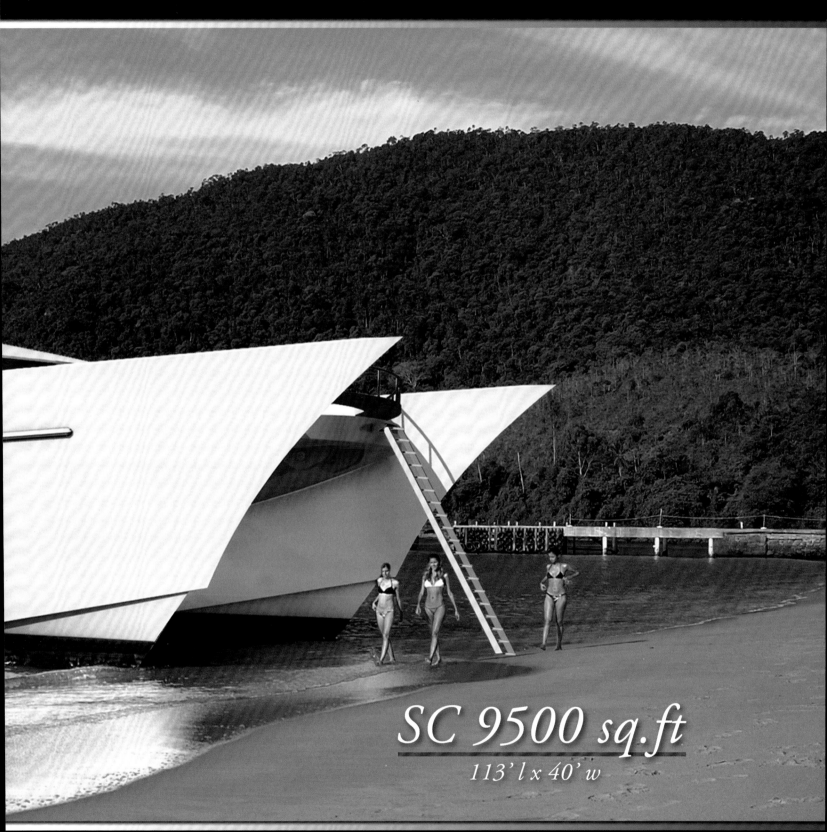

SC 9500 sq.ft

113' l x 40' w

SUNBOATS

LUXURY CATAMARANS

SORAYA
— YACHTS —

THE FUTURE IS GRACEFULLY GLIDING IN

46,5 meters • Stunning appearance • Sleek design & clutter free
Cutting-edge technology and innovations • IP communication
& control • Trans-oceanic range 5.000 n. miles • Stable and
silent • 6,5m diameter helipad • 100m² shaded sundeck with
jacuzzi • 30m² swim platform + 30m² lazarette • 21ft guest tender
and 15ft crew tender • Automatic inflatable fenders • Energy & fuel
efficient Safe & reliable • Classification RINA Charter Class & MCA

To achieve perfection,

we are prepared to invest a great deal of time. But not your time.

68m Motor Yacht
Aviva, launched 2007

»»» Admittedly, when it comes to figures, calculations and deadlines, we are extremely precise. But that is the only way to create a yacht that fully lives up to the strict expectations of our clients.

⊜wallypowerrange

SPECIAL FEATURES

NEW
YACHTS

PICCHIOTTI-VITRUVIUS EXPLORER YACHTS

The Picchiotti-Vitruvius series is a new explorer philosophy born from the alliance of Perini Navi and Philippe Briand. A complete concept of motor yacht design that combines unique aesthetics with efficiency and seaworthiness, these explorer vessels are perfectly proportioned for cruising the world's oceans. This project marks the return of the historical Picchiotti Brand and is already leading the next generation of explorer yachts.

Since the first announcement, two units of this distinctive brand of yacht have already been sold and are currently under construction, namely a 50m aluminium explorer yacht as well as a 55m steel ice class yacht that is able to navigate with strength and elegance through the presence of an ice pack 40cm thick.

www.vitruviusyachts.com

OCEANCO Y708

The latest addition to Oceanco's tailor-made luxury yachts under construction is Y708 – an 85.50m (280.52ft) yacht with an innovative exterior design by Igor Lobanov. With a sleek and elegant silhouette, Y708 is the first superyacht in the 85m range to feature a layered deck design. The design of this spectacular yacht has been based on the notion of privacy which is evident in the layout of both the interior and the exterior deck area. Each deck has its own balcony allowing guests to enjoy themselves in complete privacy.

Y708, which is scheduled for delivery in 2012, is also the first Oceanco yacht to feature an Environmental Protection Notation from Lloyd's Register which serves as a mark of environmental quality. In addition, the yacht's waste, sewage and clear water treatments have been optimized to ensure compliance with the latest environmental rules and regulations.

www.oceancoyacht.com

HAKVOORT YN 246

Hakvoort's Project YN 246 will measure 44.90m in length and have a 9.30m beam with a draught of 2.90m.

This yacht will be suitable for blue water cruising all over the world and will provide stylish accommodation for ten guests and eleven crew.

Designed with a displacement-type hull shape, this yacht will feature flared V-sections in the bow, large overhangs, a moderate deadrise amidships and a canoe stern. Hakvoort and Diana Yacht Design BV are striving to keep the yacht as low as possible, especially where the freeboard and superstructure are concerned.

www.hakvoort.com

Above:
The Picchiotti-Vitruvius 50M.

Left:
Oceanco's Project Y708.

Far Left:
Hakvoort's YN 246.

PLATINUM YACHTS 'TRITON' PROJECT

Next on the drawing board at Platinum Yachts, 'The 'Triton' Project' is an 88m diesel / electric yacht, soon to be constructed in Dubai. With exterior design and styling by the well-respected Sam Sorgiovanni Designs in Australia, and with the naval architecture under the supervision of Azure Naval Architects from The Netherlands, this stunning yacht will have a pedigree second to none. The project started towards the end of 2007 in close collaboration with the yacht's owner, the aim being to develop a superior looking mega-yacht with the ability to utilise the basic parameters of the vessel as a platform for future developments at the shipyard. Platinum's strategy for this project was to use well-known and experienced subcontractors for all the design and intrinsic works and couple them with the yard's experienced local workforce in Dubai in order to economise on outlay.

www.platinumyachts.ae

HARGRAVE 125 RPH

Already the market leader in fully customised yachts in the 70' – 100' range, Hargrave Custom Yachts is continuing to expand upwards, first with the launch of the new Hargrave 114RPH 'Sea Legend' and later this year with the launch of the new Hargrave 125RPH and the Hargrave 135 Tri-Deck. These yachts are being built for existing Hargrave owners who appreciate the time and attention to detail that Hargrave takes to ensure they receive their dream yacht.

The new Hargrave 125' Raised Pilothouse 'Cocktails' is being built for an existing Hargrave owner who likes to entertain. Featuring an extensive fly bridge, a huge interior and plenty of areas for open-air dining, she has European styling with full 'wrap-around' windows and will have luxurious accommodation for at least ten guests. As with all Hargrave yachts, the new 'Cocktails' is being built to the highest quality and safety standards and will soon be gracing the warm waters of Florida and the Caribbean.

www.hargrave.org

Right:
Platinum Yacht's 'Triton' Project.

Below Left:
The Hargrave 125 RPH.

Below Right:
The Peri 41T.

PERI 41T

Peri Yachts is taking its ultra-cool brand of high-tech luxury to new lengths with its first 41m triple-deck yacht. This superyacht is now in production and is scheduled for delivery in 2010. Designed as the crowning glory of this dynamic Turkish shipyard's range of cutting-edge composite yachts, the Peri 41T will arguably leave traditional luxury yachts in its wake.

In terms of construction, the Peri 41T uses the latest in high-tech yacht building materials. Its glass-reinforced epoxy sandwich structure makes it lighter and stronger than traditional yachts of its size making it capable of remarkably high speeds.

The Peri 41T is recognisable by its swooping profile giving it a sleek racy look. Expected to deliver a maximum speed of 25 knots from its twin MTU 12V4000M93L engines, together with superb handling, stability and safety, at a cruising speed of 20 knots, she will achieve a 1250 nautical mile range.

www.periyacht.com

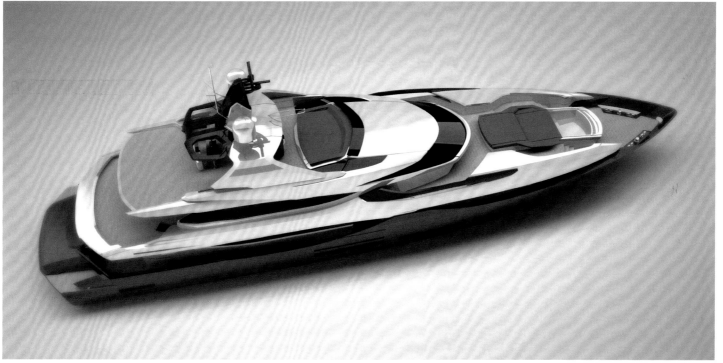

The Briand 181 was designed with a discerning yachtsman in mind - one who is seeking to combine the performance and sea presence of a racing yacht with the comfort and sophistication generally associated with a twin-deck vessel. The very sleek modern hull lines enhance the performance and the waterline length has been stretched to maximum capacity thanks to the vertical bow. With a length of 55.12m (180' 10"), the Briand 181 is a light displacement yacht with Alustar construction and with her lifting keel, she is expected to have unrivalled upwind performance for this type of sailboat.

Comfort and practicality are ensured by a streamlined twin-deck layout. On her lower deck, the spacious guest and master cabins have been designed to meet the demands of today's experienced yacht owner. Built with originality and style the floors of the main-deck cockpit and deck salon are on the same level, both areas opening out onto the exterior, whilst remaining completely sheltered. A fixed hard top protects the cockpit from all weathers and a cutting edge glass superstructure covers the whole of the deck salon area.

With a ketch sail plan and a mast height of less than 59 m (194'), the Briand 181 is able to pass under the Panama Bridge and with a roached mainsail and mizzen, the large upwind sail area is approximately 1,485 m² (15,985 sq ft). She is the ultimate yacht for an experienced owner who is looking for a yacht with the highest standards of craftsmanship as well as the speed associated with a 50m+ (165'+) yacht with a gross tonnage of less than 500.

www.philippebriand.com

SPECIFICATIONS:	**S/Y BRIAND 181**
Length overall:	55.12m (180' 10")
Beam:	10.68m (35')
Draught:	4.80m / 6.80m (22' 4" / 15' 9")
Displacement:	300 ton
Upwind sail area:	1,485 m² (15,985 sq.ft)
Downwind sail area:	2,823 m² (30,387 sq.ft)
Accommodation:	6 guests + 2 crew
Hull Construction:	Composite

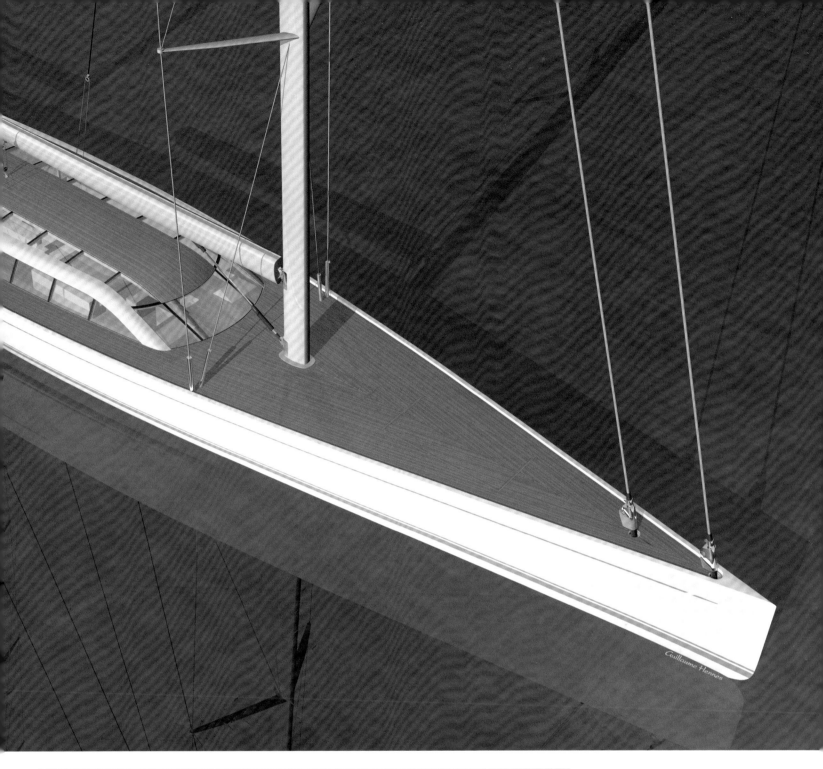

Above & Left:
The Briand 181 is a light displacement yacht with Alustar construction and with her lifting keel, she is expected to have unrivalled upwind performance for this type of sailboat.

SUNSEEKER 'ZEUS' YACHTS

With its 2009 announcement of Project Zeus, the ever evolving, UK-based Sunseeker International took that single step so significant in large yachting – across the 150ft (46 metre) threshold. And the pace hasn't let up. The project has now launched an entirely new brand - the Zeus range of tri-deck motor yachts.

Never shy of committing to investment in product development, Sunseeker is set on following the first 150ft Zeus (46 metre) launching in 2011, with proposed launches of the 164ft Zeus (50 metre) in 2012, and then the 180ft Zeus (54 metre), again just one year later in 2013.

That is quite some roll-out, and the last and biggest of the trio will mark yet another significant first for the yard, the move into aluminium construction, - the necessary expertise is already in place with top metal yacht practitioners on board.

The first two Zeus models, the 150 and 164, will however, be built in composite material. Because of the less space-hungry structural constraints of composites compared with metal fabrication, these first Zeus yachts will achieve far greater accommodation and engineering spaces than any metal equivalent. Building at a level that would make even the world's largest custom yacht builders jealous, for the Zeus yachts, yacht owners can even specify a completely different superstructure, should, for example, a more traditional European or US 'feel' be desired.

With large-yacht owners increasingly looking for reduced fuel and maintenance costs, the Zeus range also introduces a new modified form of displacement hull, optimising displacement speeds of around 11-14 knots, yet still delivering near optimised top-end 28-knot performance. The first-in-line Zeus 150 will be powered by twin MTU 12-cyliner 4000 engines which have so many ratings they will match any owner's view on performance. And range? An easy 4,000 miles for that all-important non-stop transatlantic range.

There are many unique features planned for these extraordinary looking yachts, with clamshell balconies to the main deck master suites being a prime example. Without doubt the yachting world will wait with baited breath for the 2011 launch of the first 'Zeus' Yacht.

www.sunseeker.com

Right & Below:
Combining sleek looks, spacious luxury and high performance, Sunseeker's Zeus Yachts are keenly anticipated.

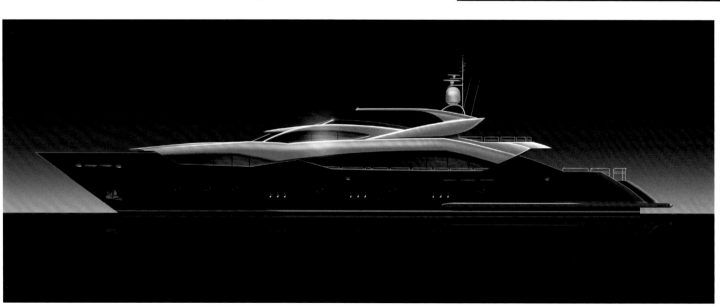

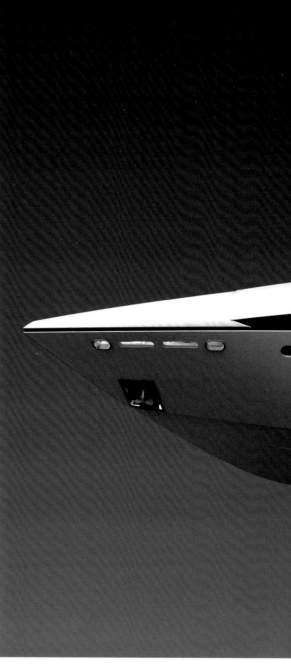

NEW YACHTS

SUNSEEKER PREDATOR 130

The Sunseeker Predator 130 is due to be launched in the autumn of 2009. Following the highly successful introduction of the 37 Metre, 34 Metre and 30 Metre Yacht range, this new performance orientated design provides customers with even greater choice.

Created for those who revel in high living and relish the freedom of extended cruising, the Predator 130 offers unsurpassed luxury and strong blue-water credentials. The bigger the boat the tougher the demands placed on it, which is why the Predator 130 is designed, built and equipped to the highest recognised standards. The Predator 130 has Sunseeker's proven hard-chine hull and trademark high decks. Sunseeker knows from experience that its deep 'V' hulls offer good sea keeping qualities, making this performance superyacht easy to handle in all sea conditions and a pleasure to travel on for extended trips.

The Predator 130 also has all the features expected on a luxury ocean-going vessel, such as the latest navigation equipment with radar/chart-plotter and colour GPS display. Built to the most stringent criteria, computerised engine management systems provide constant fine tuning, which not only improves efficiency and performance but guards against malfunction. Advanced use of hydraulics and electrical systems make the Predator 130 safe and reliable over long distances.

Ingenious layouts, deluxe features and ultra-spacious accommodation make this a vessel that ten people can share comfortably, enabling guests and crew to live aboard for extended periods. Opening side balconies, an extended beach deck and a large fly bridge add even more space for owners and guests to enjoy the seamless link between interior and exterior comfort. The ingenious design of the Predator 130 enables a crew of up to eight to move freely around the boat without intruding on guests.

www.sunseeker.com

Above & Left:
*The Sunseeker Predator 130 offers
unsurpassed luxury and strong
blue-water credentials.
Onboard, opening side balconies, an
extended beach deck and a large
fly bridge add even more space for
owners and guests to enjoy.*

DUBOIS YACHTS

'Dubois Designed' is a phrase synonymous with the very best in the world of superyachts – numerous plaudits and awards have been heaped on the design team headed by Ed Dubois.

Ed Dubois started Dubois Naval Architects in the 1970's and Malcolm McKeon became a partner in the business in 1981. They have played an integral role in the development of the modern sailing superyacht.

Dubois currently has a number of new projects in the planning or construction phase, including the stunning 46m Dubois Fast Cruising Sloop illustrated here.

This new construction has a covered cockpit lounge with just one step between that area and the interior salon, hence the unbroken line of the roof that extends over the cockpit. There is also excellent visibility from inside the salon, including when seated.

The steering stations are on the aft deck of the yacht and the levels have been worked so that there is very good visibility over the superstructure. Moreover, the steering wheels are positioned well outboard and there are clear sight lines down the wide side-decks.

This concept has an owner's cabin aft with four further guest cabins and four crew cabins.

The keel has a fixed draft of 4.5 metres with a dagger board extending to 7 metres when sailing up-wind. The sloop rig is the maximum height for clearing the Panama bridge.

Construction is intended to be in aluminium, while care will be taken to keep the interior and other weights down to improve performance, but without compromise to the noise and vibration insulation.

Below are examples of Dubois' most recent launches, the beautiful 45m 'Salperton IV' and the very elegant 51.7m 'Mondango'.

www.duboisyachts.com

Below Left:
The new 46m Dubois fast cruising sloop.

Right:
The 45m 'Salperton IV'.

Below Right:
The very elegant 51.7m 'Mondango'.

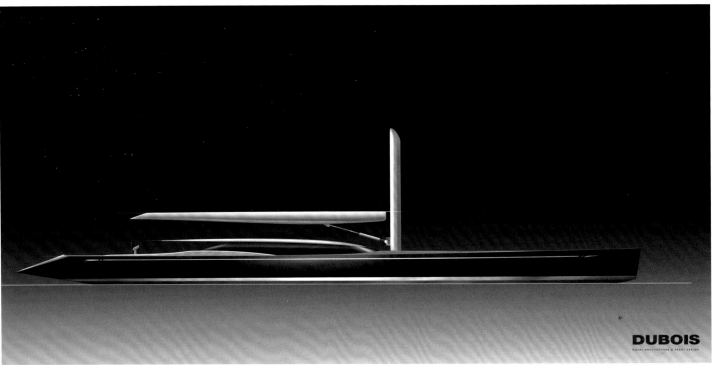

DUBOIS
NAVAL ARCHITECTURE & YACHT DESIGN

THE CREATION OF A MASTERPIECE

The inside story of the creation of 'Slipstream',
one of the world's finest motor yachts.

Early in 2009, the first of the CMN Line 60 superyachts was launched in Cherbourg. "This yacht has exceeded my expectations," declared the proud owner of his new 'Slipstream' at the recent naming ceremony at the CMN yard. He added: "My friends and colleagues in my home town of Sydney, Australia were intrigued to know why I had chosen a French yard to build my new yacht. My answer was simple. The French build the Airbus, the best aircraft in the world, so they will be able to do the same job with my boat."

The reference to Airbus is understandable as Quantas, the Australian carrier, took delivery of the massive 525 seat A380, the first of twenty A380 aircraft ordered by the company from Airbus.

'Slipstream's owner's trust in CMN was well founded. Constructions Mécaniques de Normandie is now a well established and highly respected French shipyard located at Cherbourg. Employing approximately four hundred skilled workers, the yard covers all the various specialities required for the construction of luxury yachts

or navy ships. Since the foundation of CMN in 1945, over 350 vessels in wood, aluminium, steel and advanced composite materials have been delivered. Today, CMN is able to build or refit sailing and motor yachts up to 70m.

The construction is done entirely under 48,000m² of covered facilities. CMN has significantly-sized building sheds, one of 161m x 22m and another of 80m x 22m, as well as a 3000 ton Syncrolift for moving yachts under construction prior to launch.

CMN uses the highly sophisticated computer assisted CIRCE-CATIA for modern design and shipbuilding technology. The CATIA software, also used in the aeronautics industry, is a powerful tool able to integrate complex systems resulting in optimised internal space. This software linked to modern digitally controlled plasma-cutting machines, together with modern automatic welding equipment, enables CMN to maintain a very high standard of hull construction and ensures that CMN is able to optimise designs to exactly fulfil clients' requirements.

The owner of 'Slipstream' was introduced to CMN Yachts by the broker Edmiston. The major yacht company Burgess was then engaged for the project management and building process in the capable hands of Mark Tanner.

Jonathan Beckett, CEO of Burgess recalls the purchase and the new-build programme of the 'Slipstream' project. "The client's involvement with CMN yachts began

Above:
The owner of 'Slipstream' brought with him a clear vision of how to move the Line 60 concept forward to the level of detail and innovation seen in this yacht.

Left:
The official launch of the CMN built 'Slipstream'.

Far Left:
Transporting the yacht from the yard to the water is an impressive sight to behold.

THE CREATION OF A MASTERPIECE

when 'Bernie III', a fine 58m (190ft) CMN motor yacht, came on the market. The 58m 'Netanya 8' (the original name of 'Bernie III') was under construction at the time and was the perfect opportunity to view a CMN Line 60 hull from a first hand position. Following this visit, a two-boat deal was struck with the owner of 'Slipstream', with friends of the owner taking a second yacht named 'Cloud 9'. At this point Burgess was retained by both owners to supervise the build project. Burgess was the ideal choice as the company has a complement of sixteen naval architects and engineers available to support new build projects with technical supervision and the various approval processes involved."

Jonathan continues: "Right from the start, an excellent working relationship was created with all the people at the CMN shipyard, that carried on throughout the whole build programme with full co-operation and a flexible support mentality. Although there was economy of scale with two yachts being built in the same basic time frame, we had the challenge, along with Andrew Winch Designs, who were employed as the principal designers and stylists to the project, to produce two world-class yachts within a sensible budget. Our goal, along with the yard and design team, was to deliver excellent value for money. Seeing the end result of 'Slipstream' we all feel we have achieved this and more – a truly sparkling result. Everyone involved at CMN responded to suggestions and worked hard to deliver engineering solutions. This close working relationship was the key to added value throughout all areas of the finished yacht."

A spokesman for CMN Yachts commented; "The owner of 'Slipstream' brought with him a clear vision of how to move the Line 60 concept forward to the level of detail and innovation seen in this yacht. His last 43m luxury yacht served as his bench mark and along with his experienced captain, they were able to advise us on the important features and details incorporated in this next level of the CMN Line 60 DNA."

Tested in the world's oceans 'Netanya 8', 'Slipstream's predecessor, was used as another bench mark to further develop a larger version, with a refined hull length and characteristics with specific refinements requested by the owner, his captain and team.

The redesigned 60m CMN Line 60 hull offers a wide application of custom layouts and creative thinking because of its large volume. The Andrew Winch Design solutions for this yacht are a direct evolution from the highly acclaimed 'Netanya 8' and keep many of the key features and layouts. However, with several new design features added, the experience gained on this yacht also means that the next CMN Line 60 will benefit greatly from this ground breaking work.

Andrew Winch commented on the overall design philosophy and how he and his team captured the owner's imagination and turned his dreams into reality. "The chosen style is a balance of 'classic modern' and 'tribal' as the owner did not want a 'flamboyant' yacht interior. Sensible finishes, such as matt coatings where finger-marking may occur were used, together with rich figured woods and leather panels. The careful use of mirrors not only creates spatial effects but multiplies the investment value, as seen in the master cabin where high cost leather wall coverings seem to rise up to a second level. Over time, charter guests will remember this 'tribal' feature, resulting hopefully in

Above & Far Left:
*'Slipstream' takes shape in one of
CMN's large covered building sheds.*

Left:
*'Slipstream' and 'Cloud 9' alongside
each other at CMN's quay in
Cherbourg prior to delivery.*

THE CREATION OF A MASTERPIECE

CMN Yachts

51 rue de la Bretonnière, BP539
50105 Cherbourg, France
Tel: +33 2 33 883 020
Fax: +33 2 33 883 198
Web: www.cmnyachts.com
Web: www.cmnline60.com

CMN Yachts are part of the
ABU DHABI MAR Group

future bookings. The owner himself took on the position of the 'chief of the 'Slipstream' tribe', allowing him to have his personal totem poles crafted and displayed onboard".

One point that Andrew wanted to emphasise, was how the engineers at CMN fully supported his design team both with the exterior architecture and the interior design and fit-out. "Take the fire doors as a good illustration of forward thinking and engineering understanding," he remarks. "They are fabricated larger than the apertures to ensure that the final finishing hides them to perfection. All the engineering follows this thinking and the final result is a true world-class product that makes us so pleased to work with CMN."

On sea trials, several timed runs confirmed a speed of 17 knots, a good 0.7 knots above the specified figure. The higher speed is achieved through a longer displacement length than 'Netanya 8' and a flatter aft section that provides less drag and lift. This also results in a longer potential range.

'Slipstream' was due to be in the Mediterranean in the spring of 2009 and Jonathan Beckett of Burgess outlines the charter position. "There is no doubt that 'Slipstream' will be a head-turner. Her predecessor, a black and silver 44m motor yacht also named 'Slipstream', had a strong charter following, through our own charter programme. The new yacht will certainly have the 'wow' factor and under normal charter conditions would have expected a full diary for the coming months ahead. In today's market place, the charter opportunities are greatly reduced but 'Slipstream' has charters booked and could well buck the trend for the season ahead".

On a personal note Jonathan added: "The owner of 'Slipstream' is a very personable client and we really enjoyed the whole process of building his yacht. As an anecdote, I remember the occasion when the owner, Andrew Winch and myself, all shoe-horned into a small private plane one cold, rainy day to fly from the UK to Cherbourg to visit the yacht – almost a 'boy's day out' – we

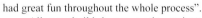

had great fun throughout the whole process".

All new-build luxury yacht projects are a very personal journey for an owner, investing time, intellect and passion over a period of many months to realise a dream. 'Slipstream' is now ready to create her own while sailing the world's oceans.

At the naming ceremony, the owner announced that 'Slipstream' was "more than a yacht, it is a work of art." Without doubt, anyone who is fortunate enough to cruise aboard this magnificent yacht will certainly agree with him.

Above:
Constructing the interior is a highly complex task.

Left:
Fairing the bow.

Centre & Left:
'Cloud 9' at her official launch.

All Photographs:
© Yvan Zedda, Superyacht Media.

ALL THE PLEASURE - A FRACTION OF THE COMMITMENT

curvelle

There is more than one way to own a superyacht. With the high cost of purchasing and maintaining a superyacht in these difficult financial times, the concept of 'Fractional Ownership' has found a highly receptive market. There are a number of differing schemes on offer, but Curvelle has developed a system that allows the owners a much greater level of flexibility and freedom of choice than other systems currently available and is therefore far closer to full ownership of a superyacht.

Up to eight owners can share the title of one of the new Curvelle 33X9 catamaran motor yachts. Each has an eighth share (12.5%) of the company which owns the yacht and as Curvelle itself retains no financial interest in the yachts the owners jointly have 100% of the equity in the vessel and full control of the asset. Each share is offered at the introductory price of 1m Euros and the scheme is structured so that no VAT is applicable to either the

Above:
Stunning to look at and highly original, the Curvelle 33X9 will turn heads wherever she cruises.

Left & Far Left:
The main salon and dining areas will be spacious and luxuriously furnished.

ALL THE PLEASURE - A FRACTION OF THE COMMITMENT

purchase of the yacht, or a majority of the maintenance and servicing costs.

Each owner has a basic entitlement to five weeks cruising - usually three weeks in the Mediterranean and two in the Caribbean - making Curvelle fractional ownership far more economical than chartering an equivalent yacht for this period. The Curvelle team has exceptional experience in running luxury yachts of this size and are capable of handling the attention to detail needed to satisfy the discerning owners of a world-class superyacht. Curvelle will undertake the management function of the yachts, providing crew, maintenance and arranging movement of the yacht from the Mediterranean to the Caribbean, taking advantage of the respective seasons and maximising the period available for cruising.

To ensure the owners can make the most of the time available to them, Curvelle has incorporated a rotating priority system to manage each owner's desired times onboard and providing a unique benefit to the purchase. The system was initially designed for British Airways for its pilot rotation and was later fine-tuned for the property market, before being structured for Curvelle by one of the original developers of the programme, Steve Last.

Luuk V. van Zanten, Marketing Director of Curvelle, commented: "Working with Steve Last, we have been able to bring his innovative and well tested system to the benefit of our superyacht owners. It provides unrivalled flexibility and is as near as possible to the freedom of owning the entire yacht without any of the worries often associated with yacht ownership. Our management will enhance the experience by ensuring the owner and his family know they are aboard their own yacht as soon as they step aboard. Details such as diet, drink preferences, family photos and furnishing layout will all be ready for the owner's arrival."

Owners can purchase more shares, if available, at any time and can, of course, sell their shares too. Any unused weeks on the yacht can be offered for charter if desired by

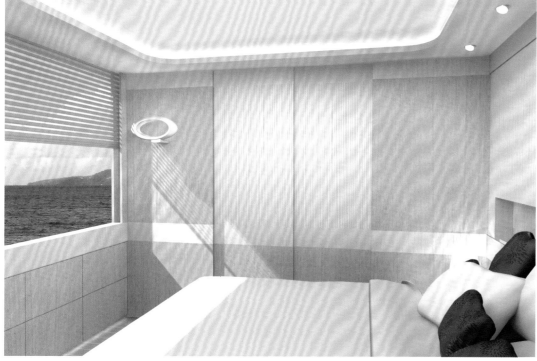

Above:
*Capable of high performance, the
Curvelle 33X9 is also very stable.*

Left & Far Left:
*All of the guest staterooms are light,
airy and command maginificent views
of the outside world.*

ALL THE PLEASURE - A FRACTION OF THE COMMITMENT

the owners, which can provide a substantial supplement to the running costs. Curvelle Fractional Ownership provides a genuine alternative to the much higher costs and concerns of full ownership. However, if an owner wishes, the exceptional Curvelle 33X9 can also be bought outright.

As a catamaran, this is no ordinary superyacht. Designed by Incat Crowther Naval Architects, with exterior styling by Luc Vernet and interior design by Lila Lou, the stunning accommodation offers 50% more space than an equivalent length mono-hull. The advantages continue when it comes to performance: speeds of up to 25 knots and a cruising range of 3000 nautical miles are achieved from the highly efficient catamaran hull design which needs around 30% less thrust to propel her to rapid cruising speeds. This results in frugal fuel demands making the Curvelle 33X9 a far greener option than her mono-hull competitors. With more space, higher performance and lower running costs, the Curvelle 33X9 represents outstanding value at about half the total cost of any similar performance mono-hull, whether purchased outright or with fractional ownership.

Built at the award winning Cheoy Lee Shipyard, the twin hulls of the Curvelle design offer her passengers a considerably more stable platform than a mono-hull, either at speed or at anchor, which will delight the less experienced guests on the yacht. Every luxury has been built into the eye-catching design, incorporating a remarkable level of accommodation flexibility. Six luxury en-suite double cabins can be swiftly changed by the crew to suit the requirements of the owner on a particular cruise: fewer guests and the accommodation can be changed to provide just three large suites, each with individual his and hers bathrooms. Whichever layout is selected, every guest space will offer superb views through extra large windows and beautifully designed glass partitions.

On deck the Curvelle 33X9 really excels with plenty of room for the owner and guests to enjoy their luxury cruising. With a 9 metre (nearly 29 feet) beam the yacht

Above:
When at anchor, the expansive deck space of the Curvelle 33X9 can be fully appreciated.

Left:
The aft upper deck is perfect for relaxing.

Far Left:
One of the guest bathrooms.

ALL THE PLEASURE - A FRACTION OF THE COMMITMENT

offers lounging and al-fresco dining on three deck levels. To board the tender, a lift takes the guest to water level where the tender is lowered into its dock area. This is also an ideal facility for less mobile guests to enjoy the yacht more fully.

This outstanding superyacht is being constructed to the very highest standards in glass fibre composite by this highly respected ISO 9001:2000 certified shipyard, ensuring that both construction and equipment are appropriate for use in warm climates and extended cruising.

The greater market available to superyacht owners at this much lower financial commitment is sure to maintain a high resale value for the Curvelle 33X9, an important factor to consider in the continuing global economic difficulties. With considerable interest from European and UAE customers, and a new design already in its latter stages, Curvelle is set to build a strong reputation in the yacht development of Full and Fractional Ownership markets in the years to come.

212 Piccadilly, London
W1J 9HG. United Kingdom
T: +44 20 7917 2976
M: +44 7509 160 234
Fax +44 20 7917 2977
W: www.curvelle.com

Specifications:	Curvelle 33X9
Length:	33m (108' 3")
Beam:	9m (28' 10")
Draught:	2.7m (8' 8")
Displacement:	130 tons
Engines:	2 x Caterpillar C32
Generators:	2 X Northern Light
Tender:	6m Limo tender
Classification:	DNV & MCA
Price:	€ 8,000,000
1/8 Fractional share:	€ 1,000,000

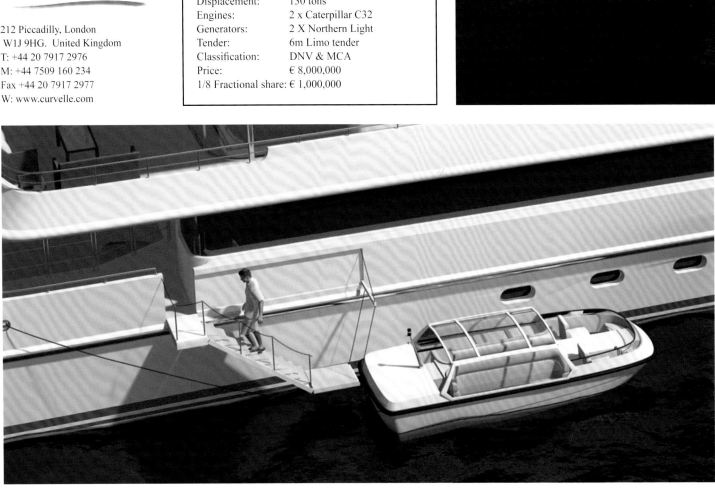

Above & Far Left:
Every detail has been thought of on the Curvelle 33X9 - including the docking of tenders alongside.

Left:
The sun deck features a Jacuzzi, a large dining table and wet bar and an abundance of loungers.

YACHT INSURANCE IS A TOPIC FOR THE BOSS

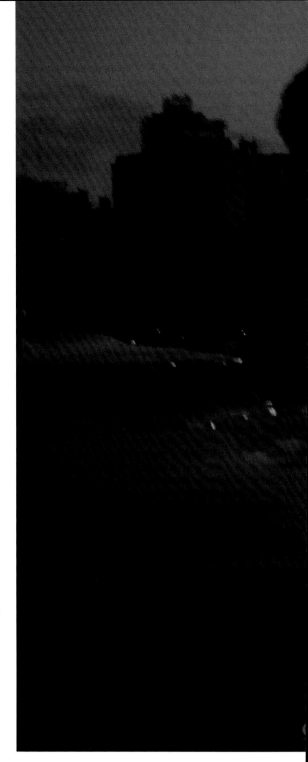

by Martin Baum,
Managing Director

There is an old saying that yacht owners love their yachts more than anything else. However, when it comes to insurance, it seems that this topic is not so close to their hearts. The owner is mainly interested in the bottom line price and assumes that the "small print" is sorted out by their captain, yacht broker, lawyers, secretary or by a professional yacht management company. The lack of interest in yacht insurance could lead to unpredictable exposure in liabilities for the owner. The owner's priority is often to protect their assets first (hull insurance) and then to think of their personal liability exposure. It is important to look at the liability side of owning a luxury yacht, as the financial risk can be considerably higher than the value of the yacht.

If, for example, a yacht has a paid crew on board, the owner can be held personally liable for the well-being of his crew. For English-flagged yachts (red ensign) it is compulsory to buy employer's liability insurance with a minimum level of £5million sum insured per employee. This even applies to seasonal workers and/or deck hands. The question that often arises is: At what point is somebody considered to be employed? A crewmember does not always need to have a written employment contract to fall

Above & Left:
Fire and collision damage are just two
factors which can lead to an owner
facing a liability claim.

under the requirements of employer's liability. To make things even more complicated, the owner must also be aware that crew protection varies with the nationality of the crewmember, beneficial owner and flag registry. For US crew members or US owners, the remedies protecting paid crew members litigating in the United States can result in damages that could be substantially higher than found in Europe. Therefore, it is very important to assess the risk properly and buy the right insurance, as well as the right limit of cover when it comes to crew liability. It is advisable for owners to consult a professional yacht insurance provider, such as Pantaenius, to assist them in protecting their exposure.

Moreover, yacht owners should understand the issue of third parties being mentioned as co-assured on their yacht policy (e.g. professional yacht management companies, marinas, etc.). Taking the example of yacht managers, there are many good reasons why they should be named on the policy as they could be seen as another "captain" ashore, and therefore they could be held liable for their actions in connection with the yacht. However, as they are professional subcontractors, they normally should have their own errors and omissions insurance and these costs should not be carried by the yacht owner. Finally, the owner must make sure that mistakes made by the professional yacht managers will not prejudice his/her insurance cover. This so called "Manager's Non-Liability" clause is a must-have for the owner and should be implemented.

Another important point is the issue of "Waiver of subrogation". Yacht owners must be very careful when signing such a clause as the owner could loose his insurance cover if underwriters have not consented to this clause. A waiver of subrogation is a means for the shipyard to transfer the shipyard's liability to the client. In other words, the shipyard does not take any responsibility for the yacht while it is based at the yard (except in the case of gross negligent and/or wilful act by the shipyard). Often the shipyard's insurance is not sufficient to insure the high values of today's superyachts. Therefore, the shipyard protects itself by requesting a waiver of subrogation from the owner's yacht insurance. With Pantaenius Yacht insurances this kind of endorsement is calculated on a case-by-case basis and varies with the length of stay, scope of refit work, professionalism of the shipyard and the scope

PANTAENIUS
Yacht Insurance

Above & Left:
Damage to the environment is a constant concern if a yacht goes aground.

Centre:
Crew can be in harm's way if there is a fire onboard or a yacht runs aground.

Far Left:
A luxury sailing yacht is a highly complex machine.

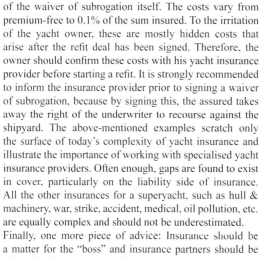

of the waiver of subrogation itself. The costs vary from premium-free to 0.1% of the sum insured. To the irritation of the yacht owner, these are mostly hidden costs that arise after the refit deal has been signed. Therefore, the owner should confirm these costs with his yacht insurance provider before starting a refit. It is strongly recommended to inform the insurance provider prior to signing a waiver of subrogation, because by signing this, the assured takes away the right of the underwriter to recourse against the shipyard. The above-mentioned examples scratch only the surface of today's complexity of yacht insurance and illustrate the importance of working with specialised yacht insurance providers. Often enough, gaps are found to exist in cover, particularly on the liability side of insurance. All the other insurances for a superyacht, such as hull & machinery, war, strike, accident, medical, oil pollution, etc. are equally complex and should not be underestimated.

Finally, one more piece of advice: Insurance should be a matter for the "boss" and insurance partners should be selected with care. A detailed individual risk assessment that takes in the legal set-up of the owning company and the manning issues of the yacht is paramount to having a "water tight" insurance cover.

A FREE POLICY CHECK FROM PANTAENIUS

Insurance contracts should be checked regularly and adapted to the current situation. Pantaenius offers all its customers and interested parties from the superyacht sector a free policy check and a detailed risk assessment.

Regular checking of the amount insured is right at the top of the list because, after all, every yacht owner would like to be reimbursed the cost of an equivalent boat from their insurer in the event of a total loss. Owners should generally avoid a drastic over- or under-insuring of their yacht in their own interest. Particular attention must also be paid to the choice of insurer: One who reimburses the insured amount as a 'fixed sum insured' without any "ifs" or "buts"

should be chosen.

It also makes sense to check some other elements of your policy regularly: For example, your cruising area. Is it still relevant? In general the cruising area should not be too wide as this could cost extra premiums. Do you really need all of Europe or the full East coast of America?

Conversely, if they have been chosen too narrowly, then gaps in cover must be closed otherwise the insurance cover is affected when it comes to making a claim. An occasional charter is also an extremely critical point if this has not been specified in the policy.

If, on the other hand, it has been contractually specified, but it is de-facto never practised, then the premium can be reduced! Have new works of art or antiques been taken on board? Are the tenders and waterborne toys sufficiently insured, including those that have been bought new? Is the crew adequately insured? Do the crew's medical and accident insurances also cover leisure activities? Is there sufficient coverage for the owner in the case of work related liability claims from the crew? Can excessive or unwarranted claims from other parties or marina operators be adequately defended in the event of a claim? Do the nautical practice and qualifications of the captain and crew suffice?

Pantaenius will help you to clarify these and many other questions free and without obligation. Just ask us and we will be delighted to respond.

Above:
Enjoy the upside of yachting without the fear of liability.

Left:
Collision damage to valuable classic yachts is always a risk at regattas.

Far Left:
Even simple tasks such as cleaning the yacht can put crew potentially at risk.

LUXURY YACHT MANAGEMENT AND THE ISM CODE

by Adrian McCourt
Watkins Superyachts

R ichard Rogers' high-tech modern Lloyd's building dominates the view from the London office of Watkins Superyachts. The sight may seem incongruous to the first time visitor seeking a large yacht service compared to the more predictable maritime locations of their competitors, but the relevance of the location soon becomes apparent and symbolises both the history and foundations of this company.

Originally established as an in-house risk management consultancy to a leading Lloyd's marine underwriter, the enterprise developed in an environment where safety, risk management and financial transparency were absolute pre-requisites. The business's integrity and stability were soon seen as appealing attributes to clients and demand for consultancy spread to assureds, established yacht management companies and owners. The team were well positioned to respond to demand, having staff with strong maritime backgrounds in safety, operational support

and fleet management. Senior managers have held both commercial vessel and large yacht command.

In the early days, Watkins provided safety consultancy and designated persons ashore to a number of yachts and market-leading yacht management companies before obtaining their own 'Document of Compliance' under the ISM Code and establishing themselves as yacht managers in their own right. Staff with a background in luxury yacht support, professional legal practice and financial administration were then able to provide a sound basis for full management and expansion away from a purely City of London base.

As the company has developed, it has applied the ethos of compliance and financial transparency to asset management and offers this to clients, recognising that, in practical terms, any system introduced on board a yacht must be appropriate and user-friendly. It benefits no-one for a manager to dump a pile of manuals and contracts on a captain's desk and expect compliance with complex and seemingly irrelevant systems without question or explanation. The relationship needs to be one of partnership, mutual respect and integrity. Watkins' senior managers regularly attend managed yachts and encourage positive relationships with crews at every level, be it management support to the Captain or essential crew training.

Management has undoubtedly had a poor press in recent years, particularly with the hard-pressed Captain.

Above:
'Pelorus'.

Left:
The superyacht 'Triple Seven' is one of many operating under the guidance of Watkins Superyachts.

Far Left:
Watkins Superyachts is strategically placed opposite the world famous Lloyd's building in the City of London.

LUXURY YACHT MANAGEMENT AND THE ISM CODE

Mutual mistrust and multi-million dollar budgets usually make uncomfortable bedfellows. There are, however, compelling benefits to be gained from employing a manager, even if only for ISM and ISPS support, not least of which is that multi-million dollar assets attract massive liabilities for the owner. The owner may be better served by a partnership between a Captain and a resourceful manager that protects him professionally, rather than leaving it to an individual who is already burdened with ever increasing statutory obligations and the boat's fundamental raison d'être, a pleasing environment for the principal. Adrian McCourt, Watkins' Managing Director, comments: "There are individual Captains who have self-managed and done so to the entire satisfaction of all throughout their time in command, but this is about risk management - fiscal as well as physical - and the cost of being over reliant on a Captain may be more than the owner bargained for in an increasingly litigious and regulated world".

This became more apparent during the early days of the ISM Code. Owners of commercially registered yachts over 50m in length were suddenly faced with having to comply with a unique piece of legislation that, for the first time, brought legal responsibility ashore. The commercial shipping industry had several years' head start and Watkins' managers had been involved with this since the turn of the 1990s. By the time this became mandatory for yachts, a sub-industry of expensive and not always effective ISM consultants had developed, seemingly charging by the page for written manual text. This resulted in the misconception that the level of compliance is directly proportional to the amount of paperwork generated. Watkins' staff have clear views of how ISM should be responsibly and reasonably applied to the large yacht industry. The key remains simplicity and not losing sight of the fundamental aims of the Code - safety and prevention of pollution. Safety management systems were produced which provided full compliance with the Code, whilst the company measured its own success by the brevity of the product. Watkins' safety management system has been commented on favourably by

Right & Below Left:
The superyacht 'Triple Seven' is one of many operating under the guidance of Watkins Superyachts.

Below Right:
'Pelorus'.

both end users and flag state registries. To further improve ease of access, Watkins has had its safety management system reproduced electronically and whilst there is still a need for some on-board documents to be available as hard copies, the ultimate aim of one day producing a paperless system remains possible, if not probable.

Despite its critics, the ISM Code has undoubtedly improved safety and environmental care at sea, to the extent that owners are requesting Watkins Superyachts to provide a mini-ISM service to implement on yachts that are not required to have it by law. A simple on board reporting system, a DPA with resources and a responsible emergency response capability provide peace of mind for the owner.

An added benefit of Watkins' style of astute asset management is that there will be a beneficial impact on the resale value of a yacht that has been properly managed. This applies to management both on board and ashore, particularly when the yacht is maintained to a standard demanded by the more stringent flag states and classification societies.

Whilst there are undoubtedly 'easier' registers and classification societies, this only makes life simpler for the crew and managers. Watkins does not encourage this route as it is of no real benefit to the owner and is careful to encourage new and existing owners to take the course that is of more benefit to them, if marginally more arduous for the crew and managers.

LUXURY YACHT MANAGEMENT AND THE ISM CODE

Watkins
SUPERYACHTS

Watkins Superyachts
St Helens, 1 Undershaft
London EC3A 8EE. UK
Tel: +44 20 7886 3900
Web: www.watkinslondon.com

The ISM Code is, of course, not a cure-all for safety and environmental protection, and the smart user will recognise that it is essentially a management tool that complies with flag state regulations and provides a documented management system. Used properly, it should serve for both manager and seafarer to work in partnership for the greater good. Watkins recognises that the principle ingredient of a successful yacht, and indeed the management company, is the people, and puts the human factor above all others. Training, both in-house and external, is essential to maintaining and improving crew performance. Indeed, crew retention is an important factor to many owners and the company encourages owners who wish to retain good manning to support formal training, private health schemes and cost effective but attractive remuneration and leave packages.

Any company is only as good as its employees and partners, and Watkins Superyachts has been fortunate enough to secure quality staffing from yacht and commercial ship management companies. Acting under the premise that a company should only do what it can do well, Watkins Superyachts has entered into agreements with a number of independent market leaders to support and enhance its service to its clients. Continuing the theme of London based quality services, the company has joined with Air Harrods - who provide the highest standards of safety and service - to provide aviation to their clients, with MAST for the provision of unparalleled maritime and asset security services and with Masters, who are able to offer innovative time charter solutions.

The company's unique relationship to the insurance market allows clients access to first class insurance cover at competitive rates. Indeed, one yacht under full management is considered to be one of the world's most comprehensively covered boats. In this case, the owner is happy to pay the appropriate premium in order to avoid any inappropriate financial surprises in the event of a claim. Of course, cheapest is always best when buying insurance if the buyer has absolutely no intention of suffering a loss

and making a claim. Caveat emptor!

As the business has progressed from a management company to a wider service company within the large yacht industry, clients have been particularly drawn to Watkins Superyachts' ability to execute discreet yacht acquisition or disposal through its London or overseas offices. This has been of particular interest to owners who wish to purchase existing yachts, projects under construction, or yachts within a certain specification that may not be for sale on the open market, and similarly for owners who wish to dispose of assets without attracting publicity.

The company takes a particularly keen interest in bringing new owners and projects into the market. In the case of aspiring owners, there is a need to walk through the entire process with the client to avoid the many pitfalls, cliques and jargon that await the newcomer. Similarly, the company is pleased to bring new ventures to the market as central agents, such as the forthcoming Kestrel Superyacht project. This will introduce an innovative Ron Holland design encompassing space, grace and pace into a 106' sailing yacht.

Watkins Superyachts continues to grow in new areas, but remains firmly rooted in its core business of management with integrity, stability and simplicity.

Above & Left:
The beautiful 'Kestrel Superyachts' are being built in association with Watkins Superyachts.

Far Left:
Watkins Superyachts has a strategic partnership with Air Harrods.

MERGING INTERIOR & TECHNICAL REFITS

FOR ADDED YACHT CHARTER AND SALE VALUE

With an asset value frequently between €20million and €100million, a luxury superyacht can often earn upwards of €5million per year in charter revenues (based on 20 weeks charter at €250,000 per week).

That said, in today's challenging times, maintaining and enhancing a yacht's value is extremely important if a yacht is to be chartered or sold to her full potential value. As with any valuable asset, a yacht in 'first-class' condition will attract significantly greater charter revenues and sales revenue when sold. More than that, as a yacht is, in many cases, a visible statement of the owner's status, a well-maintained yacht says a great deal about the professionalism of the person who owns it.

In times of recession, it is easier than ever to put off much needed refit work and save the money for more lucrative times. However, this can in itself prove counter-productive, as the charter revenues and increased sales revenue of a yacht will, in most cases, far exceed the capital invested in a refit. Just as a house is often refurbished when it is sold or offered for rent, so keeping a luxury yacht in good condition is of paramount importance, if it is to be successfully chartered or sold.

MERGING INTERIOR & TECHNICAL REFITS

![AP logo] 1987-2007 vent'anni · Arredamenti Porto

More information on Arredamenti Porto's services may be obtained from:

Arredamenti di Porto
Tel: +39 010 2770410
Fax: +39 010 2461103
Web: www.arredamentiporto.it

Arredamenti Porto is arguably the Mediterranean's leading specialist in building and installing new interiors onboard yachts. With a huge 2,000m² interior workshop located directly next to the company's yacht berths in Genoa, Italy, and backed up by another expansive 4,000m² workshop close by, where complete interiors may be assembled prior to installation, Arredamenti Porto boasts one of the finest yacht interior refit facilities in Europe.

Many luxury yachts, and particularly charter yachts, have only limited periods of downtime if they are to maintain their charter or operating schedule. This frequently leads to case scenarios whereby a yacht can only be out of service for 2-3 week stretches. To resolve this frequent problem, Arredamenti Porto has pioneered a system for 'Interim Refits', where refits are undertaken in several 'stages', with for example, the second stage of a refit being planned while work is being undertaken on the first stage of the refit.

This revolutionary concept can be applied even to the most complex of interior refits, so that for example, a yacht's salon can be refitted in, say April, the yacht could charter in the busy event season of May; have her staterooms refitted in June, then be back online for charters throughout the summer season. This fantastic interim refit system, pioneered by Arredamenti Porto, results in reduced 'downtime' and most importantly, does not affect the yacht's charter earning capacity.

WHAT ABOUT THE OTHER ASPECTS OF A REFIT?

Though one of Europe's leading specialists at refitting and renewing luxury yacht interiors, Arredamenti Porto is also a 'full-service' refit yard with on-site facilities for every refit aspect and a dry-docking facility catering for yachts up to 150m in length. These include:

i) Topside and bottom painting and fairing;

ii) Design, fitting and alteration of metal works, such as extending top decks, to fitting stern configurations;

iii) Complete electrical, mechanical and plumbing configurations, including fitting new engines and engine rooms and installing the latest navigational, communication and other bridge systems.

The key thing to ask a refit yard when planning a refit and especially when planning an interior refit is whether they are able to undertake all the work themselves on the premises, or very close to the premises. Very few yards can honestly answer, "yes" to this question. Arredamenti Porto can, which is why over the years it has established a reputation as one of the world's premier luxury yacht refit yards.

WHAT ABOUT REFERENCES?

Of course, another great way to check out whether a refit yard is as good as it says it is, is to ask for references from other yacht owners and captains. Over the past few years, Arredamenti Porto has refitted many beautiful superyachts.

If you are looking to refit or convert any aspect of your yacht, give Arredamenti Porto a call. They will be pleased to provide you with all the information you need and all the references you will require.

Above:
When drydocking is required, the company has one nearby suitable for all sizes and types of superyacht.

Left:
Most structural works can be undertaken alongside Arredamenti Porto's workshops, without the expense of drydocking the yacht.

Far Left:
Arredamenti Porto's highly experienced craftsmen ensure a high quality job every time.

ENVIRONMENTALLY FRIENDLY REFITS

Traditionally, refitting a luxury yacht created a lot of mess and used a large amount of power, both of which had adverse effects on the general environment. With global concern on environmental issues such as climate warming and sea pollution at an all time high, luxury yacht owners are increasingly demanding that luxury yacht refit yards take an active stance to become more environmentally friendly.

As one of the leading superyacht refit facilities in the world, Marina Barcelona 92, located right in the heart of Barcelona, Spain, decided to adopt a pro-active environmental policy to not only reduce the environmental impact of its business activities, but also to lead the way and introduce better environmental practices in the superyacht industry.

Obtaining its ISO 14001 environmental management certification through Lloyd's Register in 2008 was only the start of the company's broad spectrum of initiatives towards environmental sustainability. Recently, a dedicated Environmental Working Group within the company was created. This group, consisting of a team of three of its dedicated managers, is studying, proposing and implementing sustainability programmes in the yard.

An example of one of these programs is Carbon Offsetting. For this, the yard offers its clients the option to offset the carbon emissions from the shore power electricity consumed during the yacht's stay at the yard. Through its Carbon Offset partner, Yacht Carbon Offset, the money is used to support independently verified emissions reduction projects, such as green energy. This way, each tonne of CO_2 emissions from the yacht is balanced by an equivalent tonne of atmospheric CO_2 reductions from the project. Moreover,

SPECIAL FEATURES

Above & Left:
Marina Barcelona 92, located right in the heart of Barcelona, Spain, has decided to adopt a pro-active environmental policy to not only reduce the environmental impact of its business activities, but also to lead the way and introduce better environmental practices in the superyacht industry.

ENVIRONMENTALLY FRIENDLY REFITS

for every kWh that its clients offset, MB´92 will match this by making an identical investment in order to offset office, business travel and other yard energy consumptions. In addition, Marina Barcelona 92 has recently employed an external company to carry out a full environmental audit of the shipyard and its activities, so as to assess where energy savings can be made and how the yard's business impacts on the air, soil and sea quality. Most importantly, it will also recommend how these effects can be reduced. It is expected that the outcome of this audit will allow for decisions to be made that will benefit both the environment and also the efficiency of the business itself. Put simply, if the energy, water and fuel costs can be reduced within the yard, then so the yard's costs will be reduced and ultimately the costs to its valued clients.

With its vast sun oriented roof surfaces covering both its main building and its 120m paint shed, Marina Barcelona 92 is studying the feasibility of installing a considerable number of solar panels to generate part of its own electricity. Taking matters a stage further, 'recycling' is a key word within the yard. Waste separation for recycling is facilitated by providing every yacht in the yard with three different containers; one for plastic, one for paper and one for general garbage. A glass container and reception points for oil, paint and other contaminated materials are also located on site. Other subjects being studied include a recycling plant for fresh water being used for pressure washing yachts on the hard and rainwater capture facilities.

As one of the founding members of the recently established ICOMIA SuperYacht Refit Group, Marina Barcelona 92 is acting as a driving force to improve the environmental best practice issues, not just with the other members of the Group, but throughout the operational and maintenance side of the superyacht sector. In close co-operation with ICOMIA, the yard is currently working on compliance with the European Union's solvents emissions legislation. The ICOMIA SuperYacht Refit Group will also aim to improve waste reception facilities, both in their own facilities and in marinas. It is now the case that more and more yachts are willing to adopt waste separation policies on board, but are unable to then dispose of their separated waste due to a lack of shore-side facilities. Under the ICOMIA umbrella, Marina Barcelona 92 is actively co-operating with marina associations worldwide to improve

Right:
MB'92's 120m state of the art covered paint shed is in constant demand by the world's largest yachts.

Below Left:
Superyachts like the 73.3m (240')
'Silver' can take advantage of MB92's modern synchrolift system.

Below Right:
Many refits and maintenance work can be undertaken without the need to drydock the yacht.

ENVIRONMENTALLY FRIENDLY REFITS

their practices as well. With a lot accomplished and currently under way, there is still a large array of possibilities that are yet to be explored and implemented. MB'92 feels that through the co-operation with other major players in the Refit Group, a momentum can be created towards more sustainability in the industry, both in the shipyards and the marinas, on board and at sea.

MARINA BARCELONA 92

Marina Barcelona 92 provides refits, repair, service and maintenance works to more than 70 superyachts per year with a length from 35m up to 125m. This unique service is located in the port of Barcelona, a strategic stop-off point for the yachts on their journey between the Mediterranean and the Caribbean.

The company's facilities cover a surface area of 36,000m^2, making MB'92 one of the largest yacht yards in the Mediterranean and one of the most important facilities in the world specialising in megayacht repair, refitting and maintenance. One of the shipyard's important areas is the 12,000m^2 zone utilised for dry docking works, for which the 2,000-ton Syncrolift is used. A dry dock system that was built according to the specifications of Lloyd's Register was delivered in the year 2000 and has a transfer system with sufficient capacity for up to seven yachts measuring up to a length of 80 metres each. In addition, a 150-ton Travelift with a hard standing area of 15,600 m^2 is available for dry-docking works, while a floating dock is available, capable of handling the world's biggest yachts up to a maximum length of 117m (384ft) with a maximum weight of 4,300 tons.

Finally, Marina Barcelona 92 boasts a covered and afloat paint shed with the capacity to accommodate vessels of up to 125 metres in length. Managed by the prestigious company PINMAR, the paint shed has been designed to paint yachts completely afloat, meeting the most stringent quality requirements and environmental standards.

With a staff of 80 direct employees distributed throughout the company's various departments, an additional 800 contractors working in the shipyard spread over workshops and sub-contracted services repairing and maintaining the yachts, Marina Barcelona 92 offers a warm welcome to yachts to visit its wonderful facilities.

More information on refitting and maintaining luxury yachts may be obtained from:

Marina Barcelona 92
Tel: +34 93 224 02 24
Email: info@mb92.com
Web: www.mb92.com

Above, Left & Centre:
The motor yacht 'Sedation' recently underwent a full interior and exterior refit at MB'92, with stunning results. Photographs: Thierry Ameller.

Far Left:
The extensive MB'92 facilities.

ZERO SPEED™
AND BEYOND

Quantum

Back in 1999 a small but enterpprising fourteen year old company based in Florida, Quantum Marine, implemented the first successful application of a stabilization system that could not only stabilize the vessel when the ship was sailing, but also when the yacht was at anchor. This innovation would prove to have some far reaching impacts on the global market for owning and chartering mega yachts. It is well known that the majority of time spent aboard these yachts is with the yacht either in a port or when the yacht is at anchor.

In the past, owners, their guests and charter parties accepted the fact that the yachts would roll when they were at anchor and sometimes in port as well. The fact that the yachts would roll when anchored did serve to restrict the market somewhat, due to the fact that many people are very sensitive to such motions. After all, who in their right mind would spend hundreds of thousands of dollars per week to expose themselves to the discomfort and inconvenience of living aboard a constantly rolling platform?

Given that challenge, the group of technicians at Quantum brought to bear all of their experience, knowledge and most of their resources to explore this opportunity. The company had a significant amount of experience in improving conventional stabilizer performance by upgrading the control systems. Over the relatively short period of three years, Quantum supplied its control technology to over 350 yachts with remarkable success and the company gained a reputation as somewhat of a miracle worker for yachts fitted with older and outdated

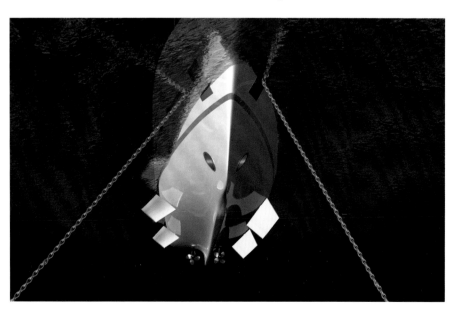

systems. Quantum's control designer, a Dutchman, had developed what was, at that time, the most sophisticated control technology that was commercially available for the private sector. He had also been involved in a previous but unsuccessful attempt to provide stabilization with a vessel at anchor and he therefore understood the challenges. The first application did not go without its ups and downs and, after several false starts, the system was eventually tested and proven in the year 2000 - to the great relief and satisfaction of both the customer and the Quantum team. Word of this first application spread rapidly and, within a very short time, Quantum had orders from other owners who wished to have this unique enhancement installed on their yachts.

The term, "Zero-Speed™" was added to the nautical dictionary and it helped define a new chapter to nautical knowledge, called roll stabilization. Since its introduction in 1999, Quantum's Zero-Speed™ stabilization has added immeasurably to luxury yachting and expanded cruising options, particularly when encountering exposed anchorages. Currently, there are over 500 yachts enjoying

Above:
Quantum Zero Speed™ Stabilizers are fitted to many of the world's largest superyachts.

Far Left:
An artist's drawing showing Quantum Zero Speed™ Stabilizers in action with the yacht at anchor.

Left:
A Quantum Zero Speed™ Stabilizer in its extended position.

ZERO SPEED™ AND BEYOND

the system, varying in size from 28m (92') to 164m (540'). From a performance standpoint, no other stabilizer company comes close to delivering the roll reduction performance; hence approximately 80% of the world's superyachts have Quantum's Zero Speed™ systems on board!

During the past few years, the engineers at Quantum have not been idle. They continue to innovate with new technology and have broadened the range of yachts that can benefit from Zero-Speed™ Stabilizers.

Quantum recently developed a new patented extendable fin system called the "XT™ fin". This system has been designed to overcome a number of challenges when fitting these dual-purpose systems to larger vessels. The modern yacht designs are calling for higher volume hull forms that are not always conducive to fitting the stabilizer fin area required for stabilizing ships at rest (zero speed). Additionally, most of these vessels have designed speeds in excess of 20 knots, dictating that appendage drag be minimized.

The XT™ fins are designed to reduce the fin footprint by having extendable foils that are only deployed for stabilizing the vessel at anchor. When the yacht is underway the foils are retracted, thus reducing drag. When deployed, the XT™ fins have a vastly more efficient geometry due to the fact that the area of the foil is aft of the shaft and in the best position to deliver the force required for roll damping at anchor. An additional benefit of these XT™ fins is the ability, in some cases, to fit two fins instead of four based on the total area requirements.

During the planning stages for the yacht 'Mary P', Quantum met with the yacht owners and builder to plan and design a custom solution for this unique sport fisher. At 122' and built with an aluminium hull, 'Mary P' was designed for serious sport fishing with the ability to go anywhere in the world so the owners could pursue their passion for the sport. The owners also wished to be able to enjoy their time onboard in ultimate comfort. This created a challenge for Quantum to develop a system that could deliver excellent motion control at the vessel's high end

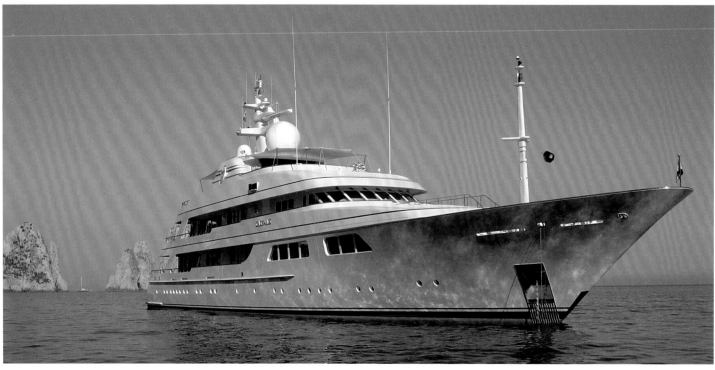

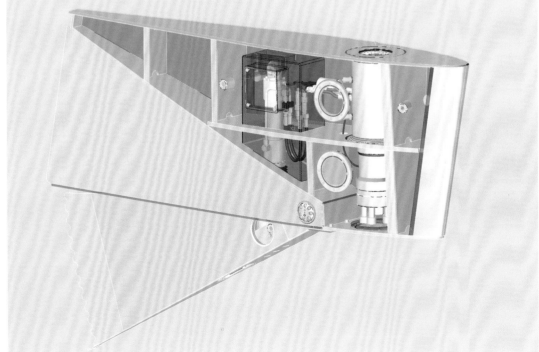

Above:
The luxurious yet functional 69.5m (228') Oceanfast aluminium motor yacht 'Aussie Rules', shown underway.

Far Left:
The 62.3m (204') Feadship motor yacht 'Cakewalk' is fitted with Zero Speed™ Stabilizers.

Left:
A cut-away illustration of an XT™ fin unit with extendable fin shown.

ZERO SPEED™ AND BEYOND

operating speed in the mid 20 knot range, while offering the same control while the yacht was trawling at low speeds in the 4 – 7 knot range. In addition to the high speed and low speed motion control requirements, was the owner's desire to have the same Zero Speed™ performance that earned Quantum its excellent reputation for the mega yacht market.

Quantum's latest innovation is the MagLift series of rotary stabilizers perfectly suited to high-speed yachts, large sports fishers and several other applications including the military.

Based upon the "Magnus Effect" discovered in the 19th century, which basically states, "the Magnus effect is the phenomenon whereby a spinning object moving in a fluid creates a whirlpool of fluid around itself, and experiences a force perpendicular to the line of motion and away from the direction of spin." In essence, the Magnus effect can be observed when a golfer hooks or slices a shot.

Using this principal, Quantum has invented and patented a completely new cylinder stabilizer that delivers full functionality both underway and at anchor. The MagLift systems offer the option of retracting the rotors into the hull for high speed, no drag travel. When deployed, they deliver a level of low-drag performance at slow speeds (3 - 16 knots) not achievable using conventional fins.

Stabilizer fins require a lot of power delivered quickly, which is why stabilizers use hydraulic power. Quantum began building its own high-capacity power packs several years ago. With the smallest footprint available, greatest flexibility of operation and highest level of redundancy, Quantum's Integrated Hydraulic Systems have earned a reputation for superior quality and reliability.

With bespoke electronic controllers and hydraulic power packs perfectly matched to the demands of its own fins or MagLift cylinders, Quantum confidently proclaims, "No one does it better."

Quantum
3790 SW 30th Avenue
Fort Lauderdale FL 33312. USA
Phone: +1 954 587 4205 or +1 954 608 0155
Mike Perkins - VP, Business Development
Email: mperkins@quantumhydraulic.com
Web: www.quantumhydraulic.com

Above:
The 37.7m (122') Trinity sportfisher 'Mary P' is a high performance sports fishing yacht.

Far Left:
Quantum's MagLift™ Stabilizer.

Centre:
Quantum's Archer™, active trim tab ride control fin can be seen to the right of the yacht's propeller.

Left:
A Quantum MagLift™ Stabilizer on 'Mary P'.

ST. MAARTEN

MUSTIQUE

VIRGIN GORDA

ST. BARTS

CAPRI

SEYCHELLES

MALDIVES

BORA BORA

Watkins Syndicate

London - Dubai - Singapore - Hong Kong - British Virgin Islands - Chicago - Houston

Independent yacht management from the City of London

Design by superyachtart.com

The Large Yacht Management Professionals

MEGAYACHT
PROFESSIONAL

Jotun Megayacht Professional: A Global Presence

'Dubois designed' is a phrase synonymous with the very best in the world of Super Yachts

Dubois Yachts was formed in 2001 as a result of a growing demand from many Dubois owners and satisfied design clients who were interested in a 'one stop shop' for the sale, purchase, charter and management of their yachts.

Ed Dubois started Dubois Naval Architects in the 1970s and Malcolm McKeon became a partner in the business in 1981. They have played an integral role in the development of the modern sailing super yacht and numerous plaudits and awards have been heaped on the Design team headed by Ed.

James Troup manages Dubois Yachts and heads the brokerage side of the business while Sarah Fraser brings more than 20 years of experience to the charter division. Mil Reid provides full marketing, PR and administrative support to the office.

Dubois Yachts specialises in the purchase, sale, charter and management of Dubois designed yachts. Working closely with the design studio gives unrestricted access to technical information and design expertise that is simply not available to the competition. Dubois Yachts is the logical place for interested parties to contact.

Dubois Naval Architects' well deserved reputation for high standards of knowledge, experience, service and integrity (which has been built up over thirty years) continues at Dubois Yachts.

Yacht insurance
as **unique**
as **your yacht**.

PANTAENIUS
Yacht Insurance

Germany · Great Britain* · Monaco · Denmark · Austria · Spain · Croatia · Sweden · USA

34, Quai Jean-Charles Rey · 98000 Monaco · Tel. +377-97 98 43 43
Grosser Grasbrook 10 · 20457 Hamburg · Tel. +49-40-37 09 10
Marine Building, Victoria Wharf · Plymouth, Devon PL4 0RF · Tel. +44-17 52 22 36 56
c/. Torre de Pelaires, 5 · 07015 Palma de Mallorca · Tel. +34-971-70 86 70

www.pantaenius.com

BROKERAGE

The purchase of a super yacht can appear daunting to a buyer. Dubois Yachts' aim is to make the purchase of a yacht both simple and pleasurable. Dubois Yachts is the logical company to handle the sale and purchase of a Dubois designed yacht. Being fully supported by the sister company, Dubois Naval Architects, their knowledge of Dubois designed yachts is second to none – they literally know the boats from the keel upwards!

Dubois Yachts not only offer advice during the selection process, they are pleased to make recommendations for finance houses, surveyors, lawyers and crew. They are experienced in successful negotiations with all parties and understand value.

Through their experience in the management of Dubois yachts, they are able to provide accurate predictions of running costs and in the event that the new owner wishes to offset some of the running costs the Dubois Yachts charter department can offer advice, recommendations and management of this service.

The industry standard fees are typically paid for by the Seller although they also act on behalf of the Buyer.

Dubois Yachts' aim is to make the purchase of a yacht both simple and pleasurable

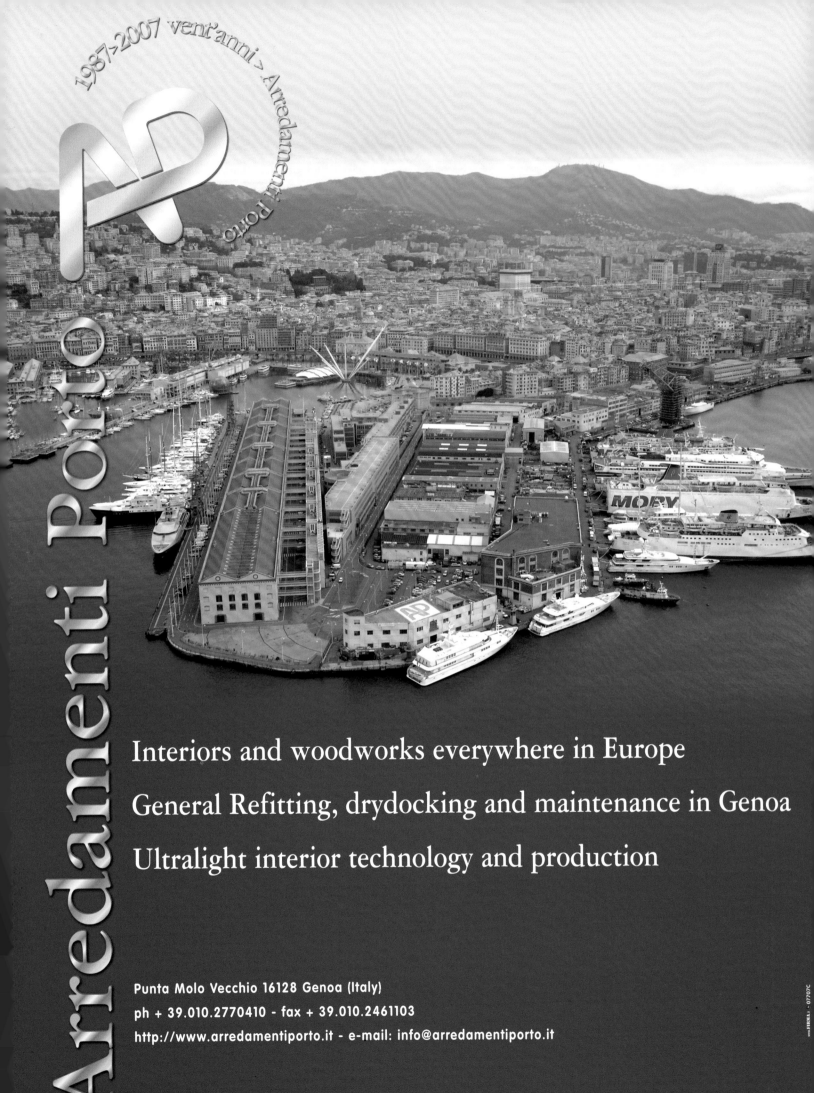

CHARTER MARKETING

Offsetting some of the running costs by chartering their yacht is a very good solution for some owners. Dubois Yachts recognise that it is of paramount importance that a yacht's charter activities in no way detract from an owner's enjoyment of his yacht. To this end Dubois Yachts take a great deal of trouble to understand the objectives and expectations of the owner. Only once this is done is a marketing strategy developed maximising the charter revenue within these agreed parameters.

Some Owners require the maximum possible number of weeks chartered; others give limited charter availability. Charterer's are vetted and recommendations on location, crew, pricing and itineraries are offered. In all cases, the Owner's wishes are the primary concern and a programme is tailor made to suit.

Dubois Yachts works closely with large retail brokers to ensure maximum exposure for their yachts.

YACHTS FOR CHARTER

Experience the pleasure, thrills and luxury of a Dubois yacht. Choose from an excellent selection of Dubois designed yachts available for charter worldwide from 95' to 180', both power and sail. Alternatively, Dubois yachts has access
to a wide range of other yachts to suit all requirements.

Dubois Yachts Ltd
Beck Farm
Sowley
Lymington
SO41 5SR

Tel:+44 (0)1590 626688
Fax: +44 (0)1590 626696

yachts@duboisyachts.com
www.duboisyachts.com

BRISTOLIAN

P2

The World
Superyacht Awards

Sailing yacht of the Year
Best exterior styling - Sailing yacht
Best sailing yacht in 30m to 44m size range

PHILIPPE BRIAND

1 Gledhow Gardens - London SW5 0BL - U.K. - Phone: + 44 207 373 36 24 - Fax: +44 207 460 36 22 - yachts@philippebriand.com - www.philippebriand.com

Welcome
to Excellence

Welcome to MARINA BARCELONA 92.
Because at MB'92 we emphasize the unique objective:
to continue being the best shipyard in refit, repair and
maintenance for megayachts.

www.mb92.com

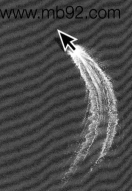

barcelona
world race

OFFICIAL SUPPLIER

antibes
yachtshow

photo: vertige

the only yacht show in europe
for brokerage & charter!

 port vauban VILLE D'ANTIBES Juan-les-Pins  INTERNATIONAL YACHT CLUB D'ANTIBES Mercedes-Benz

brokerage • charter • equipment • services

antibesyachtshow
côte d'azur

april 2010

antibesyachtshow

9 avenue saint roch   06600   antibes   france
t: +33(0)4 92 90 59 15   f: +33(0)4 92 90 58 90
e: info@antibesyachtshow.com   www.antibesyachtshow.com

brokerage   •   charter   •   equipment   •   services

Yacht insurance
as **unique**
as **your yacht.**

FEATURED
YACHTS

We go to extraordinary lengths

A bold new era of luxury motor yachts has arrived. One where imagination knows no limits. Where conventions of design, elegance and performance are continually challenged. Where the Princess 32M and 40M are the shape of beautiful things to come.

LEAVE THE WORLD BEHIND.

You have been to the edge of the world. You have seen everything.
Now it is time to find out how to be astonished, again. Distance yourself
from the earth, with the perfect mix of technology and style:
you will realize what it is you truly need.

CRN S.p.A. - Ancona, Italy - phone +39 071 5011111
Monaco Office - phone +377 97975282

The finest art on water

www.crn-yacht.com

a Ferretti brand

Premier 130⁺

Built to go wherever your dreams take you...

DEFINE YOUR HORIZON

DEFINE YOUR HORIZON

Horizon Group-Premier Series +886 7.571.6500 #100
Horizon Yachts Inc 561.346.5966
WWW.HORIZONYACHT.COM

Premier 105. 130⁺ . 150⁺. 160⁺

The secret of our success is a white sheet of paper.

SD92

That is the *carte blanche* that we give to all our owners.

SANLORENZO®

Tailor Made Only

Roma - Venezia - Antibes - Monte Carlo - Mallorca - Hamburg - Sukošan - Ft. Lauderdale

www.sanlorenzoyacht.com

Ameglia Shipyard   Viareggio Shipyard

STEEL YACHTBUILDING   REFIT   BROKERAGE   MANAGEMENT   CHARTE

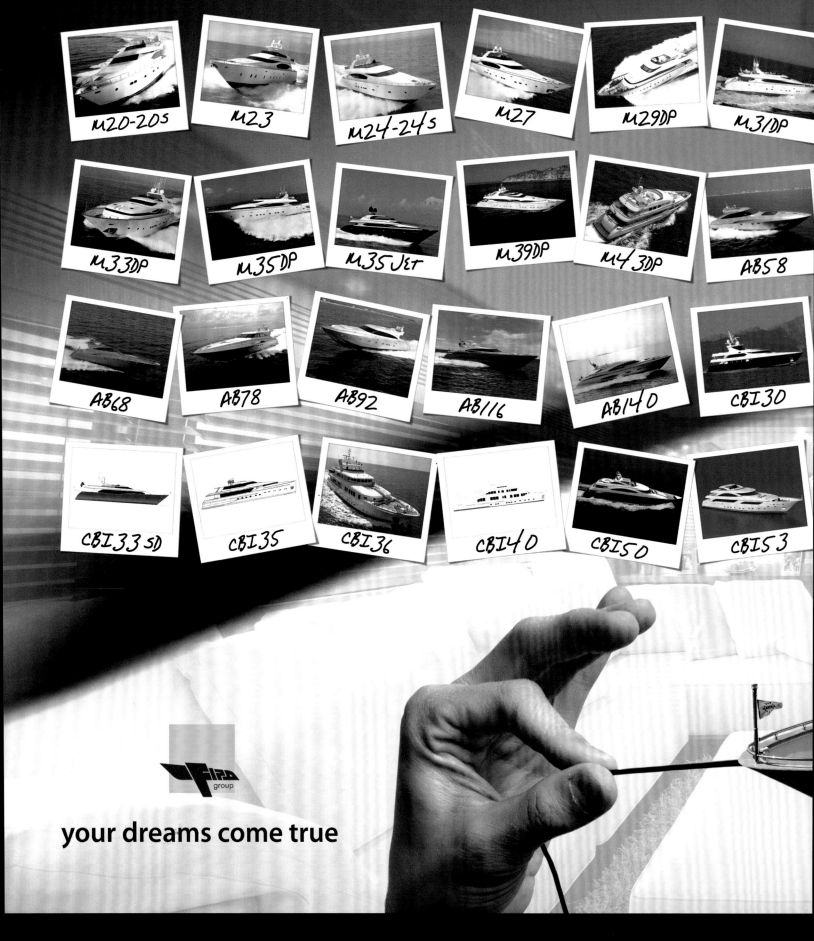

your dreams come true

SALES DEPARTMENT:
Fipa Group - Via Marina di Levante 12-14-16 - Viareggio 55049 (LU) - ITALY - tel. +39 0584 38191 - fax +39 0584 3819333
info@maiora.net - info@abyachts.com - info@cbinavi.com - www.fipagroup.com

M.35 JET

AB140

M35DP

MAIORA®

AB YACHTS

Cbi Navi

ISABEAUTIFULDAYINSEYCHELLES.   ISA**470**

TÒ-KALÒN
31m (101 ft.) Enclosed Bridge Motor Yacht

INGOT
47m (153 ft.) Tri-Deck Motor Yacht

SYCARA IV
46m (151 ft.) Classic Fantail Cruiser

Become part of the Burger family.

Sunboats Premium

M/Y Catamarans

SC 9500 sq.ft

113' l x 40' w

Projeto:
Equipe Thierry Stump

FAIRLINE

Everyone at UK-based Fairline is passionate about the way they develop and build their boats - and it's an emotion that has played a vital role in driving the international success of the Fairline marque. In fact it is probably the unique ingredient that helps create such a clearly quantifiable difference in quality.

Recent research has confirmed that the unusually high level of customer loyalty to Fairline is largely a result of two key factors: the commitment to building yachts that genuinely lead their class in terms of design, technical integrity and quality - and an appreciation of the focus placed on customer satisfaction and service at every stage of ownership.

All of this was born from one man's vision over 40 years ago, but the very same dedication to excellence, cutting-edge technology and peerless craftsmanship still runs through the company today, resulting in a luxury brand recognised and appreciated the world over.

The company's specialist Yacht Division works closely with the design and production teams at the magnificent new Oundle headquarters, opened this year, staying abreast of the latest trends and developments, as well as the advanced construction and engineering techniques used in the nearby production centres.

In partnership with your dealer, they will advise on the practicalities of production and ownership and consult with you throughout the build, to achieve the perfect end result - making sure the path to ownership is a smooth, unruffled and stylish experience.

In short, Fairline build a line-up of world class motor yachts that win many awards for their innovation and quality, but even more importantly, deliver matchless pleasure and enjoyment to their owners. Put simply, they build your boat with pride - and with a rare passion true to the original ethos and heritage of the Fairline marque.

Right & Below:
The Fairline Yacht Division makes buying, building and owning a luxury yacht an enjoyable and memorable experience.

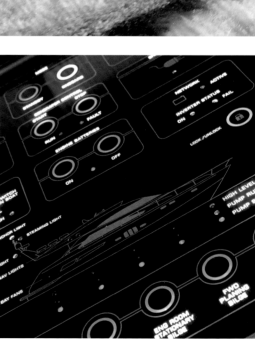

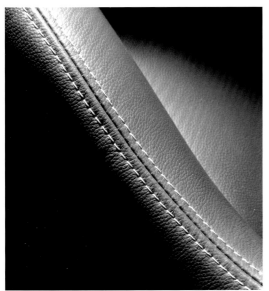

FAIRLINE
YACHT DIVISION

SQUADRON 65

The moment you step on board this magnificent Squadron, a wonderful 'large yacht' feeling embraces you. Stylish. Elegant. Substantial.

The long central window running the full length of the sunpad on the foredeck not only floods the forward cabin with light, but adds a unique look to the exterior. Up top, the huge flybridge is a masterpiece of practical design, with fabulous entertainment facilities and two large, luxurious day beds.

The spacious single level salon, with its sumptuous furnishings and elegant cabinetry, merely hints at the stunning quality and standard of finish to be discovered throughout this extraordinary yacht. Whether to use the master stateroom or the forward cabin will be a dilemma for the owners, such will be the attractions of both, with their airy, light-filled atmosphere, spacious open-plan en suite layouts, elegant 'floating' bed designs and massive wardrobe and storage space.

The panoramic windows and sheer luxury of the master en suite may make the choice easier though. Occupants of the aft cabin too, whether extra guests or crew, will enjoy their own en suite facilities and have a great view from the unusually large panoramic windows.

A true Squadron in every sense - and a fine example of the ultimate in British marine engineering and craftsmanship.

Right and Below:
The Squadron 65 is a superbly luxurious cruising yacht that is also exhilarating to drive.

SPECIFICATIONS:	SQUADRON 65
Length Overall:	20.41m (66' 11")
Beam:	5.24m (17' 2")
Draught:	1.37m (4' 6")
Guests:	6 - 8
Propulsion:	Twin (from 2030mhp to 2300mhp)
Max Speed:	36 knots

FAIRLINE
YACHT DIVISION

Right:
The main salon on the Squadron 65 is open and inviting.

Below Left:
The well equipped galley.

Below Centre:
The main helm station.

Below Right:
The luxurious master stateroom.

FAIRLINE
YACHT DIVISION

SQUADRON 78 CUSTOM

Everything Fairline has learned in over 40 years of building fine motor yachts is to be found in the breathtakingly elegant, award-winning Squadron 78.

From the well-proven hull to the smallest detail of cabinetry, Fairline has drawn on lessons learned from the creation of over 11,000 boats, in order to create a peerless luxury motor yacht. From design concept through to full-size mock-up, nothing has been left to chance, so that every detail of this boat fits a precise design purpose.

The Squadron 78 embodies everything you would expect in a luxury performance motor yacht and more, thanks to her impressive array of 'standard' equipment, a class-leading feature much remarked upon and appreciated by owners. As is the fabulous ambience of the whole boat. Large, airy 'public' spaces; grand private staterooms that combine light and space to stunning effect; and everywhere, a dazzling interplay between the finest materials - hand-selected granite work surfaces, hand-matched burrs and exotic woods - and state of the art design accents and features.

In summary, the Squadron flagship took three years to develop and countless thousands of man-hours to reach such a pinnacle of excellence ... and it shows. Everywhere you look. As its name implies, a high level of customisation is a feature of this stunning yacht and clients can rely on the specialist advice, experience and exclusive services of the Fairline Yacht Division throughout the order and commissioning process.

SPECIFICATIONS:	SQUADRON 78 CUSTOM
Length Overall:	24.37m (79' 11")
Beam:	5.70m (18' 8")
Draught:	1.61m (5' 3")
Guests:	6 - 13
Propulsion:	Twin (from 2720mhp to 3144mhp)
Max Speed:	35 knots

Above:
The Squadron 78 Custom is a stylish and powerful luxury yacht.

Left & Far Left:
A yacht built for entertaining.

FAIRLINE
YACHT DIVISION

Above:
The main lounge on the Squadron 78 Custom is warm and relaxing.

Left:
The main lounge leads out onto an open aft deck with stairs leading up to the flybridge.

Centre:
The galley.

Far Left:
The luxurious owner's suite.

FAIRLINE
YACHT DIVISION

SQUADRON 85

With such a loyal following from Fairline's clients, it is hardly surprising that they have been asked, on a regular basis, to build ever larger yachts for them. Not content merely to build a 'larger' yacht however, Fairline has responded by creating something extra special - and genuinely extraordinary. Make no mistake, the new Squadron 85 is a serious statement of intent on the world stage and a yacht without parallel in its class.

This is a yacht of considerable substance and sea-going capability, with a large 'open' transom area and a magnificent, expansive flybridge. She will feature the unique boat-management systems pioneered on the latest Squadrons, as well as a host of innovative solutions for practical enjoyment of the boat. Examples are the hi-lo bathing platform and tender-lifting facility, the elegant side-boarding balcony with integral access ladder - all designed to make life easy and relaxing for those on board.

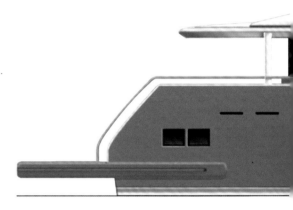

Full length deck glazing and a magnificent central atrium, complete with a glazed stairway, will reflect and disperse light throughout the interior from where guests will be able to enjoy magnificent panoramic views. Originality is a key factor here, design concepts for both exterior and interior having been created to ensure that each yacht will be elegant and truly individual to its owner.

In fact, the brief to Fairline's design team was for a semi-custom build, allowing clients to choose from a variety of layout, interior style and fit-out options, creating a yacht which precisely matches their individual accommodation preferences; the Squadron 85 is therefore offered in a 3, 4 or 5-cabin layout.

Without doubt, the Squadron 85 will achieve new levels of international recognition for Fairline - because this is a world-class yacht indeed.

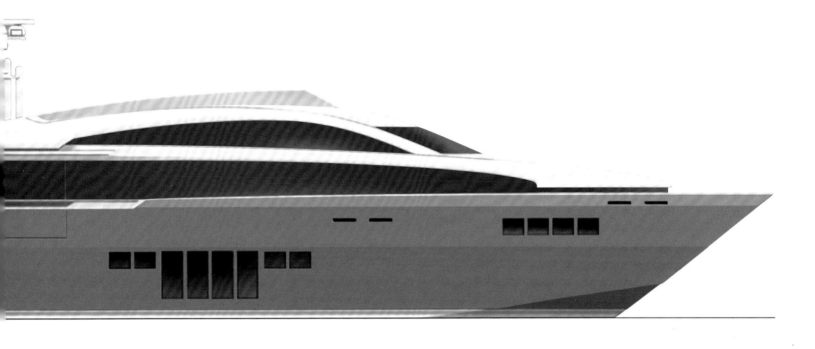

Above:
The new Squadron 85 Custom will become the flagship of the Fairline range.

Left:
Private consultations, customised design and individual attention is what the Fairline Yacht Division is all about.

FAIRLINE

Fairline Boats Ltd.
Oundle, PE8 4HN
UK
Tel: +44 1832 273 661
Fax: +44 1832 273 432
Web: www.fairline.com

SPECIFICATIONS: FAIRLINE SQUADRON 78

Length Overall:	24.37m (79' 11")
Length of Hull:	22.35m (73' 4")
Beam:	5.70m (18' 8")
Guests:	6 - 13
Draught:	1.61m (5' 3")
Dry Weight:	45.52 tons (approx.)
Engine Options:	Twin (from 2720mhp to 3144mhp)
	2 x MAN 1360mhp each
	2 x Caterpillar C32-1572mhp each
Max. Speed:	33 - 35 knots

SPECIFICATIONS: FAIRLINE SQUADRON 55

Length Overall:	17.31m (56' 9")
Length of Hull:	16.87m (55' 4")
Beam:	4.81m (15' 9")
Guests:	6 - 7
Draught:	1.50m (4' 11")
Dry Weight:	21.81 tons (approx.)
Engine Options:	Twin (from 1550mhp to 1800mhp)
	2 x Volvo Penta 775mhp each
	2 x Volvo Penta 900mhp each
Max. Speed:	31 - 32 knots

SPECIFICATIONS: FAIRLINE SQUADRON 65

Length Overall:	20.41m (66' 11")
Length of Hull:	18.48m (60' 8")
Beam:	5.24m (17' 2")
Guests:	6 - 8
Draught:	1.37m (4' 6")
Dry Weight:	29.53 tons (approx.)
Engine Options:	Twin (from 2030mhp to 2300mhp)
	2 x MAN V10 1100mhp each
	2 x Caterpillar C18-1150mhp each
Max. Speed:	34 - 36 knots

SPECIFICATIONS: FAIRLINE PHANTOM 48

Length Overall:	15.18m (49' 10")
Length of Hull:	14.50m (47' 7")
Beam:	4.46m (14' 8")
Guests:	6 - 7
Draught:	1.12m (3' 8")
Dry Weight:	15.35 tons (approx.)
Engine Options:	Twin (from 1150mhp to 1340mhp)
	2 x Volvo Penta 575mhp each
	2 x Volvo Penta 670mhp each
Max. Speed:	32 - 33 knots

SPECIFICATIONS: FAIRLINE TARGA 58GT
(provisional)

Length Overall:	17.81m (58' 6")
Length of Hull:	17.70m (58' 1")
Beam:	4.92m (16' 2")
Guests:	6
Draught:	TBA
Dry Weight:	23.74 tons (approx.)
Engine Options:	Twin (from 1550mhp to 2400mhp)
	2 x Volvo Penta 775mhp each
	2 x MAN V8 1200mhp each
Max. Speed:	31 - 38 knots (estimated)

SPECIFICATIONS: FAIRLINE TARGA 47GT

Length Overall:	14.78m (48' 6")
Length of Hull:	14.35m (47' 1")
Beam:	4.00m (13' 2")
Guests:	4 - 6
Draught:	1.05m (3' 5")
Dry Weight:	14.18 tons (approx.)
Engine Options:	Twin (from 1000mhp to 1340mhp)
	2 x Volvo Penta 500mhp each
	2 x Volvo Penta 670mhp each
Max. Speed:	33 - 36 knots

SPECIFICATIONS: FAIRLINE TARGA 44GT

Length Overall:	13.68m (44' 11")
Length of Hull:	13.12m (43' 1")
Beam:	4.04m (13' 3")
Guests:	4 - 6
Draught:	1.01m (3' 4")
Dry Weight:	11.12 tons (approx.)
Engine Options:	Twin (from 740mhp to 870mhp)
	2 x Volvo Penta 370mhp each
	2 x Volvo Penta 435mhp each
Max. Speed:	33 - 35 knots

SPECIFICATIONS: FAIRLINE PHANTOM 40

Length Overall:	12.53m (41' 1")
Length of Hull:	12.05m (39' 6")
Beam:	3.95m (12' 11")
Guests:	4 - 6
Draught:	0.97m (3' 2")
Dry Weight:	11.42 tons (approx.)
Engine Options:	Twin (from 740mhp to 870mhp)
	2 x Volvo Penta 370mhp each
	2 x Volvo Penta 435mhp each
Max. Speed:	30 - 32 knots

SPECIFICATIONS: FAIRLINE TARGA 38

Length Overall:	12.13m (39' 10")
Length of Hull:	11.06m (36' 3")
Beam:	3.64m (11' 11")
Guests:	4 - 6
Draught:	1.02m (3' 4")
Dry Weight:	7.57 tons (approx.)
Engine Options:	Twin (from 520mhp to 740mhp)
	2 x Volvo Penta 260mhp each
	2 x Volvo Penta 370mhp each
Max. Speed:	33 - 42 knots

OYSTER MARINE

O yster Marine was founded in 1973 and spent its early years developing and marketing a range of cruiser racers, with the emphasis on performance. Thirty-six years on, it has grown to become an international market leader of world-class cruising yachts. With their distinctive 'Deck Saloon' design, Oyster yachts are recognised throughout the sailing world for quality, comfort and performance.

The Holman and Pye designed UFO range got the company off to a flying start with many racing successes. In 1978, Oyster launched the Oyster 37 and the following year the centre cockpit, flush deck Oyster 39 became Oyster's first full cruising design. The subsequent year the Oyster 46 was launched with its unique deck saloon design, one that has become a hallmark for Oyster yachts to this day.

These days, around half of the company's new construction is for existing owners. This loyalty sends a strong message to new customers thinking of joining what Oyster now likes to refer to as 'the Oyster family'.

Today's Oysters are very different from the yachts the company built over 35 years ago, but the core values of strength, seaworthiness and a multitude of practical, seamanlike features remain, testament to the experience the company has gained from sailing hundreds of thousands of miles in Oyster yachts.

Today, the Oyster fleet represents several design generations, each one building on the experience and success of its predecessor. The company's business is truly international and Oyster has already won two Queen's Awards, Britain's top industrial accolade.

Above & Left:
Oyster Marine has grown to become an international market leader of world-class cruising yachts.
Shown here, above then clockwise, are the Oyster 82, the Oyster 72 and the new Oyster 100 Superyacht designed by Dubois.

OYSTER MARINE

OYSTER 575

The all-new Oyster 575 is about evolution and experience. Evolution in design terms means an exceptionally sleek deck saloon with a spacious cockpit with twin wheels. It also means that every inch of space below deck has been optimised to provide comfortable, practical accommodation.

Experience meant Oyster talking to its owners and benefiting from their experience as well as its own. With over fifty Oyster 55's and over seventy Oyster 56's in commission, Oyster's experience of quality blue water cruising yachts in this size range is probably unsurpassed.

Pure hull lines from Rob Humphreys will ensure this yacht is a fast passage maker, resulting in effortless blue water cruising and exhilarating performance, while the four cabin layout and spacious saloon and dining areas will appeal to families and those wishing to sail with crew.

Oyster are confident that the new Oyster 575, with her twin-wheel configuration, will soon set the standard by which cruising yachts in this size range are judged.

OYSTER 655

With the Oyster 655, performance was an established criterion from the outset. Designer, Rob Humphreys, created a set of hull lines with a relatively fine entry forward and a clean run aft.

Add a low centre of gravity keel, a modern high aspect rudder and powerful sail plan and the result is a fast yacht that is a pleasure to sail.

The twin helm configuration puts the helmsman in exactly the right place and means that the spacious forward cockpit is safe and uncluttered. It is also much easier to get on and off the working deck, since there is virtually flat deck access from the stern into the cockpit.

The saloon makes best use of the yacht's 5.62m (18' 5") beam, and with the U-shaped galley to port, creates a spacious and contemporary open-plan living environment, with plenty of counter surfaces and stowage space.

The 655 has a spacious owner's suite aft, with its own private access to deck, and three guest cabins.

Right:
With the Oyster 655, performance was an established criterion from the outset.

Below Far Right:
Pure hull lines from Rob Humphreys will ensure the Oyster 575 is a fast passage maker.

Below Left & Centre:
The interior on the Oyster 655 is spacious and luxurious.

SPECIFICATIONS:	OYSTER 575
Length Overall:	17.99mm (59')
Beam:	5m (16' 5")
Draught - Standard:	2.70m (8' 10")
Draught - Shoal:	2.10m (6'10.5")
Displacement:	28,000 kg (61,729 lbs)
Accommodation:	8
Naval Architecture:	Rob Humphreys
Design:	Rob Humphreys / Oyster Design

SPECIFICATIONS:	OYSTER 655
Length Overall:	20.60mm (67' 7")
Beam:	5.62m (18' 5")
Draught - Standard:	2.95m (9' 8")
Draught - Shoal:	2.21m (7' 3")
Displacement:	39,000 kg (85,980 lbs)
Accommodation:	8
Naval Architecture:	Rob Humphreys
Design:	Rob Humphreys / Oyster Design

OYSTER MARINE

OYSTER 72

The Oyster 72 was conceived from the outset to blend the live-aboard and seamanlike qualities of a typical Oyster within a design where high performance was of equal or greater priority. Modern composite engineering has produced a hull and deck that are both light and stiff, without compromising the strength, durability and ease of handling for which Oysters are well known.

The Oyster 72 has one of the sleekest deck and cockpit designs ever produced for an Oyster yacht, with her rolled edge side decks, transom stairwell and a host of 'superyacht' style features. Most owners of this size range will appreciate the advantages of separating the crew and galley from the owner's and guest accommodation, a proven configuration that works really well, with few compromises. The Oyster 72 saloon is spacious and complements the large cockpit.

The standard layout makes best use of space, but the company is also pleased to configure a custom layout to best match an owner's individual needs and priorities.

OYSTER 82

The Oyster 82 is a fine example of what can be achieved by combining the naval architect's art and the builder's experience, a yacht that really does compare favourably with many larger vessels.

From any angle, the Oyster 82 looks refined and stylish. An exceptional sailing yacht that will do 240-mile days on passage, she is beautifully balanced and light on the helm with equally impressive light airs performance.

The 82's split cockpit really does have a big yacht feel with twin wheels and a spacious, protected guest cockpit with large fitted tables for some serious al-fresco dining. Offering full standing headroom under the cockpit floor this stylish yacht displays a combination of comfort and performance, with a wealth of practical sea-going features, that are the hallmark of the entire Oyster range.

Now available in a 'supershoal' centreboard variant with a board-up draught of just 2.14m (7ft), the Oyster 82 is also the perfect yacht for secluded anchorages unavailable to many other yachts.

SPECIFICATIONS:	OYSTER 72
Length Overall:	22.77mm (74' 9")
Beam:	5.85m (19' 2.5")
Draught - Standard:	2.90m (9' 6")
Draught - Shoal:	2.29m (7'6")
Displacement:	48,000 kg (105,820 lb)
Accommodation:	10
Naval Architecture:	Rob Humphreys
Design:	Rob Humphreys / Oyster Design

SPECIFICATIONS:	OYSTER 82
Length Overall:	24.99mm (81' 11")
Beam:	6.32m (20' 9")
Draught - Standard:	3.29m (10' 10")
Draught - Shoal:	2.55m (8'4")
Displacement:	61,000 kg (134,481 lb)
Accommodation:	6 guests + 4 crew
Naval Architecture:	Rob Humphreys
Design:	Rob Humphreys / Oyster Design

Above & Far Left:
The Oyster 72 looks refined and stylish.
whether inside or out.

Left:
The beautiful interior of the Oyster 82.

OYSTER MARINE

Oyster Marine
Fox's Marina
Ipswich, IP2 8SA. UK
T: +44 (0)1473 688 888
F: +44 (0)1473 686 861
W: www.oystermarine.com

OYSTER SUPERYACHTS BY DUBOIS

The new range of Oyster Superyachts is being created by the combined resources of three long-established teams, double Queen's Award yacht builder Oyster Marine, Dubois Naval Architects and RMK Marine.

The choice of Dubois Naval Architects was no accident, since Ed Dubois and his team have emerged as the world's leading designers of cruising yachts over 100 feet. There are over 40 Dubois superyachts in commission and many more in the process of design and under construction.

Dubois' progress over 30+ years has in many ways mirrored that of Oyster's 35 years building some of the world's finest blue-water cruising sailboats. Owners of the new Oyster Superyachts can be confident that these yachts will not only look fantastic, but will have great sailing performance.

Both the Oyster 100 and 125 will be built in modern composite materials using the resin infusion system to ensure optimum strength-to-weight ratios and then post cured to an oven temperature of 100°C to ensure overall laminate quality. Lloyd's will be auditing quality carefully and each vessel will be issued with the appropriate classification.

A very comprehensive specification will be offered on both yachts, including carbon spars, hydraulic winches, bow thrusters, twin generators, and a fully appointed interior designed and configured to each owner's requirements, while options will include a water jet tender stowed within a specially recessed pit in the vessel's foredeck, and underwater lighting.

The Oyster 100 and 125 will offer almost all the benefits of a commissioned one-off but with predictable quality and sailing performance, less risk and expense and of course Oyster's renowned after sales service and support.

The new series of Oyster Superyachts, namely the Oyster 100 Deck Saloon; the Oyster 125 Deck Saloon; the Oyster 125 Raised Saloon; and the Oyster 125 Flybridge, will complement the existing Oyster range. With their handsome, Dubois designed, outboard profiles they will be stunning additions to the Oyster fleet.

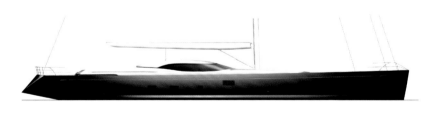

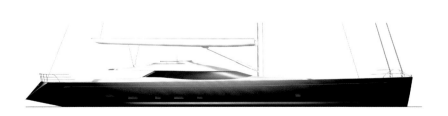

SPECIFICATIONS:	OYSTER 100
Length Overall:	30.80m (101')
Beam:	7.57m (24' 10")
Draught - Standard:	3.70m (12' 2")
Draught - Shoal:	2.70m (8'10")
Displacement:	87,000 kg (191,800 lb)
Accommodation:	6 guests + 4 crew
Naval Architecture:	Dubois Naval Architects
Design:	Dubois / Oyster Design Team

SPECIFICATIONS:	OYSTER 125
Length Overall:	38.10m (125')
Beam:	8.78m (28' 10")
Draught - Standard:	4.0m (13' 2")
Draught - Shoal:	n/a
Displacement:	155,000 kg (341,717 lb)
Accommodation:	8 guests + 6 crew
Naval Architecture:	Dubois Naval Architects
Design:	Dubois / Oyster Design Team

Above & Left:
With handsome, Dubois designed, outboard profiles, the Oyster 125 Flybridge and Oyster 100 will be stunning additions to the Oyster fleet.

Far Left:
Profiles for the Oyster 125 and Oyster 125 Flybridge.

DRETTMANN GROUP

Founded nearly four decades ago in 1970, the family owned Drettmann Group from Germany has developed into one of Europe's leading suppliers of luxury yachts. Working with the highly respected Horizon Group from Taiwan, constant product innovations, the latest technology and a highly skilled workforce have resulted in the firm's ongoing expansion and success. As well as owning its own state-of-the-art facility directly on the River Weser in Bremen-Hemelingen, Drettmann also has satellite offices throughout Europe and farther afield in prime locations, such as Palma de Mallorca in the Balearic Islands, Golfe Juan near Cannes in the South of France, Croatia and in Dubai in the United Arab Emirates.

Drettmann sells five major brands of yachts, namely, Elegance Yachts, Elegance Open Sportsyachts, Bandido Yachts, Premier Yachts and Vision Yachts, all of which are featured overleaf. All of these yachts are motor yachts ranging in size from the 16.5m Elegance 54, to the stunning new 52m Bandido 170. Now with a hugely respected international yachting company, Claudia and Albert Drettmann maintain a very close relationship with their valued clients, going way beyond handing over the keys at the time of sale. Service is a top priority at Drettmann, particularly when important issues such as financial services, insurance or boat registrations are concerned. The 'Refit by Drettmann' programme also provides new possibilities on how to modernise and upgrade 'older' yachts – with modern interior designs, for instance. Customer satisfaction is a top priority for Drettmann, while understanding and implementing the wishes of customers are the core focus of the company. This accounts for the unique success of the Drettmann Group as a whole.

Clockwise From Above:
The Drettman Group's yacht portfolio includes yachts such as the Elegance 130 (above), the Elegance Open 60 (left), the Elegance 80 (centre) and the Bandido 90 (far left).

DRETTMAN GROUP

ELEGANCE YACHTS

Elegance Yachts are the epitome of an ideal lifestyle on the water. Traditional shipbuilding artistry combined with technical innovations and modern spatial concepts create superbly spacious, luxurious and good value yachts. All Elegance yacht innovations have been designed with a single goal in mind – to offer owners the perfect yacht for entertaining and relaxing with family and friends on the water, in consummate luxury. Every Elegance yacht is built without compromise and is as individual and unique as its owner.

ELEGANCE 60

The Elegance 60 has excellent accommodation for 4-6 guests in a yacht that performs as agreeably as she looks. Boasting a semi-displacement hull with extremely good planing characteristics, even at low speed, her deep V-shape bow ensures a clean entry for sharp and stable manoeuvrability. Her open salon features a selection of high quality leather furnishings and a wealth of beautifully finished wood cabinets, while further forward the main helm station is modern and purposeful, dominated by the specialist Recaro sports helm chair. Outside on the aft main deck, a table and chairs provide a relaxing area for an al-fresco lunch, while up a few stairs, a large fly bridge, featuring a second helm station and an array of loungers and chairs, is definitely the place to enjoy the sun.

SPECIFICATIONS:	ELEGANCE 60
Length Overall:	18.60m (61')
Beam:	5.30m (17' 4")
Height above water:	4.70m (15' 5")
Weight:	38 tons
Fuel capacity:	3,700 l
Fresh water:	950 l

ELEGANCE 80

The latest yacht in the Elegance line up, the Elegance 80, showcases top workmanship and exceptional furnishings. With accommodation for eight guests, the uncompromisingly luxurious living ambience captivates with innovative design and exquisite materials. The Elegance 80 has been designed for real fun on the water. A sun lover's delight, she boasts a huge fly bridge with a topside helm station protected from the sun by a large hardtop canopy. Down below, her accommodation is light and spacious where the full beam owner's suite features an en-suite bathroom and a large flat-screen TV and entertainment centre. Available with a wide choice of engines, owners can create the yacht of their dreams, regardless of whether they require high performance or extensive cruising.

SPECIFICATIONS:	ELEGANCE 80
Length Overall:	24.40m (80')
Beam:	5.70m (18' 8")
Height above water:	5.20m (17' 1")
Weight:	60 ton
Fuel capacity:	7,000 l
Fresh water:	1,600 l

Above & Left:
The Elegance 80 is a modern stylish motor yacht.

Far Left:
The Elegance 60 offers excellent performance and handling.

DRETTMAN GROUP

ELEGANCE 98

Considerably larger than the Elegance 60, the Elegance 98 naturally offers significantly more accommodation. A full beam duplex owner's stateroom forward on the main deck, has steps leading down to a huge en-suite bathroom featuring a full size bath and shower-room.

Guests are also well looked after. A well-equipped galley and lobby separate the master stateroom from the luxuriously furnished main lounge and dining area that, in turn, leads out to the aft main deck through a large glass door. On the lower deck, two double cabins and two twin cabins are all equipped with en-suite bathrooms, giving the yacht total accommodation for ten guests.

At the forward end of the fly bridge deck, the wheelhouse is modern and offers wonderful visibility. The helmsman is well provided for with a stylish Recaro helm seat and a full array of the latest technology, while guests can relax on the sumptuous leather sofa to the side of the helm station. Further aft, the fly bridge features plenty of seating and lounging areas, a wet bar and a large Jacuzzi to relax in while enjoying the tropical sun. Even with all this, there is still space on the aft end of the fly bridge to store a good-sized yacht tender while underway. With a wide choice of MTU or MAN diesel engines, providing total power of up to 4,400hp, an owner of an Elegance 98 can also match the luxury onboard with outstanding performance.

ELEGANCE 130

The third of these Elegance models, the Elegance 130, puts Drettmann firmly into superyacht territory and does not disappoint. A magnificent three deck motor yacht, the Elegance 130 is one of three yachts in the Elegance 'Premier' range, her sisters being the Elegance 125 and the Elegance 140.

Like all Elegance yachts, the Elegance 130 is built to the highest specification and can have the option of a range of interior designs, including a five to seven cabin layout tailored to whether the yacht is to be chartered or used primarily for private use. As one would expect from a yacht that has three decks and a large fly bridge, space on the Elegance 130 is certainly not in short supply.

Above, Far Left & Centre:
With total power of up to 4,400hp, an owner of an Elegance 98 can also match the luxury onboard with outstanding performance.

Left:
The impressive Elegance 130.

DRETTMAN GROUP

ELEGANCE OPEN 60

The Elegance Open is the sports yacht range of the Drettmann line-up. This series is characterised by first-class engineering, generously sized living areas and modern design with classic elements, without foregoing an ounce of comfort or luxury. The huge glass sunroof and the enormous glass door transform the deck salon and cockpit into an integral unit, suffused with air and light. Three Recaro sport seats provide a genuine sporty feeling with optimal all-round visibility.

The salon of the Open 60 is high-tech in all the details. The large area with concave glazing not only creates a wonderful opportunity to see the excellent views but also gives an impressive appearance both from inside the yacht and from the outside.

With so much light, electrical shutters can be lowered and protect guests from the sun or intruding eyes as the need exists, giving guests the chance to relax in the very spacious main salon on the comfortable lounge seats provided. Generous stowing compartments below the seats and all over the interior can make everything disappear in an instant ensuring a contemporary tidiness onboard.

The Elegance Open 60 is particularly roomy for a sports yacht, yet is also comfortable and very luxurious. Unique and incomparable in this class is the master cabin featuring a 2m high ceiling. A well-appointed VIP cabin, en-suite bathrooms and galley all present not far off the same size and comfort as that found on a fly bridge yacht.

The Elegance Open 60 comes with a particularly impressive equipment list including a GPS, map plotter, autopilot, climate control generator, hydraulic bathing platform, tender garage, hydraulic gangway and electrical sunroof.

SPECIFICATIONS:	ELEGANCE OPEN 60
Length Overall:	18.30m (60′)
Beam:	5.30m (17' 4")
Draught:	1.75m (5' 9")
Accommodation:	6 in 3 Cabins
Weight:	33 ton
Fuel capacity:	3,200 l
Fresh Water:	965 l

Above & Left:
The Elegance Open 60 is part of the sports yacht range of the Drettmann line-up.

DRETTMAN GROUP

BANDIDO YACHTS

What makes a Bandido Yacht so irresistible? In secure and uncompromising fashion, Drettmann's explorer line brings discoverers and individualists to their desired goal. This line of yachts has been designed for a target group that enjoys freedom in a quiet and streamlined fashion, but will not accept any compromises in terms of luxury and aesthetics. Fast-paced sailing styles play a subordinate role. As a displacement yacht, the Bandido's endurance and range are unbeatable. All Bandido yachts have transatlantic capability regardless of the sea conditions. Indeed, many of the larger Bandido's are being built even stronger than that and are constructed to BV Classification, ICE Class!

BANDIDO 75

The 'baby' of the Bandido range is the Bandido 66 which will be revealed at the 2010 Düsseldorf boat show. Next up is the Bandido 75, the second of which was built for a well-known German sportsman. Spacious luxury is the best way to describe this impressive yacht. Boasting a large fly bridge complete with a forward open-air helm station, the Bandido 75 is a go-anywhere yacht and with her impressive height, provides guests with a wonderful view of the surrounding scenery. On her main deck she features perhaps the finest pilothouse of any yacht of this size, while her expansive main salon and dining area is wonderfully luxurious and relaxing.

Right & Below Right:
The Bandido 90 is a luxurious global cruiser which offers an abundance of space onboard.

Below Left & Centre:
Spacious luxury is the best way to describe the Bandido 75.

SPECIFICATIONS:	BANDIDO 75
Length Overall:	23.60m (77' 5")
Beam:	6.60m (21' 7")
Height above water:	7.30 m (24')
Weight:	105 ton
Fuel capacity:	18,000 l
Fresh water:	3,000 l

BANDIDO 90

Like her 'baby sister', the Bandido 90 is a consummate explorer at 27.90m long, with a weight of 160 tons and an impressive height of 8.80m above the water line. With such a high freeboard, the Bandido 90 is a dry boat capable of handling the worst that the world's oceans and seas can throw at her. Luxurious too. A tri-deck motor yacht, she has a huge amount of guest space and an almost commercial sized pilothouse, making long ocean cruises a real enjoyment. The spaciousness and luxury on board naturally extend to the wonderful main salon and guest staterooms, all of which are furnished to each client's taste with high quality wood cabinetry and luxurious fabrics. There are six double-bed cabins, plus one for the crew. Powered by two powerful Caterpillar engines, the Bandido 90 is a true global cruiser.

SPECIFICATIONS:	BANDIDO 90
Length Overall:	27.90m (91' 6")
Beam:	7.70m (25' 3")
Height above water:	8.80m (28' 10")
Weight:	160 ton
Fuel capacity:	35,000 l
Fresh water:	6,000 l

DRETTMAN
GROUP

BANDIDO 148

The Bandido 148 carries forth the axiom of pure classical design. The visual characteristics of the yacht make guests feel at ease, while the clear lines confirm the yacht's strength and character.

As you would expect, the interiors can be custom furnished according to the owner's specifications and equipped with the latest in modern technology or even specialist equipment, such as diving compressors and chambers, in line with the philosophy that stands behind this highly distinctive Drettmann yacht.

As a true ocean-going vessel, the Bandido 148 is built to stringent MCA LY2 regulations as well as certified to BV Classification – ICE class. Powered by twin MTU 12V4000M60 1,800hp engines, she has a range of some 4,500 nautical miles at a cruising speed of 12 knots.

SPECIFICATIONS:	BANDIDO 148
Length Overall:	45.00m (147' 6")
Beam:	9.10m (29' 10")
Height above water:	10.00m (32' 8")
Weight:	390 ton
Fuel capacity:	70,000 l
Fresh water:	10,000 l

Right:
As a true ocean-going vessel, the Bandido 148 is built to stringent MCA LY2 regulations.

Below Left & Centre:
The flagship of the Bandido range, the Bandido 170 has been designed for owners who enjoy experiencing life to the full and who value the privacy of long voyages with family and friends.

BANDIDO 170

The flagship of the Bandido range, the Bandido 170 will take its guests to their destination with consummate ease and without compromise. Its high cruising range and extraordinary spaciousness turn even long ocean-going trips into pleasurable experiences.

Designed for owners who enjoy experiencing life to the full and who value the privacy of long voyages with family and friends, the owner of the first Bandido 170 to be built is very familiar with the Bandido series as it was he who was the first to own a Bandido yacht.

For the past few years he has enjoyed his Bandido 90 yacht so much, that he has commissioned the largest yacht yet in the series to accommodate true worldwide cruising capabilities with all of the amenities that he has come to expect from a Bandido. An immense tri-deck motor yacht, space onboard is vast and luxurious, including, on the top deck, the provision of a huge sky lounge where guests can enjoy panoramic views of the surrounding scenery.

SPECIFICATIONS:	BANDIDO 170
Length Overall:	51.80 m (170')
Beam:	9.65m (31' 7")
Height above water:	10.20 m (33' 6")
Weight:	600 ton
Fuel capacity:	80,000 l
Fresh water:	10,000 l

DRETTMAN GROUP

Drettmann GmbH
Arberger Hafendamm 22
28309 Bremen
Germany
T: +49 421 56607 - 0
F: +49 421 56607 - 600
W: www.drettmann.com

VISION YACHTS

A new brand of yachts to the Drettmann range, the Vision 68 and 74 have been designed by American designer Gregory C. Marshall as go-anywhere sports-fishing cruisers, combining luxurious accommodation, high sea-keeping capabilities and sports-fishing facilities. At 68' and 74' in length both of these yachts have been created for long, comfortable sea voyages for owners wishing to venture further afield than most yachts of this size would dare.

Below deck, the yacht's owner and his discerning guests can take advantage of a truly opulent living area. Both the master and VIP cabins present luxurious and spacious accommodation, while the portside cabin, with its two single berths is no less comfortable.

Highly different from the other yachts in the Drettmann Group's stable of yachts, the Vision 68 and 74 offer yet another choice to the discerning yachtsman.

PREMIER YACHTS

Leaving the best to last, Drettmann Group is now proud to present the wonderfully luxurious Premier range of yachts. Following its successful launch of the Premier 135 this summer, Drettmann has now commissioned the construction of its first 50-metre yacht, the Premier 163.

Designed by the well-known yacht architect and Florida resident JC Espinosa, this new flagship of the Premier Yachts range will be equipped with twin 2,680hp Caterpillar engines for a maximum speed of 20 knots.

On three decks, a total of ten guests will be accommodated in five suites, in addition to the salon, master cabin, crew area, dining room, hot tubs, bar and generously sized lounge.

A distinguishing feature of the Premier 163 is the presence of large-scale windows in all living quarters for an optimal view of the sea. Completion of the yacht is currently planned for 2011.

Above & Inset:
The Premier 135 and Premier 163 (inset) are the largest craft in the Drettmann Group yacht portfolio.

Left:
The Vision 74 combines luxurious accommodation, high sea-keeping capabilities and sports-fishing facilities.

PRINCESS YACHTS

One of the leading brands in the world motor yacht market, Princess Yachts is also one of the most respected names in the marine industry.

Founded in 1965, the British company has built on the maritime heritage of its Plymouth base with an uncompromising commitment to design, engineering and manufacturing excellence.

Today the name is associated with timeless, elegant design and impeccable build quality. Every Princess craft is the result of a rigorous and uncompromising approach that blends cutting edge technology with traditional craftsmanship to set new standards in performance, sea-keeping, comfort and safety.

Renowned in its early years as a builder of exceptional flybridge motor yachts, the company's history has been marked by milestones ever since. 1994 saw the introduction of the V class high-performance sports yachts that range in size from 42 to 85 feet. In Spring 2007, the company launched its flagship Princess 95 Motor Yacht, swiftly followed by the 85 and 78.

Now, the company is entering a bold new era, with the construction of a new range of technically advanced, long range bespoke cruising yachts over 100 feet. The first model off the line will be the Princess 105 flybridge cruising yacht in 2010, followed by the unprecedentedly luxurious Princess 40M in 2011.

For over 40 years, the Princess name has been synonymous with some of the finest luxury sports and motor yachts of their age. The 40M and 32M extend an already impressive range of large craft for an ever-increasing network of loyal Princess owners.

Right:
The Princess V78.

Below Left:
The Princess 40M

Below Right:
The Princess 85 Motor Yacht.

PRINCESS 85
MOTOR YACHT

Designed with luxurious, long-range cruising in mind, the Princess 85 Motor Yacht combines astonishing good looks with superior performance and truly spacious accommodation.

Her sleek lines and advanced deep V-hull deliver a top speed of 30-32 knots with superb sea keeping qualities. But this is a motor yacht that is equally comfortable at 12 knots or 25, particularly with the optional TracStar hydraulic stabiliser system fitted, which significantly reduces motion at both displacement and planing speeds – ideal for serving lunch or sundowners while on passage.

The elegant layout offers the ultimate flexibility for enjoying life on deck. The vast teak-laid flybridge incorporates a fully equipped bar, teak table, generous seating, sunbed and optional hot tub. The flybridge crane can hoist a substantial tender up top, and also serves the hydraulic bathing platform. A large additional sunbathing area on the foredeck has the option of a Bimini sunshade.

The cockpit provides a covered area for alfresco dining, opening up through triple sliding doors to a bright, roomy saloon and dining area, resplendent with satin-varnished hardwood and soft leather upholstery. The galley is hidden from the saloon but opens to the wheelhouse which not only boasts a generous and beautifully arranged helm, but also an excellent dinette offering extensive views.

Below decks, the luxuriously appointed owner's suite amidships makes full use of the yacht's generous beam, with a walk-in wardrobe, dressing table, LCD TV and private breakfast area. The en-suite bathroom features twin marble or granite top washbasins with a shower and optional bath. The forward VIP stateroom is also beautifully furnished and includes a walk-in wardrobe and extensive stowage space. A choice of layouts allows either two twin en-suite guest cabins or a third stateroom with a further twin berth cabin, which could be fitted out as an office.

Right & Below:
The Princess 85 Motor Yacht combines astonishing good looks with superior performance and truly spacious accommodation.

PRINCESS YACHTS

The crew are accommodated in a double and twin cabin in the stern, with access via the cockpit or transom. Doors on both sides of the wheelhouse mean that the crew also have direct access to the helm and galley without disturbing the guests.

Elegantly designed and impeccably finished, the Princess 85 Motor Yacht is the ultimate cruising machine for the owner who really does want to go places.

SPECIFICATIONS:	PRINCESS 85 MOTOR YACHT
Length Overall:	25.93m (85' 1")
Beam:	6.30m (20' 8")
Draught:	1.65m (5' 5")
Accommodation:	8 guests + 4 crew
Propulsion:	2 x CAT C32A 1925hp
Speed Range:	30-33 knots
Fuel Capacity:	8,400 l (1850gal.)
Fresh Water Capacity:	1,500 l (330 gal.)

Above & Left :
The main saloon is spacious, light and luxurious.

Above Left:
The wheelhouse not only boasts a generous and beautifully arranged helm, but also an excellent dinette offering extensive views.

Far Left:
The luxuriously appointed owner's suite amidships makes full use of the yacht's generous beam.

PRINCESS V78

Unveiled to widespread acclaim in Cap d'Antibes in May 2009, the latest member of the V-Class range, the V78, is one of the most dynamically capable models that Princess has conceived. Delivering an intoxicating blend of speed, comfort and pure, unadulterated style, this sports cruiser can really fly.

The V78 is the first of the Princess V class models to benefit from resin infusion moulding - a highly advanced manufacturing system that has shaved some three tonnes from the weight of the hull, resulting in faster speeds and lower fuel consumption.

With its muscular profile and a powerful deep V-hull, the V78 also combines superb seaworthiness and precision control with a genuine long-range cruising capability that puts the most exclusive locations within easy reach.

On deck, the enormous cockpit boasts everything needed to relax and entertain in the most remote of anchorages, from a wetbar, coolbox and electric barbecue, to a large seating and dining area. The capacious stern garage, located beneath the sunpad, is big enough for an additional tender or wetbike, easily launched and stowed via the hydraulic platform.

With its clean, contemporary lines, panoramic windows and sliding sunroof, the V78's light, spacious saloon positively invites the outside in. Triple sliding doors open onto the cockpit creating a superb space for entertaining while giving the feeling of true open boating – albeit the kind that provides shade at the touch of a button.

Forward of the saloon, with its hardwood flooring, soft leather sofas and high-spec entertainment system, is a dinette seating eight in comfort, with glorious views. To starboard, the comprehensively equipped two-seat helm station provides optimum visibility for the helmsman. Below, the galley is stylishly fitted to a professional standard and finished in hardwood with a choice of granite or marble worktop.

Right & Below:
With its muscular profile and a powerful deep-V hull, the V78 also combines superb seaworthiness and precision control with a genuine long-range cruising capability.

PRINCESS YACHTS

The sleeping accommodation is arranged in four en-suite cabins to achieve new levels of space and light, with the unique reversed layout of the master suite providing a feeling of real exclusivity.

The owner enjoys a large en-suite bathroom with twin washbasins and a cavernous shower, together with a walk-in wardrobe, dressing table and chaise longue. Guests are treated to similar levels of luxury in the forward VIP stateroom and two twin berth cabins. There is an en-suite twin crew cabin aft of the machinery space.

A go-anywhere performance cruiser that combines unbeatable sports boat handling with the ultimate in relaxed on-board living, the V78 sets new standards for a class that is already in a class of its own.

Right & Below Right:
The V78's light, spacious saloon positively invites the outside in. Triple sliding doors open onto the cockpit creating a superb space for entertaining while giving the feeling of true open boating.

Below Left:
The owner's stateroom is fitted with a large en-suite bathroom with twin washbasins and a cavernous shower, together with a walk-in wardrobe, dressing table and chaise longue.

SPECIFICATIONS:	PRINCESS V78
Length Overall:	23.83m (78' 2")
Beam:	5.66m (18' 6")
Draught:	1.65m (5' 5")
Accommodation:	8 guests + 2 crew
Propulsion:	2 x CAT C32A 1825hp / 2 x 1825hp
Speed Range:	37-40 knots
Fuel Capacity:	5,846 l (1206 gal.)
Fresh Water Capacity:	1,112 l (245 gal.)

PRINCESS YACHTS

PRINCESS 78 MOTOR YACHT

Princess Yachts International plc
Newport Street, Plymouth
Devon PL1 3QG. UK.
Tel: +44 1752 203888
Fax: +44 1752 203 777
Web: www.princessyachts.com

The brand new 78 Motor Yacht bears all the hallmarks of her larger siblings, artfully arranged into 78 feet of thoroughbred living space.

Embodying the very latest in Princess design and technology, the 78 also delivers exceptional performance for a motor yacht of its size. Around 70% of her GRP structures are moulded using high-tech resin infusion, enabling an engineered weight reduction to achieve higher speeds, lower fuel consumption and increased cruising range. Sleek lines and sophisticated underwater sections deliver an assured, stable ride for fast and efficient passagemaking.

Upstairs, the expansive flybridge is the perfect place to unwind with its flexible seating and sunbed arrangement and large wetbar. There is also the option of a hot tub for soaking up your surroundings at private anchorage – and a further substantial sunbed on the foredeck for soaking up the sun.

Making full use of the 78 Motor Yacht's generous beam and panoramic windows, the sumptuous saloon is ideal for relaxing and entertaining, opening onto the cockpit with its additional seating and alfresco dining table. Forward of the saloon, the large formal dining area can be opened or closed for privacy and is conveniently located next to the superbly equipped galley. There is an additional dinette next to the helm – perfect for keeping the skipper company while enjoying breakfast or lunch underway. The helm itself has been designed for optimum visibility with clear sightlines and an intuitive controls layout, incoporating the latest electronics.

Down below, the sleeping accommodation is voluminiuous and the four en-suite cabins immaculately presented. The full beam master stateroom amidships includes a private breakfast area, large vanity unit and walk-in wardrobe. Accommodation for crew is found aft of the machinery space with separate access. These quarters feature an en-suite twin cabin with options for a large lazarette area, crew mess or second cabin.

With her elegant contemporary profile, class leading dynamic ability and uncompromising layout, the 78 Motor Yacht opens up a whole new world of cruising in comfort to Princess' loyal followers.

Right:
The Princess 78 Motor Yacht.

Below Left:
The Princess 32M.

Below Right:
The Princess 40M

PRINCESS 32M & 40M

Precision engineering, superb craftsmanship, exemplary performance and extraordinary design flair. The hallmarks of Princess Yachts have been perfected through decades of dedication to quality, strength and integrity in both design and build. Now they are being applied to a new range of technically advanced, long range cruising yachts that will stamp Princess' mark firmly on the market for superyachts over 100 feet.

The first craft due for completion in the second half of 2010 will be the Princess 32M, followed by a new flagship, the Princess 40M in 2011. Both will be unmistakeably Princess in terms of design and performance, while offering an exceptional level of personalisation. Just as Princess yachts are one of a kind, each of these superyachts will be recognised as truly individual.

The Princess 105 is a powerful flybridge cruising yacht with a separate raised wheelhouse that combines

unparalleled sea-keeping with an exceptional cruising range.

Offering sumptuous living quarters and entertaining spaces for up to ten guests, the 32M delivers class-leading levels of space and accommodation.

It can be configured with either three or four en-suite staterooms, in addition to the vast owner's suite which takes pride of place forward of the main deck. Either way, the intelligently designed layout ensures the utmost privacy for guests while providing the perfect sanctuary for relaxation.

The Princess 40M is a 40m long-range tri-deck cruising yacht offering an unprecedented level of luxury and build detailing. The three-deck configuration delivers a sublime expanse of interior and exterior living space, and can comfortably accommodate up to twelve guests in complete privacy, with separate quarters for up to eight crew.

The owner is accommodated in a magnificently appointed suite on the main deck, while on the lower deck, several configuration options provide ample scope for customisation.

Princess yachts have always commanded attention. Combining a unique heritage with extraordinary vision, the 32M and 40M tri-deck look set to commandeer the market for 100 feet-plus yachts.

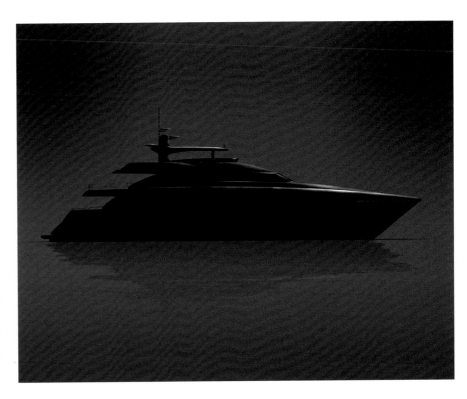

WALLY POWER

Since 1994, Wally has delivered some of the most stylish and technologically advanced luxury yachts in the world. With its headquarters in Monaco, Wally initially concentrated on state-of-the-art sailing yachts but has now designed and built one of the most prestigious ranges of motor yachts on the market, including the new 55 wallypower and 64 wallypower yachts featured overleaf.

Throughout its range, Wally offers a high degree of bespoke styling, for both the exterior and interior of its yachts. A wide palette of unique metallic hull colours for example, or a matt black paint finish, provide for a highly distinctive appearance on the water, while a variety of hi-tech fabrics as well as a range of specially developed heat, waterproof and UV resistant natural leathers allow the owner to personalise the open air seating and sunbathing areas.

Inside its yachts, the flooring options for the cabin include light oak veneer and carbon weave, while a selection of hand crafted finishes can be chosen for the cupboards and joinery such as wood veneer, carbon weave and lacquer. The interior upholstery choices range from durable hi-tech fabrics to natural leathers and fibres.

Such is the power and reputation of the Wally brand, that whenever Wally announces a yacht, the yachting industry as well as the world's elite group of luxury owners, sit up and take notice.

1 PS 002 TEMP

Above, Left & Centre:
*The stunning, powerful 64 wallypower
is capable of speeds of up to 50 knots.*

Far Left:
*The 55 wallypower makes the most of
the open air.*

55 WALLYPOWER

The new 55 wallypower completes the wallypower range filling the gap between the 47 wallypower and the recently introduced 64 wallypower.

This model introduces the full-open concept and is super-sporty and aggressive, featuring a huge windscreen that replaces the hard top and surrounds the entire cockpit area.

Four Volvo D6 engines each producing 435hp, coupled with the Volvo IPS 600 drives offer great manoeuvrability, 30% increased performance and 20% increased range providing the innovative propulsion system on the 55 wallypower. The predicted maximum speed of the yacht is over 40 knots.

The cockpit features two comfortable and symmetrical seating and relaxing areas, one on each side, completely sheltered by the windscreen. The entire cockpit can be covered by a Bimini or by a hard top as an option, sheltering the open areas from the sun. The vast aft 'beach' measures approximately 10 m² (108 ft²) and offers the signature Wally 'terrace-on-the-sea' feeling.

Another innovation onboard is the immense hydraulic retractable aft passerelle that serves as a boarding platform or swimming ladder depending on its position, similar to that on the 118 wallypower. The passerelle also serves to easily handle and lift a jet ski onboard from the water.

The interior layout of the yacht features a salon, two or three cabins with en-suites depending on the option chosen, a galley and a crew cabin with en-suite.

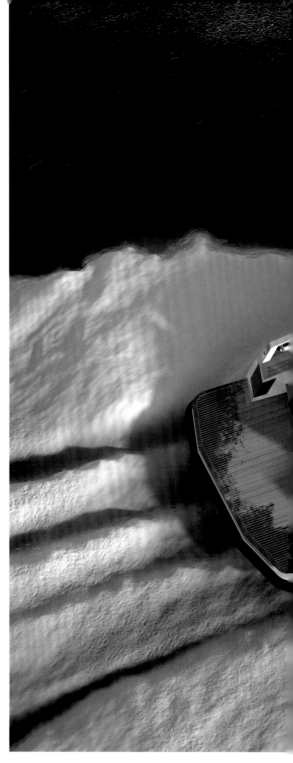

SPECIFICATIONS: 55 WALLYPOWER	
Length Overall:	17.40m (57' 1")
Beam:	5.40m (17' 9")
Draught:	0.94m (3' 1")
Displacement:	22/24 ton
Engines:	4 x Volvo Penta D6 - 435 HP
Propulsion:	Volvo Penta IPS 600
Accommodation:	5 guests + 1 crew (3-cabin ver.)
	4 guests + 1 crew (2-cabin ver.)

Above & Left:
The 55 wallypower introduces the full-open concept and is super-sporty and aggressive, featuring a huge windscreen that replaces the hard top and surrounds the entire cockpit area.

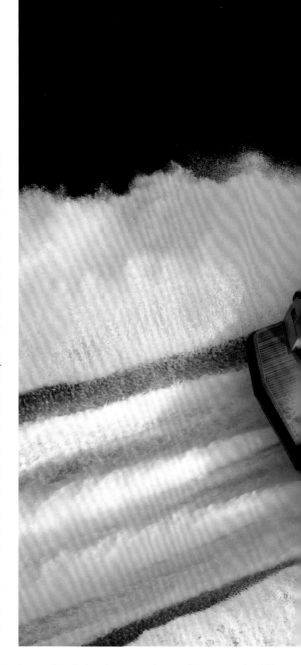

WALLY POWER

Wally
6 av. Albert II
MC 98000, Monaco
Tel: +377 93 10 00 93
Fax: +377 93 10 00 94
Web: www.wally.com

64 WALLYPOWER

This 19m yacht represents the transition between the wallytender and the larger wallypower yachts. The design fully exploits the concept of the wallypower line integrating form and function and combining large interior volumes with high performance, excellent sea-keeping, and wide open areas.

The 64 wallypower features the unique and distinctive characteristics of the Wally motor yacht models. The vertical bow improves performance and comfort in all sea conditions, while her sleek profile and perfectly proportioned hull and deckhouse are unquestionable marks of style and elegance. Indeed, the unique shape of the hull provides for wider decks than those usually found on boats of similar size, whilst keeping the same beam at the water line and therefore the same performance.

Transparency and open views are the key points of the superstructure design. There are two choices of propulsion. The standard equipment with two MAN 1,360 Hp engines gives a maximum speed of 43 knots, while two MAN 1,550 Hp engines offer the yacht a maximum speed of 50 knots. Both engine options drive KaMeWa water-jets and provide a 300-mile range at cruising speed.

The forward deck of the yacht has been designed as a sunbathing and social area. The glass superstructure, a unique and distinctive feature of the wallypower line, offers shelter and protection for the cockpit and main living areas and can be closed with the folding door aft.

Under the glass superstructure, the navigation and helm control station is located on the starboard side. The central social area has a six to eight person dining table to starboard and a sofa to port, with a coffee table that can be converted into a second large dining table.

There are three interior layout options depending on the number and type of cabins with the cabins in all three versions having en-suite bathrooms. The two-cabin layout features the owner's suite aft and the VIP stateroom forward. The owner's en-suite bathroom is particularly

impressive, being the same size as the one on the 118 wallypower.

The three-cabin twin layout has the owner's full beam stateroom forward with two identical guest twin bed cabins aft, while the three-cabin VIP layout features the full beam owner's stateroom forward, an oversize VIP guest cabin to port with queen-size bed and a guest cabin with twin bunks to starboard. This version perfectly meets the requirements of families with children.

All three layouts feature the galley amidships to starboard, and a double crew cabin with en-suite forward with direct access from the deck.

SPECIFICATIONS:	64 WALLYPOWER
Length Overall:	19.40m (63' 8")
Beam:	6.03m (19' 9")
Draught:	0.94m (3' 1")
Displacement:	30 ton
Naval Architecture:	Wally / Allseas
Styling:	Wally / Stefano Pastrovich
Interior Design:	Wally / Wetzels Brown Partners
Propulsion:	2 x MAN V12 1,360 hp
	2 x MAN V12 1,550hp optional
Waterjets	Rolls-Royce KaMeWa A45
Maximum speed:	43 / 50 knots depending on propulsion

Above & Left:
The 64 wallypower yacht represents the transition between the wallytender and the larger wallypower yachts.

Far Left:
Under the glass superstructure, the navigation and helm control station is located on the starboard side. The central social area has a six to eight person dining table to starboard and a sofa to port, with a coffee table that can be converted into a second large dining table.

SUNBOATS LUXURY CATAMARANS

The Godoy and Iervolino families of Brazil have been in love with the sea for more than 30 years. During a family gathering in Tahiti in 2001, the family rented a catamaran for day sailing and discovered this special type of vessel. It was just a matter of time before the entire family fell in love with catamarans. When they returned to Brazil, they started looking for catamaran motor yachts but could find only sailing catamarans. When the French company Lagoon launched its first 43' Powercat, the Godoys were one of the the first owners.

Unfortunately, a 43' yacht was too small for them so they began a new search for someone who could build them a larger Powercat. By coincidence, they had just become the new publishers of 'Offshore' magazine and a press release sent to the editorial department announced a catamaran motor yacht designed by Thierry Stump for Rolim Amaro, owner of TAM Airlines, the biggest airline in Brazil. It wasn't long before the Godoys bought an 80' catamaran motor yacht from Thierry. About two months after the build started, friends of the Godoys also expressed interest in the vessel due to its increased spaciousness over a monohull of the same length. After a short visit to the shipyard, Lucia Iervolino, Erothides Godoy's business partner, decided to buy a catamaran, too.

Soon after and recognising a good business opportunity in luxury catamaran motor yachts, Madames Godoy and Iervolivo, together with Godoy grandsons Enisson and Fernando, entered into a partnership with Thierry Stump, and Sunboats was formed.

Sunboats Catamarans is now firmly on track to launch the first of its first hybrid catamarans, the SC 113 and to release the Sunboats brand to the yachting world.

Above:
The Sunboats SC113 will be the first luxury catamaran to be launched by the company.

Far Left:
The master stateroom on the SC113 offers panoramic views and an abundance of space.

Left:
The SC83 is the perfect yacht for seeking out deserted bays and beautiful white beaches.

SUNBOATS LUXURY CATAMARANS

SUNBOATS SC83

The Sunboats SC83 is an agile tri-deck catamaran that gives all the comfort and space you would expect from a much larger monohull. With a length of 25.3m (83') and a beam of 10.97m (36'), the total living space onboard is an incredible 7,600 square feet. A pilothouse with owner observation lounge, a king-size bed in the master suite, a skylounge, a Jacuzzi and a bar on the fly bridge are just a few examples of the spaciousness this model offers.

With a Sunboats custom interior, this yacht is equipped with all the luxury features a first class yacht this size can hold. Its unique attributes include home theatre seating, a submersible lower aft deck for water access when afloat and easy disembarkation directly on to the beach through the bow area. A hallmark of Sunboats yachts is that all the interiors can be customised to each owner's individual tastes.

Sunboats has chosen to work with the best names in the market, such as Dee Robinson for interior design, Caterpillar for engines and Raymarine for electronics. Other well-known brands like Headhunter, Grohe and Kohler, Sub-Zero, Cummins Onan, Atlas, Dometic and Wesmar are also to be found onboard.

An optional helipad is also available on this yacht, suitable for small-sized helicopters such as the Robinson R-44 or R22.

All this space and luxury comes with great speed and efficiency. When necessary the SC83 will be able to reach 27 knots thanks to the technology of a new hybrid hull design that allows the yacht to plane at high speeds or travel in displacement mode at an economic cruising speed of 11 knots.

The SC83 will have a transatlantic range of 4,000 nautical miles, while at the same time will be 20% more fuel efficient than a monohull equipped with the same engine. As to comfort at sea, twin hulls plus Wesmar stabilizers drastically reduce pitching and rolling in comparison to a monohull of similar length.

SPECIFICATIONS: SUNBOATS SC83

Length Overall:	25.30m (83')
Beam:	10.97m (36')
Draught:	2.04m (6' 7")
Accommodation:	8 guests / 4 crew
Hull Design:	Equipe Thierry Stump
Engines:	2 x Caterpillar C18 Acert 1015hp
Maximum Speed:	27 knots
Cruise Speed:	14 knots
Range:	4,000nm @11 knots
Fuel Capacity:	20,000 l (5,283 gal)
Fresh Water:	5,600 l (479 gal)

Above & Left:
The Sunboats SC83 is an agile tri-deck catamaran that gives all the comfort and space you would expect from a much larger monohull.

Far Left & Centre:
With an interior created by Dee Robinson Interiors, this yacht is equipped with all the luxury features a first class yacht this size can hold.

SUNBOATS LUXURY CATAMARANS

SUNBOATS SC113

The Sunboats SC 113 accomplishes the impossible. This 113' yacht offers its owner the same square footage of living area as a 141' monohull but in a design with far greater luxury of space, stability and comfort. The SC 113 is a first class private yacht with a submersible lower aft deck for ease of boarding from a tender and enhanced water sports activity.

For those who prefer to fly to their yacht, the SC 113 can land a Bell 206L Long Range helicopter on its optional helipad. With its relatively shallow draft and disappearing bow gangway, you will also have the possibility of disembarking directly on to the beach, something that is certainly unique for a vessel that offers a staggering 9,500 square feet of total guest area.

All Sunboats catamarans are powered by dependable Caterpillar engines. That power, coupled with the reduced drag of the SC113's hybrid multi-hull design, allows the yacht to plane and reach a top speed of 26 knots. Yet in super economic mode the vessel has a range of over 5,000 nautical miles.

As with all Sunboats Catamarans, its interior designs are by Dee Robinson Interiors. Benefitting from the substantial beam, the yacht even offers a full commercial galley with substantial Sub-Zero cold storage and a chef's prep table to support elegant, gourmet-style entertaining on a grand scale.

The almost unimaginable spaciousness of this tri-deck yacht allows a palatial owner's suite on the main deck, an observation lounge behind the helm station, plus a multi-function sky lounge and a salon of unprecedented proportions. Topside, the flying bridge deck offers multiple seating and dining areas, a Jacuzzi and a bar.

Accommodation onboard includes four spacious guest staterooms in addition to the master suite and quarters for up to eight crew. A true globe circling superyacht, the SSC 113 is due for launch later this year and will be certified to both ABS and MCA classification.

Right:
The Sunboats SC113 offers its owner the same square footage of living area as a 141' monohull but in a design with far greater luxury of space, stability and comfort.

Below Left & Centre:
As with all Sunboats Catamarans, its interior designs are by Dee Robinson Interiors.

Below Right:
Disembarkation on to a deserted beach is easy on a Sunboats SC 113.

SPECIFICATIONS:	SUNBOATS SC113
Length Overall:	34.44m (113')
Beam:	12.19m (40')
Draught:	2.06m (6' 8")
Accommodation:	10 guests / 6 crew
Hull Design:	Equipe Thierry Stump
Engines:	2 x Caterpillar C32 Acert 1825hp
Maximum Speed:	26 knots
Cruise Speed:	16 knots
Range:	5,000nm @11 knots
Fuel Capacity:	30,000 l (7,925 gal)
Fresh Water:	8,800 l (2,325 gal)

FEATURED YACHTS

SUNBOATS LUXURY CATAMARANS

Sunboats Catamarans Ltd.
Praca das Tulipas 8
C.C. Alphaville, Barueri SP
Brazil
Tel: +55 11 4195 4545
Fax: +55 11 41951661
Web: www.sunboats.com.br

Right & Below Left:
The Sunboats SC230 is one of the most extraordinary yachts to be have been designed in recent times.

Below Right:
The SC230 will have features such as a vast 30+ seater cinema boasting the latest audio visual entertainment and Kaleidescape control.

SUNBOATS SC230

One of the most extraordinary yachts to be have been designed in recent times, the SC230 is a yacht of truly epic proportions. Measuring 80m (262') in length the SC230 has a staggering beam of 21.1m (69') covering almost her entire length, thanks to the twin hulled catamaran format that Sunboats are rapidly becoming renowned for.

As one would expect on such a vessel, the interior will be totally custom designed and with such a large amount of available space, can be constructed to accommodate any number of guests and crew.

Truly massive inside, with features such as a vast 30+ seater cinema boasting the latest audio visual entertainment and Kaleidescape control, the outside deck areas are equally impressive, topped off with a spacious semi-covered sun-deck.

SPECIFICATIONS:	SUNBOATS SC230
Length Overall:	80m (262')
Beam:	21.1m (69')
Draught:	3.45m (11' 4")
Accommodation:	Please enquire
Hull Design:	Equipe Thierry Stump
Engines:	4 x Caterpillar C32 Acert 1825hp
Maximum Speed:	18 knots
Range:	4,500nm
Fuel Capacity:	140,000 l (37,037 gal)
Fresh Water:	32,400 l (8,571 gal)

HORIZON GROUP

Founded in 1987 in Taiwan by naval architect John Lu, Horizon has grown to be one of the world's top luxury yacht builders with a range which now extends to yachts over 48m (148') in size. Initially employing just 30 craftsmen, Horizon is now a big business with over 1200 employees and has built in excess of 600 luxury motor yachts for highly satisfied clients all over the world. The yachts featured here, range from the fast and stylish Horizon Elegance 88 to the graceful Horizon Bandido 148, the largest fibreglass yacht ever to be built in Taiwan.

HORIZON ELEGANCE 88

The inspiration for the new Horizon Elegance 88 derives from the designer John Lindblom's earlier designs in the Horizon 73', 78', 82' and 84' motor yachts. Over the years these designs have proven to be both successful and appreciated by customers.

Horizon's vision with this new design is to capture a younger clientele whose taste is typically more modern, but still with the quality one expects from a Horizon yacht. The first impression of the Horizon Elegance 88 design is how well the sky-lounge harmonises with the yacht's profile. A successful sky-lounge motor yacht must be much more than a motor yacht with an enclosed flying bridge.

Not only must the proportions be pleasing in profile, the sky-lounge must provide truly useable and luxurious space without compromising the sea keeping qualities of the yacht. To complete the package, the main deck must also be reconfigured to take full advantage of the extra space afforded by moving the inside helm station to the upper deck.

Above and Left:
The Horizon Elegance 88 is a sleek, fast yacht which offers an abundance of open air deck space for relaxing and entertaining.

The design of the new Elegance 88 does all this and more. Its hull is performance oriented. The sharp bow entry angle transitions smoothly to a well-balanced semi-planing bottom aft to provide low resistance, while a unique concave shape in the mid-section gives good manoeuvrability in either calm or rough seas.

The interior layout inherits the theme of the Elegance 82 and 84, providing unbroken sightlines on the main deck from the aft deck lounge through the salon to the country kitchen.

On the lower deck the accommodation features a full-beam master stateroom amidships, a VIP stateroom opposite and two guest staterooms in between. All staterooms feature private bathrooms, while crew accommodation and working spaces are separated from the owner and guest areas and are aft of the engine room to provide maximum guest privacy.

On the upper deck, the sky-lounge features a well-protected helm station where the owner or crew can enjoy operating the boat regardless of the weather and socialise with guests at the same time.

An extended aft deck provides ample space for tender stowage and a well-designed al-fresco bar is sure to be a popular spot to watch the sunset over cocktails.

The brand new 88 is going to be built in two versions – with or without a sky-lounge, depending on the client's specific requirements. Horizon's all new 88 delivers the true spirit of 'Elegance' without compromise.

SPECIFICATIONS: HORIZON ELEGANCE 88	
Length Overall:	27.2m (89' 4")
Beam:	6.4m (21' 1")
Draught:	1.91m (6' 3")
Displacement:	82 ton
Engine:	2 x CAT C32A - 1600 HP

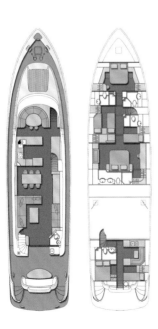

Above and Far Left:
The accommodation on board the Horizon Elegance 88 is both luxurious and spacious.

Left:
The elegant aft deck dining area.

HORIZON GROUP

HORIZON 97 RAISED PILOTHOUSE MOTORYACHT

The idea to build a 97' Horizon Raised Pilothouse yacht grew from brainstorming sessions between customers and Horizon's in-house design team.

The proof of the benefits of this collaborative approach is the five confirmed orders Horizon received for the model while the 97 was still on the design board. This sort of feedback proves that the 97 was the right model to fill the gap that existed between the Horizon 94' and 105' yachts.

The Horizon 97 maintains the line's elegant and stylish profile and its 21'6" beam provides plenty of interior space onboard. The aft main deck offers a built in settee and table for al-fresco dining or relaxing under cover in the fresh air. Sliding doors open to a spacious salon designed with a comfortable portside seating area featuring an L-shaped sofa opposite a full wet bar, and a well appointed entertainment centre on the starboard side showcasing Horizon's exquisite joinery and craftsmanship. Adjacent to the salon is a separate dining salon designed to seat eight people.

The raised pilothouse can be reached either by stairs up from the galley or down from the fly bridge. The helm console provides ample room for multiple large-screen monitors, while a small settee to port creates a cosy conversation area.

While customisation is always possible, the typical arrangement includes a full-beam master stateroom located amidships featuring a walk-in closet and an en-suite bathroom. A pair of large, vertical port lights provide maximum natural lighting. Two guest cabins, each with en-suite facilities, are located between the master and the equally spacious VIP stateroom positioned forward. Two private crew cabins are located aft.

Right:
The Horizon 97 has an elegant and stylish profile.

Below Left:
The upper deck is both expansive and very well equipped.

Far Left:
The oppulent master cabin is beautifully furnished.

SPECIFICATIONS: HORIZON 97	
Length Overall:	29.6m (97')
Beam:	6.6m (21' 6")
Draught:	1.98m (6' 6")
Displacement:	88 ton
Engine:	2 x CAT C32A - 1600 HP

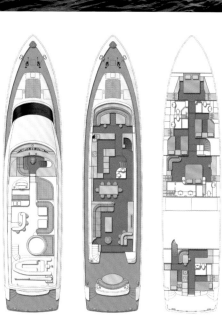

HORIZON GROUP

HORIZON PREMIER 105+

Horizon Group's Premier Series is dedicated to building custom mega-yachts of extraordinary style and luxury taking into account each client's unique requirements. The Horizon Premier 105+ is the first tri-deck model of this luxurious mega-yacht series.

As with all Horizon yachts, the Horizon 105+ is built using SCRIMP resin infusion technology, resulting in a strong but light hull. In addition however, the Horizon 105+ is also built under DNV classification and MCA compliance so that the owners can be reassured knowing they can go wherever they desire without hesitation.

In addition to the stylish exterior lines and reliable hull structure, the well thought out layout and state-of-the-art technology combine to ensure the yacht operates seamlessly and silently, leaving the owners and guests free to enjoy their time aboard together.

Making full use of the 23'6" beam, this vessel is truly grand. The huge swim deck allows for the easy use of water toys and tenders, while the lush, expansive interior features a full beam, versatile main salon, ideal for entertaining and family use. An open and fully equipped country galley, plus two king-size guest staterooms forward and a master stateroom amidships are just some of the accommodation features onboard. Six elliptical windows allow natural light to stream into the generous master stateroom, which features a king-sized bed and a Jacuzzi tub in the en-suite bathroom.

The pilothouse control station includes state-of-the-art communication and navigation systems, while the expansive fly bridge, not usually found on motor yachts of this size, features a commanding 360-degree view complete with helm and settee loungers.

As always, Horizon Group builds each yacht to meet each owner's dream.

Right:
The Horizon Premier 105+ is a hugely impressive tri-deck motor yacht.

Below Left:
The luxurious master suite.

Below Centre:
A large Jacuzzi is a central feature of the swim deck.

Below Right:
The galley is cleverly connected to a forward dining area, for informal dining.

SPECIFICATIONS: HORIZON PREMIER 105+	
Length Overall:	32m (105')
Beam:	7.16m (23' 6")
Draught:	1.93m (6' 4")
Displacement:	125 ton
Engine:	2 x CAT C32A - 1600 HP

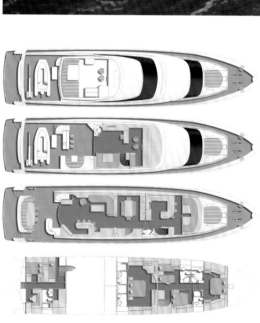

HORIZON
GROUP

HORIZON ELEGANCE 106
RAISED PILOTHOUSE

Designed by J.C. Espinosa, the new Elegance 106 Raised Pilothouse inherits the styling themes of the 120RP. This yacht marries a sophisticated, streamlined look with impressive interior volume and the luxury of numerous accommodation options.

The 106RP shares the same luxurious interior finishes and weight saving, state-of-the-art construction techniques of all new Horizon yachts. The most notable design change for the 106RP is in her advanced hull shape. The fabulous result is the comfort and enjoyment of high speed cruising. Unlike most mega-yachts which have given up the pursuit of the speed in exchange for luxury amenities, Horizon's new Elegance 106RP is designed with an innovative double-chine hull to provide great performance in both low and high speed ranges. For this new hull design, Horizon collaborated with Donald L. Blount and Associates, an internationally recognised naval architecture/marine engineering firm that specialises in high-speed hull design, structure calculations and stability evaluation, to create a comfortable and efficient high-speed hull.

In typical Horizon fashion, the Elegance 106RP offers owners many interior options, such as the choice of a roomy country kitchen on the forward main deck with the master below, and various arrangements for four en-suite staterooms and two crew cabins on the lower deck.

Among the features found on the 106RP are a tender garage, a six-person spa tub, sunbathing pads, day heads on the main deck and flying bridge, BBQ, a relaxing alfresco bar, two outdoor dining venues, a state-of-the-art pilothouse and much more.

The new Elegance 106 Raised Pilothouse is another of the exquisite designs from Horizon Group, combining a stylish exterior, well-appointed interior layout, high-tech equipment, with a fast, seaworthy performance.

SPECIFICATIONS: HORIZON ELEGANCE 106RP	
Length Overall:	32.8m (107' 7")
Beam:	7.62m (25')
Draught:	1.95m (6' 9")
Displacement:	120 ton
Engine:	2 x CAT C32A - 1800 HP

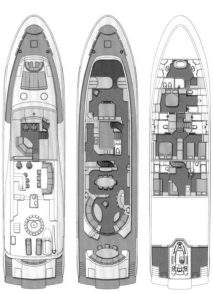

Above & Left:
The Horizon Premier 106 RPH has a
sophisticated and streamlined look as
well as being luxuriously furnished.

HORIZON GROUP

HORIZON ELEGANCE 120 RAISED PILOTHOUSE

Designed by JC Espinosa, the new Horizon Elegance 120' Raised Pilothouse motor yacht was born from the need to satisfy Horizon's ever-increasing international client list with a sleek but voluminous yacht built with well-appointed accommodation.

A generous beam of 26' 2" (7.98m) provided the designer with sufficient space to accommodate four guest staterooms with en-suite bathrooms on the lower deck. This accommodation area is linked to the main deck by an innovative atrium stairway. In the style of much larger mega-yachts, the owner's stateroom is located forward on the main deck, guaranteeing privacy. This stateroom opens to a large owner's bathroom a half-level below.

Aft of the master stateroom, the main deck space flows into a large and well appointed salon and dining room, which in turn leads to an aft deck perfectly suited to al-fresco dining. It is worth noting that all of the windows in the main salon have been made as large as possible to maximise the outside views. Behind the raised pilothouse is an expansive flying bridge, large enough to accommodate parties for dining or relaxing by the hot tub, or enjoying a refreshing drink from the well-designed bar. Located aft, crew quarters consist of three double cabins with their respective bathrooms, as well as a crew lounge. The fully enclosed tender garage is big enough for a 19' 8" (6m) tender, aft of the crew area. One of the special design and engineering features worthy of special note, is a clever elevated swim step that helps deploy the tender as well as provide divers with safe and easy access to the water.

The Horizon Elegance 120 Raised Pilothouse is built to full classification certification by Det Norske Veritas (DNV). Its design criteria and construction standards are in compliance with HSLC (High Speed Light Craft) Rule with +1A1 R1, Yacht Notation and MCA LY2 Code.

Right:
The new Horizon Premier 120RPH boasts a huge amount of interior volume, yet maintains a bold and striking appearance.

Below Left:
Space and warmth are the words best used to describe the luxurious master suite.

Below Centre:
The master bathroom.

Below Right:
The main salon is exotically furnished with beautiful woods and warm fabrics.

SPECIFICATIONS: HORIZON PREMIER 120RPH	
Length Overall:	36.58m (120')
Beam:	7.98m (26' 2")
Draught:	2.4m (7' 10")
Displacement:	182 ton
Engine:	2 x MTU 2160 HP

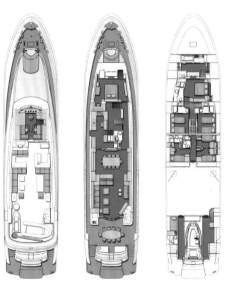

HORIZON GROUP

HORIZON PREMIER 130+

Flagship of the Horizon Group's Premier series of luxury motor yachts, the Horizon Premier 130+ combines industry-leading design with advanced construction technologies to create a yacht of extraordinary style and luxury.

Exterior lines styled by J.C. Espinosa present a balanced, refined look that is both contemporary and elegant for lasting appeal. As a world leader in the application of SCRIMP resin-infusion technology, Horizon has executed the design in a hull of superior strength, excellent sea keeping ability and impeccable finish.

The Horizon Premier 130's extraordinarily large interior volume allows owners to select from a variety of interior layouts to suit individual requirements. Choices include formal dining, on-deck master suite, five guest staterooms below, full crew accommodation, commercial galley and storage for enough water toys to suit even the most avid enthusiast. Thanks to Horizon Group's flexible approach to construction, the interior can express classic elegance, fresh contemporary styling or a blend of both. The tri-deck design incorporates a full-beam sky lounge and oversized salon, allowing the owner to create formal and informal areas for relaxed pleasure and unsurpassed enjoyment for guests.

Utilizing the patented SCRIMP resin-infusion technology to build the hull, the Horizon Premier 130+ is also built to the full Det Norske Veritas (DNV) classification and MCA LY2 code compliance. Its design criteria and construction standards are in compliance with HSLC (High Speed Light Craft) Rule with +1A1 R1, Yacht Notation and MCA LY2 Code.

The Horizon Premier 130+ includes a long list of premium equipment and features for long-term dependable performance.

Right:
Built to the strongest safety standards, the Horizon Premier 130+ is a luxurious ocean going yacht.

Below:
The yacht's interior is well laid out and takes advantage of the large spaces available.

SPECIFICATIONS: HORIZON PREMIER 130+	
Length Overall:	40.2m (132')
Beam:	8m (26' 2")
Draught:	2m (6' 8")
Displacement:	225 ton
Engine:	2 x MTU 1800 HP

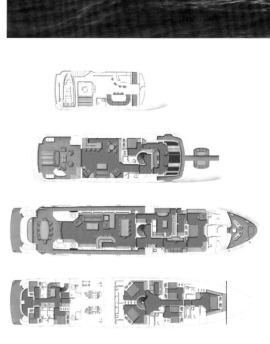

HORIZON GROUP

Horizon Yacht Co. Ltd.
No. 8 Kuang Yang Street
Hsiao Kang, Kaohsiung 81257
Taiwan, R.O.C.
Tel: +886 7 860 7770
Fax: +886 7 802 1207
Web: www.horizonyacht.com

Right:
Currently Horizon's largest yacht, the Horizon Bandido 148, has the strength and capability to cruise any ocean in the world.

Below:
The yacht's interior is customised to each owner's exact specifications and requirements.

HORIZON BANDIDO 148

The Horizon Bandido 148 Explorer is a long-range mega-yacht with worldwide cruising capability in all types of weather, while affording luxury yacht comforts to all onboard. Built with a steel hull and aluminium superstructure, the Bandido 148 Explorer mega-yacht leads Horizon Group into a new era by expanding its current model lines to include large steel luxury mega-yachts in its yacht portfolio. To meet every need and to assure superior sea keeping, the Bandido 148 will be designed, built and certified to BV Classification, ICE Class as well as MCA LY2 compliance. Powered by twin MTU 12V4000M60 1,800hp engines, the Bandido 148 will have a maximum speed of 15.6 knots, a cruising speed of 12 knots and a true oceanic range of 4,500 nautical miles. This mega-yacht will also feature ABT's TRAC stabilisers, whereby four 22sq/ft fins driven by Tracstar technology will provide perfect stability whether the yacht is at anchor or underway.

While each yacht will receive a customised interior designed according to its owner's requirements, the first Bandido 148 Explorer mega-yacht will house an expansive interior throughout its rugged, though elegant, superstructure. The layout of the first Bandido 148 includes accommodation for eight guests in four staterooms on the lower deck amidships, while a full-beam master suite with king-size bed, office, and his and her baths with Jacuzzi is located on the main deck forward. The upper deck of the yacht features a large sky-lounge, an exercise room and a sauna - both of which are designed with fold-down balconies - as well as the pilothouse and the captain's stateroom.

Connecting all the decks, an atrium staircase leads upwards to an expansive fly bridge with a spa pool for ten, lounging areas, a bar and excellent dining amenities.

The first Horizon Bandido 148 Explorer is scheduled to be shipped to Europe in 2010

SPECIFICATIONS: HORIZON BANDIDO 148	
Length Overall:	45m (148')
Beam:	8.85m (29')
Draught:	2.6m (8' 6")
Displacement:	385 ton
Engine:	2 x MTU 1800 HP

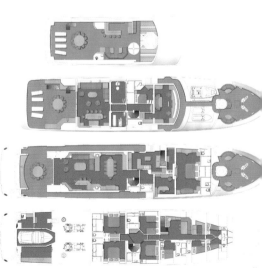

SUNSEEKER 30 METRE YACHT

Sunseeker has honed its skills over the past four decades, creating hundreds of the most distinctive luxury yachts that push the boundaries of expectation. Innovators in technology, yet guardians of traditional boat-building skills, Sunseeker's teams have always been pioneers of high performance and groundbreaking interior design.

Following the hugely successful launches of Sunseeker's 37 Metre Yacht and 34 Metre Yacht comes the latest yacht to be introduced by the company – the 30 Metre Yacht. Striking lines, up to 28 knots and 500 nautical miles, guest accommodation for ten or twelve, a crew of five or six, and serious big yacht appeal. These were the parameters Sunseeker started with when designing this exclusive 100' yacht.

At a glance, the distinctive styling follows that of her 34 Metre big sister, but in plan she is more the spiritual successor to the highly successful 105 Yacht. Yet despite her slightly shorter length, she is actually a much bigger boat, due to a completely new hull profile optimised to the absolute maximum permitted under the 24-metre load-line ruling. In addition, as Category 2 rather than LY2, this means not only cost-effectiveness in build, but also easier crew placement for a charter-compliant yacht because of the lower certification requirements.

Once again, globally active Sunseeker International has stretched the boundaries to deliver very credible benefits in a motor yacht through design ingenuity. A prime example of this is the big hull-inset windows. Everyone wants bright, naturally lit cabins with great views, but few get it on such a grand scale because designers must deal with more than aesthetics – there are stringent rules

Above & Far Left:
The Sunseeker 30 Metre Yacht's distinctive styling follows that of her 34 Metre big sister.

Left:
The wheelhouse offers superb 270⁰ visibility through sleekly angled screens, that almost creates the sense of an aircraft cockpit.

SUNSEEKER 30 METRE YACHT

to protect against the disaster scenario of breakage and water ingress. However, Sunseeker wanted to move the goal posts to show that shapes complementary to hull and superstructure lines were achievable within the naturally sought bounds of safety. So Sunseeker set to work with the relevant authorities, demonstrating its design and safety innovation with the result that the yard has once again broken new ground for this unique design.

Entering via the aft cockpit, with its spacious floor and seating plan and gorgeous architectural stainless steel hardware, the sheer scale of the accommodation is revealed through vast sliding doors, as does the inimitable Sunseeker interior styling, now so advanced. The walnut matt flooring with deep-velvet carpet inserts and leather panelling; the fixed furnishings finished with concealed lighting and glass and steel detailing; the carefully selected seating and tabling; the intelligent lighting systems; the customised cabinetry with racking for the crockery and glassware; the drop-down 50-inch LCD screen that is just one element of an extensive top-line AV system that can be enjoyed from every cabin and social space - all these are features of the new Sunseeker 30 Metre.

It is a truly holistic approach in which every owner can choose to be involved because, between the main structural bulkheads of this highly individual boat, virtually any floor plan and furnishing can be specified.

Moving forward to port, there is a steward's servery with crew-door though to the side-deck, and, of course, the galley. Here, satin-finished marble flooring, glass work surfaces, lacquered cabinets, and a wall of huge, custom cold-storage units make this area practical for extended cruising with a full complement of guests.

Below, the spacious and very comfortable crew accommodation has three sleeping cabins for six, and a separate mess area.

Forward, still on the main deck, the owner has a remarkable full-beam suite, an upside down duplex arrangement with a brilliant, daylight bright upper lounge and a lavish lower bedroom with vast bedside windows to

Above & Left:
The main salon and dining salon are beautifully designed and furnished.

Far Left & Centre:
The VIP stateroom on the lower deck is spacious, luxurious and features a beautifully designed en-suite bathroom.

SUNSEEKER 30 METRE YACHT

Sunseeker International Ltd
27 - 31 West Quay Road
Poole, Dorset, BH15 1HX. UK
T: +44 1202 381 111
F: +44 1202 382 222
W: www.sunseeker.com

Right, Below Left & Centre:
The owner has a remarkable full-beam suite, an upside down duplex arrangement with a brilliant, daylight bright upper lounge and a lavish lower bedroom with vast bedside windows to either side.

Below Right:
One of the two luxurious twin cabins.

either side. It is astonishing all this can be achieved in the bow of a not particularly deep-footed 30-metre yacht. The detailing impresses too, from the winged leather headboard with inset controls for AV, lighting and climate control systems, to the pivoting LCD TV screen which cunningly doubles as a room divider and which, with a simple twist, serves TV entertainment to either floor-level. Then there is the stunning en-suite with its enchanting mix of bronzed granites and glass.

The guest cabins are accessed from the central staircase that leads up to both the wheelhouse and fly bridge, and down to the lower-deck.

First, looking aft from the central foyer, the full-beam VIP suite has its own inner lobby formed by the large island bed floating in this expansive cabin. This area is flooded by daylight through the enormous span of portholes left and right. Surface finishing includes not only the generic satin-finished American walnut and neutral tones, but also radius-upholstered waffle-board panelling that is not only attractive but also conveniently sound deadening. Sunseeker has always been hot on power for speed, but always with low noise and vibration for comfort. In plan, this single full-beam cabin can be swapped for twinned double cabins that may be attractive to charter operators.

Forward through the foyer, the two mirrored, twin-bedded cabins have a clever, sliding mechanism, enabling conversion to double beds still with cabinetry in the right position on either side, with an optional fold-down Pullman berth potentially boosting guest accommodation from ten to twelve.

Moving up the central stairway to the wheelhouse, the superb 270-degree visibility through sleekly angled screens almost creates the sense of an aircraft cockpit. A generous sweep of observation sofas breaks the spell but makes for a fabulous view of operations.

Controls are the latest available with computerised ship's management and navigation systems, hi-tech communications and fingertip thrusters for bow and stern.

The sliding door to the back of the wheelhouse leads

up to the fly bridge that presents a huge area with a whole range of optional layouts. Of course, full dual controls have been fitted with the latest in helm seating, but the main focus is sure to be on the great new superyacht spa pool and bar arrangement. There is also the new hardtop arrangement with opening centre section, with an aft extendable canopy ensuring the entire deck area can be fully shaded.

Twin 2400 PS MTU diesels provide 28-knot performance, and for guest comfort TRAC zero-speed stabilisers are fitted as standard. For the unfamiliar, this means stabilisers abating the rocking not only at speed but, even more significantly, when at rest, anchored in the bay for a lunch-stop and play.

SPECIFICATIONS:	SUNSEEKER 30 METRE YACHT
Length Overall:	29.8m (97′ 9″)
Beam:	6.9m (22′ 8″)
Draught:	2.22m (7′ 3″)
Displacement:	102.6 ton
Guests:	10-12
Propulsion:	Twin 2400PS MTU diesels
Max. Speed:	28 knots

WALLY
SAIL

Wally is the world's leading builder of advanced composite luxury yachts. Founded in 1993 by Luca Bassani Antivari, Wally introduced a new stylish range of sailing yachts that, over the past few years, has successfully challenged and changed the entire design concept of how a luxury sailing yacht should look.

In 2001, emulating the success of its sailing yachts, Wally entered the motor yacht market and, sharing the same concept of combining technology with innovative design, created a new range of modern, stylish motor yachts. As a result, Wally has now built many luxury sailing yachts, most of which are over 80' in length and even more motor yachts ranging in size from 45' to 118' and beyond.

With several yachts under construction at any one time, this specialized builder is definitely one of the most popular among luxury yacht owners. Featured here are just two of Wally's latest launchings. Commissioned by an experienced and passionate yachtsman, the new 30m (100') sloop 'Indio' was designed to feature all the characteristics of a round-the-world high performance cruiser that can comfortably accommodate the owner and his family complete with small children.

The second yacht featured, the Wally 130 'Dream', is a revolutionary sloop rigged performance yacht. Using the latest state-of-the-art construction and advanced material technology, she is a lightweight rocket. Only recently launched she is widely anticipated to be the fastest sailing yacht ever to sail upwind.

Whatever her performance, one thing is for sure. Like all Wally yachts, she will receive plenty of admiring glances wherever she sails.

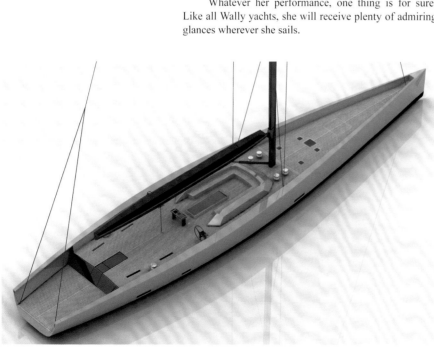

Above, Left & Centre:
Commissioned by an experienced and passionate yachtsman, the new 30m (100') sloop 'Indio' was designed to feature all the characteristics of a round-the-world high performance cruiser that can comfortably accommodate the owner and his family complete with small children.

Far Left:
The Wally 130 'Dream', is a revolutionary sloop rigged performance yacht designed by Wally and Javier Soto Acebal.

WALLY SAIL

WALLY 101 'INDIO'

Commissioned by an experienced and passionate yachtsman, the new 30m (100') sloop 'Indio' was designed to feature all the characteristics of a round-the-world high performance cruiser that can comfortably accommodate the owner and his family complete with small children.

As requested by the owner, the result is a 'family friendly' blue water sailing yacht that features on deck a social cockpit where the young kids can safely enjoy the open-air. However, this yacht is no slowcoach. Her high performance characteristics have been achieved by using the latest advanced composite pre-preg carbon construction technology in her construction, a 5m fixed keel featuring a trim tab, a mast in super high modulus and titanium deck fittings. As a result of this weight-saving technology, her displacement is only 59 tons.

On deck 'Indio' combines some design and styling elements of the previous 80-footer 'Indio', as well as those of the Wally 'Tiketitan'. Her layout features two separate cockpits, a social one amidships and the terrace on the sea aft, which gives access to the main salon. A central skylight runs from the mast foot all the way to the terrace on the sea, giving an abundance of light below deck, while the aft coamings are covered in teak to merge with the rest of the deck, thus making the yacht lines even sleeker.

Down below, the interior layout features, from bow to stern: a double berth crew cabin with head and shower; a large owner's stateroom; a guest/children double cabin on the port side with two beds and one Pullman; a guest double cabin to the starboard side with a queen size bed and one Pullman; the galley to port; the engine room amidships; a nanny/children's cabin with two bunks; a second crew cabin with two bunks to starboard, and the main salon aft. All cabins have en-suites, while the interior styling combines teak and wengé woods with ecru fabric resulting in a light yet cosy feel.

Without doubt, 'Indio' represents another significant achievement for this revolutionary yacht builder.

SPECIFICATIONS: WALLY 101 'INDIO'	
Length Overall:	30.50m (100' 1")
Beam:	6.80m (21' 2")
Draught:	4.90m (16' 9")
Displacement:	59 ton
Sail area Upwind:	542 m² (5,834 ft²)
Downwind:	1,259 m² (13,552 ft²)
Accommodation:	10 guests + 4 crew
Design:	German Frers
Interior Design:	Wally
Construction:	Composite pre-preg carbon
Mast and Boom:	Hall Spars
Rigging:	PBO Future Fibres

Above, Left & Far Left:
*'Indio' combines some design and
styling elements of the previous 80-
footer 'Indio', as well as those of the
Wally 'Tiketitan'.*

Centre:
*The modern main salon is light
and airy and looks out aft on to the
'terrace-on-the-sea'.*

WALLY SAIL

Wally Yachts
6 av. Albert II
MC 98000, Monaco
Tel: +377 93 10 00 93
Fax: +377 93 10 00 94
Web: www.wally.com

WALLY 130 'DREAM'

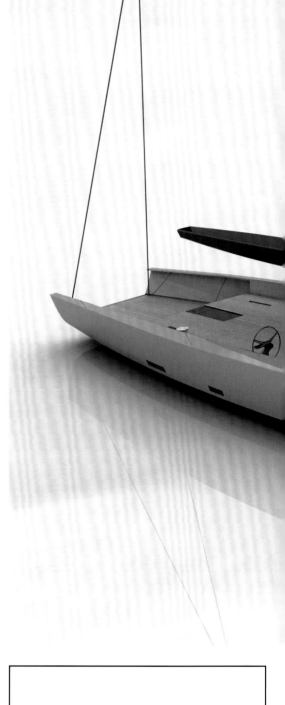

Recently launched, the Wally 130 'Dream' is a breakthrough sloop developed by Wally with the lines by Javier Soto Acebal. Such was the technology involved in this extraordinary yacht, that she is expected to be the fastest sailing yacht ever to sail upwind.

This 40m (130') megayacht's revolutionary stability is down to a combination of movable water ballast combined with a state-of-the-art trim-tab lifting keel. The innovative movable ballast combination was selected by Wally's Research & Development department to optimise safety and performance in such a large yacht. The 11 ton (24,251 lbs) water ballast improves the stability of this light displacement boat that weighs in at only 84 tons (185,200 lbs) while the 6m deep keel fitted with a trim tab improves the lift. However performance was not the only thought on the designer's mind. The draft can be reduced to 4m by hydraulic rams to allow the yacht to access shallow waters and secluded anchorages, for private social moments.

The deck on 'Dream' is similar to that of the Wally yacht 'Esense' and is characterised by the bulwark that leaves the hull lines pure, while offering more privacy and protection. Furthermore, the bulwark amidships backs on to both sides of the water tanks. The deck layout reveals a continuous uncluttered area, a sort of huge open cockpit. A distinctive styling element is the red coloured PBO rigging.

There are no social areas defined for specific uses, but instead the whole deck can be used for any purpose thanks to innovative movable components. The stern of 'Dream' features the so-called 'Terrace On The Sea', while the interior layout features a large owner's stateroom, three further guest suites as well as three twin cabins for the crew. The interior design is contemporary and is characterised by some strong architectural elements such as the natural grey oak-veneered joinery. Some interior structures have been visually enhanced to reflect the high performance of the yacht. The sides have a carbon look, the bulkheads are in light grey matt painted oak while the flooring is in wengé wood, giving the interiors a warm feeling.

SPECIFICATIONS:	WALLY 130 'DREAM'
Length Overall:	39.95m (131')
Length Waterline:	34.95m (114')
Beam:	7.90m (25' 11")
Draught:	4.00-6.00m (14' 7"- 19' 8")
Displacement:	84 ton
Ballast:	25 ton
Water Ballast:	11 ton
Sail Area:	727.5m² (7,831ft²)
Accommodation:	8 guests + 5 crew
Naval Architecture:	Javier Soto Acebal
Exterior Styling:	Javier Soto Acebal
Interior Design:	Wally
Construction:	Advanced Composite pre-preg carbon
Mast and Boom:	Hall Spars
Rigging:	PBO Future Fibers
Sails:	One Sails
Engine:	MAN D 0836 LE 401 EDS 450BHp @ 2600RPM

Above & Left:
*Recently launched, the Wally 130
'Dream' is a breakthrough sloop
developed by Wally with the lines
by Javier Soto Acebal. Such was
the technology involved in this
extraordinary yacht, that she is
expected to be the fastest sailing yacht
ever to sail upwind.*

CYRUS YACHTS

Cyrus Yachts is a prominent builder of semi-custom and custom yachts under the management of the renowned and highly respected Vitters Shipyard. Established in 2004 in Antalya, Turkey, the first semi-displacement motor yachts built by the yard achieved worldwide acclaim from the yachting industry and have already established the shipyard's reputation among the pre-eminent superyacht builders.

Antalya was chosen due to its strategic and convenient location of being next to the Mediterranean Sea, while the sales office for the company is located at the Vitters shipyard in The Netherlands.

Cyrus builds yachts that comply with the highest quality standards of systematic, precise manufacturing and now offers both custom and semi-custom yachts in lengths varying between 30 metres and 42 metres in length.

Cyrus Yachts' semi-custom model range comprises the Cyrus 30, Cyrus 34, Cyrus 38 and Cyrus 42. The Dutch designer Réne van der Velden is responsible for the exteriors of this striking range, while the leading naval architect, Piet van Oossanen, developed the lines of these extraordinary craft and is responsible for their excellent performance. Cyrus Yachts offers clients complete freedom in designing the general arrangement of each semi-custom model and they are also welcome to work with the interior designer of their choice.

With long experience in the yacht building industry, Cyrus management knows that excellent quality can only be achieved with superior working conditions. For this reason Cyrus Yachts does not compromise on quality in any of its facilities, work force or work scheduling. With more than 10,000m² of building facilities, the shipyard is

Above Left & Centre:
The semi-custom model range comprises the Cyrus 30, Cyrus 34, Cyrus 38 and Cyrus 42. The Dutch designer Réne van der Velden is responsible for the exteriors of this striking range, while the leading naval architect, Piet van Oossanen, developed the lines of these extraordinary craft and is responsible for their excellent performance.

Far Left:
Cyrus Yachts' modern yacht building facility in Antalya, Turkey, is close by the blue waters of the Mediterranean.

able to construct different and challenging projects at the same time. The yard currently has three construction halls, including a 112m (368') hall and a special painting shed in which they can build up to five yachts at the same time.

Cyrus Yachts' preferred hull construction material is composite and it collaborates with SP Gurit in order to secure its high quality standard. The shipyard uses the most advanced vacuum methods and infusion techniques available to ensure the best weight / stiffness ratios. This lightweight construction results in higher fuel economy, higher speed and, by saving weight in the deck and superstructure, a lower centre of gravity and superb stability. Similarly, the engineering and systems design is also carried out to the highest technological standards by an experienced group of mechanical and systems engineers. Many of the components fitted to the yachts are supplied by well-known Dutch yacht and ship building companies.

The excellent quality and craftsmanship of the shipyard has been proven by the award winning 'Angel of Joy', which is the very first yacht built by Cyrus Yachts. While the first two yachts 'Angel of Joy' and 'Fansea' shared the same 33m length, each yacht features very different custom styling and interior layouts. The overall styling of 'Angel of Joy', is contemporary classical and the distinctive dark metallic aubergine paint finish underlines her looks. The outside of the superstructure is covered with mahogany to give an extra touch to the warm classical appearance and feeling of the yacht. The interior is designed in cross veneered anigre wood panels which are set off by the wengé floor while light wood tones give the interior a very open and relaxing atmosphere. It is a harmonious design, following the theme and lines of the exterior profile.

The main aim for 'Fansea' was to build a cruising yacht that would be comfortable under all circumstances. 'Fansea' has excellent sea-keeping qualities, is easy to handle in all sea conditions and a pleasure to cruise aboard for extended trips. 'Fansea' is equipped with zero speed stabilizers that provide optimum stabilisation whether the yacht is at anchor or underway.

On 'Fansea', whatever the occasion is, you can choose between several generous and well-appointed areas for outside entertaining, from cocktails to gourmet dining, or simply relaxing in the Jacuzzi. The vast deck space provides endless options for leisure, fun and relaxation.

Above & Centre:
'Angel of Joy' has contemporary classical styling, while the distinctive dark metallic aubergine paint finish underlines her looks.

Left & Far Left:
'Fansea' is a pleasure to cruise aboard for extended trips.

CYRUS YACHTS

CYRUS ONE - CYRUS 34

Cyrus One is an immediate head turner and comes with the combination of performance, stability, sophistication, space and style. The semi-custom Cyrus 34 was launched in June 2008 and features a spacious fly bridge onboard offering a superb area for private relaxation. Cyrus Yachts created the Cyrus 34 to provide more storage space for water toys and to benefit from more opportunities with regard to the increased interior and exterior space.

The full width owner's cabin and three full width guest cabins all have en-suite facilities and are equipped with fully integrated entertainment systems. Each cabin has a separate stairway to the main deck and is finished in a different colour design. Prospective owners can customise a semi-custom yacht with ease and they are also welcome to bring their own interior designer, as did the owner of Cyrus One. The interior designer, Digital Space, comes from the hotel industry and created a yacht layout in close cooperation with Cyrus Yachts.

The yacht's hull and superstructure is constructed in composite with carbon fibre reinforcements to increase the stiffness and to reduce the weight. She has a displacement of 150 tons and is built to RINA and MCA requirements. Powered by twin 1,825-hp Caterpillar C32, V12 engines, Cyrus One has a range of 2,875 nautical miles at 13 knots and a maximum speed of 25 knots. Like every Cyrus yacht, Cyrus One is equipped with zero-speed stabilizers to ensure maximum comfort onboard.

SPECIFICATIONS:	CYRUS ONE - CYRUS 34
Length Overall:	34.30m (112' 6")
Beam:	7.10m (106' 3")
Draught:	1.65m (5' 5")
Displacement:	150 tons
Construction:	Composite
Accommodation:	8 guests / 4-5 crew
Engines:	2 x Caterpillar C32, 1,825hp
Maximum Speed:	25 knots
Range:	2,875 nm @ 13 knots

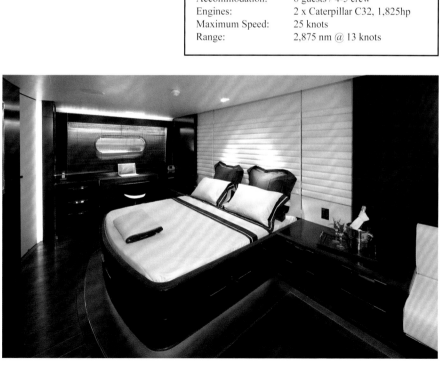

FEATURED YACHTS

Above & Left:
The Cyrus One is an immediate head turner and comes with the combination of performance, stability, sophistication, space and style.

CYRUS YACHTS

CYRUS 30

The semi-custom model range of Cyrus Yachts is well-known for excellent performance, superb craftsmanship, quiet operation, low maintenance and economical fuel consumption.

The semi-custom Cyrus 30 composite yacht has been specially designed for cruising with the same space, comfort and elegance that guests might find at home.

Highlights will include three double bed cabins on the lower deck, multiple outdoor dining arrangements, spacious sunbathing areas, easy water access and a huge fly bridge with Jacuzzi and bar. Powered by twin 1,015hp Caterpillar C18 engines, this RINA-classed and MCA-compliant motor yacht will cruise easily at 13 knots and have a maximum speed of 24 knots.

CYRUS 38 RAISED PILOTHOUSE

Cyrus Yachts created two semi-custom Cyrus 38 models in co-operation with René van der Velden to offer a raised pilothouse and a tri-deck design to clients. The open interior of the raised pilothouse yacht will provide both casual and formal atmospheres for varied entertainment and she will accommodate eight guests and up to six crew-members in true luxury.

Located on the main deck, a luxurious panoramic owner's suite will feature a private office and his and hers en-suite bathroom, while the guest accommodation on the lower deck will feature two double cabins and one twin bed cabin, all with en-suite baths and ample storage space. The dining room will be on the main deck in the aft section of the salon.

Enormous side windows will provide guests with unforgettable views of the seascapes, while the salon will extend out through a wide opening on to the outside deck and a large sheltered sun terrace where nine people will be able to enjoy the outside scenery sitting around a long mahogany table. For those guests wanting even more space, a Cyrus 38 Tri-Deck has also been designed.

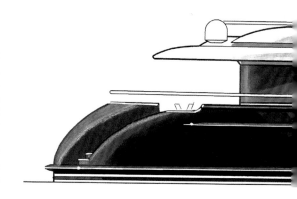

Right:
The Cyrus 38 Tri-Deck.

Below Left:
The Cyrus 38 Raised Pilothouse.

Below Right:
The Cyrus 30.

CYRUS 38 TRI-DECK

This elegant semi-custom Cyrus 38 Tri-Deck motoryacht will feature a semi-displacement composite hull. Built to RINA and MCA certifications the Cyrus 38 will be equipped with zero-speed stabilizers. Her interior and exterior day areas will be extremely impressive and spacious, allowing guests to feel comfortable and uncrowded. The expansive fly bridge will provide a very tranquil refuge from hustle and bustle of life, while on the upper deck the yacht will feature a dining table for ten guests and a stylish salon with bar and generous lounge areas. The upper deck salon will extend out through a wide opening onto to the outside deck and a large sheltered sun terrace where guests can sit and dine al-fresco as well.

A yacht built with entertaining in mind, an abundance of water sports equipment will provide for the active whilst those preferring to relax in the sunshine only have the problem of choosing where to do so.

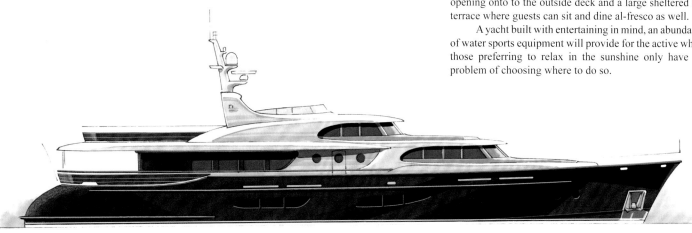

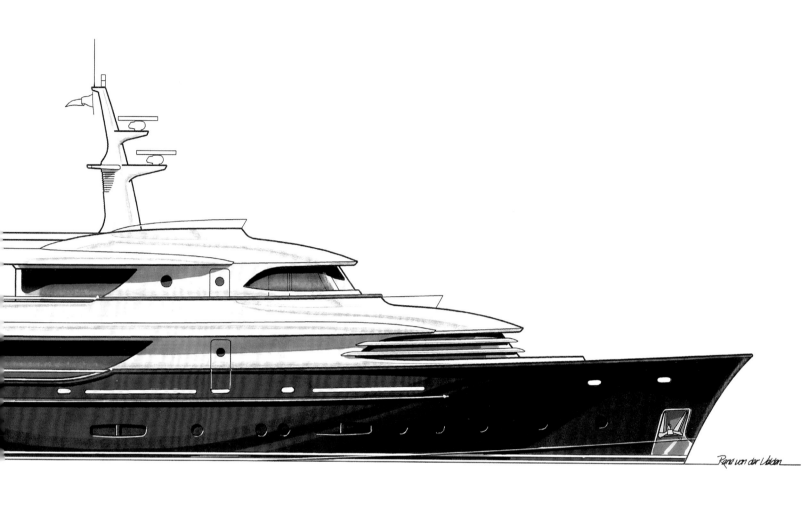

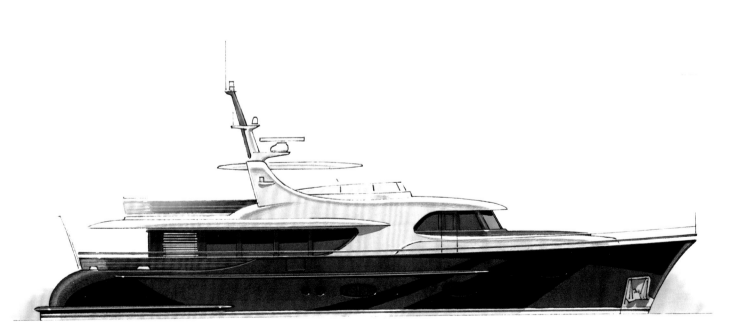

CYRUS YACHTS

Cyrus Yachts
Stouweweg 33
8064 PD Zwartsluis
The Netherlands
T: +31 38 38 67 145
F: +31 38 38 68 433
W: www.cyrusyachts.com

Right:
The custom Cyrus 32
by Guido de Groot.

Below Right:
The semi-custom Cyrus 42

Below Left:
The custom Cyrus 37 sailing yacht by
René van der Velden.

CYRUS 42

The flagship of the Cyrus semi-custom fleet, the Cyrus 42, has been designed to be a true ocean cruising tri-deck motor yacht built to the finest quality standards. Like all Cyrus yachts she will be built of composite material, be custom built according to each client's exact requirements and will feature a huge amount of space on her three decks to cosset her guests in consummate luxury.

With accommodation for ten guests and ten crew, she will have transatlantic crossing capability. Her twin Caterpillar C32 engines will give her a cruising range in excess of 4,000 nautical miles at a cruising speed of 14 knots, while her streamlined hull and high-tech construction offer good performance with a maximum speed of 19 knots.

CUSTOM YACHTS

CYRUS 32

This striking 32m custom project has been developed by the designer Guido de Groot in response to an enquiry for a displacement composite motor yacht with modern lines. A raised pilothouse motor yacht, the Cyrus 32 has a beam of 7.4m and has been designed to comply with both RINA and MCA regulations. The main deck features a large split level master cabin, with the master bathroom placed below and ahead. This layout creates an airy space, with panoramic views. Aft of the owner's cabin is a generous galley, a day-head and corridor leading through to the dining / main salon area. Further back, the aft deck allows for great outdoor entertainment. Up a level, the fully equipped raised pilothouse leads aft to an ample sun deck. This uppermost deck features enormous sun lounging areas, a large Jacuzzi, bar and seating areas.

The Cyrus 32 will be powered by twin Caterpillar C18 engines that will provide a cruise speed of 13 knots

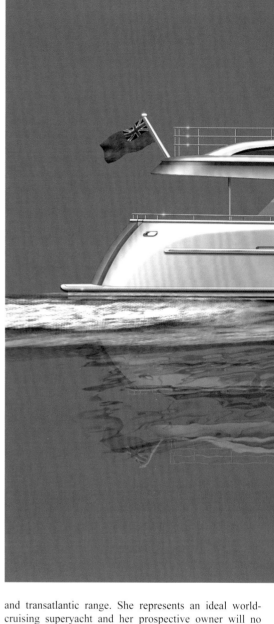

and transatlantic range. She represents an ideal world-cruising superyacht and her prospective owner will no doubt wander the oceans at will.

CYRUS 37 SAIL

This beautiful ketch rigged sailing yacht combines classic and contemporary lines with all the luxuries of a modern yacht. This custom yacht has been designed by René van der Velden Design in close co-operation with Cyrus Yachts. It incorporates an elegant and luxurious design, with wide dimensions and a purposefully comfortable layout.

The yacht has an overall length of 37.5m, a beam of 8.3m and a draft of 3.3m at full load. A luxuriant al-fresco aft deck dining area for twelve guests and a spacious sunbathing area are the centrepieces of the outdoor living space, while a generous cockpit and an elegant raised deckhouse allow guests the option of both outdoor and indoor dining, while enjoying the view in all conditions.

Below deck, a practical layout allows twelve guests to be comfortably accommodated in six en-suite cabins. The yacht features a full-beam owner's cabin aft, with study, seating area and a direct private access to the bathing platform, in addition to the four twin bed cabins and a full beam double bed cabin amidships.

As with the yard's other creations, this project has a unique exterior design and a perfect pedigree.

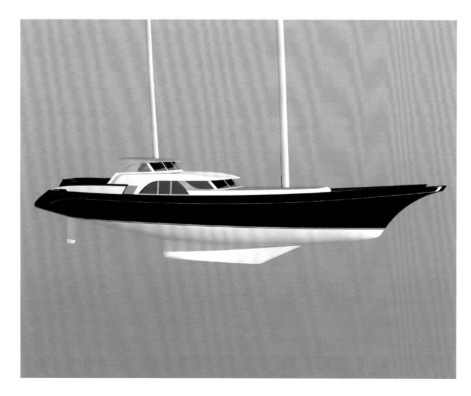

HARGRAVE CUSTOM YACHTS

Hargrave Yachts was originally known as the top yacht design firm in America when, under the direction of the legendary designer Jack Hargrave, the company played an important role in the success of other companies such as Hatteras, Burger, Amels, Prairie, Atlantic, and Halmatic, to name just a few.

In 1997, shortly after Jack Hargrave passed away, Michael Joyce returned to the company after an absence of twenty years to take over as president and CEO. Recognizing that Hargrave was far more than a design office, Joyce explained to Boating Industry International Magazine that Jack's name was in fact a 'brand name' and outlined his plans to begin construction of luxury yachts under the Hargrave banner.

Michael Joyce, head of Hargrave Custom Yachts, has always been an innovator. Embracing the changing times and the technological miracles of our age, he has been able to employ technology without succumbing to it. As a visionary entrepreneur with a passion for the finest traditions in yachting, and thirty years experience as a CEO in the industry, he knew it was the right time for a range of truly custom yachts in the 80'-100' size range, with realistic pricing, to enter the market.

With more than 80 yachts already built, Hargrave has recently launched a number of new models, several of which can be seen overleaf. It is worth noting that over half Hargrave owners have built more than one custom yacht with the yard and with some now on their fourth order, there is no doubt that Hargrave delivers yachts that rank among the best in the world.

Most importantly, they are also delivered at a price that is highly competitive!

Above:
The stylish Hargrave 100RPH
'King Baby'

Far Left:
Hargrave's new 84RPH
'On A Roll' was a big hit at the last
Fort Lauderdale Boat Show.

Centre:
The new Hargrave 135 Tri-Deck will
be the largest yacht to be launched so
far by the company.

Left:
The sleek and powerful
Hargrave 114RPH 'Sea Legend'.

HARGRAVE CUSTOM YACHTS

HARGRAVE 84RPH

While large luxury yachts require a full-time crew to run them, many experienced owners often enjoy the process of manning and running the yacht themselves. The reasons for this are numerous. Not only does it reduce, or indeed eliminate, the cost of employing a full-time crew, it gives the owner greater flexibility, privacy and indeed spontaneity when cruising.

These were the motivations for the owners of the first Hargrave 84RPH motor yacht. Presenting Hargrave, and presumably several other yards, with a list of attributes they required in a new yacht, top of the list was a mid-80' length yacht they could handle and cruise themselves without the need for a crew. Hargrave's experienced design team recognised the opportunity to create a yacht for the owners that achieved these parameters and could adapt previous standard interior configurations to meet the benefits of such a crewing system.

With the ability to be handled without crew or with a small crew, Hargrave's designers realised that with an extensive fly bridge control centre there was little need for a huge interior wheelhouse that takes up such a lot of space on yachts of this size. To replace it, they designed what they call a 'disappearing raised pilothouse', whereby a helm station is located on a mezzanine landing on the starboard side of the yacht. The upside to this ingenious arrangement is that it frees up space to create a wonderful galleried ceiling above the main galley and forward lounge.

Of course a major consideration of this yacht was that it should be easy to handle and very manoeuvrable. This is achieved by matching the yacht's twin Caterpillar engines with a powerful bow-thruster. These can be controlled on the fly bridge by a remote control station giving the helmsman the freedom to walk around the fly bridge without restraint while remaining totally in control of the yacht.

Onboard the yacht, the pedigree of Hargrave shines through. There are very few yachts which match a Hargrave

Above:
The Hargrave 84RPH eliminates the need to employ a full-time crew and gives the owner greater flexibility, privacy and indeed spontaneity when cruising.

Left:
The 'disappearing raised pilothouse', helm station is located on a mezzanine landing on the starboard side of the yacht. The upside to this ingenious arrangement is that it frees up space to create a wonderful galleried ceiling above the main galley and forward lounge.

Far Left:
The extensive fly bridge features a fully equipped helm station.

HARGRAVE CUSTOM YACHTS

for equipment and build quality and this is certainly the case on the Hargrave 84RPH.

The main salon of the yacht is bathed in natural light flooding through the marvellous galleried forward lounge and galley. A blend of beautiful wooden hand-crafted light coloured sofas and chairs give this area a luxurious and relaxing feel. More seating is to be found further forward facing the enormous galley area. The positioning of a large flat-screen television above the galley means this forward lounge is the ideal area to watch the game, with the Sub-Zero fridge within easy reach!

A wonderful chrome and wooden staircase next to the galley leads first to the helm station, then up to the expansive fly bridge deck, one of the largest on a yacht of this size, incorporating plenty of seating, the main helm-station and a wet bar, as well as ample space aft to store a large tender and deck crane.

On the lower deck the sleeping accommodation is well designed and supremely luxurious. A huge master stateroom is located amidships which takes in the full beam of the yacht and comes complete with his and hers en-suite bathrooms as well as plenty of storage and seating. In the bow the VIP cabin is almost as spacious, while two other en-suite guest cabins are situated between the master and VIP cabin. In total the yacht has four full suites for the owner and guests, plus crew accommodation for when crew are required for longer trips and extended stays.

The Hargrave 84RPH has without doubt set new standards for luxury yachts capable of being handled either by a small crew or just by the owner and his guests, and has equally set the mark for a luxurious custom built craft at a truly competitive price.

SPECIFICATIONS: HARGRAVE 84RPH	
Length Overall:	25.60m (84')
Beam:	6.40m (21')
Draught:	1.67m (5' 6")
Guests:	8
Crew:	2
Engines:	2 x Caterpillar C32, 1675hp
Maximum Speed:	23 knots
Cruise Speed:	20 knots
Construction:	FRP / Composite

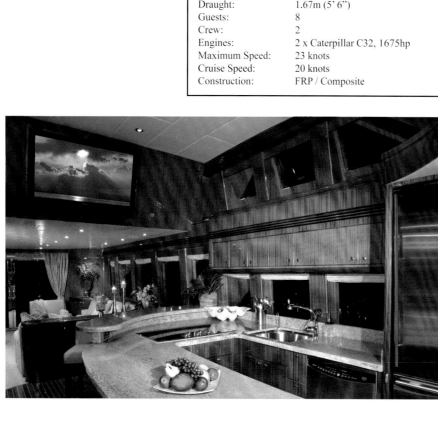

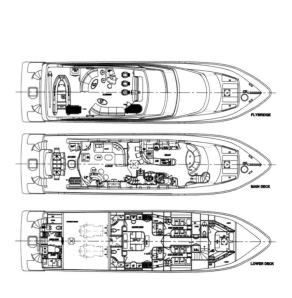

Above:
The main salon of the yacht is bathed in natural light flooding through the marvellous galleried forward lounge and galley.

Left:
The beautiful master stateroom is designed and furnished to a very high standard.

Far Left:
The positioning of a large flat-screen television above the galley means this forward lounge is the ideal area to watch the game, with the Sub-Zero fridge within easy reach!

HARGRAVE CUSTOM YACHTS

HARGRAVE 100RPH

One of Hargrave's most popular designs has been its hugely successful 100' Raised Pilothouse model. Although every yacht is different in terms of exterior styling and custom designed interiors, Hargrave still offers the yacht at a highly competitive price, which is even more astonishing considering that the craftsmanship that goes into this yacht is on a superyacht scale.

The latest Hargrave 100RPH to launch is the stunning 'King Baby', built for an owner who previously owned a Sunseeker Predator 68, but wished to upgrade to a truly custom built yacht.

Being 6' 3", one of the owner's requirements was for a yacht with a lot of headroom. Having visited the 6' 7" pro-football player Jason Taylor's 99ft Hargrave 'Katina', he asked Hargrave how they build their yachts with such good headroom. The reply came quickly – "this is a custom yacht – you can do anything you want"!

An experienced yachtsman, the owner laid down a list of items he wished to include on the yacht, such as a two storey atrium foyer, double the typical sound insulation normally found on a yacht of this size, and twin anchors for Mediterranean mooring. As the owner explains, "Hargrave brings new meaning to the word 'patience'. They simply do not know how to say 'no'."

Hargrave have a range of hull designs it can use for this size of yacht, but can also build a custom hull as required. Everything else onboard the yacht is designed and constructed exactly how the client wants it.

With a European profile, 'King Baby' would look as much at home in the Mediterranean as it does in Florida. Starting from the top, she features a huge fly bridge with plenty of comfortable seating, a dining area, loungers, a wet bar, helm-station and a good sized Jacuzzi. A large portion of the fly bridge can be covered by a retractable awning, giving guests relief from the mid-day sun when required.

Down some steps, the raised pilothouse is extremely well equipped with the latest technology, as well as a

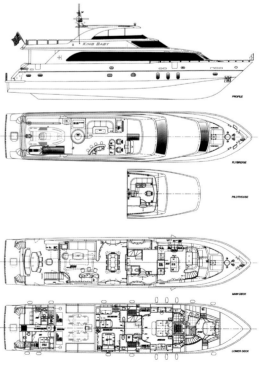

Above:
The latest Hargrave 100RPH to launch is the stunning 'King Baby', built for an owner who previously owned a Sunseeker Predator 68, but wished to upgrade to a truly custom built yacht.

Left & Far Left:
'King Baby' features a huge fly bridge with plenty of comfortable seating, a dining area, loungers, a wet bar, helm-station and a good sized Jacuzzi.

HARGRAVE
CUSTOM
YACHTS

seating area for guests to congregate and enjoy the yacht in motion.

Next deck down, the main-deck salon is large and spacious and leads forward into a separate dining area. The use of beautiful cherry wood in the cabinetry, a bar with a striking backlit white onyx top, and light coloured fabrics and carpets give this area a stylish, elegant feel. Decorated with the owner's wonderful choice of art, 'King Baby' is based on a 'rock and roll' theme, with signed pictures by several of the world's top recording artists including Sir Paul McCartney.

The advantage of the Raised Pilothouse arrangement is that forward of the main salon and galley on the main deck, there is still room for an additional 'forward lounge', ideal as a TV lounge or private 'hideaway', or even a crew lounge.

On the lower deck, there is guest accommodation for eight, all in stylishly furnished en-suite staterooms, with the owner's stateroom in particular being an impressive size. Featuring a king-size bed, his and hers bathroom, and walk-in wardrobes and dressing areas, this stateroom is bigger than that found on many larger yachts.

With ample crew accommodation aft and a large swim platform, 'King Baby' is a yacht that will give many years of pleasure, all the more so as she has been built at a very attractive price. For owners looking for a truly magnificent 100' motor yacht, Hargrave's 100RPH should be among their first ports of call.

SPECIFICATIONS:	HARGRAVE 100RPH 'KING BABY'
Length Overall:	30.60m (100' 6")
Beam:	6.40m (21')
Draught:	1.80m (5' 9")
Guests:	8
Crew:	4
Engines:	2 x Caterpillar C32, 1675hp
Maximum Speed:	21 knots
Cruise Speed:	18 knots
Range:	1,000 nautical miles @ 12 knots
Construction:	FRP

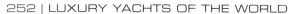

Above:
The owner's stateroom is impressive for a yacht of this size.

Left & Centre:
The main-deck salon is large and spacious and leads forward into a separate dining area.

Far Left:
The well equipped raised pilothouse.

HARGRAVE CUSTOM YACHTS

HARGRAVE 114RPH

When most yacht owners attend a boat show or study a book, such as 'Luxury Yachts Of The World', they will tell you that they like 'this on that boat' and 'that on this boat'. Constantly seeking the perfect yacht, it seems that for many yacht owners there is never a yacht that suits all their purposes – at least with a production or semi-custom yacht.

The answer of course is to build a true custom yacht, but generally these do not come cheap and very few builders construct yachts such as this under 120'.

The exception to this rule is Hargrave Custom Yachts, who specialises in building custom yachts at a very competitive price, exactly in accordance with each owner's requirements and wishes.

The new Hargrave 114RPH 'Sea Legend' is a real example of this, built for experienced yacht owners who knew exactly what they wanted. When they first started looking for a new yacht, there was simply nothing on the market that ticked all the boxes on their list of requirements.

Hargrave, however, explained to the owners that with them, they start with a clean sheet of paper and work upwards and that anything the owners wanted, they could build. This freedom sealed the deal on what was to become an 18-month construction process, during which time the owners contributed wholeheartedly to create the yacht of their dreams. For this Hargrave 114RPH, the owners started with a huge list of requirements. First, the yacht must be fitted with large fuel tanks and engines to have a cruising range over 2,000 nautical miles while cruising at 12 knots. Next, they wanted a fishing cockpit aft with a transom fitted live bait-well, as well as a dive locker complete with a Brownie Dive Compressor. Already, this set of requirements would have eliminated 90% of luxury yacht builders that normally construct yachts of this size.

On an engineering side, 'Sea Legend' has been built to last. The air-conditioning system was increased to a three

Above:
The new Hargrave 114RPH
'Sea Legend' has been built for
experienced yacht owners who knew
exactly what they wanted.

Left:
'Sea Legend' has a fishing cockpit aft
with a transom fitted live bait-well, as
well as a dive locker complete with a
Brownie Dive Compressor.

Centre:
The large fly bridge features a Jacuzzi
and wonderful views.

Far Left:
The wheelhouse has been carefully
designed for undertaking long ocean
passages when required.

HARGRAVE
CUSTOM YACHTS

ton, chilled-water Cruisair system normally found on much larger yachts, and she is fitted with a heavy duty Naiad 420 roll stabilisation system to keep the yacht perfectly level, whether at sea or at anchor.

Since much of the owner's time onboard is spent in the open air, having a high quality fly bridge 'roof' was imperative. Hargrave's wonderful fibreglass hardtop, with an automatic, retractable soft inner panel in its centre, was perfect and meant guests could enjoy the sun or seek the shade easily while still remaining on the fly bridge.

Inside, the wide elegant interior, designed by the firm 'Yacht Interiors by Shelley', features exotic marble stonework, beautiful inlaid mosaics, rich cherry wood hand crafted by Hargrave's experienced team of carpenters and light, serene fabrics. Designed with four staterooms on the lower deck, 'Sea Legend' has a huge master stateroom with full en-suite facilities, a large VIP cabin in the bow and two further twin guest cabins, each with an extra Pullman berth, all of which have en-suite facilities.

Since taking delivery, the owners have cruised the entire Eastern seaboard of the United States, while during the winter season they have cruised the islands of the Caribbean, the Yucatan Peninsula, Honduras and Belize. As the owners are keen scuba divers, the yacht carries two qualified dive instructors on board. In addition she carries a whole array of tenders, kayaks and other water sports equipment.

A truly active, custom built yacht, strong enough and highly equipped to cruise anywhere, this first Hargrave 114RPH is a winner through and through and knocks spots off most of its semi-custom competition.

Right:
The wide elegant interior, designed by the firm 'Yacht Interiors by Shelley', features exotic marble stonework, beautiful inlaid mosaics, rich cherry wood hand crafted by Hargrave's experienced team of carpenters and light, serene fabrics.

Below Left:
The elegant master bathroom.

Below Centre:
'Sea Legend's galley has been fitted out to a very high standard.

Below Right:
The stylish master stateroom is rich, warm and very relaxing.

SPECIFICATIONS:	HARGRAVE 114RPH 'SEA LEGEND'
Length Overall:	34.70m (114')
Beam:	7.00m (23')
Draught:	2.10m (6' 8")
Guests:	10
Crew:	6
Engines:	2 x Caterpillar 3412, 1400hp
Maximum Speed:	16 knots
Cruise Speed:	12 knots
Range:	2,000 nautical miles @ 12 knots
Construction:	FRP / Composite

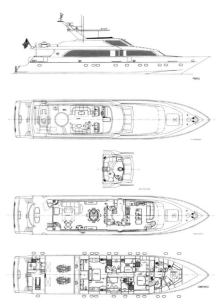

HARGRAVE CUSTOM YACHTS

Hargrave Custom Yachts
1887 West State Road 84
Fort Lauderdale. FL 33315. USA
T: +1 954 463 0555
F: +1 954 463 8621
W: www.hargrave.org

Hargrave Custom Yachts (Europe)
88 Christchurch Road
Ringwood, Hampshire. BH24 1DR. UK
T: +44 1425 473104
F: +44 1425 474368
E: info@hargraveeurope.org
W: www.hargraveeurope.org

HARGRAVE DESIGNS

Already the market leader in fully customised yachts in the 70' – 100' range, Hargrave Custom Yachts is continuing to expand upwards, first with the launch of the new Hargrave 114RPH 'Sea Legend' and later this year with the launch of the new Hargrave 125RPH and the Hargrave 135 Tri-Deck. These yachts are being built for existing Hargrave owners who appreciate the time and attention to detail that Hargrave takes to ensure they receive their dream yacht.

The new Hargrave 125' Raised Pilothouse 'Cocktails' is being built for an existing Hargrave owner who likes to entertain. Featuring an extensive fly bridge, a huge interior and plenty of areas for open-air dining, she has European styling with full 'wrap-around' windows and will have luxurious accommodation for at least ten guests. As with all Hargrave yachts, the new 'Cocktails' is being built to the highest quality and safety standards and will soon be gracing the warm waters of Florida and the Caribbean. Similarly the Hargrave 135' Tri-Deck is also due for launch this year and when launched will be the largest Hargrave so far built. Expected to set new standards for yachts of this length, both in terms of quality and price, she is eagerly awaited by all who know this prestigious yachting company.

Not resting on their laurels however, currently on the drawing board at Hargrave Custom Yachts are the Hargrave 130' Tri-Deck and Hargrave 101' Fly Bridge, both of which will soon begin construction. As one comes to expect with Hargrave, both these yachts will be built to their owners' exact custom requirements at a highly competitive price. With highly striking European styling, these yachts are ideal for not just the American market but also to take on the top European brands in their home markets.

For owners seeking a high quality custom yacht, built exactly to their requirements and at a price that is highly competitive, without doubt Hargrave is a company to contact.

Above:
The new Hargrave 125' Raised
Pilothouse 'Cocktails' is being built for
an existing Hargrave owner who likes
to entertain.

Left:
The Hargrave 135' Tri-Deck is due for
launch later this year.

Far Left:
The powerful and stylish
Hargrave 100 Fly Bridge.

BURGER BOAT COMPANY

Established in 1863, Burger Boat Company has been at the forefront of American boat and yacht building for nearly one and a half centuries. Between 1870 and the turn of the 20th century, the Burger brand appeared on almost 100 vessels including schooners, tugs, scows, steamers and barges. Throughout this time the Burger name was, and still is, synonymous with innovation, quality and craftsmanship.

Burger Boat Company continues the tradition started in 1863, that of building custom yachts ranging from 75' to 200' (23m to 60m) in both steel and aluminium. Today, each custom Burger is a reflection of her owner's specific requirements and embodies the latest in technology and innovation.

Burger Boat Company remains one of the most successful yacht yards in the world. In the last 16 years, 33 vessels ranging from 76' to 153' have been launched by the yard, all built to the highest quality standards.

Continuing in that vein, the last couple of years have arguably been the greatest in the company's history, with the launchings of some of the finest yachts the company has ever built, such as the twin 38.5m 'Areti I' and 'Areti II', the 31m 'Tò-Kalòn', the 47m 'Ingot' and the stunningly beautiful 46m 'Sycara IV'.

Above & Centre:
The 47m (152') 'Ingot'.

Left:
The 46m (151') classic fantail cruiser 'Sycara IV'.

Far Left:
The 31m (101'6") 'Tò-Kalòn'.

BURGER BOAT COMPANY

'ARETI I & II'

Even for such an experienced and knowledgeable yard, the construction of the yachts 'Areti I' and 'Areti II' was somewhat different. A young Russian industrialist, impressed with the yard's previous work, asked the yard to build him not one, but two identical yachts. The client's reasoning was simple. Because he spent a good deal of time in both the USA and in Europe, he wanted a yacht in both regions at all times, so that he and his family and clients could enjoy a yacht at any time and without the need for their yacht to continually cross the Atlantic.

With this plan in mind, designs for the yachts, which to all intents and purposes are identical, were drawn up. Named 'Areti I' and 'Areti II', the yachts are 38.5m (126' 4") in length with aluminium hulls and superstructures. Naval architecture and interior design was all undertaken by the highly professional Burger Design Team - the exterior of the yachts are classically styled and the traditional interiors feature recessed panelled makore and wonderful fluted column details throughout.

Combining a simple, uncluttered elegance by using soothing tones of cream, rust and brown, the interiors of the yachts have been designed with main deck level master suites and four large guest staterooms below decks. Powered by twin Caterpillar engines, each yacht delivers a respectable 15.5 knot maximum speed and has a 3,360 nautical mile range when cruising at 12.5 knots. As if to reinforce their quality status, 'Areti I' and 'Areti II' have also been built to ABS A1 Commercial Yachting Standards, AMS Certification and in compliance with the MCA Code of Practice for Safety.

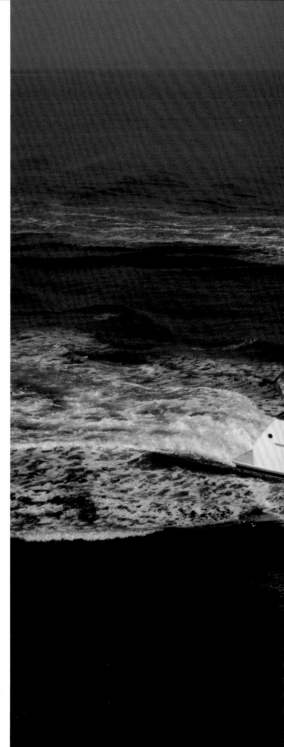

SPECIFICATIONS: 'ARETI I & II'	
Length Overall:	38.50m (126' 4")
Beam:	8.30m (27' 2")
Draught:	1.98m (6' 6")
Accommodation:	10 guests + 7 crew
Naval Architecture:	Burger Design Team
Interior Design:	Burger Design Team
Propulsion:	2 x Caterpillar 3508
Speed (max / cruise):	15.5 / 12.5 knots
Range:	3360 nm @12.5 knots

Above & Left:
'Areti I & II' epitomise Burger's reputation for strong, stylish, classic looking yachts.

Left:
The main lounge and dining area exude luxury and quality.

Centre:
The exquisite master bathroom.

Far Left:
The stylish master stateroom is decorated in light woods and furnishings, highlighting the feeling of space onboard the yacht.

BURGER BOAT COMPANY

'TÒ-KALÒN'

In September 2006 Burger Boat Company announced the signing of the contract for a contemporary-styled 31m (101' 6") enclosed bridge, high-speed motor yacht. With a team consisting of Cor D. Rover as the exterior stylist combined with the talented Donald L. Blount & Associates engineering group and the highly acclaimed Burger Design Team, this yacht promised to be absolutely incredible. Just over two years after the contract was signed 'Tò-Kalòn' was displayed at the Fort Lauderdale International Boat Show to international acclaim.

Among the top priorities for the construction of 'Tò-Kalòn' was the "need-for-speed" combined with world-class yacht quality. The unique hull design provides the necessary lift to achieve higher speeds and the soft chine ensures comfortable sea-keeping qualities. Extensive use of lightweight materials and carefully calculated design and engineering parameters ensure the yacht is capable of reaching a speed of 27.8 knots.

Onboard, 'Tò-Kalòn's interior revolves around the sapele panelling with accents of sapele pomele that flow throughout the main deck salon and guest accommodation, providing the perfect background for traditional furnishings. The owner's stateroom is located on the lower deck, while further forward there are two additional guest cabins with en-suite bathrooms, one twin cabin and one double cabin.

Twin 2,400 hp MTU-M93 engines power the all aluminium 'Tò-Kalòn'. This fully ABS certified vessel has several unique features including a comprehensive ship's monitoring and information system integrated with the entire vessel's electrical power system.

The owners of 'Tò-Kalòn' wanted a unique vessel. They loved the idea of having a one-of-a-kind vessel, unlike others docked at marinas and seen along the waterways. Having done their homework, they knew that Burger Boat Company, a custom yacht builder, could deliver. Without doubt they were proved right.

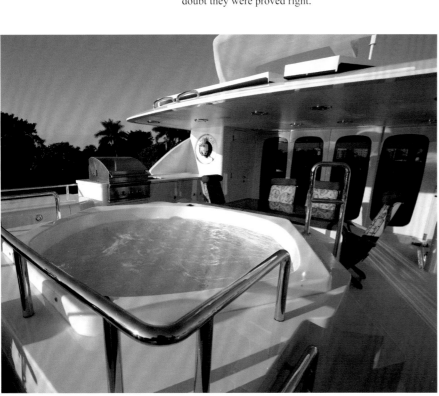

SPECIFICATIONS: 'TÒ-KALÒN'	
Length Overall:	31m (101' 6")
Beam:	6.9m (22' 6")
Draught:	1.5m (5' 3")
Naval Architecture:	Burger Design Team / Donald Blount & Assoc.
Exterior Stylist:	Cor D. Rover Design
Interior Design:	Burger Design Team / Owner
Construction:	Aluminium
Propulsion:	2 x 2,400 hp MTU-M93
Maximum Speed:	27.8 knots

Above & Left:
The owners of 'Tò-Kalòn' wanted a unique vessel - a one-of-a-kind vessel, unlike others docked at marinas.

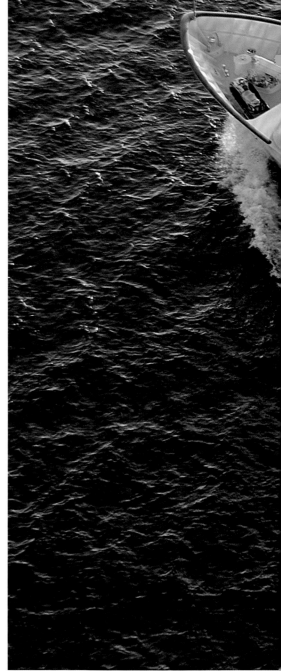

BURGER BOAT COMPANY

'INGOT'

'Ingot' is the one of the most luxurious and sophisticated Burger yachts built to date. Powered by twin Caterpillar 3508 engines, she is easily able to efficiently cruise the world privately and safely. Ingot was designed to be an environmentally friendly "go anywhere" exploration vessel with the refinement of a classic and stately motor yacht.

With an exquisite design throughout her 467m² (5,025 sq.ft) of interior accommodation and 386m² (4,150 sq.ft) of exterior deck and leisure space, she features brilliant detail and amenities ensuring pleasant cruising for owners and guests wherever she travels.

'Ingot' features a "Neo" Classical motif enriched by traditionally designed, Honduras mahogany. The interior incorporates curved, moulded joinery details throughout, accented by 104 custom built round Honduras mahogany pillars with maple burl inlaid veneers.

The lower deck accommodation includes four large VIP staterooms with king sized berths, unique joinery details, walls of raised panel mahogany and a blend of soft fabrics. Each VIP stateroom includes an en-suite bathroom with heated floors and rare marbles, granites and onyx.

A central staircase lies adjacent to a full-sized, wheelchair accessible elevator and serves all four levels. On the main deck, the salon and dining area features two large, back lit white onyx ceiling panels; one directly over the dining table and the other over the seating area in the main salon. A radius faced mahogany china cabinet with a form matching soffit above divides these spaces.

The sky deck features a large pilot house/navigation area forward with an adjacent captain's stateroom, while further aft, the sky lounge has a wealth of comfortable seating, an entertainment area and wet bar.

A yacht designed for true enjoyment and entertainment, one of the most popular areas on board is the sun deck which offers a large hot tub and sun lounge, perfect for passing time with family and friends.

SPECIFICATIONS: 'INGOT'

Length Overall:	47m (153')
Beam:	9.04m (29' 8")
Draught:	2.29m (7' 6''')
Naval Architecture:	Burger Design Team / Vripack
Interior Design:	Burger Design Team / Vripack
Construction:	Aluminium
Propulsion:	2 x Caterpillar 3508
Speed (max / cruise):	15 / 13 knots
Range:	4000 nm @11 knots

Above & Left:
'Ingot' is the one of the most luxurious and sophisticated Burger yachts built to date.

Left & Centre:
The interior incorporates curved, moulded joinery details throughout.

Far Left:
The wonderful sun-deck Jacuzzi, with surrounding sun pads, is a sun-worshipper's dream.

BURGER BOAT COMPANY

Burger Boat Company
1811 Spring St.
Manitowoc, WI 54220
Tel: +1 920 686 5117
Fax: +1 920 686 5144
Web: www.burgerboat.com

Right:
Though no longer a 'New Project', the recently launched 46m (151') classic fantail cruiser 'Sycara IV' is yet another wonderful collaboration between Burger Boat Company, naval architect Bruce King, and Ken Freivokh for interior design and exterior detailing.

Below Right:
'Sea Owl' is the result of an impressive collaboration between the Burger Design Team, Vripack Engineering and Andrew Winch Designs.

Below Left:
Hull 508 is a 42.7m (140') tri-deck motor yacht that is being built using the modular construction processes.

NEW PROJECTS

'SYCARA IV'

Recently launched, the 46m (151') classic fantail cruiser 'Sycara IV' has an appearance from a bygone age, 'Sycara IV' epitomises what luxury yachting is all about. Displaying a truly elegant profile, her exterior styling and naval architecture comes from the board of Bruce King and the Burger Design Team, while her interior has been designed by the renowned British designer, Ken Freivokh. Though classic in appearance, 'Sycara IV' carries the latest technology onboard, including twin 600hp Caterpillar C18 diesel engines, as well as Quantum 'Zero Speed' stabilizers and Quantum bow and stern thrusters.

'SEA OWL'

An experienced yachting family from Long Island, New York is commissioning 'Sea Owl' and although the family is well versed in developing and managing projects of great magnitude, this is their first custom yacht design and construction project.

'Sea Owl' is the result of an impressive collaboration between the Burger Design Team, Vripack Engineering and Andrew Winch Designs. This classic family motor yacht, being built for a charming and experienced yachting family, will have a nautical and traditional interior for a contemporary lifestyle.

This full-displacement tri-deck yacht will be configured with a transom garage for the tender and water toys, outfitted with a fog-mist sprinkler system, zero speed stabilization and will utilize the high strength, highly corrosion resistant marine alloy, Alustar.

'Sea Owl' is not intended for charter, but will be enjoyed by family and friends as their plans include extensively cruising to distant ports around the world. In the utmost luxury of course!

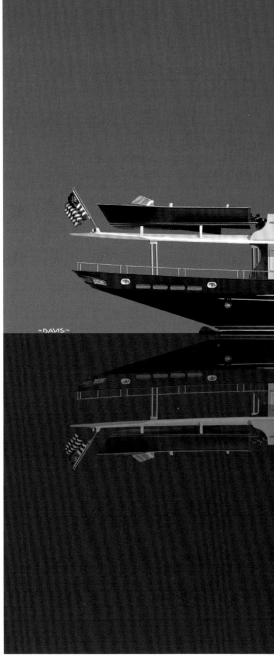

HULL 508

Burger Boat Company's Hull 508 is a 42.7m (140') tri-deck motor yacht that is being built using the modular construction processes. Each module is built to increase access to the various components while providing the ability to start outfitting each module earlier in the construction process, resulting in increased accuracy and project efficiency.

Scheduled for a 2010 launch, Hull 508 features accommodation for ten guests in the owner's party and is ideally suited for entertaining family, friends and business associates.

Designed to be fully accessible, Hull 508 features a glass enclosed circular elevator servicing all decks. The main deck consists of a full beam master suite, large formal salon, formal dining room and a teak aft deck with a large dining area.

The bridge deck consists of an owner's office situated aft of the wheel house, a butler's pantry and a large sky lounge leading to an inviting open deck area complete with a dining table.

The sundeck includes a large hot tub with sun pads; a built-in barbeque; multiple dining areas; a port side powder room and an air-conditioned all glass exercise room accessible by way of the glass enclosed elevator.

PALMER JOHNSON

P almer Johnson's foundation stems from a ninety-year history of landmark achievements - from championship sailing yachts to award winning mega-yachts. With the largest built aluminium US yacht of its time; the first Explorer of its type; the first aluminium Lloyd's/MCA compliant yacht; the first gas turbine/water jet powered yacht, notably 'Fortuna' for the King of Spain, the established firm has a proud background, incomparable to other superyacht builders.

Now in its fifth year of semi-custom Sports Yacht production, Palmer Johnson continues to expand the successful range and, in addition, provides a preview of its groundbreaking 82 metre 'PJ World'. This latest design is set to redefine the traditional concept behind exploration vessels.

Palmer Johnson launched the 120-foot express cruiser 'Cover Drive' in 2004, followed by six more 120's. The PJ 135', 150' and 170' Sports Yachts all take their styling cues from the PJ 120' to create a family of mega-yachts that are instantly recognisable with their powerful shoulders and stream-lined profiles. A sense of 'Sports Coupe' speed, style and luxury personify the Sports Yacht Series spirit. Seventeen of these yachts have now been built with three delivered in 2009.

All PJ's Sports Yachts are built to Lloyd's classification and are MCA registered. Along with PJ's reputation for superb sound and vibration reduction, all 120, 135 and 150 models have included 'at-rest' stabilizers since 2008. Italian designers Nuvolari Lenard are responsible for exterior and interior styling and work with each owner's individual personality, while MTU diesel engines continue to ensure optimum motor performance.

Above & Below:
Palmer Johnson continues to expand its successful series of motor yachts , ranging in size from the 36m PJ 120 to the groundbreaking 82m 'PJ World'.

PALMER JOHNSON

PJ 120

The PJ 120 marked the change for Palmer Johnson from fully custom projects to the semi-custom concept, setting the standard for all luxury Sports Yachts and the basis for the 135', the 150' and 170' PJ models to follow.

The fourth boat in the 120' series, 'Vanquish', was significant because according to PJ President Mike Kelsey Jr., she represents critical mass for the line. 'Vanquish' boasts balance, proportion and athleticism with windows that give the boat excellent proportion and aggressive shoulders leading the eye back to her tiered aft-deck, or rather decks, plural.

On the main-deck level, twin teak coffee tables easily convert into a single, hydraulically height-controlled dining table for the facing sofas. Outboard stairs on both sides lead down to a large, built-in sun pad. From there, a centreline staircase connects to the swim platform.

The dining area aft of the main salon takes in the views of the aft-deck and sea, much like a hillside Mediterranean café.

To ensure nothing obstructed that view while dining, as well as offering the most private sun-deck in its class, PJ engineered the stairs leading to the sun-deck to, literally, 'disappear'. With the touch of a button the top half pulls up into a hidden recess in the roofline and the bottom folds into the low-slung cabinet at its base.

'Vanquish's interior perfectly matches her streamlined minimalist exterior without becoming austere. A chocolate-coloured wengé sole anchors a masculine palette that includes washed white oak and high-gloss macasser ebony. Spinneybeck leather inserts in parque orange add an earthy energy while Rubelli fabrics throughout soften the feel. Italian-made Pole 74 sofas kick out into oversized recliners, adding another level of relaxation.

A large-screen TV acts as a divider between the salon and the dining area, the top of the cabinet containing a flush-hinged fold-out that serves as a second sideboard during meals. For movie watching, the cabinet can be

hydraulically raised to cinema-screen height and rotated towards the viewer regardless of where he sits.

The forward-facing master stateroom is amidships and entered through a dressing room that can be closed off from the sleeping area. A platform king-size bed, desk and built-in lounge are awash with sunlight from three large round port lights on each side.

With a maximum speed of approximately 30 knots and accommodation for up to eight guests and six crew, 'Vanquish' turns heads and hearts wherever she goes.

SPECIFICATIONS: PALMER JOHNSON 120'

Length Overall:	36.90m (121')
Beam:	7.62m (25')
Draught:	1.98m (6' 5")
Accommodation:	6-8 guests + crew
Naval Architecture:	Palmer Johnson
Interior Design:	Nuvolari Lenard
Construction:	Aluminium Hull / Composite Superstructure
Propulsion:	2 x MTU 12V 4000 DDEC M90
Classification:	Lloyds Register 100 A1 SSC Yacht Mono HSC G6 MCH MCA Short Range

Above:
The PJ 120 marked the change for Palmer Johnson from fully custom projects to the semi-custom concept.

Left:
The expansive aft deck is perfect for entertaining.

Far Left:
In the main salon, Italian-made Pole 74 sofas kick out into oversized recliners, adding another level of relaxation.

PALMER
JOHNSON

PJ 123

PJ 123-3 is the third in PJ's composite-built raised pilothouse yachts that marries the sleek Italian style of Nuvolari Lenard with grand American size. 'Ocean Drive' is a chic, attention-grabbing 123-foot yacht with an interior that holds voluminous, eminently liveable spaces.

Like the larger PJ 135 yacht, the 123's layout cleverly features a spacious sun-deck with bar and barbeque area, sun pads and Jacuzzi. MTU 16 cylinder twin engines power her to a speed of approximately 24 knots with a cruising capacity of 19 knots. With the same advanced insulation of the larger aluminium Sports Yachts and her fibreglass structure, this Fly Bridge model is remarkably silent underway.

The elegant interior features rare sycamore wood accented with black walnut and Rubelli fabrics in cool cream, soft gold and subtle browns and bronzes. With sugary white Thassos marble and rich Rosso Levanto marble, her interior exudes a sumptuous elegance throughout.

Forward on the main-deck is a master suite that befits a larger tri-deck yacht. There is a spacious king-sized bed suite with his and her baths running athwart-ships forward. Below decks, the guest areas offer a huge VIP stateroom along with two additional en-suite doubles.

The 123 line shows a different raised pilothouse personality. From the yacht's design, décor and construction to the innovative details and finish, Palmer Johnson has created a build that distinguishes this line with its 'big-boat' mentality and superior craftsmanship.

SPECIFICATIONS:	PALMER JOHNSON 123
Length Overall:	37.5m (123')
Beam:	7.30m (24' 6")
Draught:	2.09m (6' 6")
Accommodation:	8 guests + 8 crew
Naval Architecture:	Palmer Johnson
Interior Design:	Nuvolari Lenard
Construction:	FRP Composite Hull and Superstructure
Propulsion:	2 x MTU 16V2000
Classification:	MCA, Rina, Common Rail

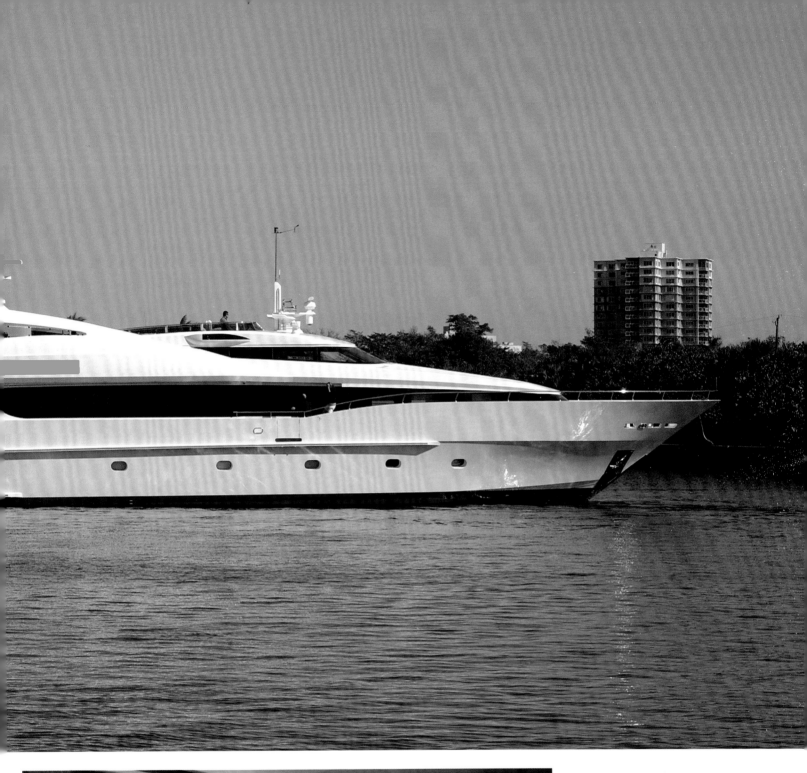

Above:
The PJ 123 marries the sleek Italian style of Nuvolari Lenard with grand American size.

Left:
The elegant interior features rare sycamore wood accented with black walnut and Rubelli fabrics in cool cream, soft gold and subtle browns and bronzes.

Centre:
Even the helm station is highlighted in high quality wood.

Far Left:
The master suite befits a larger tri-deck yacht.

PALMER JOHNSON

PJ 135

In 2006 Palmer Johnson introduced the PJ 135', a speedier, roomier version of their world-beating 120' design offering the same trademark style. She can accommodate a party of twelve in five staterooms yet offers a top speed of 30 knots – a mega-yacht for all occasions.

Massive teak covered side-decks are a welcome addition to the class allowing crew to easily access the docking stations that pop out of the forward part of the deckhouse. Incredibly quiet and smooth while underway, this is a thoroughbred with a lot of power.

The latest addition to the 135 series is PJ 135-4, named 'Coverdrive 2'. While the exterior offers immense outdoor lounging and entertainment areas as well as the trademark private sun-deck, the interior offers casually cool elegance and plenty of room.

The large swim platform has a hydraulically opening Waverunner garage, framed on either side by wide steps leading to the expansive lounging and dining area on the aft-deck. Here there is also a full bar and day head with shower, as well as a 27" TV conveniently mounted on the portside bulkhead for outdoor entertainment.

The fore-deck offers huge sun pads for lounging which open hydraulically to reveal a crane, a 16' (4.8m) diesel jet boat and two jet skis.

Up top there are more lounging areas with barbeque and Jacuzzi. All three outdoor deck areas have soft teak decks and black mesh Bimini tops that can be quickly dismantled for making fast passage.

The interior style blends beach house simplicity with sophisticated elements. White oak bulkheads and floors with the patina of driftwood, light walnut cabinetry and soft leather accents are punctuated with cabinet doors that feature an elegant pinstripe of aluminium inlay and fine Rubelli fabrics.

In the main salon, a 50" plasma TV is built into

the starboard cabinet just forward of the full bar and food service station, opening up the space even more.

The owner's suite features twin en-suite bathrooms and a large lounge and dressing area, as well as a huge king-size bed. Four more en-suite double/twin staterooms, with a Pullman berth in each of the twin staterooms, give the yacht accommodation for twelve guests and additional berths for eight crew.

The galley located below and forward of the pilothouse has stainless steel cabinetry and a stainless steel countertop. Sub-Zero refrigerator/freezers lead the appliance list.

SPECIFICATIONS: PALMER JOHNSON 135

Length Overall:	41.10m (135')
Beam:	8.40m (27' 6")
Draught:	1.80m (5' 9")
Accommodation:	12 guests + 8 crew
Naval Architecture:	Palmer Johnson
Interior Design:	Nuvolari Lenard
Construction:	Aluminium Hull and Superstructure
Propulsion:	2 x MTU 16V4000 M90 3,650hp
Classification:	Lloyds Register 100A1 SSC Yacht

Above:
The PJ 135 is a speedier, roomier version of their world-beating 120' design offering the same trademark style.

Left:
The main salon on 'Coverdrive 2' features white oak bulkheads and floors with a patina of driftwood, light walnut cabinetry and soft leather accents.

Far Left:
The owner's suite features twin en-suite bathrooms and a large lounge and dressing area, as well as a huge king-size bed.

PALMER JOHNSON

PJ150

The undisputed appeal of the dramatic 150 Sports Yacht goes beyond PJ's signature streamlined beauty. With two complete deck levels, her layout offers even greater expanses of outdoor areas for guests to enjoy as well as a raised wheelhouse.

Larger gatherings can take place on the main-deck and sun-deck, the latter of which is a truly indoor-outdoor space. It has a permanent hardtop with six large, square skylights that combine with the open aft section to provide any combination of sun and shade that guests might desire, complete with full bar, barbeque and Jacuzzi.

Within the main salon, the panoramic sea view is optimised with floor to ceiling windows and fold-down terraces on either side of the boat creating nooks for enjoying a cocktail or reading a book with an unencumbered view of the ocean. En-suite staterooms equally complement the spacious feel throughout. The 150' offers the owner the option of a private study, his and hers separate bathrooms and a spacious walk-in closet in their main-deck suite with panoramic ocean views.

PJ 150-7 features interior bulkheads and soles of rustic bleached teak, calming and soft to bare feet. With deep navy dyed high gloss Zebrano accents and passage door inserts of Wengé tiles, bulkhead accents of carved pine and metal composite panels, sophistication is added.

This model can accommodate twelve guests and has fully equipped quarters for a crew of eight. With a top speed of 28 knots she can be at anchor well before the crowd and be gone while the big boats are still beating along.

Right:
With two complete deck levels, the layout of the PJ 150 offers even greater expanses of outdoor areas for guests to enjoy.

Below Left:
The permanent hardtop covering the sundeck has six large, square skylights that combine with the open aft section to provide any combination of sun and shade that guests might desire.

Below Centre:
The PJ 150 features a huge swim deck and tender garage, ideal for water sports enthusiasts.

Below Right:
The panoramic sea view in the main salon is optimised with floor to ceiling windows.

SPECIFICATIONS: PALMER JOHNSON 150

Length Overall:	45.70m (150')
Beam:	8.40m (27' 6")
Draught:	1.77m (5' 8")
Accommodation:	12 guests + 8 crew
Naval Architecture:	Palmer Johnson
Interior Design:	Nuvolari Lenard
Construction:	Aluminium Hull and Superstructure
Propulsion:	2 x MTU 16V4000 M90 3,650hp
Classification:	Lloyds Register 100A1 SSC Yacht

PALMER JOHNSON

PJ 170

Although the PJ 170's design began in 2006, her construction began in July 2008 at the UK shipyard's interim facility. The crowning addition to the Sports Yacht series, her same slender athletic build is combined with modern refinements and a new Nuvolari Lenard designed vertical bow, allowing for even better sea keeping than her peers, with the bonus of riding dry.

The PJ 170 is without doubt the most luxurious of the Sports Yacht range emphasizing huge open spaces. A swimming beach steps up to the large, sheltered aft-deck with comfortable seating and dining areas that flow into the main salon and forward owner's private study.

The extensive main-deck salon is divided into living and dining areas by a low-profile stairwell.

The exterior layout is designed across one level with walkways leading to a fore-deck pool area that offers more lounging and a pool deep enough to really swim in with wide open views of the surrounding sea. The pool can accommodate a large tender while under way, hoisted by the hidden fore crane; jet skis and equipment are located in two fore-wells and anchor handling and mooring are sheltered in the hydraulically controlled forepeak.

Below-decks accommodates up to twelve guests in five luxurious en-suite staterooms. Forward, the tremendously spacious owner's suite stretches full beam with large circular windows letting in the natural light and sea views. Set for a summer 2010 delivery the PJ170' will reflect the maturation of the entire Sports Line.

SPECIFICATIONS: PALMER JOHNSON 170

Length Overall:	52.2m (171')
Beam:	9.50m (31')
Draught:	2.44m (8')
Accommodation:	12 guests + crew
Naval Architecture:	Palmer Johnson
Interior Design:	Nuvolari Lenard
Construction:	Aluminium Hull and Superstructure
Classification:	Lloyds Register 100A1 SSC Yacht MCA LY2
Propulsion:	2 x MTU 16V4000 M93L

Right & Below:
The crowning addition to the Sports Yacht series, the PJ 170 combines the same slender athletic build of her smaller sisterships, with modern refinements and a new Nuvolari Lenard designed vertical bow.

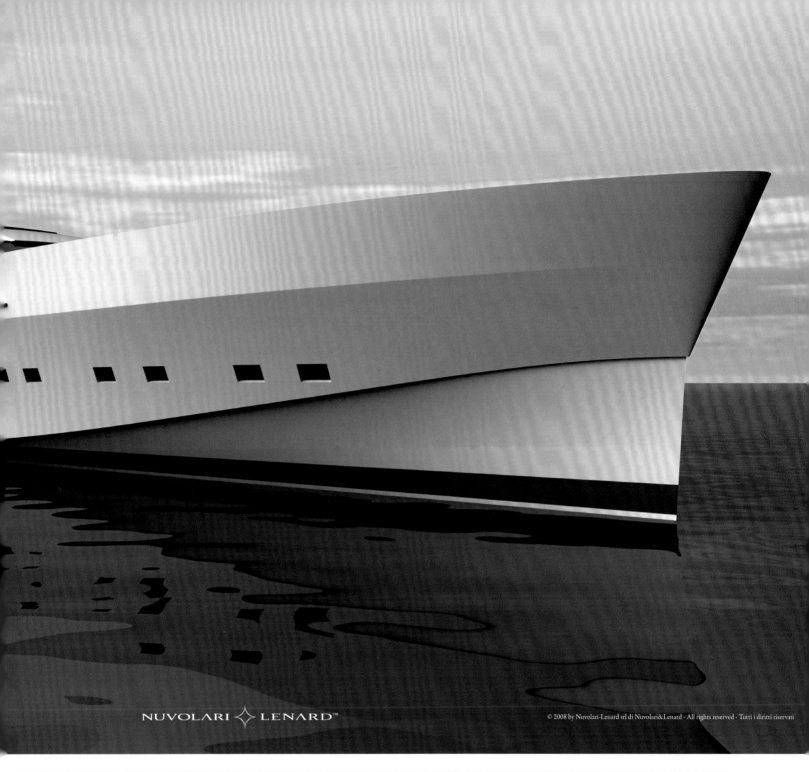

FEATURED YACHTS

PALMER JOHNSON

Palmer Johnson Yachts
128 Kentucky Street, Sturgeon Bay
WI 54235, USA
Tel: +1 920 746 6342
Fax: +1 920 743 1799
Web: www.palmerjohnson.com

Right & Below Left:
Capable of traversing the most remote regions in extreme climatic conditions, the ocean going 82m 'PJ World' vessel uses the latest Rolls Royce design technology to create the first Full Ice Class series of its kind.

Below Right:
The 'PJ World' features a six deck interior as well as large open spaces emphasized with extensive panoramic sea views.

PJ WORLD

Capable of traversing the most remote regions in extreme climatic conditions, the ocean going 82m 'PJ World' vessel uses the latest Rolls Royce design technology to create the first Full Ice Class series of its kind.

Having acquired the Norwegian shipyard, Flekkefjord Slipp & Maskinfabrikk's, one of a handful worldwide with experience in building complex seismic research and exploration vessels, Palmer Johnson Norway adopted a new approach - the starting point was to optimise the vessel's design to its operational profile. Exemplifying this groundbreaking approach, specific to the 'PJ World' yacht, a Rolls Royce UT designed hull has been optimised to a diesel-electric Azipull Propulsion system to cultivate a multitude of operational benefits. The design reduces the loss of speed in head seas, reduces vibration and noise levels, improves the vessel's manoeuvrability and control and contributes to the vessel's 'Clean Class' notification.

Exceptional station-keeping capabilities are achieved via dynamic positioning on the 'PJ World', allowing the vessel to be 'moored' in environmentally sensitive or restricted areas without the traditional use of lines or anchors. Instead, the onboard propulsion system and thrusters work together to control the position by centralised automatic responses to variations in sea conditions. Other features include a certified heli-deck and heli-hangar, an optional garage designed for a six man Discovery submarine and a superior Rolls Royce at-rest stabilization system. Security features, such as water cannons, forward scanning sonar, thermal imaging, closed circuit television and acoustic shields, are also available on this vessel.

Focusing on well-being, healthy living and relaxation, Nuvolari Lenard ensures the six deck interior and exterior large open spaces are emphasized with extensive panoramic sea views creating an open environment for ocean voyages. The owner's apartment is situated on the fourth, fifth and sixth decks, comprising of bedroom suite, walk-in dressing room, separate business and private lounges, office and a

Jacuzzi sun-deck with 360 degree viewing. One of the first features to be seen on this superyacht is the novel aft beach house that looks out to an outdoor swimming pool deck.

The layout design shows a high consideration to the separation of crew and guests. A maximum crew of twenty-seven can be accommodated according to the general arrangement of single, double and triple berth cabins.

'PJ World' is destined to be another truly iconic Palmer Johnson design. By providing environmentally friendly solutions that heighten performance whilst reducing costs, she will transform the conventional concept behind exploration-style vessels and introduce a revolutionary ocean voyager for the future.

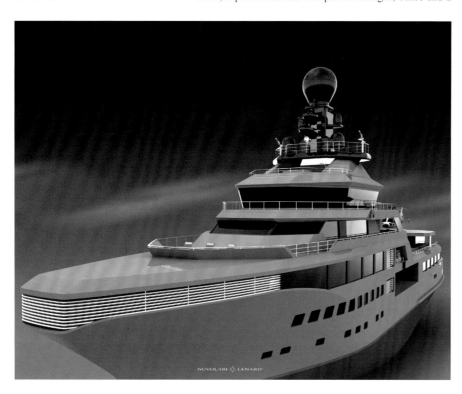

SPECIFICATIONS:	'PALMER JOHNSON WORLD'
Length Overall:	81.4m (267')
Beam:	14.60m (48')
Draught:	4.00m (13')
Naval Architecture:	Rolls Royce UT
Interior Design:	Nuvolari Lenard
Construction:	Steel Hull to Ice Class IB
Classification:	DNV 1A1, EO, LC Yacht RO Clean Comfort - V(1) HELDK-SHF
Propulsion:	Rolls-Royce Bergen C25 Type
Max. Speed:	16.5 knots
Range:	10,500 nm @ 10 knots

CRN SHIPYARD

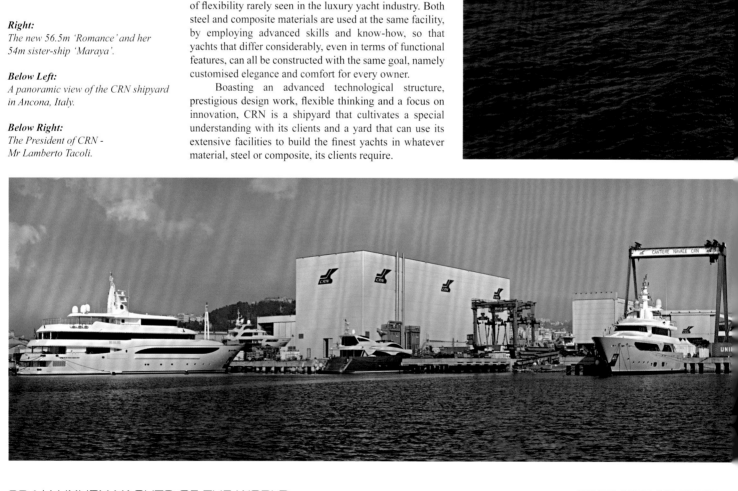

The CRN shipyard, founded in Ancona in 1963 and part of Ferretti since 1999, today builds three-deck pleasure custom and semi-custom mega yachts at lengths of 40 metres or more. At present, numerous CRN vessels are under construction simultaneously, including custom-built steel and aluminium ships measuring up to 85 metres, plus two lines of semi-custom vessels produced with composite materials at lengths of 40 and 43 metres.

The complex in Ancona, housed in an area measuring 81,000m² of which approximately 35,000m² are covered, has an extensive area equipped with three docks measuring 100, 80 and 40 metres.

Today CRN stands as one of the leading centres of Italian luxury engineering, an example of technological and stylistic research combined with structural and product development. The Ancona complex can draw on a great capacity to meet the challenges posed by ongoing innovation, being constantly stimulated to achieve the impossible by increasingly knowledgeable, demanding ship owners. The shipyard constructs vessels with a degree of flexibility rarely seen in the luxury yacht industry. Both steel and composite materials are used at the same facility, by employing advanced skills and know-how, so that yachts that differ considerably, even in terms of functional features, can all be constructed with the same goal, namely customised elegance and comfort for every owner.

Boasting an advanced technological structure, prestigious design work, flexible thinking and a focus on innovation, CRN is a shipyard that cultivates a special understanding with its clients and a yard that can use its extensive facilities to build the finest yachts in whatever material, steel or composite, its clients require.

Right:
The new 56.5m 'Romance' and her 54m sister-ship 'Maraya'.

Below Left:
A panoramic view of the CRN shipyard in Ancona, Italy.

Below Right:
The President of CRN - Mr Lamberto Tacoli.

CRN SHIPYARD   'BLUE EYES'

With its rakish, flowing bow, its impressively sized interior spaces and its extensive surface area perched over the sea, 'Blue Eyes' is a steel and aluminium mega yacht born of a joint collaboration between the CRN shipyard and the Zuccon International Project firm which designed the exterior, while the interior design was handled by the Fabrizio Smania company.

A major innovation of this stylish and elegant yacht is the aft area of the lower deck, designed to function as a fully fledged beach club with the stern hatch lowering nearly flush to the water where it can be equipped with comfortable sun-loungers to create an ideal solarium. Connected to this area is an indoor relaxation zone where guests can enjoy being close to the sea while relaxing on comfortable sofas in the shade.

Another distinctive feature of this yacht is the balcony attached to the owner's suite, designed to be nothing less than a terrace on the sea thanks to a hatch that can be lowered 90 degrees.

A strong point of CRN's yacht design and one of the custom features most frequently requested by owners, the owner's balcony is a major innovation that has quickly become an established tradition.

SPECIFICATIONS: 'BLUE EYES'	
Length Overall:	59.8m (196' 2")
Beam:	10.20m (33' 5")
Draught:	3m (9' 10")
Guests:	12
Crew:	14
Engines:	2 x Caterpillar C3512b
Maximum Speed:	15.5 knots
Cruising Speed:	14 knots
Range:	4,000 nm @ 12 knots

Above & Left:
Luxurious and stylish, 'Blue Eyes' is a
beauty to behold both inside and out.

CRN SHIPYARD   'RUBECCAN'

The third hull of the new CRN 43 composite line, 'Rubeccan' is a displacement-design maxi-yacht that can easily accommodate ten guests and nine crewmembers. Built as a joint effort involving the CRN technical staff and the Zuccon International Project Firm that handled the external layout, the interior furnishings and decorative scheme of this 43m vessel, 'Rubeccan' features a distinctive personality, having been masterfully designed to meet the needs of the yacht's owner who already has another vessel, a 35m yacht, built by this shipyard.

Discrete, natural colours, together with the use of exquisite materials, including the textiles - all manufactured by the renowned Italian label Loro Piana - characterise the stylistic choices. The curtains, the carpeting and the upholstery are all crafted from fine fibres to ensure maximum resistance, as well as the utmost in comfort, lightness and softness.

As is true with all the CRN 43 hulls, light is the key element in the yacht's architecture, thanks not only to the abundance of generously sized windows, but also the two types of fine woods used. The warm hues of walnut adorn the furniture and panelling in the lower portion of the vessel, while lighter-hued stripped oak was chosen for the upper portion of the structural facings in the two lounges.

'Rubeccan' reprises a number of the features favoured by owners of other CRN ships. The Technogym workout room and sauna in the forward portion of the lower deck combine to form a fitness and wellness area tied directly to the sea, thanks to a beach platform created by lowering the aft hatch nearly flush to the water. The balcony of the owner's suite, another must feature, is furnished with comfortable armchairs and a coffee table, making it an ideal site for exclusive breakfasts by the sea.

The desire for relaxation and comfort is also met on the sundeck, equipped in its forward portion with a Jacuzzi tub surrounded by luxuriant cushions and semicircular sofas, while the aft portion features lounge chairs for taking the sun, a dining table, a barbecue and a bar covered by a roll-bar.

The engine room in the aft portion of the lower deck, with its two Caterpillar C32 engines, powers the ship at a maximum speed of 15.5 knots and at a cruising speed of 13 knots.

SPECIFICATIONS: 'RUBECCAN'	
Length Overall:	42.6m (139' 9")
Beam:	8.65m (28' 4")
Draught:	2.35m (7' 8")
Accommodation:	10 guests + 9 crew
Engines:	2 x Caterpillar C32-C
Maximum Speed:	15.5 knots
Range:	3,800 nm @ 11 knots

FEATURED YACHTS

Above & Left:
*'Rubeccan' features a distinctive
personality, having been masterfully
designed to meet the needs of the
yacht's owner who already has another
vessel, a 35m yacht, built by this
shipyard.*

CRN SHIPYARD   'LADY BELMOR'

A week after launching the 43 meter 'Rubeccan' in October 2008, CRN launched the fifth in its 128-foot composite line, 'Lady Belmor'. Designed for owners wanting comfort and performance, this new yacht is equipped with a pair of MTU 12V4000 M90 diesels that provide a top speed of 24 knots and a 19 knot cruising speed.

Designed by CRN's technical team and Zuccon International Project, 'Lady Belmor' has three covered decks and a side-opening tender garage. Her modern interior is highlighted by numerous details in steel, such as the frames on the built-in furniture and the wooden venetian blinds. Canaletto walnut is used exclusively throughout. She is a yacht with an unmistakably distinctive modern layout featuring three covered decks. The owner's accommodation is forward on the main deck, while the guest cabins occupy the lower deck. At a length of almost 40m and a width of 7.7m, 'Lady Belmor' can accommodate twelve passengers and a crew of eight.

Further proof of the technological excellence built into every superyacht designed by CRN, is the installation on 'Lady Belmor' of five Mitsubishi Anti Rolling Gyros (MSM 4000), a stabiliser system capable of reducing the roll of the ship by more than 50%, especially when it is anchored offshore or docked alongside.

SPECIFICATIONS: 'LADY BELMOR'	
Length Overall:	39.60m (129' 11")
Beam:	7.70m (25' 3")
Year:	2008
Guests:	12
Crew:	8
Naval Architecture:	CRN Engineering
Design:	Zuccon International Project
Engines:	2 x MTU 12V 4000 M90
Maximum Speed:	24 knots
Cruise speed:	19 knots

Above:
Designed for owners wanting comfort and performance, 'Lady Belmor' is equipped with a pair of MTU 12V4000 M90 diesels that provide a top speed of 24 knots and a 19 knot cruising speed.

Left:
Her modern interior is highlighted by numerous details in steel, such as the frames on the built-in furniture and the wooden venetian blinds. Canaletto walnut is used exclusively throughout.

CRN SHIPYARD   'ROMANCE'

Beyond luxury, beyond elegance, beyond all striving for refinement and attention to detail, are all ways to describe CRN's construction project number 122, launched in April 2008. 'Romance' is a 57m luxury yacht on which the client's cultural background has combined with the shipyard's expertise in interpreting new demands and needs. The result is a return to an unadulterated concept of luxury and wealth.

A close examination of the cultural preferences of the yacht owner, the real project manager when it came to the vessel's interior decoration, made it possible for the CRN technical staff to bring to life his complex, sophisticated vision for this magnificent yacht.

Monumental in size and dashing in style, this yacht came into being like a work of art. Christened 'Romance', her external form was designed in collaboration with the design firm Zuccon International Project.

A total of twelve guests and ten crewmembers can be accommodated on this superyacht. Thanks to the hands-on role of the owner, the CRN Design Department Office was able to pin down every detail of the boat's furnishings and interior design, selecting materials and decorative elements, all of them inspired by the glamour of the baroque period that created a truly regal atmosphere.

Valuable materials such as onyx, silk and gold are customised to create grandiose, opulent effects that appear to be taken from the stage. The silk carpet found throughout 'Romance' was made by hand and customised with a variety of designs tied to the decorative motifs in the different rooms and settings. The upholstery in all six cabins, including the master suite, is handmade, bearing the name of the renowned French firm, Zuber.

In creating 'Romance', CRN has given full form to its concept of onboard well-being. The yacht's lower deck features a Turkish bath and an aromatherapy area; a sauna made of aromatic fir wood; a massage room; plus a beauty salon. In short, nothing less than a floating beauty spa!

SPECIFICATIONS:	'ROMANCE'
Length Overall:	56.5m (185')
Beam:	10.20m (33' 6")
Draught:	2.90m (9' 6")
Accommodation:	12 guests + 10 crew
Naval Architecture:	CRN Engineering
Design:	Zuccon International Project
Engines:	2 x Caterpillar 3512B
Maximum Speed:	15 knots
Cruise speed:	14 knots
Range:	4,000 nm @ 11 knots

Above & Left:
'Romance' is a 57m luxury yacht on which the client's cultural background has combined with the shipyard's expertise in interpreting new demands and needs. The result is a return to an unadulterated concept of luxury and wealth.

CRN SHIPYARD

CRN Spa - FERRETTI GROUP
Via Enrico Mattei, N. 26
60125 Ancona, Italy
Tel: +39 071 5011 111
Fax: +39 071 200 008
Web: www.crn-yacht.com

Right & Below Right:
*Measuring 80 metres, the CRN 129 will
be the largest yacht ever built at CRN's
Ancona shipyard.*

Below Left:
*The 72m 'Clarena II' continues the
successful working relationship
between CRN's technical staff and the
design firm of Nuvolari & Lenard.*

CRN 124

One of the finest yachts ever built in Italy, 'Clarena II' is a 72m displacement motor yacht being built in steel and aluminium. This completely custom build project, whose launch is planned for late 2009, is the result of a successful working relationship between CRN's technical staff and the firm of Nuvolari & Lenard. This is the same team that constructed the first boat, 'Clarena', built for this particular owner, a yacht launched in 2003 as part of CRN's extremely well received 'Magnifica' line of 46m yachts.

The design plans, developed through an attentive analysis of the owner's wishes, have made it possible to create a sophisticated, innovative vessel. The dashing shape of the hull, combined with an exceptionally modern, streamlined form, is made even more distinctive by the sharp, imposing bow and set 'Clarena II' apart from other luxury yachts of its size.

Five suites are set aside for the twelve guests who can be housed on this yacht, in addition to which there is the owner's cabin. Two additional cabins on the lower deck are meant for other guests or domestic helpers accompanying them. The owner placed great importance on the boat's staff, which counts no fewer than 28 professionals, including, in addition to the captain, onboard technicians and sailors, bodyguards, a chef trained in haute cuisine and a personal physician.

'Clarena II' has also been developed in such a way that guests can lead a perfectly convivial existence throughout the day, all the while enjoying a close relationship with the sea. To this end, a fully innovative area of more than $100m^2$ has been designed in the rear portion of the lower deck, designed to serve as a 'beach club'.

In fact, the rear hatch transforms itself into a large beach area practically flush with the sea. The extensive, adjoining internal area is outfitted for full relaxation with those onboard able to enjoy the proximity of the sea from comfortable sofas or while sipping an aperitif.

Without doubt, 'Clarena II' promises to be one of the 'launchings of the year' and one that is eagerly anticipated by many in the world of luxury yachting.

CRN 129

During February 2009 the CRN shipyard took on a brand new, extra large challenge. Vessel number 129, to be built of aluminium and steel, and measuring 80 metres, will be the largest yacht ever built at CRN's Ancona shipyard and will be yet another offspring of the fruitful working relationship between the CRN technical staff, which are handling the naval architecture, and the firm Studio Zuccon International Project, which has designed the external layout.

With an interior created by designer Laura Sessa Romboli at the request of the owner himself, this mix of talent and skill will give birth to a truly magnificent yacht capable of accommodating twelve guests, in addition to a full crew complement.

"This project represents both an amalgamation and a further development of the distinctive characteristics and the innovative soul of the most recent yachts to be turned out under the CRN name," declares Lamberto Tacoli, President of the CRN shipyard. To say this yacht is eagerly awaited, is a considerable understatement!

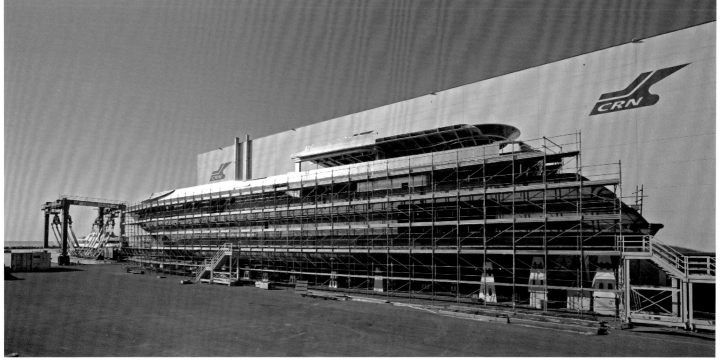

MOONEN SHIPYARDS

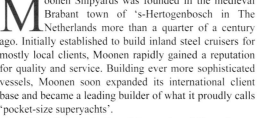

Right:
The stunning new Moonen 94 boasts both high performance and luxurious style.

Below Left:
Moonen's largest yacht to date - the elegant Moonen 124

Below Centre Left:
Moonen's modern shipyard at 's-Hertogenbosch in The Netherlands.

Below Centre Right:
The tough, ocean-going Moonen 114 Explorer.

Below Right:
Emile Bilterijst, the Managing Director of Moonen Shipyards.

Moonen Shipyards was founded in the medieval Brabant town of 's-Hertogenbosch in The Netherlands more than a quarter of a century ago. Initially established to build inland steel cruisers for mostly local clients, Moonen rapidly gained a reputation for quality and service. Building ever more sophisticated vessels, Moonen soon expanded its international client base and became a leading builder of what it proudly calls 'pocket-size superyachts'.

Since those early days, Moonen has delivered more than seventy high quality yachts to worldwide acclaim, winning many prestigious awards along the way. The current Moonen line consists of full displacement type motor yachts and rugged yet stylish explorer type yachts, built with steel hulls and alloy superstructures, as well as semi-displacement fast yachts built in alloy.

Constantly seeking perfection, Moonen continues to develop new models while also building fully custom yachts built to each client's exact specifications. Moonen's current line-up of yachts is designed and styled by René van der Velden Design with naval architecture by Stolk Marimecs or Diana Yacht Design. The company's extensive range now includes the shipyard's largest yacht ever, the first Moonen 124, launched in April 2009.

Most recently, in response to the growing client demand for even larger yachts, Moonen has acquired a state-of-the-art 60m long hall in Groot-Ammers, The Netherlands, where it will construct yachts up to 45m (148') in length. Meanwhile, the yard in 's-Hertogenbosch will continue to build the company's highly popular yachts under 35m (115'). On the following pages are recent examples of yachts that Moonen has built.

MOONEN SHIPYARDS

MOONEN 94 ALU

Moonen developed the 94 Alu, the first model in its new 'Fast Yacht Series', out of the remarkable success of the Moonen 84, of which eight have been sold since 2001. With its classic lines and popular four cabin layout, the Moonen 84 inspired several clients to enquire if the shipyard could build a Moonen quality yacht with similar accommodation, but lighter and capable of significantly higher speeds.

René van der Velden designed the 28.90m 94 Alu with a sportier flair than his Moonen 84, extending the horizontal lines for a more aerodynamic exterior. Naval architects, Stolk Marimecs, shaped a round-bilge, semi-displacement hull with a displacement of about 120 ton and a moderately higher length/beam ratio. This helps reduce resistance at cruising speed, provides a softer ride at high speed and offers good sea-keeping qualities, excellent manoeuvrability and good fuel economy - all qualities Moonen owners expect.

Moonen used the greater length over the 84' design to expand the forward accommodation, extend the swim platform, enlarge the lazarette and create a larger engine room to include more powerful engines.

For propulsion, the Moonen 94 Alu is driven by Servogear controllable-pitch propellers running in high-efficiency tunnels and steered by Servogear custom-designed rudders. These propellers, combined with the round-bilge hull, create exceptional performance.

When the yacht is cruising at 11 knots, fuel consumption is only 65 litres/hour, which, together with the yacht's 18,900-litre fuel capacity, ensures transatlantic range – an incredible achievement for a yacht with a 26-knot top speed! Furthermore, at this speed she has the same exceptional sea-keeping comfort typical of all Moonen yachts.

Moonen's advanced program of noise and vibration reduction assures silent running at all speeds when underway. Moonen builds the Fast Yacht Series in light, strong, corrosion-resistant Sealium, an aluminium alloy that has achieved wide application in aerospace, shipbuilding and commercial land construction, and which is conveniently cut, bent, and welded using the same methods as the more common 5083 alloys.

The interiors of the Moonen 94 Alu 'Nilo' and 'Infinity' are created by the highly respected company Art-Line which custom builds each interior according to each owner's specifications and requirements.

With several of these stylish yachts already built, the Moonen 94 Alu represents a remarkable design and a true success story for this highly respected luxury yacht builder.

Right:
Speed is nothing without comfort. The Moonen 94 Alu 'Infinity' is capable of a 22 knot top speed!

Below Left:
The Moonen 94 Alu 'Nilo' is a highly stylish, modern fast yacht, with a top speed of 26 knots.

Below Right:
The exquisite interior onboard the Moonen 94 Alu 'Nilo'.

SPECIFICATIONS:	MOONEN 94 ALU 'NILO'
Length Overall:	28.90m (94' 10")
Beam:	6.80m (22' 4")
Draught:	1.80m (5' 11")
Naval Architecture:	Stolk Marimecs
Exterior Styling:	René van der Velden
Interior Design:	Art-Line Interior Design
Construction:	Aluminium Hull & Superstructure
Engines:	2 x Caterpillar C32 Acert 1850hp
Maximum Speed:	26.3 knots
Cruise Speed:	19 knots
Range:	2,500 nautical miles @ 11 knots

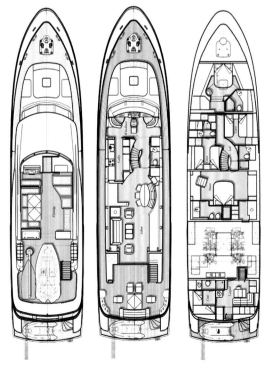

MOONEN SHIPYARDS

MOONEN 97

The Moonen 97 is a prime example of how the yard teamed up with a client to produce a model with unique features that are still universal enough to attract future clients. The Moonen 97 is an evolutionary design based on two earlier Moonen yachts, the remarkable Moonen 84 (Moonen's most successful series, with eight delivered since 2001) and the custom Moonen 96 'Clementine' launched in 2005.

René van der Velden Yacht Design sculpted the Moonen 97 with a close family resemblance to the popular Moonen 84, with a harmonious profile, nicely flared bow, sloped stern with twin stairways, graceful sheer and bold fashion plates.

The Moonen 84's highly efficient four-stateroom layout, one of the model's signature features, is often considered the starting point of other new and larger Moonen designs, as in this case. The equally strong attraction of 'Clementine' is her high volume on a waterline some four metres longer than that of the Moonen 84. Combining and rearranging the outstanding features of both designs, Moonen created the 97 for a growing number of clients seeking a medium-size, long-range cruiser midway between the Moonen 72 and the company's new flagship, the Moonen 124.

As one comes to expect of Moonen, every Moonen 97 is customised to meet the client's requirements. The first Moonen 97, 'Darsea' for example, has a fixed bimini top, a single bridge-deck tender crane, a walk-through galley open to the wheelhouse, two staterooms with double berths and two with twins. The second Moonen 97, 'Sofia II', has a folding bimini, two tender cranes, a longer bridge-deck overhang, a U-shape galley, and two twin staterooms below.

The salon and dining areas are quite different on each yacht. 'Darsea's Art-Line interior features ample use of leather and bamboo against a backdrop of fine cherry panelling, and furniture with well-rounded corners creating a soft look. The salon and dining area feature woven-suede seating, white fabric overhead liners, tight-woven fabric insets, window cabinets and carpets with bamboo surrounds. The master suite, with walk-in closet, has a large TV, 'roll-top' effect decorative panels with hand-strung fine copper strands that add warm highlights to the wood, padded leather wall segments and ripple-effect doors.

With the first two Moonen 97's already launched, the third and fourth yachts of this popular range are currently under construction, both of which will be delivered in 2010.

Right:
Room for more on the new Moonen 97.

Below Left:
The stylish owner's suite onboard the Moonen 97 'Darsea'.

Below Right:
The main salon onboard the Moonen 97 'Darsea' is beautifully furnished.

SPECIFICATIONS: MOONEN 97 - 'DARSEA'	
Length Overall:	30.00m (98' 15")
Beam:	7.30m (23' 11")
Draught:	2.18m (7' 2")
Naval Architecture:	Diana Yacht Design
Exterior Styling:	René van der Velden
Interior Design:	Art-Line Interiors
Construction:	Steel hull / Alumin. superstructure
Engines:	2 x Caterpillar C18 DI-TA 610hp
Maximum Speed:	13 knots
Cruise Speed:	12 knots
Range:	4,000 nautical miles @ 9 knots

MOONEN SHIPYARDS

MOONEN 114 EXPLORER

The Moonen 114 Explorer is Moonen's first entry into the Explorer Yacht market, and she has been built for repeat Moonen clients. The Explorer 114 has a stately top speed of 13.5 knots, appropriate for a global cruiser, and has been designed with many unusual features to maximise the facilities available for the owners and their family who enjoy outdoor living, dining, and entertaining afloat.

The first such feature is that the designers have kept the profile low, with a three-deck layout that aids stability, even as it enhances the eye-catching beauty of the design. The overall form of the yacht is an updated classic research-type craft, having a powerful, seaworthy steel hull with a pronounced forward sheer, topped by a workmanlike aluminium superstructure, all of which live up to the name 'Explorer' in style, substance, and practicality. In addition, the hull has been reinforced to receive a Lloyd's Register Ice Classification for safe high latitude cruising.

Further enhancing the owner's lifestyle, the flying bridge, with tender stowage aft, features a large settee, Jacuzzi, wet bar and dumbwaiter for food service. Interestingly, it has no helm-station that would otherwise reduce the deck area available for sunny entertainment. Similarly, the bridge deck 'footprint' has been kept relatively short to create a spacious afterdeck dining and lounging area under the flying bridge overhang that can be closed off by protective glass panels.

Inside the bridge deck, a cosy octagonal salon is coupled to the wheelhouse and its breakfast nook through a foyer with a spiral staircase. The main deck features a full-width owner's suite forward, complete with a dual office desk and a large en-suite bathroom. Amidships is a large L-shaped galley and crew mess and the main salon, dining and entertaining area aft.

Below decks, a suite of four double guest staterooms is located off a central semi-circular foyer amidships which is separated by a structural bulkhead from the captain's cabin and crew quarters forward. This ensures separation and absolute privacy for both guests and crew.

Aft of the engine room is a large tender garage. Carrying 45,700 litres of fuel, the Moonen 114 Explorer offers a huge ocean crossing range of 5,000 nautical miles at 10 knots.

A true global cruiser if ever there was one!

Right:
The Moonen 114 has trans-oceanic range through any seas.

Below Left:
The magnificent owner's suite onboard the Moonen 114 Explorer 'My Issue' is both luxurious and spacious.

Below Right:
The combination of fine woodwork and soft fabrics gives the main salon on 'My Issue' a highly relaxing environment.

SPECIFICATIONS:	MOONEN 114 EXPLORER
Length Overall:	34.70m (113' 10")
Beam:	8.10m (26' 7")
Draught:	2.40m (7' 10")
Displacement:	285 ton
Naval Architecture:	Stolk Marimecs
Exterior Styling:	René van der Velden
Interior Design:	René van der Velden
Construction:	Grade A Steel hull
	Aluminium superstructure
Hull:	Round bilge displacement hull
Keel:	Duct keel
Engines:	2 x MTU 12V2000 M60 804hp
Maximum Speed:	13.5 knots
Cruise Speed:	11 knots
Range:	5,000 nautical miles @ 10 knots
Fuel Capacity:	45,700l
Freshwater Capacity:	10,200l

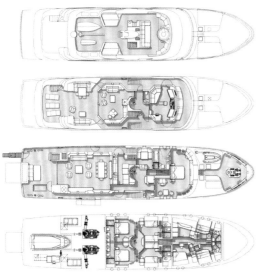

MOONEN
SHIPYARDS

Moonen Shipyards bv
Graaf Van Solmsweg 52 F
5222 BP 's Hertogenbosch
The Netherlands
Tel: +31 (0)736 210 094
Fax: +31 (0)736 219 460
Web: www.moonen.com

MOONEN 124

On 25 April 2009 Moonen launched its new flagship at its Groot-Ammers yacht-building yard. The first Moonen 124 is a tri-deck yacht built with a high-grade steel hull and aluminium superstructure. The interior onboard the Moonen 124 has been designed and furnished by Art-Line and is of 'fusion' styling, combining western cherry with eastern details. With an abundance of space, this stylish yacht provides a magnificent owner's stateroom on the forward main deck with its own veranda, a large bedroom with king-size bed, a huge en-suite bathroom and a spacious dressing room.

Moving down to the lower deck via an amidships atrium staircase linking all the decks of the yacht, there are two double and two twin guest cabins as well as excellent accommodation for the yacht's crew.

On the wheelhouse deck, an ergonomic wheelhouse has been designed with excellent all-round visibility and is equipped with the latest navigation and communication technology.

Capable of trans-oceanic passages, the Moonen 124 can cover a remarkable 5,000 nautical miles when cruising at 8 knots and powered by twin MTU 16V 2000 M60 engines, can achieve a very respectable 14.5 knots maximum speed.

The Moonen 124 is indeed, a worthy flagship for this most progressive and prestigious yachting company.

MOONEN 99 ALU

The new Moonen 99 Alu 'Phoebe' is an extended version of the award-winning Moonen 94 Alu 'Nilo' and is on target for a summer 2009 delivery.

'Phoebe' has a sleek aerodynamic profile suited to her 26-knot top speed accomplished by Servogear Controllable-Pitch Propellers running in high-efficiency tunnels.

To keep weight down, 'Phoebe', like all Moonen 'Alu' yachts, is constructed of Sealium and her antenna mast is fabricated in advanced composites. Wonderfully proportioned, she has a contemporary interior styled by Rhoades Young, another Moonen 'first' featuring fine Moonen joinery of European walnut.

MOONEN 124FT

INTERIOR DESIGN BY ART-LINE ©
-OWNER'S SUITE-

MOONEN 124FT
INTERIOR DESIGN BY ART-LINE ©
-WHEELHOUSE-

SANLORENZO

In 2008, with half a century of history behind it (1958-2008), the Sanlorenzo Shipyard in Italy launched its 500th vessel. Boasting a rich heritage is one thing, and continuously updating it is another, but this is something that Sanlorenzo has achieved better than most.

Today, Sanlorenzo's production consists of the brand's traditional fibreglass range and a range of high-tech metal superyachts built at the company's new Viareggio factory. Sanlorenzo's Ameglia Division, and the site of its headquarters, is on the banks of the river Magra near La Spezia and this is where the company builds its traditional fibreglass planing-hulled motor yachts, ranging in size from 62' to 108'.

The new Viareggio Division produces two additional lines of luxury Sanlorenzo yachts: 92' and 122' 'Navettas', and a range of steel or aluminium superyachts ranging from 38m to over 50m.

At a time when luxury yacht builders, like all prestige brands, are finding times challenging, Sanlorenzo stands as a beacon of success. In 2005, the year in which the entrepreneur Massimo Perotti took over the shipyard from his predecessor and historical owner Giovanni Jannetti, the turnover of the company was 42 million euros and the shipyard produced around 14 yachts a year.

Thanks to the opening of the new Viareggio Division, by the end of the 2008 financial year, Sanlorenzo Spa's turnover had risen to 150 million euros, a growth percentage of 250%, and had an exclusive production of around 30 yachts,

With its modern, well-built luxury yachts becoming ever more popular, the future looks set for this prestige yacht builder.

Above:
*The highly distinctive
Sanlorenzo 40 Alloy.*

Left:
The Sanlorenzo SD122.

Centre:
The Sanlorenzo SD92

Far Left:
Sanlorenzo's Ameglia fleet.

SANLORENZO

SANLORENZO SD92

The Sanlorenzo SD92 is the first model from the new range of 'Navetta' yachts, built in composite material with semi-displacement hulls, produced by Sanlorenzo's new Viareggio Division.

The SD92 arose from Sanlorenzo's intention to create a new vessel, combining charming lines with the possibility of experiencing life at sea without limits, cruising 2000 nautical miles at 12 knots on a single tank of fuel. The SD92 brings together innovative solutions and classic elements. Designer Francesco Paszkowski has succeeded in producing a highly evocative layout inspired by the transatlantic liners of the 1930s and 40s, yet meeting every requirement in terms of design and performance.

With a maximum continuous speed of 17 knots, this Sanlorenzo Navetta is unique in its class. Having designed and created the semi-displacement hull, the Sanlorenzo Technical Department did not settle for the performance capabilities typical of these rounded stern vessels ('navettas'), but carried out an extensive model testing campaign to achieve excellent results in terms of speed as well as static and dynamic stability.

For the Sanlorenzo SD92, stylistic research included the selection of the hull colour - a creamy hue that brings to mind the pastel colours of the sailing boats of the 1970s perfectly complementing the mahogany of the washboard and the teak floor of the deck.

On the upper deck, the canvas awnings protecting the fly bridge from the wind are also cream-coloured, a distinctive trait that clearly evokes the traditional navettas of the early twentieth century.

The upper deck of the SD92 features a modern layout and is characterised by an original 'black stroke' extending the glazing of the pilothouse further aft.

In keeping with the custom tradition of the shipyard, each and every model launched in the course of its half-century long history has been unique and every one of the SD92 line is styled in total concert with the owner.

SPECIFICATIONS:	SANLORENZO SD92
Length Overall:	27.60m (91' 0")
Beam:	7.15m (23' 6")
Draught:	1.80m (5' 11")
Displacement:	89 ton
Guests:	8
Crew:	4
Engines:	2 x MAN V12 CR 1200
Max. Speed:	17 knots
Range:	2000 nautical miles @ 12 knots

Above:
The SD92 brings together innovative solutions and classic style.

Centre:
The fly bridge is ideal for entertaining.

Left & Far Left:
Two stylish designs for the main salon.

SANLORENZO   SANLORENZO SL108

Built by Sanlorenzo's Ameglia Division, the Sanlorenzo SL108, with its overall length of 33 metres, represents the flagship of the Sanlorenzo fleet of fibreglass flying bridge motor yachts. Like all of Sanlorenzo's beautiful yachts, the unmistakable style and the fine lines of the SL108 have made it one of the most popular luxury motor yachts in a size sector that is highly competitive.

With the SL108, the shipyard wanted to produce a yacht that combined internal comfort and balance with high performance and which could be tailor-built to each client's exact requirements. The result is simply startling. Powered by twin MTU engines, each producing 2,775hp, the SL108 is capable of speeds of up to 30 knots, while still remaining beautifully stable and comfortable at speed.

Onboard, the Italian style and elegance that Sanlorenzo is famous for shines through. The huge fly bridge features a large Jacuzzi, plenty of loungers and a seating area, all covered by a retractable roof, and where al-fresco dining is the order of the day. At the forward end of the fly bridge, a second helm station makes open-air control of the yacht a welcome option, while stairs lead down to the latest high-tech equipped raised pilothouse.

On the main deck, a vast owner's suite takes up the forward end, complete with large en-suite bathroom and walk in dressing room. Further aft, a large and beautifully furnished main salon and dining area lead back to a set of doors to the outside onto a good sized aft deck and dining area for ten. With four additional double / twin guest cabins on the lower deck and good sized quarters for the crew, the SL108 is Sanlorenzo's entry into the superyacht class.

SPECIFICATIONS: SANLORENZO SL108	
Length Overall:	33.00m (108' 3")
Beam:	7.40m (24' 3")
Draught:	1.85m (6' 1")
Displacement:	125 ton
Guests:	10
Crew:	5
Engines:	2 x MTU 12V4000M90, 2,775hp
Max. Speed:	30 knots

Above & Centre:
The Sanlorenzo SL108, with its overall length of 33 metres, represents the flagship of the Sanlorenzo fleet of fibreglass flying bridge motor yachts.

Left & Far Left:
The SL108 features a large and beautifully furnished main salon and dining area, which may be customised to the owner's individual taste.

SANLORENZO

SANLORENZO SD122

In 2008, after the success achieved the previous year with the launch of the SD92 - the first 'Navetta' yacht from Sanlorenzo - the shipyard presented its big sister and the flagship of the new line to the yachting world, the SD122. This craft boasts a semi-displacement hull of almost 38 metres, is built in composite material and has three decks.

In keeping with the best Sanlorenzo traditions of building tailor-made motor yachts for over 50 years to suit the requirements and style of each individual owner, the SD122 also combines the best technology available with the most sophisticated hand built craftsmanship. The result is a model that is imposing, both in terms of space and dimensions, and with lines that explicitly evoke the harmony and elegance of the SD line, developed in partnership with the designer Francesco Paszkowski.

Onboard the SD122, there are many distinctive stylistic elements; from the large flying bridge hosting the wooden chaise longue and the hydro-massage tub with waterfall, to the distinctive lateral walkways and the sliding curved hatches providing access to the outside.

Internally, the large spaces offered by a semi-displacement craft such as the SD122, have enabled the Sanlorenzo technical office to position the captain's cabin directly on the upper deck near the control area, an ideal choice for craft wishing to cover long distances.

The ten guests on board are wonderfully accommodated. The internal layout features a stylish owner's suite on the main deck covering the whole width of the yacht and is generously sized, with a private office and separate bathrooms for him and her. On the lower deck there are two large VIP cabins and two cabins with double or twin beds, all beautifully furnished in true Italian style. In terms of performance, the SD122 reaches a maximum speed of 17 knots, delivered via her twin Caterpillar C32 ACERT engines, each capable of producing 1,624hp. At a speed of 12 knots, the SD122 is able to cover over 2,000 nautical miles without stopping and in complete privacy.

SPECIFICATIONS:	SANLORENZO SD122
Length Overall:	37.44m (122' 9")
Beam:	8.00m (26' 3")
Draught:	2.15m (7' 4")
Displacement:	202 ton
Guests:	10
Crew:	7
Engines:	2 x Caterpillar C32, 1624hp
Max. Speed:	17 knots

Above:
The Sanlorenzo SD120 is the flagship of its 'Navetta' line.

Left:
The accommodation and wheelhouse is all beautifully furnished in true Italian style.

SANLORENZO

Sanlorenzo SpA
Via Armezzone, 3
19031 Ameglia (SP)
Italy
Tel: +39 0187 6181
Fax: +39 0187 618316
Web: www.sanlorenzoyacht.com

SANLORENZO 40 ALLOY

One of the most distinctive yachts to be launched in recent years, the first Sanlorenzo 40 Alloy was launched by the company's new Viareggio Division.

Sanlorenzo entrusted the interior layout to Francesco Paszkowski, who conceived a totally innovative project while maintaining Sanlorenzo's stylistic traits. The result is a superyacht in a class of its own, featuring elegant flowing lines and totally innovative elements, such as the exclusive bathing terraces that can be lowered down onto the sea, and the distinctive gull-wing doors.

Having decided to enter the field of building yachts out of metal alloy, the choice of aluminium as the construction material for the Sanlorenzo 40 Alloy was dictated by a two fold need: to widen the size of the company's fleet of yachts and to maintain the performance and quality levels the company is well known for.

The Sanlorenzo 40 Alloy, in line with Sanlorenzo's traditional approach, was designed in concert between the shipyard and the owner and custom built exactly to the owner's individual requirements.

With accommodation for ten guests, the owner's suite is positioned at the forward end of the main deck and is equipped with a huge en-suite his and hers bathroom, a walk-in dressing room, several seating areas and an owner's study.

One of the yacht's distinctive gull-wing doors opens on the starboard side of the owner's suite to provide a private sun balcony. The remainder of the accommodation is on the lower deck including a large VIP suite forward.

In keeping with the stylish exterior appearance of the yacht, the interior is equally elegant, featuring a clean modernistic style with fine leather couches and warm woodwork throughout.

A yacht that typifies the progressive, forward thinking nature of this successful Italian yacht builder, Sanlorenzo's 40 Alloy is a yacht that deserves the worldwide acclaim bestowed upon it over the past year.

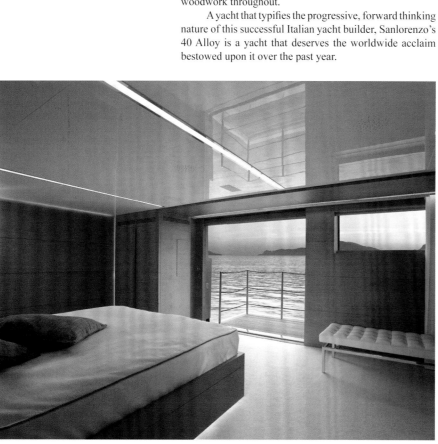

SPECIFICATIONS:	SANLORENZO 40 ALLOY
Length Overall:	40m (131' 3")
Beam:	7.90m (25' 11")
Draught:	3.05m (10' 0")
Displacement:	190 ton
Guests:	10
Crew:	6
Engines:	2 x MTU 12V4000M93
Max. Speed:	28 knots
Range:	800nm at cruising speed

Above:
The Sanlorenzo 40 Alloy is one of the most distinctive yachts to be launched in recent years.

Left:
The main salon is very elegant, featuring a clean modernistic style with fine leather couches and warm woodwork throughout. The wonderful balcony invites the outside world in.

Far Left:
The owner's suite is positioned at the forward end of the main deck and is equipped with a huge en-suite his and hers bathroom, a walk-in dressing room, several seating areas and an owner's study.

IAG YACHTS

IAG Yachts was founded in 2005 by Michael and Bernard Chang as an autonomous division of the well established IAG Group, the world-leader in the production of consumer and professional audio, lighting and video products. From the beginning, the goal was to create a modern shipyard that would build world-class luxury yachts, with the huge advantage of being located in China. The geographical position in Zhuhai, Southern China, close to Hong Kong and Macau, facilitates the import of equipment and technology from Europe and the USA, being easily accessible from everywhere on the mainland or abroad.

The IAG Yachts shipyard is about 67,000m² in area, including a 6,800m² fibreglass production shed, a 7,100m² outfitting workshop and 7,600m² ancillary workshop, plus office buildings. A third construction shed is being built to enable the construction of even bigger yachts in steel and aluminium.

Yacht construction is conceived and organized in a series of well-planned steps that include a major input from the owner in order to personalise the design. The fibreglass production is concentrated in a dedicated temperature and humidity controlled shed while the interiors and furniture are fully prepared and assembled ashore. Complete mock-ups of all the decks are prepared in the wood workshop in order to guarantee the level of quality and to maintain the strict schedules.

The company has gathered together the most experienced and skilled engineers, designers and craftsman, both locally and internationally, to form a team that can manage the total project from the initial conceptual stage through to the final delivery of the yacht to the client.

Above:
The high performance and truly luxurious IAG 100 will boast a top speed of some 30 knots through her twin Caterpillar C32 Acert engines.

Left & Centre:
The company's new state-of-the-art shipyard, located in Zhuhai, near Macau in China, incorporates the very latest yacht building equipment.

Far Left:
The stunning IAG 127 under construction.

IAG YACHTS

IAG 127 - 'PRIMADONNA'

IAG Yachts started production with the IAG 127 model, a 40m tri-deck motor yacht specially conceived for charter operations. Despite keeping down the overall dimensions, she is able to accommodate twelve guests with nine crew, while still providing huge salons and recreational spaces, quite incredible for a yacht of this size.

However, thanks to the clever design concept developed by IAG Yachts, the format of the IAG 127 is flexible enough to allow easy customisation to an individual owner's requirements for their private use.

To ensure the highest possible standards of construction, all the materials and equipment on-board have been selected from well-known manufacturers and all the employees involved were chosen for their excellent skills and craftsmanship. Based on the highest safety and quality standards, the yacht's design, materials, equipment and construction processes were surveyed and checked by RINA to achieve the highest-class notation. The IAG 127 has also been designed to comply with the MCA LY2 code for unrestricted navigation, the most important code for large yachts operating under charter.

The IAG 127 is equipped with two Caterpillar C32 Acert main engines, each rated at 1800 bhp. Based on a tank test at half load, the yacht can achieve a top speed of 20 knots at maximum engine output, with a cruising speed of 17 knots. Furthermore, at an economical speed of 10 knots, the IAG 127 can deliver a range of 3,500 nautical miles. Electrical power is supplied by two 90kw Northern Lights generators fitted to provide parallel operation. The 50 KVA SEA Electronics shore power converter also provides a parallel function with the generators for power transfer capability.

Special attention has been paid to noise and vibration reduction during the design, construction and outfitting. The materials and technical solutions adopted are such that they confer the greatest comfort to guests on board and in

Above & Left:
The first Italian styled IAG 127 motor yacht is currently being built in Zhuhai, near Macau and Hong Kong and will be delivered in March 2010.

Far Left:
The exquisite main salon.

IAG YACHTS

addition, CMC Marine stabilizers with zero speed function have been installed.

In keeping with modern ideas, the style and the interiors have been designed by the Italian company YD&AS using a linear and sophisticated scheme, light being the guideline. Ample windows and clear colours give the impression of widening the spaces on all the decks.

Boarding the yacht from the stern, there is a large swim platform behind which is a big tender garage accessed by a hydraulic door that, when opened, reveals a space large enough for a Castoldi Jet 15 tender. A wide passerelle allows access to the main deck and the salon and dining area through a large crystal aft door.

The light and the blue of the sea flow from the large windows all around but, by closing the remotely controlled curtains in the luxurious salon, the atmosphere can easily become more intimate to enjoy the high quality entertainment system provided by IAG. She features a comprehensive audiovisual system, including a central movie server that also supplies all the cabins.

Proceeding forward, a pantry leads to a well-equipped galley completed in bamboo veneer and finished in stainless steel. On the right, the lobby provides access to the owner's stateroom forward, to the guest area on the lower deck and to the upper deck. The owner's full-beam apartment is astonishingly wide, and benefits from having two distinctive ceiling windows. On the upper deck, the salon is comfortably arranged in the wide area aft, while the forward part is dedicated to the fully equipped wheelhouse, luxuriously finished in leather.

The incredibly spacious sun-deck, is devoted to unwinding and enjoying life to the full- a Jacuzzi, sun pads, bar, sofas and a large table for al-fresco dining complete the relaxation area.

The presentation of the IAG 127 to the European and American markets at the boat shows was an unmitigated success - both professional operators and private clients alike appreciated the style and the characteristics, confirming a real interest in this new "Italian style yacht coming from China".

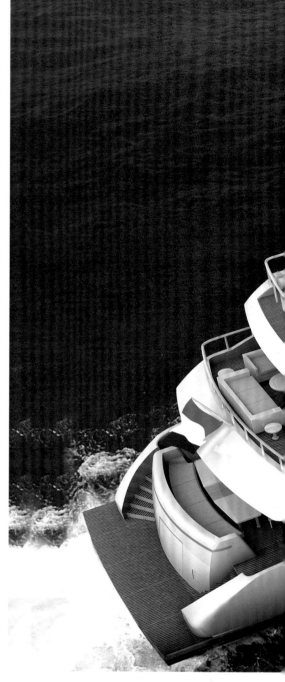

SPECIFICATIONS: IAG 127

Length Overall:	38.80m (127' 3")
Length Waterline:	35.00m (114' 9")
Beam:	8.00m (26' 4")
Draught:	2.10m (6' 10")
Displacement:	180 ton
Construction:	FRP
Guests:	12
Crew:	9
Engines:	2 x CAT C32 Acert 1800bhp
Max. Speed:	20 knots
Classification:	RINA, C HULL; MCA (Ych)

Above & Left:
At a length of 40m and with an
8m beam, the IAG 127 can easily
accommodate twelve guests and nine
crew members on her three decks.

Far Left & Centre:
The dining area is separated from the
main salon by a stylish glass screen
and entertainment counter.

IAG YACHTS

IAG 100

IAG Yachts Ltd
Pingsha Yacht Industry Park
Zuhai 519055
China
Tel: +86 756 7720720
Fax: +86 756 7725511
Web: www.iagyachts.com

Even as the construction of the third hull of the successful IAG 127 series is commencing, IAG Yachts presents its new model – the IAG 100.

This yacht is the result of close cooperation between the shipyard's technical office and the Italian companies YD&AS and REDS, well known and respected in the yacht design world. YD&AS, who previously designed the IAG 127 series, developed the design of this two-deck yacht with raised wheelhouse, and maintained a classic style in a modern context. REDS took care of the engineering with great attention to performance and safety. The IAG 100, as with all the yachts produced by IAG Yachts, is constructed to the highest RINA class and is fully compliant with the MCA rules for charter.

The vessel, 30m LOA and with a beam of 6.5m, accommodates eight passengers plus four crew on two decks sailing in full safety at a maximum speed of 30 knots, thanks to the two Caterpillar C32 Acert main engines. As with the IAG 127, all the materials and equipment installed on-board are from well-known brands, granting reliability and safety.

Inside, the huge salon benefits from panoramic windows and a superb sound-video system, and with the stylish dining area in a separate room, enjoyment is assured. The outdoor of the IAG 100 is no less inviting, with the comfortable sun-deck, the sun pads in the fore-deck and the main-deck aft salon.

Definitively, the IAG 100 is built for yacht owners who appreciate true quality and the best things in life.

SPECIFICATIONS: IAG 100

Length Overall:	31.00m (101' 8")
Beam:	6.80m (22' 4")
Draught:	1.30m (4' 3")
Displacement:	115 ton
Construction:	FRP
Guests:	8
Crew:	4
Engines:	2 x CAT C32 Acert 1800bhp
Max. Speed:	30 knots
Classification:	RINA, C HULL; MCA (Ych)

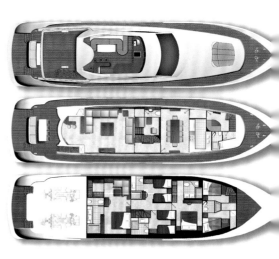

Above & Far Left:
The IAG 100, as with all the yachts produced by IAG Yachts, has been designed in accordance with the highest RINA class regulations.

Left:
A 'cut-away' rendering cleverly shows off the layout of the yacht.

PERI YACHTS

Peri builds its high-tech yachts in one of the most advanced yards in the eastern Mediterranean. The company's shipyard is located in Antalya on the Turkish Riviera, where it builds its performance yachts, ranging in length from 29m (96') to 41m (135').

Peri's business philosophy is to manufacture composite yachts under the right conditions and to the highest standards. The company invests in the most advanced tools for composite production and quality control and is determined to become, and remain, one of the world leaders in this field.

The quality of the Peri team is enhanced by constant training, either on the job or in specialised courses given by international experts. In addition to the shore teams, a support team of professional mariners contribute their vast experience gained through thousands of miles at sea.

Peri yachts are not mass-production creations. All yachts, whether built to Peri's own lines or custom-designed to the owner's specifications, are constructed to the latest classification rules and thus qualify for the approval required for charter.

Modern to the core, the Peri yachts embody the advantages of E glass and epoxy resin construction. This composite material possesses outstanding properties of lightness, stiffness and strength translating into a vessel that delivers impressive speed for the power used while maintaining great stability and ease of handling, in addition to expanding the living space available.

These high-tech luxury craft are designed by Turkey's avant-garde Scaro Design group and engineered by the British naval architect, Bill Dixon, with all the composite construction processes laid down by High Modulus.

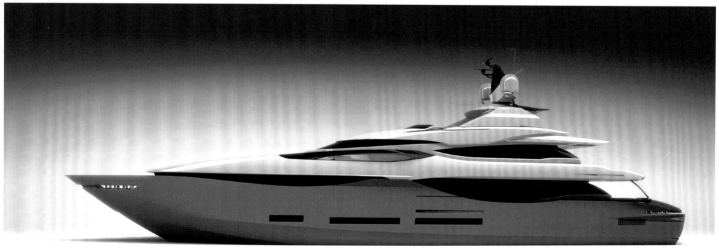

Above:
The beautiful, sleek Peri 29 is capable of speeds of up to 28 knots!

Left:
The Peri 37 is distinctive in her modern, contemporary design.

Far Left:
The Peri 41T is the crowning glory of this dynamic Turkish shipyard's range of cutting-edge composite yachts.

PERI YACHTS   PERI 29

With a length of 28.6m and a beam of 6.48m, the Peri 29 is the lightest and fastest model of the Peri line. Combining the design flair of Scaro Design and Bill Dixon, the high level engineering of High Modulus and the craftsmanship of Peri Yachts, the Peri 29 is distinguished by her modern sleek lines, vast volumes and strong epoxy composite sandwich structure. Contrary to the majority of composite yacht builders, Peri Yachts prefers to use the more expensive epoxy resins instead of polyester or vinylester resins to guarantee strength, durability and performance. The result is exhilarating speed, formidable resistance to wear and tear and a hull that remains completely free from the threat of osmosis.

The Peri 29's interior is a masterpiece of contemporary design. The composite construction's lightness and strength frees up interior space and removes the conventional design boundaries. This is a totally new take on luxury living and a major advantage over yachts built using conventional materials.

The main salon has two distinctive areas. The lounge area is furnished with two sofas to relax in, while the comfortable dining area is perfect for entertaining guests. Also on the main deck and adjacent to the main salon, the galley is well located to serve the needs of the guests.

The Peri 29 has accommodation for eight guests in one master, one VIP and two identical twin guest cabins, each with en-suite bathroom. All guest suites feature a sophisticated entertainment system and have spacious storage facilities. Peri Yachts has also developed a 5-cabin version of the Peri 29, accommodating ten guests while maintaining the spaciousness of the cabins. As in every other part of the yacht, all of the guest suites are equipped with an advanced climate control system. The crew area is separated from the guest quarters and is suitable for accommodating three or four crewmembers.

The outside deck areas of the Peri 29 matches the spaciousness of the interior, offering large open-air areas

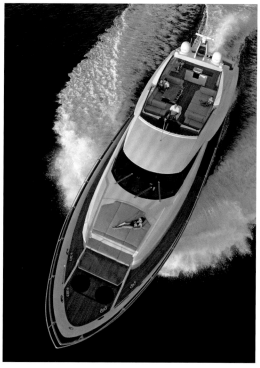

Above & Centre:
The Peri 29 is distinguished by her modern sleek lines, vast volumes and strong epoxy composite sandwich structure.

Left:
The aft deck is perfect for entertaining guests.

Far Left:
Enjoy plenty of sunsets on the spacious fly bridge.

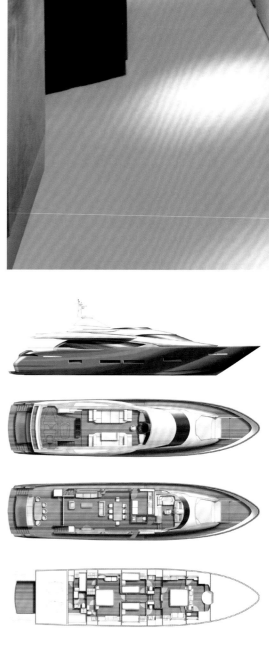

PERI YACHTS

for the guests to relax in. Guests have several options when considering where to dine. An aft dining area is perfect for open air dining, while other dining areas in the salon and on the fly bridge provide other alternatives.

The fly bridge offers a wet bar, barbeque and ample sitting and sun bathing areas. The wide area on the fore deck is another attractive area where guests can enjoy the sea and the sun with its wide sun pad and uncluttered deck arrangement.

The engine room of the Peri 29 is equipped generously with twin Caterpillar 1825hp C32 ACERT main engines, 2x CAT C2 22kW and 1x Fischer Panda generators and Wesmar hydraulic systems. The engine room is well insulated and is connected to the aft platform through a spacious storage area and a hydraulically operated transom door.

Cruising at 26 knots and with a maximum speed of 31 knots, the Peri 29 has two control stations equipped with the most modern navigation and communication instruments available. The engines, thrusters, capstans and all major functions are controllable from both control stations. The Peri 29 is built with RINA Charter Class classification and is MCA compliant

SPECIFICATIONS: PERI 29

Length Overall:	28.60m (93' 10")
Beam:	6.48m (21' 3")
Draught:	1.01m (3' 4")
Displacement:	70 ton
Naval Architecture:	Dixon Yacht Design
Exterior Styling:	Scaro Design
Interior Design:	Scaro Design
Construction:	Glass Reinforced Epoxy Sandwich
Engines:	2 x Caterpillar C32 Acert 1825hp
Maximum Speed:	31 knots
Cruise Speed:	26 knots
Range:	up to 400 nautical miles

Above :
The main salon has two distinctive areas. The lounge area is furnished with two sofas to relax in, while the comfortable dining area is perfect for entertaining guests

Left:
Twin staircases lead down to the full-width swim platform.

Far Left:
Enjoying the Peri lifestyle!

PERI YACHTS   PERI 37

As with all the yachts in the series, the Peri 37 is a distinctive vessel with her modern sleek lines, vast volumes and strong epoxy composite sandwich body reinforced with carbon fibre.

The aft-raked stern and beamy hull features much larger volumes and decks in comparison to similar vessels of her size. Indeed, the design offers accommodation comparable to the yachts of 38m – 40m in length.

Fitted with twin 2,250hp MTU 16V 2000 M92 main engines, the Peri 37 achieves a top speed of 24 knots, while at a cruising speed of 20 knots she has a range of 1,250 nautical miles. As an option, the Peri 37 can be fitted with twin 2,400hp MTU 16V 2000 M93 engines, capable of reaching a top speed of 26 knots.

The Peri 37's engine room details a generous variety of machinery and equipment of highly-reputed brands, including TRAC stabilisers and fully automated monitoring systems.

Aft of the engine room, a spacious dinghy garage for all kind of toys leads to an aft bathing platform that can be lowered hydraulically to allow easy access to the sea.

Forward of the engine room on the lower deck, there are two spacious VIP cabins and two guest cabins, each with en-suite bathroom and sophisticated entertainment systems.

On the main deck, the master stateroom is one of the best available in the market today on yachts of this size. With its wide beam and high overhead, this cabin is not only spacious but luxuriously appointed. A comfortable owner's study at the entrance to the master cabin is conveniently connected to the main salon, which consists of two large and separate areas for lounging and dining. Throughout the yacht, an advanced climate control system keeps the temperature and humidity at the optimum level, whether cruising in the tropics or colder latitudes.

The galley, equipped with an additional dining area for the benefit of the crew, is designed and equipped for

Above, Centre & Far Left:
The Peri 37 is a distinctive vessel with her modern sleek lines, vast volumes and strong epoxy composite sandwich body reinforced with carbon fibre.

Left:
The stylish fly bridge.

PERI YACHTS

needs beyond the capacity of the vessel, to ensure the comfort and high level of hospitality expected from such a yacht.

Outside, the decks of the Peri 37 have been well designed and offer large areas where guests can relax in privacy. While the aft dining area is ideal for open air dining, guests may also dine and be entertained on the spacious fly bridge which features a barbeque, wet bar and kitchen, as well as a Jacuzzi and a variety of seating and lounging areas.

The Peri 37 has two control stations equipped with the most modern navigation and communication instruments available on the market today. The engines, thrusters, stabilizers and all major functions are controllable from both helm stations. The yacht is also equipped with onboard camera, security and alarm systems, all controlled by a mainframe computer.

The Peri 37 is built with RINA Charter Class classification and is MCA compliant.

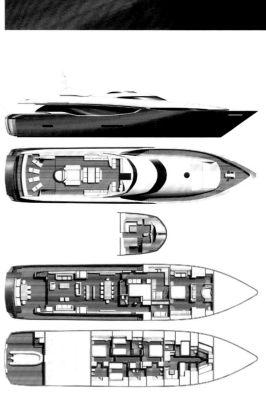

SPECIFICATIONS: PERI 37	
Length Overall:	36.93m (121' 2")
Beam:	8.10m (26' 6")
Draught:	1.57m (5' 2")
Displacement:	160 ton
Naval Architecture:	Dixon Yacht Design
Exterior Styling:	Scaro Design
Interior Design:	Scaro Design
Structural Comp:	High Modulus
Construction:	Glass Reinforced Epoxy Sandwich
Engines:	2 x MTU 16V2000M93 2400hp
Maximum Speed:	26 knots
Cruise Speed:	22 knots
Range:	up to 1250 nautical miles

Above:
The main salon is divided by a beautifully crafted TV unit into a relaxing living room and a formal dining room.

Left:
The modern owner's stateroom.

Far Left:
The VIP stateroom.

PERI YACHTS   PERI 41T

Peri Yachts is taking its ultra-cool brand of high-tech luxury to new lengths with its first 41m triple-deck yacht. This superyacht is now in production and is scheduled for delivery in 2010. Designed as the crowning glory of this dynamic Turkish shipyard's range of cutting-edge composite yachts, the Peri 41T will arguably leave traditional luxury yachts in its wake.

The Peri 41T tri-deck yacht will embody two of Peri's key assets: its leadership in composite construction and its ability to express contemporary ideals of luxury. The result is both a high-performance yacht and a palatial residence with a unique uncluttered elegance. The forceful profile and stunning interior space are the work of Scaro Design, Turkey's avant-garde design group.

In terms of construction, the Peri 41T uses the latest in high-tech yacht building materials. Its glass-reinforced epoxy sandwich structure makes it lighter and stronger than traditional yachts of its size making it capable of remarkably high speeds. The Peri 41T will deliver a maximum speed of 25 knots from its twin MTU 12V4000M93L engines, together with superb handling, stability and safety. At a cruising speed of 20 knots, she will achieve a 1250 nautical mile range.

Although glass-reinforced epoxy composites are more expensive and difficult to process than conventional alternatives, the advantages of using such materials are considerable and Peri's shipyard in Antalya is a leader in the field of composite construction.

Having proved the advantages with its earlier models, the company says firmly: "We prefer to build our yachts the hard way." The Peri 41T's design and engineering is by the renowned British naval architect Bill Dixon, while all its composite processes are laid down by High Modulus.

The Peri 41T is recognisable by its swooping profile giving it a sleek racy look despite its broad 8.8m beam. Once on board, the voluminous living space is immediately apparent. The lighter, stronger composite

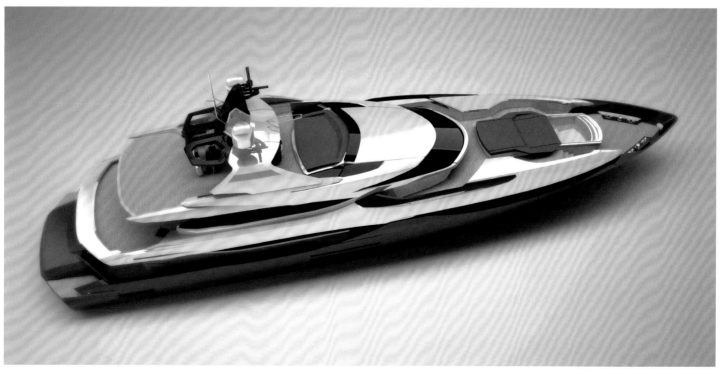

Above, Left & Far Left:
The forceful profile and stunning interior space of the Peri 41T are the work of Scaro Design, Turkey's avant-garde design group.

PERI YACHTS

Peri Yachts
Bagdat Caddesi Oncu Sokak,
Buyukhanli Konutlari B2/10 Suadiye,
34740 Istanbul, Turkey
Tel: +90 216 464 7030
Fax: +90 216 464 7020
Web: www.periyachts.com

structure dramatically increases the space available for relaxing, playing and socialising. A striking example is the 45m² sun-deck with its bar, grill and huge sunbathing area, that is adjoined by a dining area for eight, measuring a full 70m². The foredeck provides another vast and idyllic setting for dreaming, relaxing and entertaining.

The Peri 41T's interior is equally impressive. This is serious glamour and minimalism at its best - a potent concoction of bold, simple shapes, pale luxurious fabrics and sophisticated lighting. The huge main salon makes a strong central statement, with large sofas in soft, hand-stitched leather and a dining table that seats ten comfortably. Accommodation is on the same lavish but uncluttered scale. The master suite in particular is worthy of mention, taking up the whole forward section of the main deck and comprising a full beam master bedroom, a huge en-suite bathroom and a private owner's study. This in turn leads aft to the opulent main salon containing a large formal dining area, separated by a partition containing the yacht's main entertainment systems from the relaxing lounge area, boasting a variety of comfortable settees and chairs.

With five other guest suites on the lower deck, the yacht welcomes an owner's party of twelve in the six spacious cabins, while the nine crew are well catered for in five cabins and a separate crew's mess.

As a truly high-tech luxury yacht, the Peri 41T is endowed with the very latest technology.

With RINA Charter Class classification and being MCA compliant, she will indeed be a worthy flagship of this ultra-modern and progressive yacht builder.

SPECIFICATIONS: PERI 41T	
Length Overall:	41.00m (134' 6")
Beam:	8.80m (28' 10")
Draught:	1.84m (6' 1")
Displacement:	190 ton
Naval Architecture:	Dixon Yacht Design
Exterior Styling:	Scaro Design
Interior Design:	Scaro Design
Construction:	Glass Reinforced Epoxy Sandwich
Engines:	2 x MTU 16V2000M93 2400hp
Maximum Speed:	23 knots
Cruise Speed:	18 knots
Range:	up to 1250 nautical miles

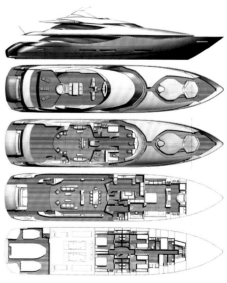

Above & Far Left:
The master suite takes up the whole forward section of the main deck, consisting of a full beam master bedroom, a huge en-suite bathroom and a private owner's study.

Left:
The Peri 41T's opulent main salon contains a large formal dining area, separated by a partition containing the yacht's main entertainment systems from the relaxing lounge area, boasting a variety of comfortable settees and chairs.

FIPA GROUP

ipa Italiana Yachts was established in Viareggio in the early 1980's, producing fibreglass hulls and structures for a yachting market that was increasingly asking for more and more of this new, strong and mouldable material. With the success of this business, Fipa's next step was to develop its yachting division in a major way, so in the mid 1980's it acquired Maiora, one of the most prestigious yachting brands in Italy.

With an already established reputation for high-quality, seaworthy craft, Maiora found in Fipa a means to grow and develop into a world leader of luxury yachts and one that continually seeks to achieve perfection.

At the beginning of the 1990's, with the Maiora brand going from strength to strength, new production sites inside the port area of Viareggio were constructed, including the historic Intermare shipbuilding yard in the Viareggio basin, where Fipa now offers its clients a full yacht service capability. Expanding further in 2001, Fipa acquired AB Yachts, a leading Italian yacht builder specialising in the design and production of high-performance, water-jet propelled 'Open' yachts.

Finally, the acquisition by the Fipa Group of CBI Navi, in March 2005, who build fully customised, displacement yachts made of steel and aluminium from 24m to 80m in length, made it possible for the company to offer a complete array of customized, luxury motor yachts.

Today, with such a wide range of luxury yachts now being built, the Fipa Group can meet any possible request for a personalised motor yacht, whether it be a stylish fly bridge yacht, a fast high-tech cruiser, or a displacement vessel for inter-oceanic routes.

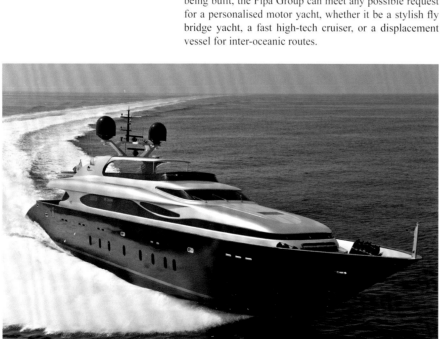

Above:
The awesome AB 140 has a maximum speed of 46 knots.

Centre:
The AB 116

Left:
The stylish CBI 50.

Far Left:
The M39 is yet another jewel to grace the Maiora range.

FIPA GROUP   AB 116

The AB 116 is the brand new model from the AB Yachts range combining strength and luxury with extraordinary performance in a yacht with a maximum speed of nearly 50 knots.

With smooth, winning lines and spacious interiors, the first AB 116 was launched in May 2009 and features an enormous sun-deck, a flying bridge with a wide-open helm station and big sun beds on the stern. In fact, all the open spaces on the yacht have been designed to be large and luxurious and to enhance the joy of being in the open air. Inside, the interiors are no less luxurious, with a salon taking up almost half the volume of the main deck. On the main deck a large open-air aft deck leads forward into the main salon that is separated from the dining area, with its table for eight guests, by a stylish panel featuring a 50" television. In front of the dining area, the well-equipped wheelhouse features three beautiful leather helm chairs and offers great views through the front windows. Moving down the staircase to the lower deck guests enter a wonderful lower deck lounge that can be used as a TV room and which is lit by the windows of the main deck. Further aft, a master stateroom takes in the full beam of the yacht and is equipped with a large sitting area as well as an en-suite bathroom. Three more double guest cabins and good crew accommodation complete the layout.

Thanks to the AB 116, AB Yachts have found a fantastic starting point to begin the process of developing its entire production range, of which the stylish AB 140' and AB 160' will be a major part, in continuing AB Yachts' success.

SPECIFICATIONS: AB 116	
Length Overall:	35.30m (118' 9")
Beam:	7.20m (24' 7")
Draught:	1.20m (3' 11")
Displacement:	110 ton
Engines:	3 x MTU 16V2000M83, 2,400hp
Max. Speed:	46 knots
Cruise Speed:	42 knots
Range:	About 500 nautical miles

Above & Left:
With smooth, winning lines and spacious interiors, the first AB 116 was launched in May 2009 and features an enormous sun-deck, a flying bridge with a wide-open helm station and big sun beds on the stern.

Far Left & Centre:
Inside, the interiors are no less luxurious, with a salon taking up almost half the volume of the main deck.

FIPA GROUP   AB 140

For the AB 140, AB Yachts' objective was to create a masterpiece of technology and performance. To achieve this result much time and expense was spent investigating both the materials to be used and the hydrodynamic properties of the yacht. Her hull lines were designed around finding the right balance between handling the power that her three 2400hp engines would produce in the craft, and yet guaranteeing optimal comfort when cruising.

After much testing, the amazing result is a yacht capable of achieving a maximum speed of 46 knots and a cruising speed of 43 knots. However, perhaps the most impressive fact is that with only the two wing engines running it is possible to achieve 34.5 knots and cruise at 32 knots for a range of 950 miles.

For her construction, the hull is entirely built in composite sandwich material using Kevlar fabrics and carbon reinforcing. This gives the yacht a weight reduction of 35-40 % compared to normal GRP hulls.

On the main deck there is the main salon, dining room, and wheelhouse as well as a small dining room for relaxing. Forward of this, the wheelhouse contains a panel made of composite and finished with carbon. The helm station features three luxurious helm chairs lined with leather, as well as the very latest navigation and communication technology.

Below the main deck, the lower deck hosts four big cabins all with en-suite bathrooms, including the huge full-beam master suite, as well as a gym and accommodation for the crew of seven.

A yacht built for luxurious excitement, the AB 140 is, without doubt, well equipped to provide just that.

SPECIFICATIONS: AB 140	
Length Overall:	41.6m
Beam:	8.0m
Draught:	1.3m
Displacement:	131 ton
Engines:	3 x MTU 16V2000M93, 2,400hp
Max. Speed:	46 knots
Cruise Speed:	43 knots

Above & Left:
A yacht built for luxurious excitement, the AB 140 is, without doubt, well equipped to provide just that.

FIPA GROUP

MAIORA M35 JET

With a group comprised of Maiora Yachts, CBI Navi and AB Yachts, the last New Year for the Fipa Group started at a brisk pace with the launch of its latest creation, the Maiora 35 Jet, taking place on February 9th 2009 at the Port of Marina di Carrara in Italy. With over thirty years experience of building prestigious motor yachts, this new model represents a fusion of elegant lines, safety, power and comfort that has always distinguished this stylish Tuscan brand.

This development of the shipyard's expertise and hard work has resulted in a truly exotic yacht that has met all of the owner's expectations and much more. The Maiora M35 is a fully customised yacht with classic lines, wonderful interior living spaces and the latest high-tech instrumentation.

On board, the interior of the first Maiora 35 features soft, pleasant colours brought together by refined lighting. The interior walls are made of light durmast wood creating a beautiful contrast to the wengé floors, while the ceilings are lined with ivory leather producing a warm and comfortable ambience.

Each room is designed to create a relaxing environment. The huge owner's suite, like all the accommodation onboard, is highly luxurious.

Powered by three MTU 16V2000M93 engines, each providing 2400hp to three 550 MJP water jets, the performance of the Maiora 35 Jet is simply startling, with a maximum speed in excess of 40 knots.

Available also without water jets, the Maiora 35, when fitted with twin MTU 2,700hp engines, still produces a highly respectable 23 knots.

SPECIFICATIONS: MAIORA M35 JET	
Length Overall:	35.00m (113' 2")
Beam:	7.50m (23' 7")
Draught:	1.40m (4' 7")
Displacement:	120 ton
Engines:	3 x 2400 HP MTU 16V 2000 M93
	3 x water jets 550 MJP
Max. Speed:	44 knots
Cruise Speed:	38 knots
Range:	Approx. 500nm at cruising speed.

Above & Centre:
The performance of the Maiora 35 Jet is simply startling, with a maximum speed in excess of 40 knots.

Left:
The Maiora M35 is a fully customised yacht with classic lines, wonderful interior living spaces and the latest high-tech instrumentation.

Far Left:
The Maiora M35 & Maiora M35 Jet make quite a combination.

FIPA GROUP

MAIORA M39

FIPA GROUP
Maiora - AB Yachts - CBI Navi
Sales Department
Via Marina di Levante 12-14-16
55049 Viareggio (LU), Italy
Tel: +39 0584 38191
Fax: +39 0584 3819333
Email: info@fipagroup.com
            info@maiora.net
            info@abyachts.com
            info@cbinavi.com
Web: www.fipagroup.com

The M39 is yet another jewel to grace the Maiora range, a name that now boasts over 30 years of experience in the construction of highly prestigious and luxurious motor yachts. This 39m yacht is noticeable, not only for its dimensions, but for its stylish design that combines comfort with luxury, safety with practicality, elegance with aggressiveness and tradition with innovation.

Designed as a yacht where open-air living is paramount, a huge flying bridge has been designed into the Maiora M39, offering comfortable sun beds, a beautiful bar and plenty of seating.

Inside the yacht, the combination of colours and light is superb. The interior walls are made of light durmast forming a harmonious contrast with the wengé floors, while the ceilings are all lined with light leather.

When entering the main salon from the aft deck through the elegant crystal sliding door, guests are greeted by a wide convivial area with sofas, floors and ceilings all in light colours creating a pleasant variation with the darker woods and details. In the main salon, a high-tech home theatre system complete with a 52" television can be lowered and hidden in the furniture, and a refreshing bar area can also hidden from view. Below deck, four comfortable guest cabins plus, in the bow, an enormous owner's suite, illustrate just how big the Maiora M39 really is.

Equipped with twin 3700hp MTU engines which are capable of producing a maximum speed of approximately 32 knots, enjoyment is the name of the game on the Maiora M39.

SPECIFICATIONS:	MAIORA M39
Length Overall:	36.20m (129' 10")
Beam:	7.60m (24' 11")
Draught:	1.90m (6' 3")
Displacement:	135 ton
Engines:	2 x MTU 16V 4000 M90
Max. Speed:	32 knots
Cruise Speed:	27 knots
Range:	Approx. 1000nm at cruising speed.

Above & Centre:
This 39m yacht is noticeable, not only for its dimensions, but for its stylish design.

Left:
The elegant master suite.

Far Left:
The spacious fly bridge is a sun-lover's dream.

ISA YACHTS

The prestigious Italian yacht company ISA began building yachts in 2001 by uniting two neighbouring shipyards located in the industrial area of the Port of Ancona under one banner. The company specializes in the design and construction of 30-80m luxury motor yachts made of steel, aluminium and composite material.

ISA is the result of a synergy between the experience and resolution of the Ancona managers, Gianluca Fenucci and Marcello Maggi, and the financial backing of the Yachting Investors Group (YIG), a UK private equity fund dedicated to the yachting industry, based in London and operating worldwide. After considerable investment, ISA now has outstanding facilities and a highly skilled work force enabling it to build different types of vessel, including those made of composite material, all to the most stringent quality standards and to the most creative of designs.

The ISA shipyard is one of Europe's finest, boasting a 45,000m^2 facility, of which 18,000m^2 are covered, including three covered building sheds, the technical and the administration offices and some workshops for on-site engineering and woodwork operations. The yard's know-how allows it to build yachts ranging in size from 40 to 100 metres in steel, aluminium and steel or all aluminium and composite. More than nine boats can be built simultaneously.

Most recently, in 2008 a new division dedicated to the maintenance and refitting of any kind of yacht, including sailing yachts, opened for business. This new division, which makes use of the vast experience of the shipyard's skilled work force, also has an adjoining marina with ten berths for yachts up to 90m in length for yachts to be refitted in or for those just in transit.

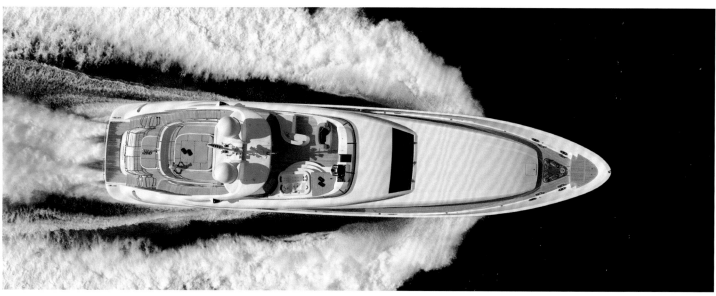

Above :
The ISA 480 'Alexander V'.

Left:
The ISA 600.

Far Left:
The ISA 120 'Firouzeh'.

ISA YACHTS

ISA 480 'ALEXANDER V'

The ISA 480 'Alexander V' is a true 'special edition' yacht that has been customised from the yard's now famous 47m range. At 48 metres long and with a steel and aluminium construction, she is an original masterpiece of style and elegance, yet maintains the yard's trademark showpiece - the stairway connecting all the decks, leading from the stern 'beach deck' to the sun-deck.

'Alexander V' is a yacht ISA can be particularly proud of, as all the internal furnishings were designed and constructed in-house, without the need to employ an external interior designer. The owner, along with the architects Daniele Socci and Rita Luzzi from the ISA technical office and project manager Sandro Spaziani, all worked together closely to produce an extremely refined interior ambience using precious woods, namely maple, ebony and teak and balanced out with valuable marbles.

The client, whose name is kept strictly confidential, is a young, dynamic entrepreneur who demanded the very best from the yard. That ISA successfully delivered with its attention to detail and quality control, is a true testament to the company's expertise.

Apart from the voluminous areas that are just waiting to be enjoyed onboard the yacht, 'Alexander V' features light, airy internal spaces – a result of the large panoramic windows on either side of the yacht. Most noticeably, the balconies on 'Alexander V's superstructure have been lengthened from those of the ISA 470. By extending these, spacious shady areas have been created both on the stern cockpit of the main deck - set up with dining table and sofas - and on the upper deck, where together with the dining table and chairs and further towards the stern, a relaxation area with white sofas, pouf and low coffee tables, has been created. Both areas are shaded by two fixed awnings that maximise guest enjoyment of these areas.

Onboard, the warm, welcoming feel to this yacht is almost tangible as you enter the main deck living area aft through the large French doors. The beautiful modern

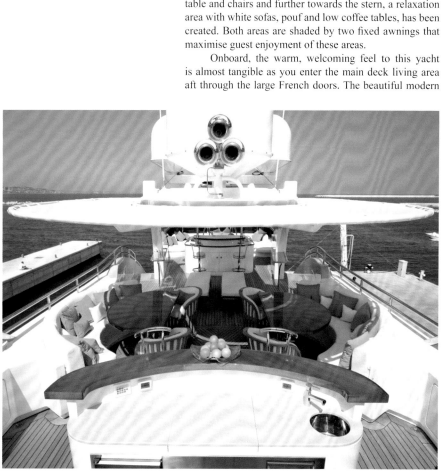

Above:
'Alexander V' is a true 'special edition' yacht that has been customised from the yard's now famous 47m range.

Far Left & Left:
The upper deck features plenty of seating and sunbathing areas as well as a bar and large Jacuzzi.

Centre:
'Alexander V' features ISA's trademark showpiece - the stairway connecting all the decks, leading from the stern 'beach deck' to the sun-deck.

ISA YACHTS

furnishings are created with exotic wooden cabinetry, luxurious white fabric and leather sofas, as well as low coffee tables in dark brown leather, ebony and with a central glass panel. A dividing structure separates the living and dining areas, at the centre of which is an etched glass panel with a design representing the boat's profile. The dining table, chairs and all the surrounding furniture are made of ebony, in striking contrast with the teak flooring.

The owner's cabin on the forward main deck is simply enormous. At the entrance, a dressing room constructed of maple with leather stands opposite the owner's study. The king sized double bed provides the heart of the room, while the en-suite bathroom is spacious and light. Built in maple and Arco Iris onyx, it is equipped with his and hers washbasins, an extra-large shower and a Jacuzzi.

Down a flight of stairs, the lower deck accommodates four guest cabins (two doubles and two twins), and the crew quarters. The style of these is in keeping with the rest of the yacht, with maple walls and furniture, and teak flooring.

The upper deck layout of 'Alexander V' is unusual and differs from that of the previous ISA 470. From the stern, an upper deck lounge is a relaxing room where guests can enjoy a cinema-style entertainment system. Further forward, a large double VIP stateroom is found complete with en-suite bathroom. Forward of this a wonderful wheelhouse is equipped with the latest technology as well as a stylish red leather sofa and armchairs, where guests may relax in the control centre of the yacht.

Finally, the sun-deck is divided up into two separate areas. Towards the bow, a dining area is located under the shade of the enormous radar arch, while large white sofas and armchairs enhance this relaxation area. Further aft, there is a wet bar with stools integrated into the enormous Jacuzzi. Just beyond this, a large and very comfortable sunbathing area is furnished with loungers.

Without doubt, this is a yacht designed for an owner who happily welcomes guests aboard, and wishes to enjoy his yacht, and particularly so in the open-air.

SPECIFICATIONS: ISA 480 – 'ALEXANDER V'

Length Overall:	48.00m (157' 5")
Beam:	8.90m (29' 3")
Draught:	2.55m (8' 5")
Displacement:	500 ton
Naval Architecture:	ISA
Exterior Design:	ISA
Interior Design:	ISA
Construction:	Steel Hull / Aluminium Superstr.
Engines:	Two MTU 12V 4000 M70
Max. Speed:	17 knots
Cruising speed:	15 knots
Range:	1,650 nm at cruise speed

Above:
The beautiful main salon's modern furnishings are created with exotic wooden cabinetry, luxurious white fabric and leather sofas, as well as low coffee tables in dark brown leather, ebony and with a central glass panel.

Left:
The owner's cabin on the forward main deck is simply enormous.

Centre:
The upper deck lounge is a relaxing room where guests can enjoy a cinema-style entertainment system.

Far Left:
The large VIP stateroom.

ISA YACHTS

ISA 120 'FIROUZEH'

The luxury yacht 'Firouzeh' is the sixth yacht of the ISA 120 series and has an overall length of 36m (120'). Constructed by ISA in collaboration with Cristiano Gatto Design, who designed the classical interiors, she was designed by Andrea Vallicelli in close collaboration with ISA's in-house technical department. Her striking external lines offer progressive and unique styling with superb deck space and functionality.

Her name, which was chosen by the owners, has an oriental origin and symbolizes a precious blue gem used as a good luck charm.

Speed and high performance are very much 'Firouzeh's main features. This planing composite built yacht has a maximum speed of 36 knots and an astonishing cruising speed of 27 knots! She achieves this through her three 2000hp MTU engines that drive two lateral water jets and a central booster jet. With a maximum beam of 7.40m and a full load displacement of 130 tons, the ISA 120 complies with all the latest MCA safety standards.

The sleek-profiled ISA 120 oozes power and offers a vast split-level master stateroom at main deck level with 180-degree panoramic views forward, together with an option of either three or four guest cabins on the lower deck, all with en-suite bathrooms. The finish throughout is naturally of the highest standard - something clients of ISA have grown accustomed to!

Right:
'Firouzeh's striking external lines offer progressive and unique styling with superb deck space and functionality.

Below Left:
The colourful main salon and dining room.

Below Right & Centre:
The master stateroom and en-suite bathroom are very spacious and opulently furnished.

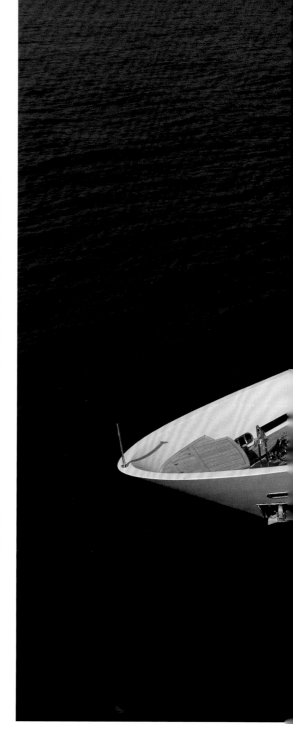

SPECIFICATIONS: ISA 120 – 'FIROUZEH'	
Length Overall:	36.45m (119' 7")
Length Waterline:	30m (98' 5")
Beam:	7.40m (24' 3")
Draught:	1.46m (4' 10")
Displacement:	153 ton
Naval Architecture:	ISA
Exterior Design:	Andrea Vallicelli
Interior Design:	Cristiano Gatto
Construction:	Composite
Classification:	MCA, RINA, Lloyd's 100A1
Engines:	3 x MTU 16V 2000 M93
Max / Cruise Speed:	36 / 27 knots
Range:	500 nm at cruise speed

ISA YACHTS

ISA
International Shipyards Ancona
Via Mattei 14
60125 Ancona, Italy
Tel: +39 071 5021 91
Fax: +39 071 5021 9210
Web: www.isayachts.com

ISA 600

After the huge success of the ISA 120 and with seven yachts already sold, ISA confirmed its position as a builder of innovation, style and quality.

In celebration of this and not being a yard that rests on its laurels, ISA recently announced a new model to its line-up - the ISA 600, a twin screw, full displacement motor yacht. At 60.50 metres long and 12 metres wide, she is, in terms of size, the largest motor yacht ever to be built by the ISA shipyard in Ancona.

Thanks to twin Caterpillar 3512 C DITA-SCAC diesel engines, this gem of a megayacht will have a maximum speed of 16 knots and a cruising speed of 15 knots.

In addition to the master cabin on the main deck, the interiors will include four other guest cabins (two doubles and two twins) on the lower deck, with one double cabin on the main deck and a VIP cabin on the upper deck. Like any ISA project, this new 60m yacht will stand out for its perfect harmony of sleek, stylish lines and extremely spacious and comfortable internal areas.

The ISA 600 was originally designed by Walter Franchini, then revised by Andrea Vallicelli, while the project management and construction will be by ISA's own team of engineers. The new ISA 600 is scheduled for delivery in the Summer 2010.

Right:
At 60.50 metres long and 12 metres wide, the ISA 600 is, in terms of size, the largest motor yacht ever to be built by the ISA shipyard in Ancona.

Below Left:
The elegant master stateroom.

Below Right:
The huge main salon will be highly luxurious.

SPECIFICATIONS: ISA 600	
Length Overall:	60.50m (198' 5")
Length Waterline:	53.95m (177')
Beam:	12.00m (39' 5")
Draught:	3.30m (10' 10")
Displacement:	980 ton
Naval Architecture:	ISA
Exterior Design:	Walter Franchini
Construction:	Steel / Aluminium
Classification:	Lloyd's 100A1 SSC YACHT
Engines:	2 x Caterpillar 3512C 1765 kW
Max. Speed:	16.5 knots
Cruising speed:	14.5 knots
Range:	2,700 nm at 14 knots

VITTERS SHIPYARD

V itters Shipyard is a well-established and respected custom yacht builder situated in Zwartsluis, The Netherlands. The facility opened in 1990 and has delivered an impressive list of yachts up to 80 metres in length, working with some of the world's top designers.

With an emphasis on delivering superior quality and providing seamless support to the owner and crew once the yacht has been delivered, lessons are learned from each and every yacht the yard launches and are merged into every subsequent project while maintaining a competitive commercial position at all times.

Situated on the original Dutch coastline, which is now located in the heart of the country, Vitters Shipyard continues to take advantage of the area's long standing boat and yacht building traditions. The yard employs the best local craftsman and also utilises the strong infrastructure of specialist technical companies that continue to grow in support of the large Dutch yacht building industry.

Of course, owners are the first and most important ingredient of every yacht-building project. Every owner has a unique vision and so each project provides unique challenges. Vitters in turn challenges its engineering and construction team to fulfil each owner's vision and at the same time deliver a strong, safe and practical yacht that complies with the stringent conditions set by the world's leading external regulatory bodies. The quality and track record of the Vitters fleet bears testament to the success of this approach.

Featured overleaf are two of Vitters recent launches, the beautiful sailing yachts 'Mystère' (43.2m) and 'Nirvana' (53.5m), as well as some of the latest projects currently under construction at this prestigious yard.

Above:
The 53.5m (176') S/Y 'Nirvana'.

Far Left:
The 43.2 m (140') S/Y 'Mystère'.

Left:
The soon to be launched
44.7m (146' 7") S/Y 'Lady B'.

VITTERS
SHIPYARD

'NIRVANA'

The challenge of building 'Nirvana' was driven by the first and foremost item in the design brief: to build a comfortable and well-performing yacht with luxurious interior spaces with a draught of no more than three metres. Because of the latter limitation, the overall design became a balance between draught and beam. 'Nirvana' combines a wider beam with a dagger board, which in the down position gives the yacht a 10-metre draught. As the ballast is in the hull rather than a bulb, the yacht has a relatively wider beam of 11.50m and carries 155 tons of ballast. The additional weight and hull volume do not have any negative consequences on her performance. On the contrary, the reduced wetted surface area and deep draught dagger board give 'Nirvana' impressive upwind speed potential.

The fluidity of the continuous space continues to the fly bridge where all the individual elements of the interior reappear, adapted to the outdoor environment and the multiple functions of the upper deck. This is a place for leisure and dining as well as the main control centre from where the captain drives the yacht under sail.

Open the transom and a vast platform unfolds. A wide theatre-like staircase gives access to this large beach area that can be lowered to water level to provide a comfortable entry from the sea. Here too, at the very end of this gracious yacht, considerable attention was given to the fluidity of the continuous space, the surrounding sea being included in the full picture.

The aft cockpit is a logical development from the luxurious salon (or maybe vice versa), showing the fluidity of space concept in its optimum form. The cockpit area is designed as an outdoor dining and lounging area with the same comfort and standard as the indoor areas. The sole difference is that the furniture needs to withstand the outdoor environment.

The yacht's interior, featuring a decor by GCA Arquitectes Associats of Barcelona, is deceptively simple, concealing a wealth of clever design. GCA's design concept revolved around comfort and flexibility, while the owner was heavily involved in the project from the general concept to specific technical solutions. The interior designer especially welcomed this contribution for the way it helped ensure maximum compatibility between high-

Above & Left:
The challenge of building 'Nirvana' was driven by the first and foremost item in the design brief: to build a comfortable and well-performing yacht with luxurious interior and exterior living spaces.

VITTERS
SHIPYARD

tech solutions and the homely character they were aiming for.

The owner's stateroom is exceptional, with the mizzen mast shown in a lacquered finish revealing the spar's carbon weave. This full beam area reveals the sheer size of the yacht, creating a space that is extraordinary for a sailing yacht. Located aft, the bathroom is rare in terms of both size and style. Highlights include a sauna and a rain-shower, while the shower compartment is finished in glass with floors in bare wood.

On the lower deck, four near-identical double en-suite cabins with sliding doors, backlit fabric panels and Japanese screens in the windows, are accessed from a broad hallway.

As a division between the salon and dining area, five leather-lined 'shelves' are suspended in toughened glass. At the flick of a switch, three leather steps appear from a leather cabinet below the shelves, offering access to the fly bridge between the twin helms. This design feature is a very clean and sophisticated solution for such a common aspect of a fly bridge yacht.

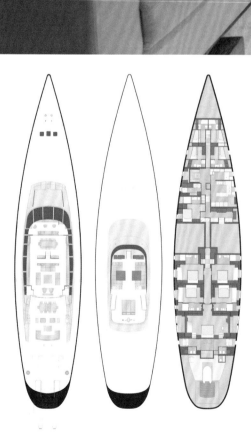

SPECIFICATIONS:	VITTERS SHIPYARD S/Y 'NIRVANA'
Length Overall:	53.5m (176')
Length waterline:	46.6m (153')
Beam:	11.5m (38')
Draught:	3.0m (10') board up / 10.0m (33') board down
Ballast:	155 ton
Displacement:	513 ton
Construction:	Aluminium
Naval Architecture:	Dubois Naval Architects Ltd
Exterior Styling:	Dubois Naval Architects Ltd
Interior Design:	Josep Juanpere Miret, GCA Arquitectes
Engine:	2 x Caterpillar C18, DITA

Above & Far Left:
The yacht's main salon features a decor by GCA Arquitectes Associats of Barcelona, which is deceptively simple, but conceals a wealth of clever design.

Left:
The full beam master stateroom reveals the sheer size of the yacht, creating a space that is exceptional for a sailing yacht.

VITTERS
SHIPYARD

'MYSTÈRE'

'Mystère' is the uncompromised outcome of a design brief to create a truly integrated modern and stylish yacht. Her 140 ton displacement extends over the 39m waterline, offering an ideal marriage of speed and ease of handling.

Benefiting from a selection of unique interior and exterior innovations, 'Mystère' ensures an unforgettable experience for all who step on board.

'Mystère's owner prefers volume in length rather than beam. This has given the yacht both the space and the capacity for easy globetrotting. The low centre of gravity optimises 'Mystère's seaworthiness and power. She sails equally well in the light airs of the Med as on lengthy ocean-going passages.

The lifting keel allows a reduction in draft from 5.75m (19') to 3.75m (12' 3"), combining access to shoal water with excellent sailing characteristics and stability. The powerful sail plan includes a fully battened mainsail on a leisure furl boom from Marten Spars, a jib and staysail on furlers, as well as a Code 1 and an asymmetric spinnaker.

The concept for 'Mystère' was to keep the decks as clean and uncluttered as possible. Her exterior styling is characterised by a low pilothouse on a flush deck, with hidden captive winches, under-deck leads for safety, and clear walkways. The main cockpit is sunk below deck level inside a coaming, affording protection yet retaining clear views forward from the wheel. A separate owner's cockpit aft doubles as a private terrace with direct access to the owner's suite. A full cockpit cover can be set or hidden away at will. The owner's 'modernist ideals' are reflected in the layout, with the distinction between interior and exterior spaces being expressly blurred.

While the design philosophy and lightweight construction required a bare minimum of detailing, the owner still desired a rich, dark and sophisticated interior ambience. To achieve this balance of modernity and comfort, a rich, flat-grain cherry wood was used throughout. This gives a strong modern structure to the bulkheads and furniture, the warmth of which counterbalances the high-contrast materials elsewhere.

The lower deck layout is calm and symmetrical, with carefully planned sightlines and focal points that lead you through the yacht. There is comfortable and flexible accommodation for seven guests and six crew-members.

Above, Left & Centre:
The concept for 'Mystère' was to keep the decks as clean and uncluttered as possible. Her exterior styling is characterised by a low pilothouse on a flush deck, with hidden captive winches, under-deck leads for safety, and clear walkways.

Far Left:
The main cockpit is sunk below deck level inside a coaming, affording protection yet retaining clear views forward from the wheel.

VITTERS
SHIPYARD

The upper salon is a magnificent social area offering a 360^0 panorama. This vast open area is divided into intimate seating and dining areas, with a bar to port.

The navigation area sees carefully matched instrumentation integrated in leather panels, complete with custom leather helm seats.

The owner's stateroom takes up the full beam aft of the yacht and includes two double beds. A double bathroom and walk-in wardrobe further enhance the sense of grandeur in this lovely area. An intimate raised seating area saddles the interface between the bedroom and the owner's private cockpit. The aft bulkhead in glass floods the bedroom with light, providing sightlines to the exterior and dramatically increasing the feeling of space.

'Mystère' benefits from the fabulous finishing that makes every Vitters yacht a treat for the eyes. Soles are the darkest wide-planked Indian rosewood wrapping up the skirting. A discreet stainless steel trim captures the light and defines the floor boundary, making the floor feel even wider than it is. Furniture tops are finished with dark leather inserts, offering contrast with the pale minimalist window linings and deck heads.

Every high performance sailing yacht with a relatively shallow bottom presents engineers with a challenge to ensure that equipment and machinery can be properly serviced. On 'Mystère', smart thinking prevails throughout and access for maintenance is assured.

SPECIFICATIONS:	VITTERS SHIPYARD S/Y 'MYSTÈRE'
Length Overall:	43.2 m (140')
Beam:	8.8 m (29')
Draught:	3.75 m (12' 3") /
With lifting keel:	5.75 m (19')
Displacement:	140 ton
Ballast:	40 ton
Naval Architecture:	Tripp Design
Exterior Styling:	Tripp Design
Interior design:	Rhoades Young
Hull:	Alustar
Superstructure:	Carbon on foam core
Engine:	MTU 12V 183TE 72
Classification:	Lloyd's SSC + 100 A1

Above, Far Left & Centre:
The upper salon is a magnificent social area offering a 360^0 panorama. This vast open area is divided into intimate seating and dining areas, with a bar to port.

Left:
The owner's stateroom takes up the full beam aft of the yacht and includes two double beds.

VITTERS
SHIPYARD

VITTERS SHIPYARD
Stouweweg 33
8064 PD Zwartsluis
The Netherlands
Tel: +31 38 386 7145
Fax: +31 38 386 8433
Web: www.vitters.com

Opposite:
S/Y 'Cinderella IV'.

Below Left:
S/Y 'Marie'.

Below Right:
S/Y 'Lady B'

VITTERS NEW PROJECTS

As well as the recent launchings of the stunning S/Y 'Mystère' and S/Y 'Nirvana', Vitters also have three other major projects nearing completion:

S/Y 'CINDERELLA IV'

For 'Cinderella IV', Vitters Shipyard, Jens Cornelsen, Donald Starkey Designs and Tripp Design have been chosen by the owner to create a 128' sloop that will fulfil the owner's thirst for long sailing passages to unseen places.

The design is a very modern boat with a new interpretation of a classic two-house deck layout, while the styling of the yacht is a modern interpretation of the classic deckhouse with a strong emphasis on all around views and sheltered areas.

With customer satisfaction in mind, sailing performance is at the heart of this design and all efforts have been made to ensure a high performance level.

To this end the yacht is fitted with a generous sail plan, a lifting keel, a light interior and a rational approach to weight control in systems design and construction. Green Marine is manufacturing the hull out of pre-preg carbon sandwich.

S/Y 'LADY B'

Combining exceptionally high performance levels with superlative comfort, this striking 44.7m sloop was designed by Dubois Naval Architects and has an excellent blend of naval architecture and ergonomics in order to offer fast speeds, state-of-the-art technology and cutting edge styling.

Her slim profile features a single-level superstructure to keep weight low and reduce windage. She is being constructed in aluminium and will have a high aspect ratio rig with carbon mast and furling boom.

Equipped with PBO standing rigging to enhance performance, her compact lifting keel system generates a variable draught from a minimum depth of four metres to a maximum depth of six. 'Lady B' is scheduled for delivery in 2009.

S/Y 'MARIE'

Vitters Shipyard, Hoek Design and David Easton were chosen by the owner to create a 180' fabulous-looking and sensational performance yacht.

The result is 'Marie', a sophisticated and distinguished sailing yacht and a sister ship to Vitters' triple award-winning sailing yacht 'Adèle'. 'Marie' will have an identical hull, keel, rudder and sail plan to 'Adèle' but will feature a new and entirely customised interior and deck layout.

'Marie' has a large main deckhouse and a vast forward deck. This allows the entire deck and interior layout to be tailored to the owner's taste and requirements.

A considerable weight saving is achieved with the use of composite rigging and high modulus carbon spars, while the lightweight interior will also improve the already outstanding performance.

The hull will be constructed in Alustar to ABS and full MCA specifications. 'Marie' is scheduled for delivery in 2010.

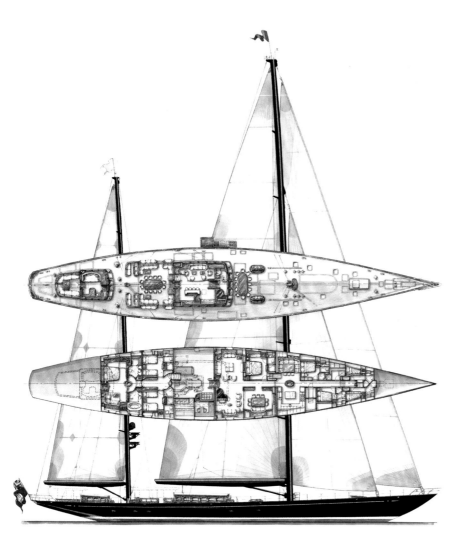

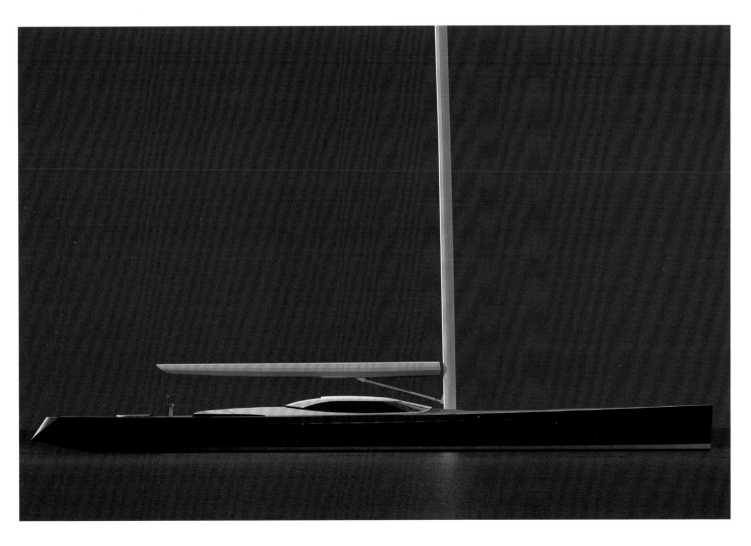

HAKVOORT SHIPYARD

Right:
The 45m 'My Trust' is the very epitome of Dutch Pedigree.

Below Left:
The 50m 'JeMaSa'

Below Centre:
The stylish 46.2m 'Flamingo Daze' features a wealth of outdoor deck space.

Below Right:
The gorgeous 38m contemporary motor yacht 'Perle Bleue'.

Located on the shores of Lake IJsselmeer, about eight miles north of Amsterdam and a mere 15 miles from Schiphol International Airport, the historic and beautiful village of Monnickendam is home to Hakvoort Shipyard.

Deriving its name from the monks who built a dam there in the 12th century, Monnickendam was granted city rights in 1355 and became a prominent port in the 1600s, the winding cobblestone streets recapturing these maritime memories.

Entrepreneurs such as Albert Klzn Hakvoort have played their part too. Nearly a hundred years ago, he bought a shipyard that had launched its first vessel way back in 1780, then proceeded to lay down the firm foundations of a thriving business that would eventually lead to the name of Monnickendam well and truly being put back on the world maritime map.

As the demand for pleasure sailing grew, Hakvoort Shipyard responded to this by moving into yacht building rather than concentrating on fishing boats, the initial business base and the yard has remained in family hands since, passing from father to son several times.

Today, Hakvoort is one of the world's leading luxury yacht builders. For many satisfied owners, the personal approach they encounter when building their yacht in tiny Monnickendam remains an abiding memory.

With two enclosed and temperature-controlled construction halls, a metal workshop, a dedicated office complex and a large quayside operation, the magnificent yacht building facilities employ about ninety highly skilled experienced staff who construct the highest quality luxury yachts, right from the design conception to the launch.

HAKVOORT SHIPYARD

'FLAMINGO DAZE'

In 2004, Hakvoort Shipyard in the Netherlands successfully delivered one of its most extraordinary yachts to date, the 46.2m (151'6") 'Flamingo Daze'. With naval architecture by Vripack Yachting International and a Glade Johnson interior, the pedigree of this twin-screw ocean going motor yacht was always going to be impressive.

Built to Lloyds and MCA classification, 'Flamingo Daze' is an extremely seaworthy yacht with a round-bilged displacement hull made of steel with an aluminium superstructure. The owner intends to cruise the world extensively over the coming years, and with a range of at least 6000 miles, the yacht's features provide the means to satisfy this desire.

The engine room, with its separate control and generator rooms, is highly sophisticated. An imposing propulsion package includes two Caterpillar 3508B DI-TA diesels, each with an MCR type B-rating of 716 kW at 1600 rpm. A Vosper 4080 non-retractable fin stabilizing system is also installed in the engine room along with a VT Naiad Marine stabilization-at-anchor control system.

The interior also benefits from this high-tech philosophy, with a computerised lighting system, touch screen drapes, a spectacular surround sound system and much more besides. Large windows and oversized portholes make 'Flamingo Daze' a light and airy boat, as well as offering excellent views. With accommodation for eleven guests in total, including the master stateroom, 'Flamingo Daze' is also used for chartering, for which she is the ideal size.

Glade Johnson Design and the owner have opted for a contemporary interior style, with the main woods being mahogany, cherry and maple burl. Onboard, the sky lounge has a huge bar and is actually more of a theatre with a large plasma screen elevating from the top of the bar, plus a large screen that lowers from the ceiling, with a suspended projector. A chic circular stairway descends to the huge main salon with formal dining area.

More casual dining is available in the breakfast area in the galley - a bright area with lots of space and two TV screens. Forward on the main deck, the owner's stateroom has a full beam bedroom with central double doors opening up to reveal a magnificent bathroom with Jacuzzi, separate shower and toilet, and a surprisingly large walk-in closet on the starboard side.

In terms of shapely elegance and effortless style, 'Flamingo Daze' takes some beating.

Right:
'Flamingo Daze' is a seaworthy ocean going yacht with a range of at least 6000 miles.

Below Left:
The main lobby.

Below Centre:
The master bathroom.

Below Right:
The huge main salon features a bar and plenty of seating.

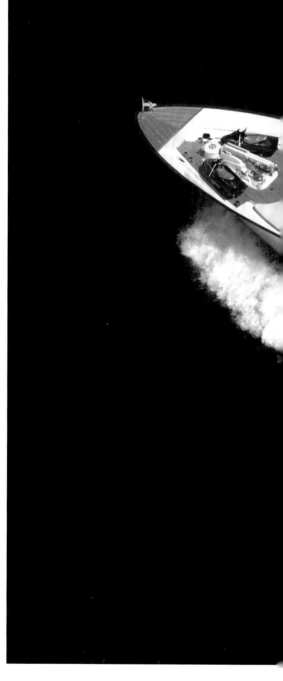

SPECIFICATIONS:	HAKVOORT SHIPYARD 'FLAMINGO DAZE'
Length Overall:	46.21m (151' 6")
Beam:	8.84m (29')
Draught:	2.7m (9' 1")
Accommodation:	11 guests + 9 crew
Naval Architecture:	Vripack Yachting International
Interior Design:	Glade Johnson
Construction:	Steel hull, aluminium superstructure
Displacement:	499 ton
Propulsion:	2 x Caterpillar 3508B DI-TA
Maximum Speed:	14 knots
Fuel Capacity:	92,000l
Fresh Water:	12,000l

HAKVOORT SHIPYARD

'JeMaSa'

Delivered in May 2006, the 50m 'JeMaSa' represented another impressive achievement by Hakvoort Shipyard. Built to Lloyd's 100A1 specifications, 'JeMaSa' has a naval architecture designed by Diana Yacht Design, while her exterior profile originated on the drawing board of designer Espen Oeino. While the interior was originally also by Oeino and Michela Reverberi, the owner's family implemented changes devised by designer Barbara Barry based in Los Angeles. According to Oeino, the yacht maximises the space available and has a high volume for her length both in and outdoors.

Onboard, the main deck foyer is located on the starboard side, parallel to the lobbies above and below. They are connected by an especially striking stairwell created by Espen Oeino's team. The main deck lobby and galley, opening onto the starboard and port-side decks respectively, divide the main deck into a full-beam owner's area forward and a dining space and main salon.

The comfortable main salon and dining room have been finished in a variety of pleasant brown and beige tones. The dining room, which can effortlessly accommodate twelve guests, is connected directly to the galley forward.

The owner's stateroom forward is finished in teak and accessed through a superb office and lounge area. This area features a king-sized bed and opens onto a cedar-walled dressing room and beautiful, full-width bathroom with his and her shower rooms and an interconnecting bath section. The accommodation deck below the main consists of five cabins: two VIP suites offer generous, well-appointed spaces with en-suite bathrooms, while two slightly smaller staterooms are set up in double layouts; a fifth cabin with a bunk bed arrangement also includes en-suite facilities.

'JeMaSa's elegant, well-laid-out wheelhouse was designed by Captain Juan Koegelenberg who was with the yacht during her construction time at Hakvoort.

The innovative split-level sun-deck doubles as an al-fresco dining area with a large table and dumb waiter going straight to the galley two decks below. At the aft-most end, a helipad platform with cunningly disguised refuelling apparatus also serves as a rescue boat berth. Further forward between the masts, 'JeMaSa's well-equipped gymnasium's glass doors open onto the whirlpool tub and sunbathing area.

Handling very well in close quarters 'JeMaSa' is extremely quiet in operation, her two Caterpillar diesel engines generating a maximum speed of 15.7 knots and a cruising speed of 13.5 knots.

Right:
'JeMaSa' has a huge volume of living space for her 50m length.

Below Left:
The master stateroom.

Below Centre:
The fabulous sun-deck features an on-deck cinema.

Below Right:
The elegant aft main deck is perfect for relaxation and open air dining.

SPECIFICATIONS:	HAKVOORT SHIPYARD 'JeMaSa'
Length Overall:	49.99m (164')
Beam:	9.45m (31')
Draught:	2.7m (9' 1")
Guests:	10
Naval Architecture:	Diana Yacht Design
Exterior Styling:	Espen Oeino
Interior Design:	Michela Reverberi & Barbara Berry
Construction:	Steel hull, aluminium superstructure
Propulsion:	2 x Caterpillar 3512B DI-TA
Maximum Speed:	15.7 knots
Cruising Speed:	13.5 knots
Range:	5200nm @ 10 knots

HAKVOORT SHIPYARD

'PERLE BLEUE'

'Perle Bleue' is a 38-metre contemporary motor yacht with naval architecture by Diana Yacht Design and interiors by Donald Starkey Design. The yacht features a round-bilge displacement steel hull with a good dead rise, level keel and flared bow with a fine entrance angle, and an aluminium superstructure.

When asked which past experiences he and his wife incorporated in this latest build, 'Perle Bleue's owner, Stanley Bey, answers without hesitation: "Everything that ever happened to us... 'Perle Bleue' distils all our 40 years of experience. For instance, while we wanted her to be relatively small and sleek compared to our previous yachts, we also recognised the importance of open areas. To create lots of open space on a smaller deck surface, we needed to rethink both hardware and layout."

Extensive outdoor spaces and lots of interior and exterior luxury enhance both the visual and the material comfort levels onboard to a striking level. As a streamlined successor to the owner's previous yacht, the 45m Hakvoort 'Campbell Bay', 'Perle Bleue' benefits from the countless insights only a lifetime of sailing on quality yachts can provide.

As Bey explains, "First we opted for a long bridge deck that reaches almost to the stern boarding platform. In this way we achieved more usable outdoor space on the 38m 'Perle Bleue' than on her 45m predecessor!"

Mr Bey had also tired of the limitations of a substantial draught, most notably the restrictions on visiting favourite places on the East Coast of the US. "This is why we insisted on a draught of just 2.1 metres this time around. Of course, this does not mean that 'Perle Bleue' sails less well. She is built to the highest standard and has the ability to cross the Atlantic on its own, right out of the box." This is confirmed by 'Perle Bleue's excellent range of 5750nm at 9 knots.

Inside, 'Perle Bleue's main salon is finished in French modern style, inspired by 1930s French salons: the

Right:
The 38m 'Perle Bleue' was built for a highly experienced yacht owner and features extensive outdoor space.

Below Left & Right:
The wonderful sun-deck features a whirlpool tub, a wet-bar and plenty of loungers.

Below Left Centre:
Cruising onboard is a real delight.

Below Right Centre:
An aerial image shows that this yacht is designed for outdoor living.

mahogany rosewood walls are enhanced by a burnished gold ceiling, while the floor is covered with carpet and leather tiles. A series of paintings representing stylish scenes of parties in Parisian apartments have been reproduced by a special process onto fabric and then placed on the walls. The full-width lobby features carpeted stairways leading up to the upper salon and down to the guest quarters.

The lower deck is St. Barth's inspired. Three guest staterooms, designed with teak floors and individual pastel colour themes, provide accommodation for up to eight guests. The bathrooms also provide unique colour schemes, each finished with a different type of marble.

The full-beam master stateroom is a continuation of the overall theme of the yacht, although with a more oriental Zen approach. Golden panels enhance the wengé and blond teak walls, while the lovely floor is made of bamboo.

The large bathroom is finished in Jerusalem stone with details of reeds, golden pearl shells and blue mosaic tiles on the walls. The separate owner's study features a large desk and plenty of locker space and bookshelves.

On the bridge deck, the upper salon is 'Perle Bleue's pièce de résistance. It is highly sophisticated and includes a surround sound theatre with a massive 64" screen. The sky lounge opens seamlessly onto the huge aft deck to create a single combined indoor/outdoor space where the partly covered exterior deck measures 11m and includes a table for eight – extendable to twelve – that is semi-surrounded by a glass enclosure.

"This is the primary dining area on 'Perle Bleue'," Bey says. "We deliberately chose to not install a dedicated dining room indoors, as it has to be exceptionally bad weather for us not to eat outdoors."

Another original area on 'Perle Bleue' is the space in front of the wheelhouse, consisting of a dining table for six and a huge all-teak patio area. "This is very handy for slow cruising in canals or waterways where you really want to soak up the surroundings," Bey points out.

On the huge sun-deck there is plenty of open deck

Right:
'Perle Bleue's main salon is inspired by 1930s French salons.

Below Left:
The master stateroom features a wonderful bamboo floor.

Below Right:
The sky lounge offers panoramic views and opens seamlessly onto the huge aft deck.

space for lounging, particularly amidships to starboard, opposite the bar. The sophisticated whirlpool bathtub forward includes a fountain as well as a waterfall arrangement streaming from the back of the forward-facing bench seat. A large built-in sun bed is installed starboard of the whirlpool.

'Perle Bleue' is indeed a yacht built for a connoisseur, by a yard that is a true artist when it comes to delivering the perfect craft.

SPECIFICATIONS:	HAKVOORT SHIPYARD 'PERLE BLEUE'
Length Overall:	38m (124' 8")
Beam:	8m (26' 3")
Draught:	2.30m (7' 6")
Guests:	8
Naval Architecture:	Diana Yacht Design
Exterior Styling:	Donald Starkey Design
Interior Design:	Donald Starkey Design
Construction:	Steel hull, aluminium superstructure
Propulsion:	2 x Caterpillar C18
Maximum Speed:	13 knots
Cruising Speed:	11.5 knots
Range:	5750nm @ 9 knots

HAKVOORT
SHIPYARD

'MY TRUST'

The 45m (147' 6") twin screw ocean going motor yacht 'My Trust' is the very epitome of Dutch pedigree: her harmonious exterior designed by Cor de Rover, the classic nautical interior from the board of Felix Buytendijk, with Diana Yacht Design responsible for the naval architecture. The accomplished technicians and craftsmen at Hakvoort Shipyard completed the yacht with the utmost care and attention to detail, characteristics on which the yard has built its international reputation.

In addition to being built to Lloyd's and MCA specifications, 'My Trust' is the first Dutch motor yacht to be constructed for chartering under the new guidelines for Commercial Cruising Vessels (CCV). As the yacht is registered in Holland and managed by a Dutch company, the owners enjoy all the fiscal and legal benefits that come from sailing the Dutch flag.

'My Trust' fits her highly dynamic appearance well within the parameters of timeless design. Classical details include the majestic blue hull as well as, more subtly, the teak cap rails and veneered recesses around the windows. More generally, 'My Trust's exterior is characterised by numerous details finished in a warm teak veneer giving her a level of warmth and personality that is rare on yachts of her size today.

As fans of sailboats, 'My Trust's owners have endowed her interior with elements of sail yacht décor not habitually found on motor yachts. The traditional nautical interior is classical without being old-fashioned and provides remarkable comfort for the owners and up to ten guests and nine crew.

Located forward on the main deck, the owner's stateroom feels very spacious. The suite features a king-sized bed, a retractable LCD flat screen TV and a comfy seating area for two to starboard. The stateroom is accessed via a roomy study centred on a large built-in desk, while the forward owner's bathroom features a good-sized whirlpool bath with shower and a separate custom-built sauna.

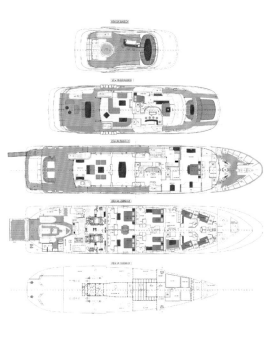

HAKVOORT SHIPYARD

Moving aft, the dining area and lounge are separated by a subtle partition, mirrored on the dining area side and inlaid with artwork on the lounge side. The convivial lounge abounds in entertainment and leisure options thanks to the large pop-up LCD TV screen on the forward wall and built-in dry bar, fridge and icemaker.

The wide aft deck is arranged as a generous seating area with a wide, straight sofa for ten and two large fixed teak tables. Handy double stairways to port and starboard lead down to the integrated swimming platform, while an integrated staircase to port leads up to the aft bridge deck.

On the bridge-deck, the wheelhouse features a fully integrated bridge by Radio Holland, including five Hatteland screens for radars, a chart plotter, and conning and alarm panel, while the full-beam bridge-deck lounge represents a continuation of the consummate style and finish found in the salon.

The sun-deck on 'My Trust' more than lives up to its name. It features a whirlpool bathtub with a teak circular top for up to six people, as well as lots of open deck space for lounging. An advanced system of awnings fixed to the mast covers the entire sun deck thanks to a smart combination of 6 stainless steel vertical pipe supports.

A lovely L-shaped bar installed between the funnels is flanked by four fixed bar stools and features a sink, icemaker and refrigerator as well as an electric stainless steel grill. The mast itself incorporates a system of cosy spotlights as well as a 15-nozzle misting system that helps cool down the entire area on particularly hot days.

The lower deck accommodates four guest cabins – double or twin, depending on preferences – each with an en-suite bathroom and extra Pullman bunk. The same joinery and whitewash scheme as in other cabins is deployed here, giving the space a feeling of intense elegance and openness. Framed historical photographs from the Beken of Cowes archives are used to great effect.

The owner's chartering experience is evident throughout 'My Trust', being equipped with features normally only found on larger yachts. All cabins feature

Creston controls that manage not only the Kaleidescape AV system but also lighting, curtains and air-conditioning. The IT network includes both hardwire and WiFi connections in all areas. There is also a VSAT video conference system ensuring that guests are given every opportunity to stay tuned into their work and the wider world, while enjoying the finer things of life.

A yacht rich in pedigree and high on technology, 'My Trust' is yet another masterpiece to emerge from the drawing board of Hakvoort Shipyard.

SPECIFICATIONS:	HAKVOORT SHIPYARD 'MY TRUST'
Length Overall:	45m (147' 6")
Beam:	8.80m (28' 9")
Draught:	2.80m (9' 1")
Accommodation:	10 guests + 9 crew
Naval Architecture:	Diana Yacht Design
Exterior Styling:	Cor de Rover
Interior Design:	Felix Buytendijk
Construction:	Steel hull, aluminium superstructure
Propulsion:	2 x Caterpillar C3508B
Maximum Speed:	13.4 knots
Cruising Speed:	11.3 knots

Above:
The owner's stateroom is spacious and luxuriously furnished.

Left:
The convivial lounge would not look out of place in a stately home.

Far Left:
The sky lounge salon features a huge TV with a Kaleidescape AV system.

HAKVOORT SHIPYARD

Hakvoort Shipyard
Havenstraat 22
1141 AX Monnickendam
The Netherlands
T: +31 299 651403
F: +31 299 651041
W: www.hakvoort.com

NEW PROJECTS

YN 243

The new Hakvoort YN 243 will make the most of her 48.77 metre length, both in terms of interior comfort and sailing performance.

Conceived on the drawing board of Diana Yacht Design, with exterior styling by Glade Johnson and with interiors by Sinot Yacht Design, YN 243 will be as ingenious as she is beautiful, featuring a clever sky-lounge, a wealth of open areas and panoramic views, a lift and a dumbwaiter serving all decks.

She will also be ideal for chartering, providing accommodation for twelve guests, while for private use she can accommodate up to sixteen guests.

YN 245

Hakvoort's Project YN 245 is a new 39-metre luxury ocean-going motor yacht. Scheduled for launch at the end of 2009, the naval architecture on this stylish yacht has been done by Azure Naval Architects, the exterior styling by Cor de Rover and she will feature a modern nautical interior by Michela Reverberi.

Very suitable for chartering, YN245 will have accommodation for ten guests including the owner, and be built according to Lloyd's regulations for Special Service Craft. The fully welded construction will consist of a steel hull and aluminium alloy superstructure.

YN 246

Hakvoort's Project YN 246 will measure 44.90m in length and have a 9.30m beam with a draught of 2.90m.

This yacht will be suitable for blue water cruising all over the world and will provide stylish accommodation for ten guests and eleven crew.

Designed with a displacement-type hull shape, this yacht will feature flared V-sections in the bow, large overhangs, a moderate deadrise amidships and a canoe stern. Hakvoort and Diana Yacht Design BV are striving to keep the yacht as low as possible, especially where the freeboard and superstructure are concerned.

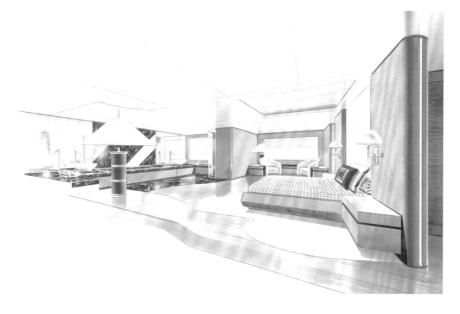

YN 247

Hakvoort signed the contract to build this 39m displacement motor yacht for a Russian client. This will be the first ever superyacht project for the owner, who became attracted to the 'Hakvoort look' after seeing its recent yachts such as 'Perle Bleue', 'Flamingo Daze' and 'Spada'.

Featuring a full-beam master stateroom and owner's study on the main deck, eight guests will enjoy first class accommodation in four cabins, with dedicated quarters for the captain and four crew.

Naval architecture, construction and engineering design for this project will be by Diana Yacht Design, which has been given the brief to optimise technical accessibility and keep maintenance requirements to a minimum.

Both the interior design and the exterior styling are from the boards of Reymond Langton Design.

Above:
Hakvoort's Project YN 246 has been designed for blue water cruising.

Left:
Project YN 247 is a 39m motor yacht being built for a Russian client.

Far Left:
Project YN 245 will feature a modern nautical interior by Michela Reverberi.

SORAYA YACHTS

Impressive and opulent, with several cutting-edge technological innovations and completely dedicated to providing the ultimate level of comfort to its passengers, the Soraya 46 is a bright new sparkling diamond among yachts of her class.

The Soraya 46 is being built by Gentech Yachts Ltd., a subsidiary of Gentech Ltd., a highly successful international corporation with businesses in a number of fields, including business aviation, real estate development, engineering and fashion retail.

With expertise in cutting-edge innovation and technology and with more than 15 years of personal experience in yachting, Gentech is dedicated to setting new standards for this range of 21st century mega yachts.

Built to Gentech's stringent quality standards at the firm's modern shipyard conveniently located in the duty-free zone near Antalya in Turkey, the Soraya 46 is the impressive result of years of planning and a worldwide collaboration of leading suppliers and contractors. Carefully selected teams of skilled and experienced staff are working in close collaboration with expert supervisors and project managers from Europe and the USA. All the suppliers and sub-contractors were chosen from renowned and experienced companies, many of which have been involved in building some of the world's most famous mega yachts.

Above & Far Left:
The Soraya 46 is the impressive result of years of planning and a worldwide collaboration of leading suppliers and contractors.

Left:
The expansive aft deck is the perfect place for entertaining.

SORAYA
YACHTS

Offering contemporary yet timeless design, Jure Bukavec, founder of Uniellé Yacht Design, has created the ultimate showcase for Gentech's innovative use of technology.

The Soraya 46's exterior is without doubt a real eye-catcher. Ultra-modern yet elegant, she exudes an eclectic mixture of timeless elegance and impressive high-tech naval appearance.

A thoroughly modern yacht, an innovative, state-of-the-art IP network has been custom-designed for the Soraya 46 by Cisco Systems and Goap d.o.o. The "nerve system" of this magnificent yacht, every major function, from engines and power generators to CCTV security systems, HVAC and much more can be monitored in real-time by the crew, as well as from any onshore location with Internet access, anywhere in the world. Special attention is given to the monitoring of the engines by Caterpillar experts onshore, enabling prompt and accurate advice and prevention of potential problems, as well as an efficient delivery of spare parts.

The IP system also channels and controls VOIP telephony, fixed and wireless intercom, Internet access, HVAC control, interior and exterior illumination and the TV/audio/entertainment system. The security system consists of CCTV and movement sensors with onboard and ashore monitoring and alarms, as well as allowing real-time monitoring of the yacht's location.

The Soraya 46's spacious layout is comfortable and functional for both private family holidays and charter commitments and is well designed for special corporate or entertaining events, with crew operational paths and accommodation located completely separately from the guest facilities.

With her multi-functional and generous layout, the Soraya 46 offers both privacy and expansive social areas for owner and guests alike. Throughout her spacious and elegantly furbished decks, the passengers will be able to enjoy a wide variety of activities as well as enjoying a peaceful and relaxing atmosphere throughout the yacht.

Right & Below:
The Soraya 46 will turn heads at any time of night & day.

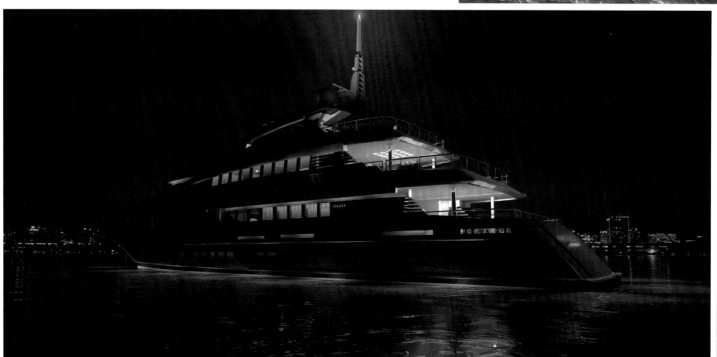

SORAYA
YACHTS

A careful choice of machinery and supporting systems, combined with a special battery-powered "Night mode" and soundproofing of guest's cabins, will ensure an exceptionally silent and relaxing environment.

Among the technology onboard the yacht, zero speed stabilizers will keep the Soraya 46's sturdy steel hull stable not only while sailing but also at anchor, allowing an enjoyable seagoing experience, even for more sensitive guests.

With a great deal of research and thought having gone into her design, every feature of the Soraya 46 adds practicality while enhancing her visual appearance. A prime example of this is the retractable hydraulic helipad at the bow that, while providing excellent private access to the yacht for the owner and guests, also serves as a highly practical and safe operational space for the crew when storing and handling the yacht's tenders and other equipment. Right behind the helicopter pad is a double hatch where the crew/rescue tender is stored.

A large garage at the stern also helps to keep this beautiful yacht clutter-free. As the main stern door opens horizontally to allow easy access to tenders and water-sports toys, it also creates a huge swim platform, providing an ideal setting for fun and relaxing water activities for the yacht's guests. At night, the Soraya 46's spectacular exterior and underwater illumination is mostly provided through energy efficient LED technology and presents a warm and inviting beacon for the yacht's guests.

Throughout her spacious and elegantly furnished decks, the guests will be able to enjoy a range of activities as well as a peaceful and relaxing atmosphere in different areas.

A full custom yacht, the lower deck may be constructed with five or six guest cabins depending on the owner's preference, each carefully designed and luxuriously furnished for the maximum relaxation and comfort of the guests, with the latest entertainment equipment supplied in all rooms. Each cabin is connected to an IP system that

Right & Below:
The revolutionary retractable helipad is positioned on the yacht's bow.

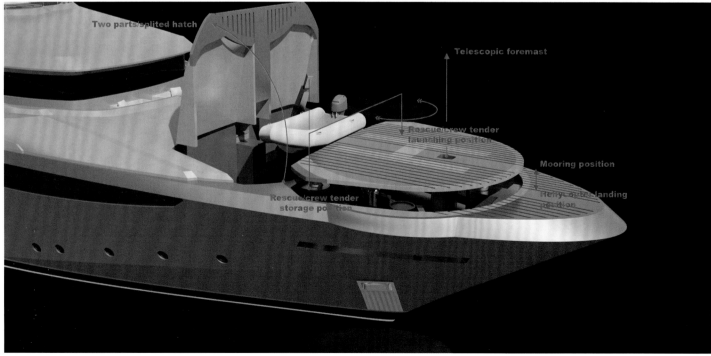

SORAYA YACHTS

Gentech Ltd.
Aelestrasse 5
FL-9490 Vaduz
Liechtenstein
Tel: +386 41660760
Web: www.sorayayachts.com

enables all guests to control the air conditioning functions and lighting in their cabin as well using the vessel's intercom, telephone and Internet connections.

The main deck features the yacht's main salon and dining areas, which will be furnished according to the owner's exact requirements. Built with full height windows for panoramic views, the main salon will be bathed in a profusion of natural light and furnished luxuriously.

Forward of the main salon, an extremely well-equipped galley with a large cold room features stainless steel surfaces and is equipped with top-quality appliances. Due to its location, it also serves as a buffer, preventing noise and disturbance caused by other guests from interfering with the privacy and peace of the owner's stateroom situated on the forward main deck.

This cleverly positioned and spacious 54m² owner's stateroom, with en-suite bathroom and dressing areas, is exquisitely furnished for onboard living with maximum privacy and comfort.

The upper deck of the yacht offers additional areas for socialising and entertaining, capable of hosting twelve guests for al-fresco dining with sweeping panoramic views. A large, wonderfully furnished 70m² salon is perfectly suited for both corporate events and private parties. There is a second cocktail bar located here, with separate seating areas and a superb audio/video system, suitable for everything from sales presentations to simply providing background music.

Above the upper deck, the sun deck is the sun-lover's paradise. A 2.3m Jacuzzi is surrounded with large sun loungers and will certainly be a popular area of the yacht all day, and well into the night. Guests will also find a well-equipped wet-bar on this deck - a must in such a popular socialising location. Above the sun deck, the large radar arch supports a vast sun awning, which in turn provides the shade for the sun deck dining and socialising area.

A truly modern yacht, the launch of the first Soraya 46 is certain to be eagerly awaited by yacht owners worldwide.

Right & Below:
The main aft deck and upper deck are the main outdoor social areas of the yacht.

SPECIFICATIONS:	SORAYA 46
Length Overall:	46.5m (152')
Length Waterline:	37.6m (123')
Beam:	9m (29' 6")
Draught:	2.45m (8')
Displacement:	430 tons
Naval Architect:	Meccano Engineering
Exterior Styling:	Uniellé Yacht Design
Interior Design:	Ales Bratina
Construction:	Steel Hull
	Aluminium Superstructure
Engines:	2 x Caterpillar C32ACERT 1300hp
Maximum Speed:	16 knots
Cruise Speed:	13 knots
Range:	5,040 nm @10 knots

PERINI NAVI

PERINI NAVI

Right then clockwise:
All Perini Navi yachts are unique and feature the trademark specifications of the brand, whether automation of the sails; cutting edge styling; a swinging keel; ample space on deck; liveability and comfort; high quality and safety; or in the case of the yacht 'Salute', the world's tallest aluminium mast!
Yachts featured here include:
'Salute' (56m)
'Baracuda' (50m);
'Maltese Falcon' (88m);
'P2' (38m).

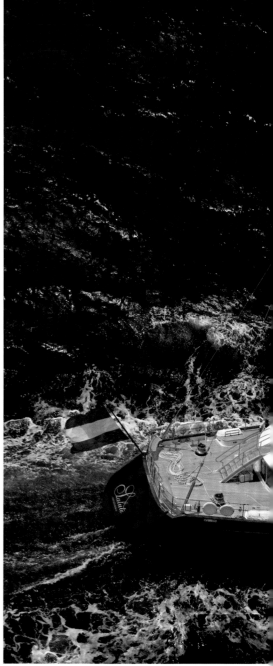

Perini Navi, arguably the world leader in the luxury sailing yacht industry, was established in the early eighties thanks to the intuition of its founder, Fabio Perini. He created a new breed of sailing yacht that could be handled by a single person thanks to a revolutionary sailing system. Fabio Perini himself designed and created a completely automated sailing system that allows a single person to handle the impressive sail area of a large yacht in complete safety. Specifically invented for the purpose was a new type of automatic winch now known as the captive reel winch, which is controlled by specially built electrical motors.

His technological vision allowed the company to overcome one of the basic limitations of the development of large sailing yachts, namely the need to have a large crew of expert sailors, required to handle the sails.

This spectacular technological breakthrough was achieved by applying various solutions to the operating system of the sail plan, all of which were inspired by developments in other industrial activities in which the Perini Group had achieved world leadership.

All Perini Navi yachts are unique and feature the trademark specifications of the brand, namely automation of the sails; cutting edge styling; a swinging keel; ample space on deck; liveability and comfort; high quality and safety.

The first Perini Navi sailing yacht, the 40m 'Felicità' (now 'Clan VI'), launched in 1983, radically exceeded the normal length of sailing yachts of the time. This first Perini Navi model also had a fly bridge that significantly increased the living area of the vessel and which, together with the aft cockpit, allowed a more comfortable and ample use of the open spaces. This new concept of internal space, sail handling automation and comfort had never been seen before in sailing yachts of this size.

Following on from the success of this first launching, Perini Navi has gone on to build numerous yachts. It then proceeded to increase the size of the yachts it built with a series of boats of 46m, 48m, 50m, 52m, 58m, 64m in length as well as the instantly recognisable 88m sailing yacht 'Maltese Falcon', which has featured in every volume of 'Luxury Yachts Of The World'.

Perini Navi always invested significant resources in research and development, with a particular focus on new product design, in order to constantly develop its yachts to satisfy both the market demands and the company's own spirit.

The 'Maltese Falcon', launched in 2006, represents a prime example. She is an 88m clipper, with a revolutionary sailing system consisting of three carbon fibre freestanding and rotating masts, each with five independent sails for a total sail area of 2,400m². This project represented a milestone in the Perini Navi development, which twenty

five years after the captive reel winch, again introduced a new revolution to sailing technology.

In April 2009, S/Y 'Riela', a 56m aluminium ketch and the 46th sailing yacht of the Perini Navi fleet was launched. Four of Perini Navi's most recent yachts, 'Baracuda', 'P2', 'Selene' and 'Salute' are featured in this volume of 'Luxury Yachts Of The World'.

A significant tribute to the company's success is the series of 56m yachts that have now been launched, which, with seven models delivered and three models sold and under construction, is a unique, matchless example of a successful series in the world of superyachts.

PERINI NAVI

PERINI 50M 'BARACUDA'

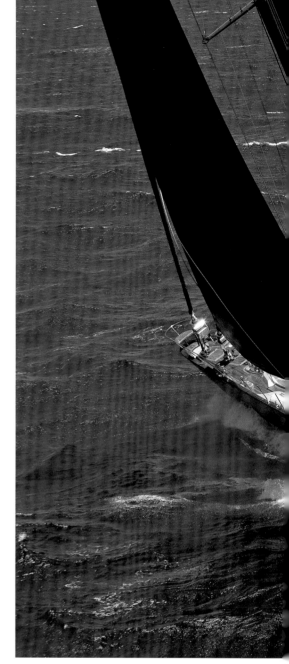

With her high-performance aluminium hull, S/Y 'Baracuda' is the latest evolution of Perini Navi's successful 50m series and might be considered a summation of all the innovations that Perini Navi has achieved in over 25 years. 'Baracuda' was conceived by Perini Navi in collaboration with the naval architect Ron Holland whose co-operation with Perini Navi had started with the building of the 64m ketch rigged 'Felicità west'.

In the words of Ron Holland: "The design development for Baracuda has included a relatively long waterline. This incorporates hull lines with forward waterline angles to minimise sailing resistance in rough sailing conditions and firm mid-ship sections. This hull shape, combined with a high aspect ratio centreboard, maximises sailing stability. These features are not only designed to improve speed and close-winded ability under sail, but are also intended to create a comfortable yacht for all aboard."

'Baracuda's interiors are by John Pawson, a guru of modern minimalism. The main deck is conceived as open living space with no partitions, the aim being to keep a much clearer, unencumbered visual field than is conventionally the case on ships of this type. The parchment wall covering was chosen not only for the subtle beauty of its colour and texture, but also for the way it serves to dematerialise the central stair volume. An emphasis on spatial fluidity also characterises the connection from the main cabin through to the aft cockpit, with the lines of floor and ceiling timbers continuing unbroken across the threshold. The furniture is a carefully chosen anthology of bespoke pieces mixed with classic designs. The lower deck hosts the full beam owner's suite with central king-size bed and his and her bathrooms. Eight guests can be accommodated in four guest cabins: two VIP cabins with queen size beds and two twin-bedded cabins with additional Pullman berths. All guest cabins have en-suite bathrooms, while the crew area accommodates 8 crew in 4 cabins, plus a captain's cabin.

Right & Below Centre:
'Baracuda' was conceived by Perini Navi in collaboration with the naval architect Ron Holland whose co-operation with Perini Navi had started with the building of the 64m ketch rigged 'Felicità west'.

Below Left:
'Baracuda's interiors, including the main salon, are by John Pawson, guru of modern minimalism.

Below Right:
The expansive fly bridge.

SPECIFICATIONS: PERINI 50M 'BARACUDA'

Length Overall:	50m (164')
Length Waterline:	42.65m (139' 10")
Beam:	10.52m (34' 6")
Draught:	4m (13' 2") / 9.79m (32' 2")
Main Mast Height:	56.75m (186' 2")
Hull / Superstructure:	Aluminium
Displacement:	430 ton
Total sail area:	1418 m²
Mainsail area:	398 m²
Classification:	LY2 / ABS: Malta Cross
	A1 Yachting Service + AMS, MCA

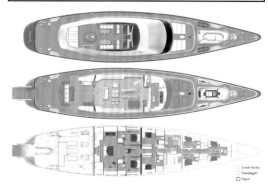

PERINI NAVI

PERINI 38M 'P2'

The new Perini Navi 38m (125') is the first of a new series of yachts with a clear inclination towards performance achieved in comfort and safety. The first of this new line, named 'P2', combines Perini's design and build philosophies with enhanced sailing characteristics. The designer Philippe Briand explains: "While designing the new Perini 125' line we had in mind the image of a really well-performing gentleman's yacht. What makes a sailing yacht special is the elegant look and the sensation of performance and acceleration of the boat under sail. If you add to that a refined and comfortable interior the yacht becomes a passion. A performance sailing yacht needs to be sensitive in light air and powerful and stiff in heavy winds."

The project's hull is constructed of an aluminium alloy, Sealium, which provides greater structural strength and improved corrosion characteristics while reducing weight. The total material weight in regatta mode does not exceed 133 tons. The design includes a lifting keel with bulb for a draught that goes from 3.50m (11' 6") to 5.50m (18' 1"). For the stability of the boat, the yacht is equipped with 7 tons of water ballast, while for sail power, she has a 50m carbon fibre mast and a sail area of about 734m² upwind.

In the Perini tradition, the 38m line has a pleasing and comfortable layout. The vast cockpit and luminous deck salon create an inviting living area. The cockpit can be fully protected when necessary and can also be converted into a sun bathing area. The deck salon faces the dining area and the salon and allows for panoramic views.

'P2' is the first of a line of racing yachts. The project is proposed with four possible layouts. One includes two guest cabins and a large owner's suite, while another layout includes four guest cabins, perfect for racing or charter.

The Perini 38m has already proved that she is able to finish well in regattas and can also sail around the world safely, in comfort and true Perini Navi style.

Right:

The new Perini Navi 38m 'P2' is the first of a new series of yachts with a clear inclination towards performance achieved in comfort and safety.
A real prize winner at the World Superyacht Awards, 'P2' won 3 awards for the 'Best Sailing Yacht Of The Year'; the 'Best Exterior Styling for a yacht in the 30m - 44m size range'; and the 'Best Sailing Yacht in the 30m - 44m size range'. She also won the 2009 Newport Bucket Regatta confirming her high performance credentials!

Below Left:
The stylish owner's suite.

Below Right:
The main salon is light and modern.

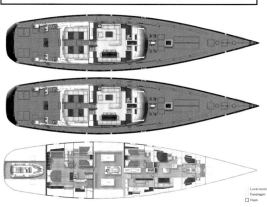

SPECIFICATIONS: PERINI 38M 'P2'	
Length Overall:	38m (125')
Length Waterline:	34.66m (113' 8")
Beam:	8.36m (27' 5")
Draught:	3.5m (11' 6") / 5.5m (18')
Construction:	Alumin. Hull / Composite SuperStr
Displacement:	155 t / 133 ton (Regatta Mode)
Mast:	52m Carbon-fibre Marten Spars
Sail Area Upwind:	734 m²
Classification:	LY2 compliance ABS: Malta Cross A1 AMS Yachting Service + MCA

PERINI NAVI

PERINI 56M 'RIELA'

The ketch rigged sailing yacht 'Riela' is the 46th in the Perini Navi fleet and the 7th in Perini's highly successful 56 metre series.

With a choice of customised layouts, the Perini 56 metre series offers owners a creative licence to have a yacht built to their specific tastes and requirements, while maintaining Perini's signature appearance and technical excellence on the yacht.

When guests first set eyes upon Riela, it is clear that she is a vessel like no other. The design for this beautiful yacht was developed by Perini Navi in collaboration with Ron Holland, with the aim of producing a yacht which would offer a fast cruising speed while still providing a luxurious and comfortable lifestyle for the owner and his guests.

'Riela' is a ketch rigged yacht and is equipped with two aluminium masts and carbon-fibre booms. She holds a sail plan of approximately 1,500m², offering her superb performance, especially downwind.

Boarding via a retractable aft gangway on to the open main deck mooring area, circular staircases lead down either side to the aft cockpit. The aft cockpit is shaded by the upper deck and is fitted with a large dining table perfect for al-fresco lunches, as well as a number of comfortable chairs.

Moving inside, the versatile and spacious interior design is by Rémi Tessier. A large salon is stylishly furnished with cream leather sofas and exquisite wooden cabinetry, as well as a dining area forward.

All the sleeping accommodation is located on the lower deck and includes the master stateroom with a full beam bedroom, a sitting room, walk-in closet and two bathrooms. Two double guest cabins and two twin guest cabins with an extra Pullman berth, all en-suite, complete the line up.

The flying bridge on this yacht is quite spectacular and includes extensive sunbathing areas with facing corner sofas, a hot tub and a covered helm and sail control station.

A quite superb ocean sailing yacht, 'Riela' is yet another masterpiece from arguably the world's leading luxury sailing yacht builder.

SPECIFICATIONS: PERINI 56M 'RIELA'

Length Overall:	56m (183' 4")
Length Waterline:	46m (151')
Beam:	11.52m (38')
Draught:	3.65m (13') - 9.73m (32')
Interior Design:	Rémi Tessier
Naval Architecture:	Perini Navi / Ron Holland
Hull:	Aluminium
Superstructure:	Aluminium
Displacement:	530 ton
Engines:	2 Caterpillar C32
Max. Speed:	15.50 knots
Range:	3,500 nm @ 13 knots
Fuel capacity:	59,000 l
Main mast height:	59.14m (194')
Total sail area:	1,500 m²

Above & Far Left:
The 56m aluminium ketch 'Riela'
represents the latest evolution of
Perini's successful 56m series.

Far Left:
The interior of the yacht is modern,
warm and stylish.

PERINI NAVI

Perini Navi
Via Coppino 114
55049 Viareggio
Italy
Tel: + 39 0584 424 1
Fax: +39 0584 424 210
Web: www.perininavi.it

PERINI 45M 'HELIOS'

'Helios', the result of a collaboration between Perini Navi's naval architects and Ron Holland, is the second steel-hulled 45m yacht to be launched by this Italian shipyard. The third yacht in this class will be delivered to her owners in 2010. The extra displacement and, hence, increased wetted surface area of the steel hull was ingeniously absorbed into the design to ensure that added drag was kept to an absolute minimum. This was achieved by incorporating fine entry at the bow and a careful balance between generous beam in the aft sections and a long, clean run to the extended counter.

The Perini Navi-built aluminium mast that rises over 50 metres above the waterline carries a sail area of almost $1,200m^2$ which is handled by seven of Perini Navi's reel captive winches. Perini Navi electric furlers handle the in-boom furling system that stores the $432m^2$ main sail within the carbon fibre boom.

'Helios' has two main differences in comparison with her sister-ship 'Heritage', the first yacht in the 45 Metre series that was launched in May 2006. The $36m^2$ fly bridge now offers a comfortable sunbathing area aft and a helm station forward, while the opening stern reveals a structural staircase that descends to a $7m^2$ swimming platform.

The interior of 'Helios', designed in-house by the Perini Navi Design Department, is a pure classic. Mainly fashioned from mahogany and mahogany briar, the cabinetry features an octagonal motif, a geometrical figure created specifically for the owners. The owner and guest quarters, are particularly versatile in that each stateroom can be transformed into a variety of configurations.

SPECIFICATIONS:	PERINI 45M 'HELIOS'
Length Overall:	45m (148')
Length Waterline:	37m (121' 4")
Beam:	9.73m (32')
Draught:	3.9m (12' 9") / 8.75m (28' 6")
Interior Design:	Perini Navi
Naval Architecture:	Ron Holland / Perini Navi
Construction:	Aluminium
Max. displacement:	358 ton
Engines:	1 x CAT C32

Above & Centre:
'Helios' is the second of Perini Navi's 45m series.

Left:
The interior of 'Helios', designed in-house by the Perini Navi Design Department, is a pure classic.

Far Left:
The 36m² fly bridge offers a comfortable sunbathing area aft.

PICCHIOTTI VITRUVIUS EXPLORER SERIES

Right & Below:
Designs for the Picchiotti-Vitruvius series have already been drawn for several yachts ranging in size from 44m to 73m, with (from right then clockwise) the Picchiotti-Vitruvius 55, Picchiotti-Vitruvius 73 and Picchiotti-Vitruvius 44.

The Picchiotti-Vitruvius series is a new explorer philosophy born from the alliance of Perini Navi and Philippe Briand. A complete concept of motor yacht design that combines unique aesthetics with efficiency and seaworthiness, these explorer vessels are perfectly proportioned for cruising the world's oceans. This project marks the return of the historical Picchiotti Brand and since its first presentation to the yachting press, is already leading the way for the next generation of explorer yachts.

In 2007, Perini Navi, one of the most celebrated designers and builders of large sailing yachts, teamed up with Philippe Briand, a French expert in the design of fast sailing boats and announced an exciting new project. The union of these two names has already generated a new series of Perini racing yachts, but in this case, the project being announced was for a series of motor yachts. However, these yachts were not your average craft, but a very distinctive series of motor yachts, with the name taken from the father of all architects, Vitruvius, the Roman architect whose theory of proportions and beauty are the basis of modern architecture. Now, with the respected Italian brand of Picchiotti part of the Perini Navi Group, the brand re-emerges to mark a new generation of explorer vessels.

Since the first announcement, two units of this distinctive brand of yacht have already been sold and are

PICCHIOTTI VITRUVIUS EXPLORER SERIES

currently under construction, namely a 50m aluminium explorer yacht as well as a 55m steel ice class yacht that is able to navigate with strength and elegance through the presence of an ice pack 40cm thick.

The first 50m yacht will be launched in the spring of 2010 with the 55m soon after in 2011. With several designs already completed, the Picchiotti-Vitruvius series now offers yachts from 44m to over 73m in length, creating a generation of yachts with the same style and philosophy.

In the words of Philippe Briand: "My architectural work is based on the conviction and principle that efficiency is the reason for all forms of transportation and I believe that aesthetics are the only "raison d'être" of a luxury superyacht. In addition, in the true Vitruvius spirit, these yachts have been designed to stand for quality, comfort, elegance and harmony".

The Picchiotti-Vitruvius yachts are true blue-water yachts and their excellent seaworthiness has been optimised through a vertical centre of gravity, reducing the rolling and pitching. The sleek profile is a direct result of their streamlined superstructures and the outcome is characterised by the purity of proportion. Efficiency is the key. The optimised stretched hull design allows for the minimisation of water friction, while the vertical bow maximises the waterline length. The distribution of volume and weight follows the same principle. The result is a drastic reduction in fuel consumption and this, combined with the application of forward thinking systems in the field of propulsion and recycling systems, makes the Vitruvius yachts able to cruise the globe while respecting nature.

The continuous quest for the best hydrodynamic configuration and overall efficiency, comes from the sailing roots of this project; sailing roots that are also evident in the distribution and rationalisation of the space and in the optimisation of the volumes. The pursuit for a deeper contact and proximity with nature is also present in the wide glass windows that characterise the upper deck of the Vitruvius series.

The series, is composed of four main models:

PICCHIOTTI-VITRUVIUS EXPLORER 44M

In this version, the BOS (Briand Optimised Stretched) aluminium hull is combined with all the characteristics of the Vitruvius series. The comfortable arrangements include four double guest cabins with en-suite bathrooms on the lower deck, while the full beam owner's suite is located on the main deck forward, together with a wide salon and living area. On the upper deck, surrounded by ample glass windows, the dining room dominates the landscape with spectacular 360° views. Two main engines of 720 kW offer the yacht a range of 4,500 nautical miles at a speed range of 11 knots. The maximum speed is in the order of 14 knots. This flexible and dynamic explorer yacht features a 16' tender and a rescue boat of 14' for the use of guests and crew.

PICCHIOTTI-VITRUVIUS EXPLORER 50M

The aluminium hull of this yacht is designed for more efficient and effortless navigation in all cruise and long-range conditions, thanks to a low gross tonnage of

Above:
The revolutionary
Picchiotti-Vitruvius 50.

Left & Far Left:
The first Picchiotti-Vitruvius 50
under construction.

500 tons and an optimised draft of just 2.50m. The BOS Hull – Briand Optimised Stretched hull, gives a maximum speed of over 15 knots and a cruising speed of 12-14 knots with 2 x 970 kW engines. The range of the yacht exceeds 4,500nm when cruising at 12 knots. This yacht has two decks: the upper deck being both a bridge deck and sky lounge, and as it is glazed, appears to float. The interior spaces are open to each other and through the extensive glazing that visually opens to the sea and the scenery surrounding the yacht, the passengers are connected to the surrounding spaces and the environment.

The yacht has a full beam owner's quarter cabin with separable studio, located in the centre of the main deck, with full large windows on both sides. The upper and main salons are connected to the outdoors through oversized windows and transparent screens. The aft main and upper deck areas offer large spaces for the enjoyment of the owner and guests, including sitting and sunbathing areas. On the lower deck, the four double guest cabins with en-suite bathrooms are located mid-ships, while the five crew cabins are placed forward. The main equipment onboard includes a 16' tender fully recessed on the main deck forward and a 21' tender in the stern garage, accessible via the aft transom door.

PICCHIOTTI-VITRUVIUS EXPLORER 55M

The Picchiotti-Vitruvius Explorer 55m is the ice class version of the series. This 55m explorer yacht has an optimised draught of 3.0m, a gross tonnage of 720 tons and a reinforced steel hull as per ICE Class notation. The perfect vessel for exploring extreme areas where others tend not to venture, such as in the presence of an ice pack 40cm thick, this Philippe Briand designed yacht features a typical stretched waterline hull and gives a maximum speed over 15.5 knots and a range of 6,000nm when cruising at 11 knots with an installed power of 2 x 1174kW.

Far Right:
The Picchiotti-Vitruvius Explorer Series.

Right:
The fine bow entry of the Picchiotti-Vitruvius 50.

Below:
Every Picchiotti-Vitruvius yacht will have interiors custom built to each client's specific tastes and requirements.

The lower vertical centre of gravity and the fine entry of the water line will give a smoother motion, with the high forward freeboard contributing to the feeling of safety. The yacht has a full beam master cabin with a studio located in the centre of the main deck that are furnished with large panoramic windows on both sides.

The four guest cabins are located on the lower deck amidships. As befits a yacht of this kind, a large space is dedicated to leisure and sport activities, with particular attention given to two elegant sun-decks.

The lower sun-deck is very special, providing easy access to the sea and containing a heavenly infinity pool. The yacht is also very functional and boasts unusually large storage areas to house three tenders - 31', 21' and 14', and multiple toys such as lasers and kayaks.

PICCHIOTTI-VITRUVIUS EXPLORER 73M

The flagship of the Vitruvius family, this 73m vessel is equipped with electrical propulsion for a maximum speed of 16.5 knots, while her range at 12 knots, is an incredible 7,500 nautical miles.

This extraordinary vessel features five wide decks where the owners, guests and the twenty-two crew have their own space, comfort and privacy.

EXPLORER 44m

EXPLORER 50m

EXPLORER 55m

EXPLORER 73m

VITRUVIUS

PICCHIOTTI

PERINI NAVI

AEGEAN YACHT S/Y 'GALILEO'

There are few better sights than a magnificent three-masted schooner under full sail, her sleek hull moving swiftly through the waves under the power of her complement of eight beautifully cut white sails. A vessel indeed to dream of.

However, while most of us only ever realise this vision as a dream, one man made the dream a reality. The initial idea and concept for this dream was the brainchild of Aegean Yacht's owner, Sinan Ozer. With more than 30 years experience in yachting, Mr. Ozer and his company had become well known for the many stylish custom-built yachts they had delivered to a distinguished international clientele, including Turkish businessmen, Arabic sheikhs and Russian oligarchs.

So it was that, during the summer of 2007, a grand celebration took place at the Bodrum Marina in southern Turkey, as Aegean Yacht unveiled its new vessel, the beautiful 50m classic three-masted schooner 'Galileo'. This superyacht became the 40th yacht to be launched at the Aegean Yacht boatyard and is the biggest yacht of her type to be built in the history of Turkish boatbuilding.

Aegean Yacht is based in the refined Mediterranean resort of Bodrum, the ancient city of Halicarnassus, where boats have been built for centuries. The company started by building hand-made traditional wooden 'gulets', motor-sailers with a traditional round stern. Now it is a full

Above & Centre:
The 50m steel-hulled 'Galileo' was designed completely in-house, and features over 500m² of luxurious interior and 400m² of open deck space.

Left:
Aft of the main deck dining area, a huge 'day-bed' creates the perfect atmosphere for an afternoon siesta.

Far Left:
On the main deck, wide sidewalks connect the vast aft dining and lounging area to the teaked foredeck.

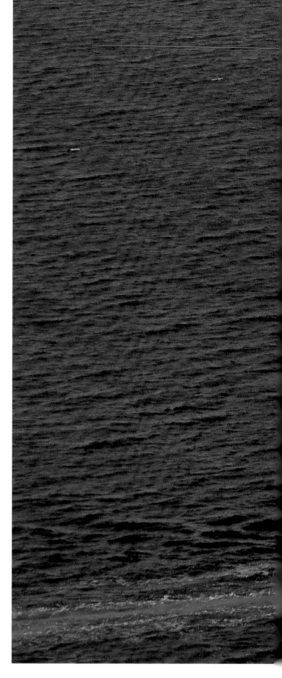

AEGEAN YACHT

service boatyard producing classic sailing and modern motor yachts up to 60m in length, mainly from steel.

The 50m steel-hulled 'Galileo' was designed completely in-house, and features over 500m^2 of luxurious interior and 400m^2 of open deck space. The exterior of 'Galileo' was designed by veteran naval architects Yavuz Mete and Tansel Taskiran, while the interior design was created by Osman Aslandere.

The initial brief for the designers at Aegean Yacht was to recreate the classic elegance of the schooners of the 1930's of the last century and combine it with modern flair and high technology.

Stepping aboard, the decks are all finished in high-grade Burmese teak and stretch right around the vessel. On the main deck, wide sidewalks connect the vast aft dining and lounging area to the teaked foredeck where there is a good-sized Jacuzzi with yet more loungers. Ahead of the foredeck, the long bowsprit anchors three foresails and takes guests back to a much-missed bygone age when sailing was THE way to travel and relaxation was the order of the day. Such is the size of the foredeck that there is still room to store the yacht's tenders while underway.

Back to the spacious aft deck, guests are entertained with a wet-bar, a full entertainment centre featuring a 42" plasma screen TV and a large dining area, where al-fresco lunches are frequently enjoyed. Further aft of the dining area, a huge 'day-bed' creates the perfect atmosphere for an afternoon siesta. This whole expansive deck area is covered with a huge sun awning, keeping the yacht cool even in the strong Mediterranean sun.

As if this was not enough deck space, stairs alongside the wide companionway lead up to the huge upper deck where sunbathing may be enjoyed while watching 'Galileo's beautiful white sails capture the wind.

'Galileo's three steel masts carry a sail area of 1,100m^2, giving her the ability to make fast passages under sail. When the wind drops however, twin MAN 760 HP engines also propel the yacht at a generous pace. In addition, three generators (twin Kohler 55 kW and one

Above & Left:
*'Galileo's three steel masts carry a sail
area of 1,100m², giving her the ability
to make fast passages under sail.*

Far Left:
*Stairs alongside the wide
companionway lead up to the huge
upper deck where sunbathing may
be enjoyed while watching 'Galileo's
beautiful white sails capture the wind.*

AEGEAN YACHT

emergency Kohler 23 kW) make sure that the yacht always has plenty of power to run the extensive electrical systems onboard. The high-tech nature of the yacht also extends to the yacht's sailing systems. All the booms are built in lighter aluminium allowing for easy handling, while the sails are manufactured by Prima Sails and the deck hardware by Harken, arguably the world leaders in luxury sailing yacht hardware.

The yacht's stunning interior design can be best described as classic contemporary with the use of African cherry wood (Makoré) throughout. Inside the 80m^2 main deck salon, guests can take advantage of a highly spacious and luxurious environment with gorgeous carpet flooring providing luxury underfoot. In the main salon, there is another large dining table for twelve guests and two separate sitting areas where oversized sofas offer maximum comfort in a very relaxing atmosphere. All the carpets and deck heads are furnished in light colours, contrasting beautifully with the rich woodwork evident throughout the yacht. A wide 60" plasma TV mounted on a wall separating the main salon from the galley can be watched from any seat in the main salon.

Unusual for a yacht of this size, 'Galileo' has only five staterooms, all of which are located on the lower deck. Two of these are the luxurious owner's and VIP suites, each offering a huge 60m^2 of living space. The owner's suite is located at the aft end and encompasses the full 10m beam of the yacht. This majestic stateroom features a king-size bed, a well-designed corner office as well as a make-up table and a sitting area with a semi-circular sofa. A retractable plasma TV is also sited right in front of the bed. The cabin's decor is beautifully crafted with an abundance of high quality woodwork merging with luxurious fabrics and carpets creating a very intimate environment. Naturally, this stateroom also boasts an immense full marble en-suite bathroom complete with a Jacuzzi, as well as a walk-in dressing room.

Located at the bow, another equally large VIP suite is equipped to an equally luxurious standard. In between these two staterooms, there are two other double guest suites and one triple guest suite. Also located below, what could easily serve as a sixth cabin has been converted into a scuba storage area and diving compartment, fully equipped with scuba compressors, diving gear and a hydraulic diving platform.

Above, Left & Far Left:
Three views of the main salon, where there is a large dining table for twelve guests and two separate sitting areas where oversized sofas offer maximum comfort in a very relaxing atmosphere.

AEGEAN YACHT

Aegean Yacht
Icmeler 54
Bodrum 48400
Turkey
Tel : + 90 252 313 26 55
Fax : + 90 252 313 84 68
W: www.aegeanyacht.com

In total, more than 150 craftsmen and engineers were employed to create 'Galileo'. The yacht has been designed and built to the classification standards of RINA (Registro Italiano Navale) and all the construction work was carried out under their supervision. The result is an absolutely world-class yacht, which is supremely comfortable and hugely spacious. Classic, elegant, attractive and strong, she blends old-world charm with modern day technology and is without doubt a yacht that dreams are made of.

Building a custom line yacht is the realisation of every luxury yacht owner's dream. It is easy to build a dream, if you have enough inspiration, innovation, necessary knowledge, faith and, of course, the right team. Last year Aegean Yacht celebrated its 30th anniversary. With the knowledge and experience gained from building 'Galileo' behind them, this unique luxury yacht builder is looking forward with confidence to building many more dream yachts over the next 30 years!

SPECIFICATIONS:	AEGEAN YACHTS 'GALILEO'
Length overall:	50m (164') exc. bowsprit
Length waterline:	39.26m (129')
Beam:	10m (33')
Draught:	3.60m (12')
Displacement:	420 ton
Concept:	Sinan Ozer, Aegean Yacht
Naval architect:	Yavuz Mete, Aegean Yacht
Interior design:	Osman Aslandere, Aegean Yacht
Construction:	Steel hull, Steel superstructure covered by mahogany
Engine:	2 x 760 HP MAN
Maximum speed:	13 knots
Cruising speed:	11 knots
Range:	800nm at cruising speed

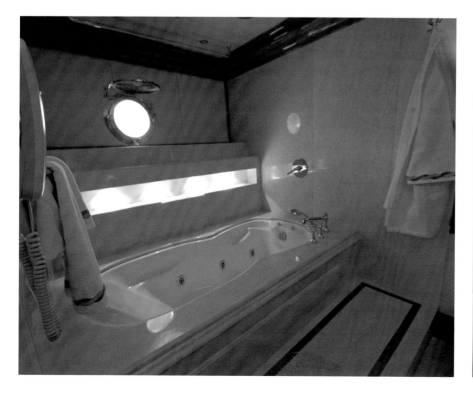

Above:
The majestic owner's stateroom features a king-size bed, a well-designed corner office as well as a make-up table and a sitting area with a semi-circular sofa.

Left:
The VIP stateroom.

Centre:
A triple guest cabin.

Far Left:
The beautiful owner's bathroom.

TRINITY
YACHTS

Centrally located on the Gulf Coast of The United States, Trinity Yachts has earned its place as one of the world's elite builders of custom superyachts with an emphasis on European quality steel and aluminium constructions. The company's goal is to build truly custom yachts that fulfil all of its clients' unique cruising desires.

Trinity Yachts was purchased in 1988 from Friede Goldman Halter by John Dane, former CEO of Halter Marine Inc., Felix Sabates and Billy Smith and became a private company in the year 2000. Continuing the company's proud traditions, high quality craftsmanship, state of the art construction and engineering techniques have been acquired from many years of experience with thousands of boats and ships designed and built by other Halter divisions, as well as technology transfers from Halter's ultra fast, ultra quiet military vessels.

Trinity's first launch was the motor yacht 'Leda' in 1991. A few years later, during the 1997 Fort Lauderdale International Boat Show, Trinity and Victory Lane debuted the first of their Legend Series Motor yachts - the 150' Tri-Deck 'Magic' (ex-'Noble House'). Now one of the world's most sought after yacht builders, Trinity Yachts continues to build its magnificent vessels at its yard in New Orleans. This facility is situated on 38 acres of waterfront property and includes 200,000ft^2 of fabrication area and 84,000 ft^2 of outfitting area, all undercover.

In a world where most yachts are constructed on a semi-production basis, Trinity Yachts has the ability to build to any design and to any size up to 123m (400') in length and to work with many of the world's most renowned naval architects and interior designers.

The following yachts are just some of the recent launchings by this extraordinary luxury yacht builder.

Above then clockwise:
Trinity Yachts has the ability to build to any design and to any size up to 123m (400') in length:
'Foxharb'r Too' (49.1m / 161');
'Mary P' (37.20m / 122');
'Anjilis' (49.08m / 161');
'Norwegian Queen' (49.9m / 164')

TRINITY YACHTS

'DESTINATION FOX HARB'R TOO'

Built for a legendary Canadian entrepreneur, the 161' Trinity motor yacht 'Destination Fox Harb'r Too' adds a new dimension to the world of luxury yachting. Boasting five luxurious staterooms there is an adaptable sixth stateroom able to accommodate additional guests, or act as a private office, gymnasium or private lounge area.

With an interior by Patrick Knowles Design, she has a refreshingly cool style, similar to that of a luxury spa and features sophisticated fabrics, hand carved glass and wood work consisting of redwood burl, lacewood, macasser ebony and Honduran mahogany. The stonework onboard is equally exotic, showcasing Beaumaniere limestone, River Rock pebbles and walnut travertine.

Onboard, her split-level owner's suite offers magnificent 180-degree views and features dual private en-suite facilities (his with shower, and hers with Jacuzzi tub). Four additional guest staterooms, featuring three king beds, two twin sized beds, and one Pullman, are located below decks with equally impressive facilities. The sixth adaptable stateroom adjoins the owner's suite on deck, and features a queen bed sleeper-sofa, and full en-suite facilities.

As befitting a yacht of this stature, 'Destination Fox Harb'r Too' has many areas in which to relax, including a spacious aft deck which is superb for shaded dining, two large salons and a huge sun-deck well equipped with sun loungers, a Jacuzzi, a bar and shaded dining areas.

For propulsion, she is fitted with two highly dependable Caterpillar 3512B engines, each delivering 2,250hp and giving the yacht a 20-knot top speed and an excellent 3,000 nautical mile range at 12 knots.

State of the art electronics onboard include V-SAT constant WiFi Internet, the latest Crestron video and audio equipment, and iPod docking stations throughout the yacht.

Right:
The 161' Trinity motor yacht 'Destination Fox Harb'r Too' was built for a legendary Canadian entrepreneur.

Below Left:
The split-level owner's suite offers magnificent 180-degree views and features dual private en-suite facilities.

Below Left Centre:
The large aft deck.

Below Right Centre:
The expansive fly bridge.

Below Right:
The main salon has a refreshingly cool style.

SPECIFICATIONS:	'DESTINATION FOX HARB'R TOO'
Length Overall:	49.1m (161')
Beam:	8.6m (28')
Draught:	2.2m (7' 3")
Displacement:	250 ton
Naval Architecture:	Trinity Yachts, LLC
Interior Design:	Patrick Knowles Design
Accommodation:	12 in 6 staterooms
Crew:	10 in 6 cabins
Propulsion:	2 x Caterpillar 3512B 2,250hp
Max. Speed:	20 knots
Cruising Speed:	18 knots
Range:	3,000nm at 12 knots
Construction:	Aluminium

TRINITY YACHTS   'NORWEGIAN QUEEN'

The 164' tri-deck yacht 'Norwegian Queen' is the latest "ultra-contemporary" design to come from the Trinity Yachts yard. Designed with fun very much in mind, all the parties involved, Trinity, Evan Marshall and of course, the owner, have not been afraid to break with convention to achieve the desired result, which is a stylish, spacious and light-filled yacht.

'Norwegian Queen's modern interior has been designed by Evan K. Marshall and is characterised by the extensive use of leather and fabric for wall and bulkhead coverings, creating a soft, warm feel throughout. The striking sky-lounge, with black carpeting and black leather furnishings lashed in red, is the ultimate expression of the yacht's white, black and red colour scheme, while the split-level master suite on the main deck features an en-suite bathroom with a Jacuzzi and a large shower stall. On the lower deck, four guest staterooms are luxuriously furnished to a very high standard, while the crew cabins are all spacious and modern.

Constructed in aluminium, 'Norwegian Queen' has a shallow draft of just 7.4 feet, making her ideal for cruising the shallow waters of the Bahamas and for anchoring in secluded anchorages other yachts are unable to visit.

Powered by twin 2,250hp Caterpillar 3512B engines, this stylish and powerful yacht is capable of achieving a top speed of 21 knots and has a transatlantic range when cruising at 12 knots.

SPECIFICATIONS: 'NORWEGIAN QUEEN'	
Length Overall:	49.9m (164')
Beam:	8.6m (28')
Draught:	2.22m (7' 4")
Displacement:	206 ton
Naval Architecture:	Trinity Yachts, LLC
Interior Design:	Evan K Marshall
Guests:	10 in 5 staterooms
Crew:	9-10 crew in 5 cabins
Propulsion:	2 x Caterpillar 3512B 2,250hp
Max. Speed:	20 knots
Cruising Speed:	18 knots
Construction:	Aluminium

Above:
Constructed in aluminium, 'Norwegian Queen' has a shallow draft of just 7.4 feet, making her ideal for cruising the shallow waters of the Bahamas and for anchoring in secluded anchorages other yachts are unable to visit.

Far Left & Centre:
The striking main salon and dining area features the yacht's white, black and red colour scheme.

Left:
The split-level master suite on the main deck features an en-suite bathroom with a Jacuzzi and a large shower stall.

TRINITY YACHTS   'UNBRIDLED'

One of the largest yachts ever to be built in the United States, the 191' motor yacht 'Unbridled' was designed and constructed as a luxurious expeditionary yacht, capable of cruising the globe in the utmost comfort and privacy. Unusual in this day of concealing all accessories in stern garages or behind hydraulic side doors, 'Unbridled' flaunts her toys on deck, including her twin 31' Novurania RIB tenders, making a bold statement that this is a yacht built for fun and exploration. A yacht that will seek out the corners of the world without compromise.

With her impressive length and 34' beam, her living areas are simply huge, especially on the enormous sun-deck where the 360-degree views are complemented by seemingly acres of relaxing lounging areas. On the upper deck a wonderful lounge is located behind the well-equipped pilothouse and leads aft through sliding doors to a huge deck area perfectly suited to al-fresco lunches.

The vast master stateroom is located on the forward main deck, which has been designed as one might expect with a luxurious en-suite his and hers bathroom. However, with a walk-in dressing room, an owner's office and yet another room that serves as a gym or extra guest accommodation, the space afforded to this area is quite astonishing. Four further en-suite guest staterooms are situated on the lower deck along with accommodation for a crew of ten, together with a spacious crew lounge.

Built to MCA standards and equipped with twin 2,200hp Caterpillar engines, 'Unbridled' offers ocean-crossing range, which is exactly what she is expected to do on a frequent basis.

SPECIFICATIONS: 'UNBRIDLED'	
Length Overall:	58.23m (191')
Beam:	10.45m (34' 4")
Draught:	2.98m (9' 10")
Naval Architecture:	Trinity Yachts, LLC
Interior Design:	Patrick Knowles Design
Guests / Crew:	12 in 6 staterooms / 14 in 6 cabins
Propulsion:	2 x Caterpillar 3512B 2,012hp
Max. Speed:	16 knots
Construction:	Aluminium

Above & Left:
With her impressive length 191' length and 34' beam, 'Unbridled's living areas are simply huge, especially on the enormous sun-deck where the 360-degree views are complemented by seemingly acres of relaxing lounging areas.

TRINITY YACHTS   'ANJILIS'

Launched in 2009, the 49m (161') Trinity luxury motor yacht 'Anjilis' features a sophisticated interior designed by Glade Johnson Design with Art Deco inspired creative elements exuding style and comfort.

Featuring custom marquetry, stone inlays and elegant luxurious furnishings, 'Anjilis' is a highly modern yacht with state-of-the-art audio-visual systems fitted throughout.

With a streamlined aluminium displacement hull, this large Trinity motor yacht can reach a highly impressive cruising speed of around 18 knots, with power supplied by her twin Caterpillar 3512B, 2,250hp diesel engines. Whether at speed or at anchor, this stylish yacht remains comfortably stable with her two active Zero-Speed capable stabilisers.

Designed with sweeping outdoor entertainment areas, 'Anjilis' is ideal as both a private or charter yacht. These spaces include a bar and day head on the sundeck as well as superb outdoor dining areas on the aft upper deck. There is also a further outdoor dining and bar area on her aft main deck.

Further aft her innovative beach style swim deck features chairs, cocktail tables and a sunshade for those who like relaxing close to the water. Another innovative feature onboard is the wonderful riding seat located forward of the pilothouse, from where guests may take in the scenery as it develops over the horizon.

This elegant yacht can accommodate eleven guests in five luxurious en-suite staterooms, all outfitted with custom Italian linens and amenities.

The full width main deck master stateroom, complete with owner's study, is especially elegant with hand-tufted wool and silk carpeting and luxurious furnishings.

With state-of-the-art audio-visual and surround sound throughout the yacht and a full array of water toys, she is quite simply the perfect yacht for entertaining guests, whether privately or on charter.

SPECIFICATIONS: 'ANJILIS'

Length Overall:	49.08m (161')
Beam:	8.53m (28')
Draught:	2.28m (7' 6")
Naval Architecture:	Trinity Yachts, LLC
Interior Design:	Glade Johnson Design
Accommodation:	11 guests + 9 crew
Propulsion:	2 x Caterpillar 3512B 2,250hp
Max. Speed:	20 knots
Construction:	Aluminium

Above:
Designed with sweeping outdoor entertainment areas, 'Anjilis' is ideal as both a private or charter yacht.

Far Left:
The full width main deck master stateroom, complete with owner's study, is especially elegant with hand-tufted wool and silk carpeting and luxurious furnishings.

Left:
'Anjilis' features a sophisticated interior designed by Glade Johnson Design with Art Deco inspired creative elements exuding style and comfort.

TRINITY YACHTS   'BIG CITY'

Launched in 2009, the 42.97m (140' 11") 'Big City' offers everything one would expect of a contemporary Trinity motor yacht. A semi-displacement, aluminium hulled built motor yacht, 'Big City' features an interior design by Patrick Knowles.

'Big City' has been designed with an open plan main salon and dining area. At the aft end of the main salon, sliding doors open up on to the main aft deck which features two tables that can be joined together to seat eight to ten guests. From this position, a circular stairway leads up to the upper aft deck and sun deck, while a dual stairway leads downwards to the oversized 'beach style' swim platform.

Moving up the stairs to her upper aft deck, another large dining table seats ten to twelve guests. The upper-deck sky lounge also has ample seating, a large screen HD/TV, and a large semi-circular wet bar to port.

Above the upper deck an expansive sun-deck provides an L-shaped bar with six stools, a casual dining banquette to port for six and a powder room in the support arch. Further forward on the sundeck, a Jacuzzi together with a seated area can be shaded with three removable awning "sails".

Totally luxurious throughout, the master suite is quite exceptional and is ideally positioned on the main deck. It is outfitted with a walk in closet, a desk, an L-shaped sofa and his and hers bathrooms forward with a central Jacuzzi bath and a shower. On the lower deck there are another four guest staterooms.

A yacht built for entertainment, all the main salons and staterooms feature high quality audio visual systems, including a Kaleidescape central movie/music server with universal touch screen remote control, remote lighting control by Crestron touch screen, and iPod docking stations.

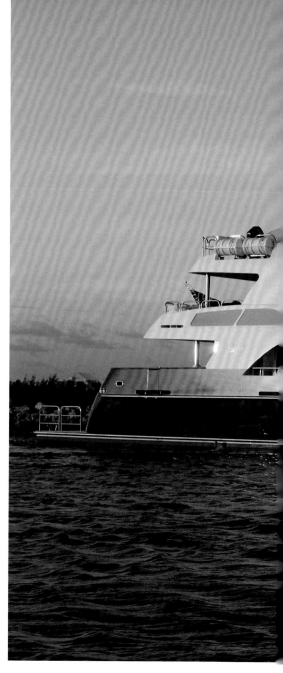

SPECIFICATIONS: 'BIG CITY'

Length Overall:	43m (141')
Beam:	8.51m (27' 11")
Draught:	2.28m (7' 6")
Naval Architecture:	Trinity Yachts, LLC
Interior Design:	Patrick Knowles Design
Accommodation:	10 guests + 8 crew
Propulsion:	2 x Caterpillar C32
Max. Speed:	17 knots
Cruise Speed:	14 knots
Construction:	Aluminium

Above:
A semi-displacement, aluminium hulled built motor yacht, 'Big City' features an interior design by Patrick Knowles.

Far Left:
On the sundeck, a Jacuzzi together with a seated area can be shaded with three removable awning "sails".

Centre:
The master suite is quite exceptional and is ideally positioned on the main deck.

Left:
'Big City' has been designed with an open plan main salon and dining area.

TRINITY YACHTS   'MARY P'

Trinity Yachts LLC
13085 Seaway Road
Gulfport, MS. 39503 USA
Tel: +1 228 276 1000
Fax: +1 228 276 1001
Web: www.trinityyachts.com

Launched in 2009, the 37.2m (122') 'Mary P' is one of the world's largest sports fishing yachts and yet another pedigree yacht to be built by Trinity Yachts.

Built in aluminium, with naval architecture by Doug Sharp of Sharp Designs, 'Mary P' truly answered an extensive client brief through extensive research, including tank testing of the hull-model while going astern. The transom has been designed to increase the seaworthiness of the yacht and maximise her performance while going astern, a movement frequently required when big game fishing.

There are many other unique details which enhance her role as a sports fishing yacht, such as a fully automated anchor deployment and retrieval system, specially designed underwater lighting to enhance her performance when night fishing and a fly bridge that maintains a good line of sight for the captain, which is especially important when backing down on a fish.

Onboard, 'Mary P' accommodates an owner's party of eight in four staterooms and a crew of three in two cabins in the stern. The interior features highly finished custom woodwork using exquisite woods such as oak burl, African zebrano and Japanese sen.

Propulsion is provided by twin Caterpillar 3512B-HD engines, each producing 2540hp. Combined with her aluminium hull, this provides 'Mary P' with a highly respectable top speed of approximately 25 knots. A minimum of 7,000 gallons (26,460 l) of fuel allows for a large cruising range.

'Mary P' has a very advanced stabilizing system featuring the Quantum MagLift® with 3 axis digital control and Zero Speed ™ as well as high-speed stabilization utilizing Archer® active trim tabs. This combination of two types of stabilizers enables 'Mary P' to be highly stable at high speed, trolling, at anchor and, a first for any yacht, active stabilization while going astern and when backing down on a fish.

SPECIFICATIONS:	'MARY P'
Length Overall:	37.20m (122')
Beam:	7.30m (24')
Naval Architecture:	Doug Sharp Designs
Interior Design:	Judy Bell Davis
Accommodation:	8 guests + 3 crew
Propulsion:	2 x Caterpillar 3512B-HD 2,540hp
Max. Speed:	25 knots
Construction:	Aluminium

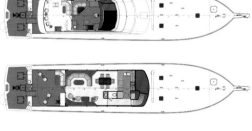

CMN YACHTS 'SLIPSTREAM'

CMN has a heritage that dates back to 1912 when Felix Amiot Aircraft construction put the French region of Normandy on the aeronautical stage. Aircraft design and production gave way to shipbuilding, both commercial and military.

It was in the sixties that CMN started to bring its attention to the then emerging yachting market with the construction of a series of sailing boats such as the 'Maïca', an 11-metre sailing boat designed by Illingworth and Primrose.

In the 1970's and 1980's, among other racing projects for famous yacht skippers, CMN launched 'Paul Ricard' for Eric Tabarly and 'Kriter IV' for Olivier de Kersauzon.

With the luxury yacht market expanding into larger and larger yachts in the nineties, CMN Yacht Division undertook projects over 140' such as the schooner 'Friday Star' and the expedition yacht 'French Look II'.

The new millennium saw CMN Yachts launching larger motor yachts like 49m 'Bermie II' and 43m 'Héloval', and sailing yachts such as 32m 'Attimo' and 32m 'Lady Barbaretta'.

Today, with the development of the CMN LINE 60 with 3 recent launches – 'Netanya 8', 'Slipstream' and 'Cloud 9' - CMN Yachts is rapidly developing a marque brand name and setting new standards in the world of luxury yacht construction.

Right & Below:
"More than a yacht – a piece of Art,"
is how the owner described his 60m
(197') superyacht 'Slipstream' on her
launch in 2009.

CMN YACHTS 'SLIPSTREAM'

'SLIPSTREAM'

"More than a yacht – a piece of Art," is how the owner described 'Slipstream' on her launch in 2009. "This yacht has exceeded my expectations," he further declared. And it is not surprising. 'Slipstream's design offers a huge level of accommodation and incorporates many impressive features, such as the full beam panoramic sky lounge and the full beam owner's suite, while the bridge deck VIP suite boasts a private foredeck with sweeping ocean views.

'Slipstream' is the second yacht of the CMN Line 60 series to be launched and is a result of the collaboration between CMN Yachts and Andrew Winch Designs. At 197' in length, this exceptionally stylish displacement yacht is the largest yacht ever to be launched by CMN and is packed full of innovative and original features.

The sheer volume on 'Slipstream', such as her 2.25m – 2.3m headroom on the main deck and bridge decks, exceeds that of most other yachts, while her exterior deck spaces include a huge open plan sun-deck equipped with a large Jacuzzi, gym equipment and sun-pads.

Indeed, the first impression on boarding 'Slipstream' is one of space and volume. A hallmark of the CMN Line 60 series is the flexibility of creating unique custom interiors within a tried and tested seaworthy hull design. With 'Slipstream', Andrew Winch Designs not only used this flexibility to create the optimum use of the space available, but by the clever use of colour and textures, painted an illusion of a yacht that is even larger than her impressive stature actually is.

Throughout the yacht there is a recurring motif of 'waves' seen in the carved wooden panels, in the fabrics, the carpets and even in the glazing. All the guest staterooms have a rich focus set in a classically simple setting, with small pieces of art providing colour enhancement to a relaxing and highly luxurious environment created by the use of carefully selected woods, fabrics and marble.

'Slipstream's dramatic exterior architecture,

Right & Below:
'Slipstream' is the second yacht of the CMN Line 60 series to be launched and is a result of the collaboration between CMN Yachts and Andrew Winch Designs.

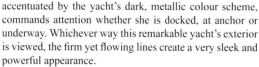

CMN YACHTS 'SLIPSTREAM'

accentuated by the yacht's dark, metallic colour scheme, commands attention whether she is docked, at anchor or underway. Whichever way this remarkable yacht's exterior is viewed, the firm yet flowing lines create a very sleek and powerful appearance.

Moving onboard, a central atrium reaching up three decks high creates a highly impressive entrance to the yacht, which is emphasised by three uniquely carved totem poles, produced by the British Columbian artist Stanley E. Hunt. These totem poles depict the spirits of the yacht's owners and are topped by a soaring eagle with wings spread wide – ready to fly across the oceans.

The huge full beam owner's suite on the main deck, is actually a duplex stateroom and includes an office, his and hers bathrooms, separate dressing rooms and a private observation lounge giving panoramic views forward.

The bridge deck VIP stateroom also has its own private teak floored terrace, offering unsurpassed views of the sea and surrounding scenery. Also equipped with a large en-suite bathroom and dressing room, this may well be the finest VIP suite on any yacht of comparable size.

Four more spacious guest staterooms on the lower deck are all en-suite and all highly luxurious. Two of these staterooms have twin beds that can be easily converted into double suites when required.

Like the staterooms, the public areas are also very spacious and luxurious. The main salon is endowed with large panoramic windows that invite the outside light in while maintaining the relaxing air that this stylish space was designed for. Forward of the main salon, the formal dining room has a large dining table which seats twelve to fourteen guests comfortably and is separated from the main salon by an ornate screen.

Up one deck, the bridge deck features a wonderful sky lounge that is serviced by its own pantry and is equipped with a state-of-the-art cinema boasting a 2.5m high-resolution screen as well as a high-tech surround sound system. The cinema, as well as the other television systems throughout the yacht, features a centralised 'Sensory'

Right:
The ultra-luxurious main deck dining area.

Below Right:
The main salon benefits from large panoramic windows.

Below Left & Centre:
The owner's bedroom is spacious and rich in colour and features a wonderful private lounge with panoramic views forward.

CMN YACHTS 'SLIPSTREAM'

CMN Yachts

51 rue de la Bretonnière, BP539
50105 Cherbourg, France
Tel: +33 2 33 883 020
Fax: +33 2 33 883 198
Web: www.cmnyachts.com
Web: www.cmnline60.com

CMN Yachts are part of the
ABU DHABI MAR Group

system offering over 300 DVD's and music albums on demand. Satellite communication and iPod connectivity are also available in all public areas and staterooms. Astern of the cinema, a stylish dining area can be enjoyed either in the open or closed off from the elements.

A yacht very much built for entertainment, the huge 150m^2 sun-deck is a sun lover's paradise. As well as the large Jacuzzi and sun loungers, the aft section of this deck, with a large dining table and seating, can be protected from the sun, wind and rain by an innovative 'Targa' roof and lateral fixed windows.

A yacht designed for cruising, 'Slipstream' is powered by twin Caterpillar 3516B engines, each producing 2,230hp at 1600 rpm. These deliver a maximum speed of 17 knots and an ocean crossing range of 5,000 nautical miles at a cruising speed of 12 knots.

A truly inspiring yacht built to the highest standards by CMN, 'Slipstream' has just joined the elite group of luxury charter yachts offered by the world-class charter broker Burgess. There is little doubt she will be amongst the most popular yachts afloat.

SPECIFICATIONS:	CMN LINE 60 'SLIPSTREAM'
Length Overall:	60m (197')
Beam:	11.10m (36' 5")
Draught:	3.45m (11' 4")
Naval architecture:	CMN
Design:	Andrew Winch Designs
Guests:	14
Crew:	16
Hull:	Steel
Superstructure:	Aluminium
Classification:	Bureau Veritas
Engines:	2 x Caterpillar 3561B 16V, 2230hp
Maximum Speed:	17 knots
Cruising Speed:	15 knots
Range:	5,000nm at 12 knots

Above:
The bridge deck features a wonderful sky lounge that is serviced by its own pantry and is equipped with a state-of-the-art cinema boasting a 2.5m high-resolution screen as well as a high-tech surround sound system.

Far Left & Centre:
The bridge deck VIP stateroom has its own private teak floored terrace.

Left:
Astern of the cinema, a stylish dining area can be enjoyed either in the open or closed off from the elements.

All Photographs:
© Guillaume Plisson (exterior)
Simon McBride (interior).

ABEKING & RASMUSSEN

In September 2007, at the end of Germany's sailing season, a huge party took place at Lemwerder near Bremen on the banks of the Weser River. Abeking & Rasmussen celebrated its 100th birthday with the yard's owner Hermann Schaedla, grandson of founder Henry 'Jimmy' Rasmussen, fully in charge and with great-grandson, Hans Schaedla, ready to follow.

Nearly 100 years is a long time and very few shipyards in the world can claim to have built yachts of all kinds and sizes for that length of time.

Throughout its remarkable history, Abeking & Rasmussen has built up a unique reputation for quality, craftsmanship and reliability. Yard number 1 was an unnamed 15' working boat built in 1907.

In 2008 number 6479, 'Eminence', featured overleaf, was launched - an elegant five deck 257' (78.4m) twin-screw motor yacht. No less than 6477 vessels have been built in between, with many of them still sailing today and kept in excellent shape.

As well as building traditional luxury motor yachts, Abeking & Rasmussen have for some time, been one of the world's leaders in the development of SWATH ships, (small waterplane area twin hull) with their characteristic torpedo shaped displacement hulls providing low rolling and pitching motions even in rough seas.

Taking the lead with SWATH technology, last year Abeking & Rasmussen launched the world's first SWATH Expedition Yacht, the 41m 'Silver Cloud'.

Boasting the space and performance of a much larger yacht, the first Atlantic crossing in just 10 days by this yacht with the owner onboard, demonstrated and confirmed the real advantages of this new luxury yacht concept.

Above & Far Left:
The magnificent 78.4m motor yacht 'Eminence'.

Left & Centre:
The revolutionary 41m SWATH yacht 'Silver Cloud'.

ABEKING & RASMUSSEN

'EMINENCE'

'Eminence' is one of the newest and largest luxury yachts to be built so far by Abeking & Rasmussen. Measuring in with a length of 78.40m and a 12.40m beam, this outstanding yacht has extensive interior space over her five decks, yet still appears slender due to her outstanding exterior design, embodying style and elegance from every perspective.

A masterpiece of craftsmanship and planning, 'Eminence' was designed and styled by the British firm Reymond Langton Design, a highly experienced and professional design studio with talents in both the exterior styling and interior design of some of the world's finest superyachts. With a brief for a yacht designed with a comfortable modern contemporary style, enlivened with the lightest touch of art deco, attention to detail was paramount throughout the build, right up to the yacht's mast being shaped resembling the tailfin of a whale.

The use of beautifully crafted woods such as walnut, mahogany and striped macassar ebony is evident throughout the yacht, while lightness and colour have been maintained onboard the yacht by the designers using cream and white upholstery, carpets and deck-heads. Marble and rich honey onyx also endow the hallways and bathrooms with a warm and luxurious feel.

While the styling and interior design of the yacht generally demand all the headlines, note should be taken of 'Eminence's steel hull designed by Abeking & Rasmussen's own naval architects. With a fine entry at the waterline and flared, high bow sections, the bow of this yacht provides low hydrodynamic resistance and excellent seaworthiness, characteristics of a true classic yacht.

At the top of this magnificent yacht, the sun-deck provides ample space and amenities for guests to relax and take in the open-air. Five decks up from the waterline, the views are, as one would expect, panoramic. At the aft end of the sun-deck, curved sofas provide a circle of seating next to a bar area surfaced in marble, above which awnings

Above & Left Centre:
'Eminence' has the lines of a truly classic superaycht.

Left:
The main entrance lobby features an elevator which connects all the decks.

Far Left:
The large aft upper deck is the perfect place for al-fresco dining.

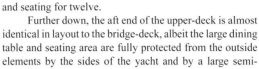

ABEKING & RASMUSSEN

can be remotely deployed to provide shade at the hottest time of the day. Further forward more seating is arranged near an elevator linking all decks of the yacht.

Below the sun-deck, a stylish sky-lounge features seating, another bar area forward and games tables. Aft of the sky-lounge, an area perfect for open-air dining on a huge expanse of deck has a modern outside dining table and seating for twelve.

Further down, the aft end of the upper-deck is almost identical in layout to the bridge-deck, albeit the large dining table and seating area are fully protected from the outside elements by the sides of the yacht and by a large semi-circular door which, when left open, allows the feeling of open-air dining. Outside the circular doors, yet more deck areas can be found for social entertaining.

Beneath this, the main-deck aft provides access to the huge transform platform that can be lowered down when at anchor and retracted when underway. This arrangement not only gives the yacht's stern considerable protection from the elements, but also from the threat of piracy, an ever-increasing consideration of yacht owners worldwide.

The major benefit of a yacht of this magnitude however, comes with the size and scope of the interior layout and the provision of additional spaces that have been utilised for purposes 'outside the norm'. A fully functional cinema with a 'Kaleidescape' film database and high-end surround sound on the main-deck and a well-equipped gymnasium on the upper-deck ensure full use of space.

At 136m², the hugely impressive owner's suite, consisting of a spacious bedroom, a choice of sitting areas, a stylish office and his and hers bathrooms, is one of the largest to be found on a yacht of this size.

The sleeping accommodation on board the yacht is further enhanced with two VIP suites on the main deck and four more guest suites on the lower deck, all fitted with full entertainment and communication systems.

A yacht constructed to the highest standards and with meticulous planning, 'Eminence' is a truly unique and superbly built yacht.

Opposite:
The main salon is light and welcoming.

Below Left:
The cinema features a 'Kaleidescape' film database.

Below Right:
One of the luxurious VIP cabins.

SPECIFICATIONS:	ABEKING & RASMUSSEN 'EMINENCE'
Length Overall:	78.4m (257')
Length Waterline:	68.1m (223')
Beam:	12.4m (40'8")
Draught:	3.30m (10'10")
Construction:	Steel hull and aluminium superstructure
Displacement:	2054 ton
Naval Architect:	Abeking & Rasmussen
Interior Design:	Reymond Langton Design
Exterior Styling:	Reymond Langton Design
Accommodation:	14 in 6 staterooms
Crew:	20 in 10 cabins
Max. Speed:	16.5 knots
Cruising Speed:	14 knots
Range at 12 knots:	6,000 nm
Fuel Capacity:	180,000l
Water Capacity:	35,000l
Main engines:	2 Caterpillar C3516B DITA Series II 1492 kW each
Stabilisers:	Quantum zero-speed (2 pairs)
Classification:	Lloyd's 100A1, SSC Yacht (P), Mono G6, LMC, UMS, MCA LY2

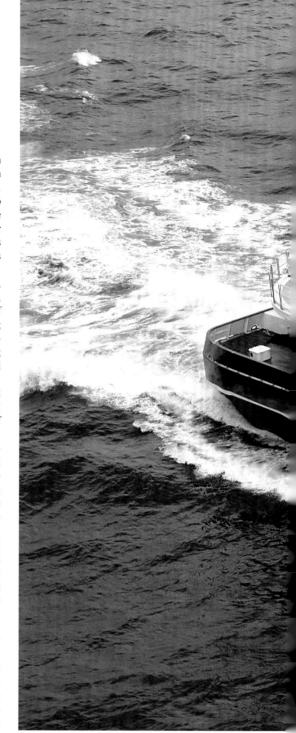

ABEKING & RASMUSSEN

'SILVER CLOUD'

When designing and constructing an expedition yacht, the comfort on board and the behaviour of the ship in high seas and when at anchor have significant importance. One option is to equip the yacht with stabilisers in order to dampen the rolling motions during the journey. To achieve this, smaller mono-hull yachts need two fins, while larger yachts are normally equipped with four. These special fins have to prove their efficiency during the voyage, as well as when anchoring at so-called 'zero-speed'.

While the fitting of fins is without doubt successful, especially when fitted to larger mono-hulled mega-yachts, in most cases the level of comfort achieved in terms of movement is still some way off that of an ocean going cruise liner. While most stabiliser fins fitted onboard mega-yachts effectively decrease trolling movements, pitching and slamming motions are not always effectively reduced in a mono-hulled yacht under 100m in length.

In the early 1990's Abeking & Rasmussen started to investigate the further development of the SWATH principle in order to improve the motion behaviour of luxury yachts and small ships

The calm behaviour of the SWATH ship, the so-called 'soft ride', is achieved as a result of the special design of the SWATH or semi-submersible ships. The two lower hulls, built in a torpedo shape, are designed to be 1m to 3.5m under water, depending on the vessel's size. The lion's share of the vessel's displacement (about 80% of the ship's weight) is carried by these two hulls.

Having successfully built these craft in the commercial field for pilot boats and supply boats among others, it was a natural progression for Abeking & Rasmussen to develop this concept and recognise a SWATH type yacht as being a worthwhile contribution to their classic mega-yacht program, utilising the vastly improved motion control afforded by this type of craft.

Finding a client to try out this innovative technology however was another thing.

However, as is often the case, a breakthrough came when an experienced American yachtsman, Mr Alex Dreyfoos, who had already owned yachts built by some of the world's leading yacht builders, undertook extensive research on minimising a yacht's motion, due to his wife's

Above & Left:
The revolutionary 41m SWATH yacht
'Silver Cloud'.

ABEKING & RASMUSSEN

Abeking & Rasmussen
PO Box 1160
Lemwerder 27809, Germany
Tel: +49 42 16 733 531
Fax: +49 42 16 733 115
W: www.abeking.com

tendency to be seasick. An Australian shipyard owner that he wrote to suggested he explore the SWATH design, while a Google search and further inquiries led to visits to a naval architect firm and three shipyards that had designed or built SWATH commercial vessels. It soon became clear that Abeking & Rasmussen had the most developed and sophisticated technology and the most experience of building such craft. Moreover, they were also one of the world's leading luxury yacht builders.

Moving ahead to a day in June 2005 in the North Sea, on a 25m (82') Abeking & Rasmussen built SWATH pilot boat and in conditions that would have made his wife seasick had they been on their current Feadship, Mr Dreyfoos found his wife happily reading and knitting onboard, while he discussed the technology with the yard's management and the boat's captain. It soon became clear that the SWATH design was what they had been looking for, with the result that in March 2006 a contract was signed with the yard to built a 41m (134') long SWATH yacht to be named 'Silver Cloud'.

Two years later, in August 2008, the yacht began sea trials with the owner onboard. At a time of year of normally calm seas, they were fortunate to find some 2m (7') seas in the North Sea, and it was immediately clear that he had made the right decision in commissioning Abeking & Rasmussen to build a SWATH yacht.

As well as giving far greater motion control, this first SWATH yacht, with a length of only 41m, provides internal and deck space comparable with a conventional 50m yacht and offers a top speed in sea behaviours equivalent to a much larger vessel of over 100m in length.

Beginning the passage to the yacht's home base in Palm Beach, Florida in October, the yacht cruised from the A&R shipyard on the Weser River, north of Bremen, Germany to Gibraltar; Gibraltar to the Canary Islands; the Canary Islands to St Thomas (US Virgin Islands) and from St Thomas to Palm Beach. During the passage, 'Silver Cloud' experienced heavy seas on all quarters and, at times, head seas of 3m to 5m with an occasional 6m to 7m wave. Incredibly, vases remained in place during the entire trip - quite a remarkable ride. Most importantly none of the guests, including the owner's wife was seasick. In short, the owners remain delighted with their 'Silver Cloud' SWATH and in early 2009 began a voyage around the world!

SPECIFICATIONS:	ABEKING & RASMUSSEN 'SILVER CLOUD'
Length Overall:	41m (134'6")
Length Waterline:	37m (121')
Beam:	17.8m (58'5")
Draught:	4.10m (13'5")
Construction:	Steel hull and aluminium superstructure
Displacement:	601 ton
Designer interior:	Abeking & Rasmussen
Designer exterior:	Abeking & Rasmussen
Accommodation:	8 in 4 staterooms
Crew:	10
Max. Speed:	14 knots
Cruising Speed:	10 knots
Range at 12 knots:	3,500 nm
Main engines:	2 Caterpillar C32 820kW
Classification:	GL 100 A5 'MOTOR YACHT'/ MCA, LY2

Above & Left:
Both the main salon and the owner's stateroom are characterised by their huge size.

Far Left:
All the guest cabins are beautifully appointed.

LÜRSSEN
YACHTS

More beautiful, faster, better, first: these are the qualities that the Fr. Lürssen Werft Boatbuilding Company has been cultivating for more than 130 years and that have raised it to the pinnacle of the luxury yacht industry. From the beginning quality, performance and innovation have been the features that have made Lürssen what it is today - an internationally renowned, complete shipbuilder, with sales, design, manufacture, development, yacht management, service and logistics facilities.

The goal of being first and best in all classes was achieved early on and repeated over and over again. In 1886, for example, Friedrich Lürssen, together with the legendary engineers Gottlieb Daimler and Wilhelm Maybach, constructed the world's first motor boat, the 'Rems'. Another early success was the construction in 1905 of the speedboat 'Donnerwetter', beginning a series of successes for the shipyard at all of the European motor boat races. The 1912 'Saurer Lürssen' with Otto Lürssen at the helm, was able to win a string of trophies at the famous 'Prix de Monte Carlo'- another true racer.

Nowadays, Lürssen leads the way in the construction of many of the world's finest luxury superyachts. The names of yachts such as 'Izanami', 'The One', 'Limitless', 'Carinthia VII', 'Pelorus', 'Octopus', 'Rising Sun', 'Ice', 'Eos' and 'Kismet', stand for taste, perfection, purity, grace, dignity, beauty and character. Working with world famous architects and engineers such as Sir Norman Foster, Jon Bannenberg, Tim Heywood and Espen Oeino, every yacht built at Lürssen has the family name on it and a true pedigree of the finest quality and craftsmanship.

Above:
The beautifully stylish 95m (321')
'Carinthia VII'.

Left:
At 126m (414'), the motor yacht
'Octopus' is one of the largest yachts in
the world.

Far Left:
Just part of Lürssen's expansive luxury
yacht building and refitting facilities.

Centre Left:
The speedboat 'Donnerwetter' was
built by Lürssen in 1905.

LÙRSSEN YACHTS

'MADSUMMER'

Built by Lürssen and styled by Espen Oeino, 'Madsummer's eye-catching design and baby blue hull clearly set her apart from her peers. Once onboard you easily feel that this also applies to the Alberto Pinto designed interior. Delivered in November 2008, the owner's captain, Chris Beirne, and yacht broker, Robert Moran of Moran Yacht & Ship, had supervised the project and brought in their huge spectrum of experience.

The layout is a very 'private' one and is not what one would expect on a 78m yacht. No generous foyer, no massive staircases – it is not your typical 'show-off' yacht. 'Madsummer' is built for an owner who likes his privacy. On the one hand, the huge private area on the owner's deck with its own Jacuzzi and sunbathing spaces underlines the privacy of this yacht. On the other hand, her layout, with lots of spaces with different salons, dining and relaxation areas, allows her to entertain a large number of guests.

Guests enter the yacht through the lobby on the main deck, which has both a staircase and an elevator. A long stylish passageway, decorated in woven platane wood and maple, leads to the guest cabins forward.

Four very generous VIP suites with king-size beds, plus one regular guest cabin with twin beds are at the disposal of the guests on this deck. The guest suites are all decorated in a similar style, but using different colours and different stone – either perlatino or travertin - in each cabin. Each has a plasma TV screen, a bathroom with bathtub and shower as well as a dressing room. A possible sixth cabin has been laid out as a children's playroom and cinema.

The main lobby leads aft to the main salon, which is divided into two areas. One part is reserved for dining and, instead of one large dining table, two round tables offer the guests a very congenial place for having either a formal or a casual dining experience. The adjoining wall to the main salon separates the dining area from the more casual part of the main salon and offers four different seating areas, either for enjoying a movie, for playing cards or just for relaxing

Above & Left:
The stylish 'Madsummer' was built in 2008 for a private owner.

Far Left:
The top deck pool and pool bar are beautifully designed to take in the sunny surroundings.

Centre:
The owner's deck at night.

LÙRSSEN YACHTS

and reading a book. Outside on the aft deck another large seating area and huge sun bed offer more space to relax and enjoy the sunshine.

One deck higher is the owner's deck. The aft outside seating area is covered by the helideck above and is well protected from sun or rain. Further forward, there is another generous salon for relaxing, watching television or enjoying a drink at the bar. The panelled walls are covered with West African zebrano wood giving this space a very special and soothing effect.

The lobby on the owner's deck leads forward into the 130m² owner's private area where a 180° front view provides superb ocean views and floods the room with natural light. Two side doors give access to the owner's personal sun deck forward with a Jacuzzi and a seating area. Much space has been allocated to his and hers bathrooms as well as to the dressing rooms. The design is again very elegant and clean – instead of massive marble floors the bathroom is furnished in a variety of exotic woods.

One deck above is the bridge deck that is mainly operational. In addition to the very generous wheelhouse, the captain has his own area with an office. Two further staff cabins are available for additional personnel, such as helicopter crew. The bridge is laid out with its navigation table placed centrally and set back from the main console, flanked by two guest sofas. The large aft deck is reserved for the helipad, complete with refuelling station.

Last but not least, a stairway leads to the top deck dominated by a midships bar and two adjacent pools – one with a jet stream for swimming and the other one a large Jacuzzi for up to ten people. Recreation plays a major role onboard – there is well-equipped gym on the lower deck with a spa that extends onto a large fold-down sea terrace.

Technically, 'Madsummer', is a high-tech yacht with many interesting features, highlighted against others by the vaulted ceiling in the generously laid out engine room. Powered by two Caterpillar engines of 2,000 kW each, she reaches a top speed of 17 knots. Built to Lloyd's Register, this Lürssen can literally, cruise all around the world.

SPECIFICATIONS:	LÜRSSEN YACHTS 'MADSUMMER'
Length Overall:	78.40m (257'2")
Length Waterline:	66.70m (218'8")
Beam:	13.50m (44'3")
Draught:	3.80m (12'5")
Construction:	Steel hull and aluminium superstructure
Displacement:	1,978 ton
Designer interior:	Alberto Pinto
Designer exterior:	Espen Øino International
Guests:	12
Crew:	32
Max. Speed:	17 knots
Range at 12 knots:	6,000 nm
Main engines:	2 Caterpillar 3516 DI TA SCAC 2000 kw at 1600 rpm
Fuel capacity:	126 ton
Fresh water capacity:	40 ton
Stabilizers:	4 Quantum Zero Speed
Bow Thruster:	Brunvoll 240kW
Classification:	LRoS - + 100A1 SSC Yacht mono, G6 + LMC UMS
Year Built:	2008

Above:
The luxurious main salon combines beautiful woodwork with vibrant colours to create a highly relaxing environment.

Left:
The owner's stateroom features a 180° front facing view.

Far Left:
The sumptuous upper deck salon provides luxurious seating and dining.

LÜRSSEN YACHTS

'VIVE LA VIE'

Delivered in June 2008, and built by Lürssen together with the highly professional interior designers of Art-Line, the 60m 'Vive la Vie' is a very refreshing yacht featuring many new ideas and design features.

The first 'wow-effect' occurs immediately you enter the main foyer. The staircase dominating the foyer is in itself a piece of art. Overlooking the stairwell the spectacular glass bridges are suspended in woven steel grills. These bridges lead you from the foyer either to the main stairs or to a glass elevator. Seemingly floating carpeted steps lead up to the bridge deck or down to the lower deck. An illuminated glass sculpture is incorporated within the glass elevator where the lighting can be programmed to change colour depending on the day or night mood one would like to create.

Going aft, the main foyer leads into the main salon that, although it is designed in a very open way, incorporates four separate areas. On the starboard side there is a veranda on a raised wooden floor. The outside border of the ceiling is styled in wooden waves underlining this separate relaxing area.

The square dining table is laid out for casual dining or breakfast for eight, while a third area is reserved for TV entertainment onboard, where four fabulous lounge chairs invite you to a relaxing view of your favourite movie. Last but not least, a circular seating area in white leather and with adjustable backs perfectly completes the main salon.

Forward of the main foyer a passageway leads past a powder room to a superb fitness area offering a wonderful view outside while exercising and on to the VIP cabin on the portside. The passageway continues further forward into a raised forward facing formal dining room.

The dining room is certainly an unusual feature on a yacht this size. Besides the fact that it is forward facing and offers the dining guests sweeping unimpeded views, it also performs a dual use. The table can be raised into the ceiling to allow the room to be used as a disco. The imitation

Above:
'Vive La Vie' is a very refreshing yacht featuring many new design features.

Left:
When at anchor, tenders and watersports toys may be deployed from the side garage.

Centre Left:
The private owner's deck.

Far Left:
The sun-deck features a large Jacuzzi, plenty of loungers and magnificent views.

LÜRSSEN
YACHTS

Lürssen Yachts
Zum Alten Speicher 11
28759 Bremen
Germany
Tel: +49 421 66 04 166
Fax: +49 421 66 04 170
Web: www.lurssen.com

crocodile leather table is in itself quite spectacular - the middle part of the table includes a woven copper element lit from below, but when the table is raised up it functions as a ceiling light.

Up the stairs to the bridge deck, which although housing the bridge and captain's cabin, is mainly reserved for the owner. Forward leads to the bridge and captain's quarters, while starboard is the owner's open lobby. Adjacent to the lobby is the owner's office that is effectively separated from the lobby and stairwell by a glass wall.

The owner's area is laid out in a grand fashion. The round owner's suite contains a bed on a rotating circular platform in the centre, allowing for a selection of bed positions from night to day time mode and for adjusting position to make the most of spectacular views through the full height windows. Gold leaf on the ceiling and designer lighting make for a very impressive room.

A fireplace in a glass column on the exterior private deck runs with bio alcohol gel. A very cosy place indeed to enjoy the surroundings and gaze at the stars!

One deck higher is the sun deck, where a sky-lounge 'tunnel' connects the fore and aft deck. Different coloured light settings can be chosen, changing the mood of this lounge from a nightclub to a beach house for different styles of entertainment. Further down, the guest cabins are on the lower deck – one double and three twin cabins – and are identical in design but with different colour schemes.

On the lower deck aft, two tenders are stored and can be launched by crane from either side through the large side shell doors. A multi-functional passarelle with an integrated lifting device can handle the two motorbikes that can be stored in the tender garage. The enlarged aft platform also functions as a bathing platform where guests can use a shower hidden in the back door.

Powered by two Caterpillar engines of 1,455 kW each, 'Vive la Vie' reaches a top speed of 15.5 knots. Built to Lloyd's Register this Lürssen can cruise all around the world and this is indeed what she is doing with her highly satisfied and proud owner.

SPECIFICATIONS:	LÜRSSEN YACHTS 'VIVE LA VIE'
Length Overall:	59.40m (195'2")
Length Waterline:	51.04m (167'5")
Beam:	11.10m (36'4")
Draught:	3.50m (11'5")
Construction:	Steel hull and aluminium superstructure
Displacement:	1,070 ton
Designer interior:	Art-Line Interiors BV
Designer exterior:	Lürssen Yachts
Guests:	12
Crew:	15
Max. Speed:	15.5 knots
Range at 12 knots:	7,000 nm
Main engines:	2 Caterpillar 3512B DITA each 1455 kw at 1835 rpm
Fuel capacity:	135 ton
Fresh water capacity:	43 ton
Stabilizers:	Quantum QC-1800 Zero Speed
Bow Thruster:	Jastram BU 40 F, 200kW
Classification:	LRoS - + 100A1 SSC Yacht mono, G6 + LMC UMS, MCA LY2
Year Built:	2008

Above:
The main salon and dining area.

Left:
The owner's stateroom features a bed on a rotating platform to ensure the best outside view at all times.

Far Left:
'Vive La Vie's staircase is a beautiful piece of art.

OCEANCO

With several impressive projects currently under construction, Oceanco has carved out a niche for itself in the 80m (262ft) sector, as one of the finest builders of superyachts in Holland. In an era where clients require evermore sophisticated yachts built in the shortest time span, Oceanco provides the ultimate in yacht design – technically, mechanically and aesthetically. With a reputation for realising the vision of owners, new clients have the confidence of seeing some of the world's most accomplished yachts built on time, on budget and to exceptional standards.

In April 2008, Oceanco acquired 57 000m² of land to expand the premises of its shipyard in Alblasserdam, The Netherlands. The new property will enable Oceanco to further develop the company's already substantial construction capacity by adding covered dry docks to the existing yacht building facility which includes a shed, a hull-building facility and a private harbour with a 130m quayside.

With these new facilities, Oceanco is able to give clients more than had ever been previously possible at any shipyard, by pushing the boundaries of yacht design with new and exciting projects that attest to the company's versatility and multi-faceted vision. With Y708 and PA090, Oceanco's designers are developing new concepts for a future that is not far away.

Right:
The 75.5m M/Y 'Anastasia'

Below Left:
Project Y708

Below Right:
Project PA090

Y708
Length overall 85.50m (280.52ft)

PA090
Length overall 115m (377.30ft)

OCEANCO   'ANASTASIA'

Delivered in June 2008, Y703, the 75.50m (247' 8") 'Anastasia' is the third of the new generation of Oceanco superyachts. With distinctive interior and exterior design by the renowned Australian designer Sam Sorgiovanni, this blue-hulled superyacht was presented at the 2008 Monaco Yacht Show where she was the star attraction. Only a few short months after her delivery, 'Anastasia' received the Yachts International award for the 'Most Innovative Yacht 2008' which was presented at the Cannes Boat Show in September 2008.

With her elegant, sweeping curves and pair of 'rocket' wings on top of her superstructure, 'Anastasia's exterior is a complete change from Oceanco's previous launch, the immensely powerful 'Alfa Nero', featured in Volume 2 of 'Luxury Yachts Of The World'.

To create 'Anastasia's distinct exterior look, Sam Sorgiovanni employed a raised bow and reversed sheer line to link 'Anastasia's various deck levels. The yacht's timeless exterior evokes the elegance of timber construction with a varnished wood transom, hand painted by the craftsmen at the Oceanco shipyard, to render the wood effect even more convincing.

'Anastasia's ageless interior design exudes a feeling of warmth and elegance. The prevailing theme of the interior is a comfortable and relaxing beach house atmosphere, which Sam Sorgiovanni has employed to perfection.

The interior is light and welcoming, accentuated by bold shapes and a subtle mix of textures with a solid and refined appearance. To stay within the scope of the beach house atmosphere, Sam Sorgiovanni has utilised a variety of woods such as bamboo, eucalyptus, white oak, wengé and macassar throughout the yacht's interior. Mock crocodile lined cubes have been used for bookcases or display shelves.

Among the interesting surface effects are small squares of stone-coloured resin into which repeated designs were impressed. The sand-ripple effect carpet continues

Above:
The sleek and stylish 'Anastasia'.

Left:
Al-fresco dining for 12 on the expansive aft upper deck.

Left Centre:
'Anastasia's stern is instantly recognisable.

Far Left:
'Anastasia' is superbly equipped and has a swimming pool and an abundance of loungers on the sundeck.

OCEANCO

the coastal theme with many of the cabins featuring original stunning seascapes artwork. The furniture aboard 'Anastasia' is a reflection of contemporary shapes coupled with the occasional art deco detail.

The starting point of 'Anastasia's exceptional layout is the lower deck with nearly half its length devoted to the tender garage. A real haven for water sports enthusiasts, the tender garage houses a wide array of water toys: six competition jet skis, four two-seater WaveRunners, two kayaks, an assortment of sailboards, windsurfers, towing toys, diving equipment and fishing gear, as well as a pair of 9.5m Vikal custom launches, a general-purpose open boat and an enclosed limousine. For the diving devotee, the lazarette includes a high-tech air-bottle filling station with a Nitrox mixing facility and top-of-the-range breathing sets fitted with underwater communications, as well as Apollo underwater scooters to pull divers along.

A beautiful glass aquarium with an artificial but life-like coral reef and a variety of exotic fish divides the main salon from the formal dining area on the main deck. One of the more interesting features of the interior layout is the ability of the main salon to be converted into a dance area with a full complement of equipment, from a smoke machine to lasers and disco lights. In addition, the outdoor furniture on the aft upper deck can be rearranged and transformed into a stage for a live band whose instruments can be hooked up to 'Anastasia's state-of-the-art sound system.

The salon on the upper deck is designed for a more relaxed atmosphere, accentuated by large sofas and armchairs with a large circular card table. A splendid three-deck high, glass sculpture depicting a forest of kelp inhabited by mysterious sea creatures adorns the centre of a passageway leading forward to the main stairs.

The large rectangular windows of 'Anastasia's four guest cabins in the forward part of the main deck give an open, airy feel thanks to their location well above the waterline. While all are double bedrooms with a bed, a sofa and an additional foldaway Pullman berth, two are rated

Above & Left:
The main salon and dining room are separated by a beautiful aquarium with an artificial but life-like coral reef and a variety of exotic fish.

Far Left:
The cinema onboard 'Anastasia' is equipped to show all the latest movies.

Centre Left:
A splendid three-deck high, glass sculpture depicting a forest of kelp inhabited by mysterious sea creatures, adorns the centre of a passageway leading forward to the main stairs.

OCEANCO

VIP and have both a bath and a shower.

A split-level apartment in the forward part of the upper deck, which can be reached through the upper lobby, provides the outstanding owner's suite. The first area incorporates a study with two-deck headroom, tall windows to the side and a modern desk in macassar wood that contrasts well with the carved bamboo floor. A passageway, lying parallel to the wardrobes, leads to the other side of the yacht, where a stairway rises to an upper-level bedroom conferring fantastic panoramic views through a 180-degree curve of the windows. The owner's suite also features a two-seat breakfast table on the upper deck terrace.

'Anastasia' is powered by twin 4000 series MTU main engines that can push her along at a maximum of 18 knots, while 14 knots in a single cruise gives a range of well over 4,000 nautical miles. With large tanks and plenty of storage capacity, 'Anastasia' has everything needed for lengthy expeditions.

SPECIFICATIONS:	Y703 - 'ANASTASIA'
Length Overall:	75.50m (247' 8")
Beam:	13.40m (43' 11")
Draught:	3.80m (12' 6")
Gross Weight:	2200 ton
Guest Accommodation:	12 in 6 staterooms
Crew:	20
Naval Architecture:	Oceanco
Exterior Styling:	Sam Sorgiovanni Designs
Interior Design:	Sam Sorgiovanni Designs
Construction:	Steel hull / Alum. superstructure
Engines:	2 x MTU 16V 4000 M90 3650hp each
Max. Speed:	18 knots
Cruise Speed:	15 knots
Range:	4,000 + nautical miles

Above & Left:
The VIP staterooms.

Far Left:
All of the guest staterooms are
beautifully furnished.

Centre Left:
'Anastasia' is instantly recognisable
wherever she cruises.

OCEANCO

Oceanco Yard
Zuiderstek 40
2952 AZ Alblasserdam
P.O. Box 20
2950 AA Alblasserdam
The Netherlands
Tel: +31 78 699 5399
Fax: +31 78 699 5398

Oceanco
Gildo Pastor Center
7, Rue du Gabian,
MC 98000, Monaco
Tel: +377 93 10 02 81
Fax: +377 92 05 65 99
Web: www.oceancoyacht.com

Opposite & Below Right:
Project Y708.

Below Left:
Project PA090.

Y708

The latest addition to Oceanco's tailor-made luxury yachts under construction is Y708 – an 85.50m (280.52ft) yacht with an innovative exterior design by Igor Lobanov. With a sleek and elegant silhouette, Y708 is the first superyacht in the 85m range to feature a layered deck design.

The design of this spectacular yacht has been based on the notion of privacy which is evident in the layout of both the interior and the exterior deck area. Each deck has its own balcony allowing guests to enjoy themselves in complete privacy.

The owner of Y708 will have two private decks offering breathtaking panoramic views both aft and forward. In addition to a private sun deck with a whirlpool and a sunbathing area, the owner's deck comprises a suite, salon, study and an aft open deck with balconies all around the front.

The upper deck features sliding wing stations and an open forecastle deck with a runway. This deck also houses two VIP cabins each with its own balcony and automatic foldable bulwarks. Guests seeking privacy can relax in the library and cigar room located further aft on the upper deck.

The main deck below hosts an airy formal dining room and a sushi bar. A lounge area ideal to host and entertain guests and a large swimming pool convertible into a helicopter landing area are located on the exterior aft main deck. Further down, on the lower deck, is a gym and an exclusive health spa complete with a massage room and hammam.

Y708 can accommodate twelve guests divided over two double VIP cabins, three double guest cabins and one twin guest cabin. The captain of this impressive 85m superyacht will be accommodated in a spacious cabin/apartment with his own salon, office and bedroom.

This technically-impressive superyacht is equipped with twin MTU 20V 4000 M73L diesel engines and has a

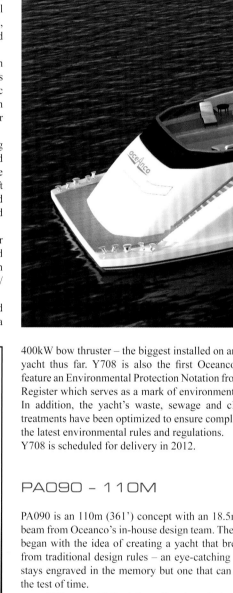

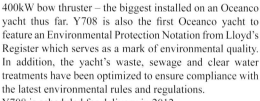

400kW bow thruster – the biggest installed on an Oceanco yacht thus far. Y708 is also the first Oceanco yacht to feature an Environmental Protection Notation from Lloyd's Register which serves as a mark of environmental quality. In addition, the yacht's waste, sewage and clear water treatments have been optimized to ensure compliance with the latest environmental rules and regulations.
Y708 is scheduled for delivery in 2012.

PA090 – 110M

PA090 is an 110m (361') concept with an 18.5m (60' 8") beam from Oceanco's in-house design team. The designers began with the idea of creating a yacht that breaks away from traditional design rules – an eye-catching yacht that stays engraved in the memory but one that can withstand the test of time.

With a sophisticated profile characterised by racy exterior lines and curves, PA090 is a unique and innovative project with the volume of a typical 110m superyacht but without the conventional design that usually accompanies a yacht of such large proportions.

One of PA090's most prominent design features is a two-deck glass atrium, which, when seen in profile, takes the form of a large glass column.

oceAnco   PA090

From the exterior, the atrium transforms into a vertical axe that cuts through the yacht's profile and intensifies the sporty look of the superstructure.

PA090 is Oceanco's first project compatible with SOLAS specifications and, as such, the preliminary interior layout allows for accommodation of twenty two guests in eight guest cabins, two VIP suites and one master stateroom with an overlooking skylight.

Some of the yacht's exceptional features include a state-of-the-art 160m² health spa, specially designed to offer comprehensive spa treatments, a 10m x 7m swimming pool on the aft main deck, a fully-equipped gym, a spacious tender garage with two 15m tender limousines and a large home theatre. The main staircase and elevator are accessible directly from the tender garage and lead all the way up to the sundeck.

This 110m yacht has been designed with an MCA-approved helicopter landing pad on the sundeck and a retractable, telescopic helicopter garage. In addition to advanced anti-pirate systems, PA090 will feature the latest green technologies developed in accordance with the current environmental rules and legislations. Thanks to a truly unique and innovative design feature, guests can enter the yacht through a glass tunnel underneath the swimming pool that leads directly into the spectacular atrium that flows through both the main and upper deck.

PLATINUM YACHTS

PLATINUM YACHTS

Platinum Yachts (PY) is a part of Drydocks World, a group of shipyards located in Dubai, Singapore and Indonesia, employing a workforce of about 30,000. The core business of Platinum Yachts is the construction of custom and semi-custom built megayachts, as well as the conversion and repair of large motor and sailing yachts. Boasting its own in-house interior design and decoration office, and fully equipped naval architecture and engineering departments, Platinum Yachts production team consists of mechanical, electrical, structural, hull treatment and interior and exterior outfitting units. A huge array of work, either in-house or in close collaboration with other specialist companies, can therefore be handled in-house using the extensive facilities Platinum Yachts have access to.

Currently Platinum Yachts is located in the free zone area of Jebel Ali port. Not only does the company have dedicated offices, warehouses and workshops for the various activities there, it also has the use of a floating dry-dock capable of serving yachts up to 200m in length and up to 10 000 tons gross weight. The company has an additional 400m of quayside space suitable for outfitting yachts alongside its facility.

In 2009 Platinum Yachts will move to Dubai Maritime City (DMC), a man-made peninsula in the heart of Dubai, specifically made for the maritime industry. The facilities within DMC include large outfitting quays, two synchro-lifts (3000 tons and 6000 tons), a transfer area and numerous smaller and larger dry berths. Platinum Yachts are commissioning three fully air-conditioned sheds - two of 100m and one of 150m. Platinum Yachts will have its new offices next to these superb facilities.

Above:
At 162m (524' 10") in length, M/Y 'Dubai' is currently the world's largest yacht.

Far Left:
The stylish 88m 'Triton Project'.

Left:
Platinum's impressive new yacht building facilities, will be a match for any in the world.

PLATINUM YACHTS

M/Y 'DUBAI'

In 2001, after purchasing the bare hull and part of the superstructure of the abandoned project 'Panhandle' from the Blohm & Voss and Lürssen shipyards, Platinum started on the completion of what was to become the world's largest yacht, the incredible M/Y 'Dubai'.

At the time of purchase, the hull had no outfitting whatsoever (no pipes or cable trays or foundations) and part of the superstructure was just stepped on the hull, not welded.

Some of the equipment including main engines and generators were stored in containers. The whole lot was transferred on a floating dock to Dubai to perform the necessary works to complete the project with a new interior design, suitable for the new owner.

It took some time to bring things to order, but the main progress happened when Platinum Yachts engaged the additional services of Drydocks World - Dubai, the biggest shipyard in Dubai, which is widely recognised as one of the finest ship refitters in the world. M/Y 'Dubai' was handed over to her owner in 2005, but final certification by Lloyd's Register of Shipping was given in 2006 after a number of materials in the interior were modified in order to meet the requisite SOLAS standards.

Though the project was completed successfully, it had proved a very steep learning curve for Platinum Yachts, who, with its efficient management and dedicated workforce, had risen to the challenge and achieved what many thought was an impossible task for such a new yard. It was, in essence, a full new-build, starting with a semi-completed hull and superstructure and an incomplete package of drawings and materials purchased from the initial yard that had begun the project.

All drawings and engineering were reviewed and completed by Platinum Yachts' own in-house engineering and design office, and the interior design was again done in-house by the company's interior design and decoration team.

Right & Below:
The 162m (524' 10") M/Y 'Dubai' has been built to the highest standards and luxuriously furnished.

PLATINUM YACHTS

S/Y 'DUBAI MAGIC'

Not content with completing the world's largest yacht, Platinum Yachts has recently completed the conversion of a 45m three-mast schooner, the 'Dubai Magic'.

Constructed in Turkey in steel, S/Y 'Dubai Magic' was stripped completely to her bare hull, then re-welded to increase her strength and to bring her up to the standard demanded.

Platinum Yachts then added more fuel tanks to increase the range, as well as zero-speed fin stabilisers, new rigging and sails, new generators and other machinery equipment, a completely new interior, new teak decks, AV/ IT equipment, and new HVAC to cope with the Middle East conditions.

Finally, she was completely faired and painted. In all, the conversion took 14 months and she was delivered to her owner at the end of 2007.

M/Y 'DUBAWI'

With the completion of M/Y 'Dubai' providing invaluable experience for the yard, in August 2007 Platinum started on the conversion of a 90m cruise-ship (ex Renaissance series, built in Italy in 1989) to a private yacht, now called 'Dubawi'.

A vessel that offers a wonderfully large volume compared to her length, Platinum completed the whole conversion in just 18 months, with the delivery in January of 2009. The work undertaken on board was extensive and included the upgrade and renovation of much of the engine room equipment, such as the replacement of the chilled water-plant and the overhaul of the main engines and generators.

Now fitted with state of the art machinery throughout, 'Dubawi's excellent manoeuvring characteristics allow access to all major marinas and bays for extensive cruising and water-sports enjoyment.

Without doubt the most important part of the

Above and Far Left:
The 90m M/Y 'Dubawi' has been converted by Platinum Yachts from a cruise ship into a highly luxurious private yacht.

Left & Centre:
The 45m three-masted schooner S/Y 'Dubai Magic', is a beautiful sight to behold when under full sail.

PLATINUM YACHTS

conversion however, was the total design and refurbishment of the interior spaces. Platinum replaced the complete guest interior with a high quality new luxury interior for the yacht's owner and his guests. The new accommodation includes one owner's cabin on the top deck, one owner's suite on the lower deck, eight VIP suites and twelve guest cabins. This luxury accommodation includes a variety of salons and dining rooms for entertaining large groups of guests. The conversion of this 90m ex-cruise ship to a luxury superyacht has proved very successful, delivering to the owners their exact requirements in record time.

THE 'TRITON' PROJECT

Next on the drawing board at Platinum Yachts, 'The 'Triton' Project' is an 88m diesel / electric yacht, soon to be constructed in Dubai. With exterior design and styling by the well-respected Sam Sorgiovanni Designs in Australia, and with the naval architecture under the supervision of Azure Naval Architects from The Netherlands, this stunning yacht will have a pedigree second to none.

The project started towards the end of 2007 in close collaboration with the yacht's owner, the aim being to develop a superior looking mega-yacht with the ability to utilise the basic parameters of the vessel as a platform for future developments at the shipyard. Platinum's strategy for this project was to use well-known and experienced subcontractors for all the design and intrinsic works and couple them with the yard's experienced local workforce in Dubai in order to economise on outlay. As a result, Platinum is using Imtech for the whole electrical package, including the electrical propulsion, Heinen & Hopman for the air conditioning, Yachting Protection (Florakis) for the painting, and some of the best European interior outfitters for the luxury interior. All the main equipment to be installed on the yacht, such as the communication, propulsion and entertainment systems, is being ordered from some of the best known companies in the world, to ensure the yacht is completed to the highest quality standards. Under

Above:
An aerial view of M/Y 'Triton' shows her expansive deck space.

Left & Centre:
The luxuriously appointed main salon.

Far Left:
One of the stylish guest staterooms.

PLATINUM YACHTS

Platinum Yachts FZCO
P.O.Box 17215
Jebel Ali, Dubai
UAE
T: +971 4 8833323
F: +971 4 8833686
E: info@platinumyachts.ae
W: www.platinumyachts.ae

Platinum's project management, Drydocks World - Dubai (DDW-D) will make use of its extensive experience when constructing the steel hull and installing the machinery, as well as undertaking the detailed engineering for the machinery spaces. Within the DDW-D scope is the construction of the aluminium superstructure that the yard has ordered as a building kit from The Netherlands.

Following the completion of the hull, superstructure and machinery, M/Y 'Triton' is scheduled to undertake full trials and following the successful completion of these, the yacht will be taken to Platinum's new installation facilities in Dubai Maritime City. There, the rest of the works will take place, namely the interior and exterior outfitting in a climatically controlled environment.

This stylish megayacht has a very high volume, with 1300m^2 of luxury space, when compared to other yachts of similar length.

M/Y 'Triton' has aesthetically pleasing lines that will always be in style. The yacht's hull is to be painted in a metallic "gold-beige" colour and, taking into account this darker colour, the HVAC has been designed for Middle Eastern conditions.

Equipped to European quality standards, 'Triton' will have many state of the art features. The single deck engine room provides a larger interior space for the given volume with better circulation, and opening bulwark flaps aft create a very large 'beach' area together with swimming pool, sunbathing area and beach bar. The yacht will be powered by diesel / electric engines with conventional shafts, a feature which incorporates the good characteristics of the diesel / electric engine system with the reliability and easy maintenance of the conventional shafts / propulsion system.

The plan for Platinum Yachts will be to capitalise on the engineering of the first M/Y 'Triton' and reproduce it, using the same hull design but with different styling, a different superstructure and alternative layout arrangements, to ensure the individuality of every yacht. By using the same tested machinery and other equipment however, owners of this new breed of superyacht will receive a yacht built to the highest quality standards at a price comparable to any yacht of this size in the world.

SPECIFICATIONS:	M/Y 'TRITON'
Length Overall:	87.30m (286' 5")
Length Waterline:	74.10m (243' 2")
Beam:	14.60m (47'11")
Draught::	4.40m (14'5")
Displacement:	2650 ton
Guests:	14
Crew:	29
Tenders:	2 x 11.00m
Max Speed:	19 knots
Cruising Speed:	15 knots
Range @ 15 knots:	5,000 nautical miles
Fuel Capacity:	250 ton
Fresh Water Capacity:	80 ton
Classification:	Lloyd's Register X 100A1 SSC Yacht (P) Mono G6 X LMC, UMS, SCM MCA Large Commercial Yacht Code (LY2) Compliant

Above:
The 88m M/Y 'Triton' is a truly majestic yacht.

Left:
The 'infinity' Jacuzzi and pool.

Far Left:
When at anchor, the stern of the 88m M/Y 'Triton' transforms into a huge swim platform.

ANTIBES SHIPSERVICES

Established for over 30 years, Antibes Shipservices supplies motor and sailing yachts with chandlery, deck hardware, marine paints, spare parts & repairs and associated services from Antibes, in the south of France, the world's YACHTING CAPITAL PAR EXCELLENCE !

The trusted partner of major yacht brokers, charter brokers and managing agents for their yachts cruising in the Mediterranean Sea, we endeavour to uphold YOUR reputation.

Reliable, prompt and cost-effective support of commercial yachts chartering in the Mediterranean.

Our own regular delivery service encompasses Monaco to Cannes with deliveries (by prior arrangement) assured between La Spezia and Marseille as well as by 24 hour courier service worldwide.

Antibes Shipservices
12/16 Boulevard d'Aguillon 06600, Antibes, France
T:+33(0)4 93 34 68 00 - F:+33(0)4 93 34 53 95
E: info@antibes-ship.com - W: www.antibes-ship.com

CHARTER & BROKERAGE

PRINCESS MARIANA
79M (257'10") | ROYAL DENSHIP | 2003/2006 | LYING: CARIBBEAN
WINTER CHARTER RATE: 610,000 EUR PW

Fraser Yachts is the world's leading luxury yacht charter company, specialising in the finest private yachts, international destinations and captivating experiences. A superyacht offers all the benefits and facilities of a floating villa enabling you to explore a variety of exciting destinations amidst luxury, comfort and privacy. As a guest on a charter yacht you're able to customise every aspect of your holiday making it a true seven-star experience.

Please contact us to request your personal copy of our limited edition 2010 Charter Portfolio.

marketing@fraseryachts.com

A Tradition of Innovation

Our experience ensures that yours is truly memorable.
The world leaders in luxury yacht charters.

Sales | Charter | Management | Construction | Crew

Monaco   Seattle
Ft. Lauderdale Newport, RI
San Diego   Mexico City
London   Auckland
Milan   Casa De Campo
Palma

FRASER YACHTS

fraseryachts.com

INTERNATIONAL YACHT COLLECTION

YACHT SALES

YACHT CHARTER

THE WORLD

...IS OUR HOME PORT

WHAT IS A GOOD DEAL IN YACHTING TODAY

Right:
The 49.9m (163'8") 'Lady Ann Magee' is currently for sale through YPI.

Below Left:
The inside of a good broker's office is a hive of activity.

Below Right:
A good deal depends on the yacht itself.

Having the time and money to invest in purchasing a yacht can be an exciting but daunting proposition especially when 'great deals' and 'price reductions' are being shouted out at you from all corners. Robert Strand has been following the trends in luxury yachting for the last 15 years and he now speaks with the team at Yachting Partners International (YPI Group) to find out more about what really makes a 'good deal' in yachting today.

'One man's meat…another man's poison'. That was how one owner described the notion of what 'a good deal' was when I first mentioned I was writing this article. I knew exactly what he meant. The concept of 'a good deal' is, after all, a particularly subjective one dependent on each buyer's perceived value of the yacht - those aspects seen as qualities rather than drawbacks; selling points rather than hindrances. And of course, it also depends on what the buyer is actually looking for from a yacht.

For many, 'a good deal' would seem to be about price – the implication being that a yacht with its price slashed by ten million dollars is a yacht offered at a heavily discounted rate. A good deal, it would seem. But Matt Albert, Sales and New Construction Broker with YPI Brokerage does not agree. "Since 2005 the yachting market has seen some fairly significant price rises. A lot of what we have been seeing over the last year or so is more of a price correction…and in some cases it is still not corrected

enough." Good news then for potential buyers, but are they all good deals? "It all depends on the yacht itself," explains Matt. "It depends on its history, age, any repair work and refits it has gone through and when. To know whether it is a good deal or not requires looking into the background of the yacht." So price drops and reductions, no matter how big, are not always the answer it would seem - if anything they might even flag up a risky investment. "It is so important now to get sound advice on the yachts you think might be worth looking at. Price should rarely be your starting point when looking for the right package for yourself," adds Matt.

In fact 'good value' is not just about the price you can buy your yacht for, but the opportunities or hindrances it may present in terms of potential future chartering, running costs, crewing, eventual upgrades and refits and of course re-sale price.

"It is useful to have experience of all the elements in the process in order to be able to really understand whether you are getting value for money or not," advises Matt. "Only then can you really make an educated decision on the

investment." The choices are very personal. Some buyers are looking purely for short-term investment opportunities. For some, the notion of chartering is almost abhorrent. Some expect to sell on within a few years or even months, some expect to keep it in the family for generations.

Matt uses the example of a classic 40-metre Feadship, a great brand from a shipyard with excellent build quality, known for building yachts timeless in their design and look. "The Feadship may represent a great deal in terms of purchase price for example," he begins. "For five or six million dollars you get a lot of boat for a relatively small amount of money. But once you have bought it, then what? The reality then is you own a yacht with a crew of eight and a bill to pay of something in the region of two million dollars a year to run it. Add to that the fact that you will probably need to put in some serious capital refit costs to keep the yacht at the level you expect, which in turn means keeping her out of the water for six months which incurs yet more costs…and before you know it, your budget to feed your passion for yachting is well and truly blown."

All of which brings us back to the notion that 'real'

WHAT'S A GOOD DEAL IN YACHTING TODAY

value is not just about price, but about finding the right yacht to suit you.

"Some clients would love that Feadship as a project," Matt continues, "they would feel as though they were getting great value for money. They have the chance to stamp their mark on the yacht and when the refit is complete, they have a superb yacht re-designed to suit their own tastes for at least another five to ten years."

For others though, far from being a dream, this would be hell on earth. "For some it really is K.I.S.S - Keep It Simple Stupid. They want a nice yacht without too much to think about and plenty of fun time. So no matter how enticing the price in my example here of the Feadship would be, it would not be the yacht for them. A Benetti, even one at a slightly higher purchase price, but with only five or six crew and no refit worries would be much more appropriate."

Buyer profiling, it would seem, more than ever, lies at the heart of today's successful yacht purchases. When advising clients, all the brokers in YPI Brokerage take great care to listen to what their clients are asking them for and how they intend to use the yacht. "In some ways we are less sales people than consultants," offers Matt. "Our business is not built on making a fast buck. Even when clients decide quickly on a yacht they like – and that happens more often than you might think – the 'deals' are just as thoroughly researched and checked as the more long term buys…in many cases even more so. We take the long view that as a business we are stronger and more solid when clients are still enjoying the benefits of their purchases long after they have forgotten how much they invested."

Brokers are there to supply you with the information you need to know when it comes to deciding which yachts best suit you. How clear and detailed that information is when choosing your yacht is key. In essence it is your broker's responsibility to present the most intelligent and accurate information about the yacht - it is important not only in terms of the acquisition but also when it comes

to selling at a later date. As Bertrand Vogèle, YPI Group Managing Director explains: "It is vital for our brokers to explain to potential owners the facts and the figures in as much detail as they have available…and if the broker doesn't know the complete story he has to say so. I believe this not only builds up trust, but it demonstrates an element of transparency."

There are few, even amongst those fresh to the yachting industry, who have not heard stories of 'overly inflated' valuations and 'over-looked' blemishes designed to encourage unwitting buyers to invest in floating assets and dream purchases worth well below what they are paying. Many will tell you that in such a competitive arena, it is commonplace for yacht brokers, as with any other brokerage industry, to retain information or knowledge they believe could in fact 'blow a deal'. But in all its 37 years, Yachting Partners International has never been accused of that. The fundamental philosophy at the core of the YPI Group has always been to make sure everything is on the table – the good, the bad and the ugly. "The truth hurts sometimes," explains Group Chairman Alex Braden, "but it's the truth. We deliver a 'warts and all' approach – a candid opinion on the true value, rather than simply delivering the answer the owner wants to hear." Alex admits this policy may have lost the Group some potential clients over the years but as he says, "it has retained our

integrity and professional relations with all our key clients and everyone they recommend us to." In yacht brokerage, if a broker or the brokerage house loses its integrity you have to ask the question...what is left?

What of those wishing to invest in a new construction? Where is the 'good deal' in that?

YPI Management consists of some of the industry's most qualified individuals and master mariners with experience in naval architecture, marine engineering, environmental engineering and project management. Franc Jansen, YPI Director and Head of YPI Management says, "You can't expect one person to be an expert in everything...in the yachting business however you have to expect everyone to be an expert in something." Franc's team works very closely with YPI Brokerage to ensure clients investing in a new construction not only get the best deal in terms of yard rates and tariffs but in terms of the yacht design, materials and engineering efficiency. "Very often the best time to save money is before you've spent it," smiles Franc. "Real savings happen in the design stage. We have saved so many clients a lot of potential outlay by working with top designers and engineers to find and research the best systems, engines and materials to bring about the most efficient running yachts of today." And this, for Franc, is the real value in know-how and team play. This is what clients find so reassuring. There are precious

Above & Left:
The YPI managed 'Aquamarina'
built at the ISA yard in Ancona, is
a fine example of a successful yacht
construction project.

WHAT'S A GOOD DEAL IN YACHTING TODAY

few, I dare say, who would ever deny that the ultimate in 'good value' is 'peace of mind.'

In fact 'peace of mind' is something all the divisions in YPI constantly work together to ensure all clients get to benefit from. YPI Crew is one Division that works very closely with all the others, its role pivotal in helping to ensure yachts are run and maintained as efficiently as possible. YPI Crew Director Laurence Reymann explains. "We get to know our clients well from all angles. The matchmaking - understanding the needs of our clients and our candidates - is a particular strength of YPI Crew. When we send out three or four CVs to a client that probably means we have interviewed ten to twelve candidates." And at times such as the world has been experiencing since the end of 2008, the time and money saved in finding the right crew for the right yachts is not negligible. "Crew, the Captain, the Engineer, the Steward, the Chef…these people are the heart of the yacht. Get those people wrong and that will cost you money and time."

So it would seem we are back to money when it comes to value and a good deal, but not money spent – money saved. Real value may actually come from the extra help, guidance and expertise we benefit from when we spend wisely.

YPI Charter is a Division that helps clients both save and earn. "Our clients are owners who want to charter their yachts and those who want to book the very best private yachts for holidays," explains Director and Head of YPI Charter, Catherine Ambrogi. "The team at YPI Charter do a lot of leg work for our clients so they can benefit from the very best advice possible. We all cruise, travel, inspect a lot of yachts and attend lots of familiarity trips in order to amass information, to find the best boats and the best crew." This information is instrumental in matching clients to yachts and crew that best suit their needs and preferences…it saves lots of time and money and heartache.

And that, one would assume, brings us back to 'peace of mind' once more.

For me, having spoken with the team at Yachting Partners International, where you will find the real value in yachting – where the really 'good deals' properly lie - is in finding 'peace of mind'. When you can turn to someone and tell them you have found the perfect yacht, because it is the one you can see delivering on all the things you hoped it would…then you have found 'a great deal'. Today, more than ever before, it will probably have been a well-informed, intelligent and brutally honest broker who, in part at least, will have helped bring you and that all important 'peace of mind' together.

If it was…remember one thing…
they are only doing their job!

YACHTING PARTNERS INTERNATIONAL

UK: T: +44 1273 571 722 - E: brighton@ypigroup.com
France: T: +33 493 34 01 00 - E: antibes@ypigroup.com
Monaco: T: +377 99 99 97 97 - E: monaco@ypigroup.com
Web: www.ypigroup.com

Above:
YPI have considerable expertise in selling and chartering sailing yachts as well as motor yachts.
Photo: Paul Coleshill / rawphoto.co.uk

Left:
The 38.7m (125') motor yacht 'Gladius' is for sale and charter through YPI.

Far Left:
When you can turn to someone and tell them you have found the perfect yacht, because it is the one you can see delivering on all the things you hoped it would...then you have found 'a great deal'.

A Cruise Aboard 'NERO'

Completed as a new build in 2008, the 90.1m (295' 6") motor yacht, 'Nero', was inspired by the 'Corsair' series of yachts owned in the early part of the last century by the financier J.P.Morgan. She truly captures the magic of that golden age with a huge sun- or promenade-deck and multiple exterior seating and dining areas and is, without doubt, one of the finest luxury yachts ever to be offered for charter.

'Nero's traditional exterior features a great deal of best quality Burmese teak. With huge capping rails, a beautifully laid swept-deck and traditionally styled deck furniture the yacht has many unique and original features.

The designer of 'Nero' was very careful to make sure that the yacht had a feel of cosiness despite her large size. It was thought important that the yacht could adapt to being a cosy family boat as well as a grand entertaining platform. To that end 'Nero' features a wide range of differently styled dining and relaxing areas to cater to the exact number of guests aboard and the mood of the occasion.

Not only beautiful to look at, 'Nero' is a strong and sea-kindly ship. With her efficient hull and the latest in stabilisation systems, she cruises through rough seas at over 16 knots with the minimum of roll and pitch. Many of the visitors and crew aboard have commented on her favourable ride compared with vessels with more modern styling. The hull was designed to help 'iron out' the typical Mediterranean swell of about two metres and ensure the greatest levels of comfort.

Beneath the skin 'Nero' is a truly modern superyacht offering all the latest developments in construction and design, resulting in low noise levels and refinements unheard of with an original classic yacht. Benefiting from the latest Naiad four-fin 'Zero Speed' stabilisation system and large bilge keels, she provides the highest levels of comfort whether underway or at anchor. 'Nero' is supremely at ease even when sitting side-on to a large and persistent Caribbean swell. In addition the owner and guest cabins have been placed as near to the mid-ships section of the yacht as possible, ensuring the most pleasant passage making for her guests.

Onboard, 'Nero' features a traditional raised and fielded wood panelled interior. The entire yacht, including the crew's quarters, is fitted out in ash and limed oak panelling with the extraordinary quality interior joinery featuring many curved panels and lobbies.

The yacht is configured with the main deck as the principle entertaining area for larger gatherings, with the aft deck table ideal for larger dinner parties. The spacious main salon, library and dining salon offer the capacity to entertain on a grand scale, while the various lobbies on the yacht illustrate the extraordinary quality of the joinery on board.

Right, Below Left & Centre:
'Nero', was inspired by the 'Corsair' series of yachts owned in the early part of the last century by the financier J.P.Morgan.

Below Right:
The boat-deck aft living area is one of the favourite gathering spots on the yacht and is very popular for relaxing and entertaining.

A CRUISE ABOARD 'NERO'

BURGESS

Right:

The spacious main salon, library and dining salon offer the capacity to entertain on a grand scale.

Below Left:

The observation lounge offers panoramic views on three sides.

Below Right:

For the water enthusiast, 'Nero' features both a large Jacuzzi on the sun-deck and a 5.7m swimming pool with swim current machine on the foredeck.

The boat deck above is used more as the day-to-day living space and the aft sky lounge and outdoor seating area seem to be the most frequently used living space, while the snug is an ideal place for a cosy dinner or just to sit out of the sun, chill out and read a good book. The boat-deck aft living area is one of the favourite gathering spots on the yacht and is very popular for relaxing and entertaining, featuring both a 50 inch pop-up plasma TV and a drop down movie screen that can make an al-fresco midnight movie a real treat. At night 'Nero' truly comes into her own with wonderfully subtle interior and exterior lighting.

Highly modern, technology wise, 'Nero' features the latest audio-video systems with large plasma screens in nearly all of the cabins and both an indoor and outdoor cinema. All areas have either 5.1, 7.1 or 9.1 surround-sound and all the audiovisual systems on the yacht have AMX hand-held remote controls with touch screens. High speed WiFi and hard cable Internet connections are available throughout the yacht, as are iPod docking stations.

The large dining table on the boat deck is the most popular on the yacht and the smaller card table can be raised for intimate dinners for two. On both sides of the yacht on the boat-deck, there are overhead 'rain' showers with an additional shower cubicle for guests forward of the snug. Two further internal day heads feature showers for day-guest's use.

Moving upwards, the sun-deck features the main sunbathing area. For the water enthusiast, 'Nero' features both a large Jacuzzi on the sun-deck and a 5.7m swimming pool with swim current machine on the foredeck – the choice is yours!

Back down to the main-deck, the owner's cabin is effectively a large duplex apartment. On the forward part of the main-deck, where the owner's quarters are full beam, there is a stateroom with his and hers bathrooms and a central shared dressing room. Aft of this there is a large owner's study containing a relaxing

area with a 65-inch plasma TV, a writing desk and a private dining area.

From here a private staircase leads up to a lobby off which is a day head and the observation lounge - a large room with windows on three sides. The forward facing sofa can be rotated and a large drop down screen in front of the fireplace lowered to complete the transformation of this room into the yacht's indoor cinema. Leading off the observation lounge is the owner's oval office with its own entry door from the port side-deck for the discreet arrival and departure of guests.

The owner's private sitting room and dining area, being the full width of the yacht, offer total privacy. This is an excellent place to retire early and catch a movie or take breakfast whilst still in your pyjamas.

The guest accomodation is on the lower deck and is composed of two very large suites separated by two centrally located twin cabins. The aft cabin has its own sitting room, stateroom, his and hers bathrooms and a central dressing room. This suite can be divided into two separate cabins with their own bathrooms when the Pullman berth in the sitting room area is in use.

The forward suite has a sitting room, stateroom, a large VIP bathroom with spa bath, walk-in shower and separate WC. Both of the yacht's twin cabins can be configured as twin or double cabins. All the cabins and sitting rooms feature en-suite bathrooms which have both

A CRUISE ABOARD 'NERO'

baths and showers and with bathroom fittings by Czech & Speake of London. Furthermore, the aft guest suite can be divided into two separate cabins, each with its own en-suite bathroom, by closing the adjoining doors in the sitting room.

To gain access to the water, 'Nero' has a large foldout side-boarding platform that is 6m (18') long. This makes an excellent "beach" from which to enjoy a swim or any of the many water sports activities on offer, or to board a tender to go ashore.

'Nero' has three tenders, including an enclosed cabin classic launch. This custom designed 9.5m (31') classic cabin cruiser was designed and built specially for 'Nero' and allows safe and dry passage ashore in most weather conditions.

Supplementing this are two rigid inflatables, one of 8m (26') and the other 5.2m (17') that were custom built for 'Nero' in the yacht's own livery. For the water sports enthusiast, 'Nero' has five jet skis aboard. There are two Seadoo RXT's - large three-seater wave riders with high-speed capability and reverse gear function. These are like mini-tenders and generally more stable and dry for beach excursions. There is also one Yamaha GP1300R - a two-seater sports waver rider, and a new Seadoo 3D DI convertible configuration jet ski. This can be used as either a stand-up machine or, with the use of a fold out seat, as a wave rider. Lastly there is one Yamaha Superjet traditional stand-up sports jet ski. All of the jet skis are top of the range models and although they are the most powerful, some of them have settings that can be changed to reduce performance when being used by children. There are also two Seabob underwater scooter / towing devices on board. These will pull a swimmer or snorkeler at up to 20km per hour either underwater or on the surface.

Now available for charter, 'Nero' has an experienced crew of 20 led by British Captain Nick Przybylski. The two professional chefs on board are able to offer international cuisine to the very highest level, while the service onboard is of an impeccable standard.

Right:
The luxurious owner's cabin is effectively a large duplex apartment.

Below Left:
The exquisite sunlounge.

Below Centre:
The library is a peaceful room to unwind and relax in.

Below Right:
The owner's private sitting room and dining area, being the full width of the yacht, offer total privacy.

As is the tradition on classic ships, 'Nero' also has a ship's cat to welcome you onboard. 'Nelson' lives in the crew's quarters and is not permitted in the guest areas. However he can occasionally be seen taking his morning and evening stroll on deck, making the most of all of his nine lives!

'Nero' is available for charter and also for sale through the worldwide central agents, Burgess Yachts. For further details, please call +44 207 766 4300 or email: london@burgessyachts.com

SPECIFICATIONS:	M/Y 'NERO'
Length Overall (including spars):	90.10m (295' 6")
Length Overall (excluding spars):	80.83m (265' 2")
Length Waterline:	64.92m (213')
Beam:	12.00m (39' 4")
Draught:	4.87m (16')
Displacement:	1775 ton
Maximum Speed:	17 knots
Cruising Speed:	16 knots
Range:	4,559 nautical miles @ 13 knots
Engines:	2 X 1740kW MaK / Caterpillar 9M20 2,333hp

A Cruise Aboard
'LINDA LOU'

Built for a highly experienced yacht owner, the 60m (197') 'Linda Lou', built by the Lürssen shipyard, is also arguably the perfect charter yacht. Originally planned as a 50m (164') shallow draft yacht, ideal for cruising the waters of the Caribbean and the Bahamas, the owners and their project team, led by Captain Ingo Pfotenhauer, the former captain of the 204' motor yacht 'Virginian', looked forward to an easy build.

However, soon after the contract was signed, the euro-to-dollar exchange rate began to favour the euro. As a result the owner and his wife decided a larger yacht would present a better resale opportunity down the road, so everything was put on hold.

Soon afterwards the owners visited the recently launched 192' Lürssen 'Capri' at the 2003 Fort Lauderdale International Boat Show and knew they had found their inspiration for their new yacht. 'Capri's expansive volume and design set the initial benchmarks for 'Linda Lou'.

The next step was to bring in a designer. Espen Oeino, who was to be the naval architect for the originally planned 50m yacht, was invited by the owners to design their new enlarged yacht.

Though the styling of 'Linda Lou' is all his, this remarkable yacht incorporates features of particular importance to the owners. For example, they specified at an early stage that they wanted a swim platform that

would provide easy access to the water for diving and the boarding of tenders and toys. Another requirement was that the yacht should have large upper deck spaces, particularly in the sky lounge. This required eliminating the familiar walk-around bridge deck often found on yachts of this size.

What the owners gained however is a yacht that has a huge spacious interior. The owners invited the interior designer, François Zuretti, to create a look with timeless appeal. As a result, the interior features both contemporary and classic elements so that the yacht will remain undated throughout her life. All the way through the yacht, Zuretti and the owners opted for a mixture of tones, materials and textures instead of using one type of wood with one type of finish.

An effective example of this is the sky lounge, where reddish-brown lacewood has been treated in a variety of ways on the furnishings and walls. Some panels are simply stained, while others are bleached and then hand rubbed to create a metallic sheen, then lacquered. The sole leading through the lobby forward into the wheelhouse is teak, while the walls are madrona wood, distinguishing the rooms from one another yet avoiding too dramatic a change.

Boarding the yacht from the stern, the aft main deck features a large dining table and chairs for eight to ten guests. The table can be ingeniously lowered for cocktails

Above & Left:
*'Linda Lou' is a very spacious yacht,
thanks in part to her lack of side decks.*

Far Left:
*The Jacuzzi is positioned on the
forward part of the panoramic
sun-deck.*

A CRUISE ABOARD 'LINDA LOU'

or split into two smaller tables for more intimate lunches.

Sliding doors lead through to the huge main salon with plenty of casual seating and a large low bar surrounded by stools – ideal for enjoying a cocktail or two. Further forward, the formal dining area has a large dining table and chairs suitable for a party of twelve.

The master stateroom on the forward main deck is quite spectacular. Styled using a wide variety of woods and fabrics it features a large sitting and office area, his and hers en-suite bathroom and a full-beam bedroom with king sized bed.

Different tones, this time from birch and elm, have been introduced below decks, where just four guest staterooms ensure friends and family will be quite comfortable. However, the yacht has been designed so that if the owners wish to invite a larger party onboard, the gym forward of the sky-lounge can be simply converted to an extra suite while the day head just aft can serve as its en-suite bathroom.

Above the main deck, the bridge deck is one of the most popular areas on the yacht, wonderful to relax in with plenty of casual seating, gaming tables and a U-shaped cocktail bar. Large panoramic windows bring the outside world inside, while the aft section of the lounge effortlessly converts to a dance floor for those impromptu parties!

For the best views however, the panoramic deck situated above the bridge deck is the place to be. Cleverly designed, this deck features a central panoramic salon that opens up to the deck space both fore and aft, but can be can be closed off from the elements with semi-circular glass doors.

Boasting the latest technology, 'Linda Lou' is fitted with a custom sound system as well as a Kaleidescape central movie/music server with extensive libraries. Operated with Crestron remote touch screen controls, these systems are available to use throughout the yacht.

The forward section of this deck is a sun lover's paradise. A large Jacuzzi with two large sun pads either side is situated to port, while to starboard a casual dining

Above:
The main lounge on 'Linda Lou' is highly luxurious.

Left & Centre:
The oppulent master stateroom.

Far Left:
One of the spacious guest suites.

A CRUISE ABOARD 'LINDA LOU'

banquette is available for those wanting a snack in the sun. Further aft, a large deck space is the setting for alfresco lunches, with yet more room for several more sun loungers.

Even though the owners paid a great deal of attention to the interior design and accommodation, they did not ignore the crew areas or technical spaces. One decision that should have other owners, captains and project managers taking notes is the way the crew mess was incorporated into the layout. Not only does it rival the space in some yachts' formal dining rooms, but there is also copious stowage beneath the seats and in the lockers. Another good example of the clever use of space onboard is the laundry room, which is the size of one of the guest suites. As Peter Lürssen, head of the shipyard, explains, the washers and dryers are outboard and forward in the narrower portion of the room, rather than aft, leaving more valuable relaxing space in the mess.

Similarly, the same attention is paid to serving meals. A dumbwaiter extends all the way up to the panoramic sun deck from the main deck, not the lower deck, therefore preserving a tank level for technical equipment. In an equally ingenious move, a closed-circuit camera permits the chief steward to monitor unobtrusively when the owners and their guests have finished with a course - and guests are sure to enjoy many a course on board.

One of the finest charter yachts available, 'Linda Lou' is a true classic in every way and one built for providing the perfect yachting vacation.

For more information on chartering 'Linda Lou' or one of the many other yachts in the IYC fleet, call +1 954 522 2323 or visit:www.iyc.com

SPECIFICATIONS: 'LINDA LOU'	
Length Overall:	60.00m (197')
Beam:	11.30m (37')
Draught:	3.5m (11' 5")
Guests:	12 in 6 staterooms
Crew:	13
Naval Architecture:	Espen Oeino
Interior Design:	Zuretti Interiors
Builder:	Lürssen Yachts
Year Built:	2006
Engines:	2 x Caterpillar 3512B 1990hp each
Cruise Speed:	12 knots
Charter Area:	Please enquire
Charter Rate:	Please enquire

Above & Left:
The panoramic sky lounge offers
wonderful views.

Far Left & Centre:
Fine dining and fine wines come as
standard onboard 'Linda Lou'.

A HELLENIC ADVENTURE

By Miriam Cain,
Camper & Nicholsons International

Camper & Nicholsons International
YACHTING SINCE 1782

Right:
The 58m 'Ethereal' is available to charter through CNI from €225,000 per week for 10 guests.

Below Left:
White washed alleys coloured with bouganvillea and hibiscus flowers are a common sight in the Greek islands.

Below Right:
Clear waters, traditional fishing boats and beach side dining are another feature of this beautiful region.

The Cyclades islands beg to be approached by sea, revealing their charms slowly or in a sudden moment of sheer drama. You could see them all in ten days, but chances are, you will be tempted to linger longer.

Its combination of steady winds, dramatic landscapes and natural harbours makes the Cyclades a perfect sailing destination. The idyllic chain, with its gleaming white villages and blue church domes piled above the sea, provides Greece with its most potent tourist clichés and postcard shots.

The islands abound with an astonishing wealth of historical sites and legacies left by countless successive civilisations over the course of five millennia. From the cosmopolitan island of Mykonos to the majestic Santorini, all the islands abound with simplicity and charm, but each is unique. Legend has it the land here was fragmented by Zeus and each island is in its own little world with its own rhythm. Fortunately, there are plenty of the Cyclades to go around, with something to appeal to everyone.

ONWARDS FROM ATHENS

After a few days ashore exploring Athens, one of the oldest inhabited cities in the world, step aboard the recently launched 58m 'Ethereal' and sail towards the Cyclades' island of Serifos. Approaching the first anchorage of your charter you will be greeted by one of the most breathtaking landfalls any Greek island can offer: the little capital of Chora with its alluring white skyline draped across a peak high above the port. The island's interior is sun-baked and a little unexciting, but the people are very hospitable

and the beaches along the eastern coast are well worth an afternoon of exploration before heading to the family-run Greek taverna, Takis. Set right on the waterfront in Chora, you can enjoy fresh fish and a fine selection of Greek wines – along with some entertaining characters.

Making your way anti-clockwise around the Cyclades to the neighbouring island of Sifnos, you will start to appreciate the laid-back charm of Greek-island cruising. Sophisticated and chilled, Sifnos is like a small piece of chic Caribbean – a mix of St Barth's and Anguilla but lying in the Eastern Mediterranean. The beaches are perfect for castle building, the sea is safe and the relaxed character of the island makes it perfect for a family charter. Split your time between the cosmopolitan port of Kamares, or the beach havens of Vathi and Platys Gialos.

Alternatively, start the day with an early morning swim or take the tender ashore. While your crew set up a breakfast picnic on the beach, you can climb to the medieval hilltop village of Kastro and watch the sunrise over the neighbouring island of Milos, your next port of call.

ASHORE IN MILOS

Following breakfast, step back on board and sail to the next island. Approaching Milos, take time to appreciate the rousing colours of the cliffs, the sea grottoes and the beaches tucked in between. Milos has an excess of the latter, with several isolated sandy inlets only accessible by boat. Stepping ashore, you can explore the ancient ruins up in Plaka where you will also find a fine museum and rare, early-Christian catacombs.

After a leisurely day of water sports or exploration, sail on to Folegandros. Just 15 kilometres wide, it is known as the 'island of peace' because of its relaxing atmosphere. The cliff-top capital, Chora, is a classic Greek village with alleys lined with bougainvillea and hibiscus, and a precipice that drops 200 metres into the sea. There is no bank and no nightlife, but Folegandros has some superb walking paths among almond groves and barley fields.

After a peaceful night's anchorage, awake early and step ashore for a morning hike followed by a Champagne brunch on the beach set up by the crew.

A HELLENIC ADVENTURE

Those guests wishing to enjoy the peace and quiet can take the tender ashore to the beach at Agios Nikolaos, which is only accessible by boat or coastal path from Vathy Bay.

VOLCANIC LANDSCAPES

Born of fire and brimstone, the vertiginous island of Santorini now envelops its visitors with peace and tranquillity. Take a cable-car ride to the island's main town of Fira, cruise around Santorini's satellite islands of Thirassia, Palea and Nea Kameni and discover some of the Cyclades' superior and most secluded beaches. In the early evening, retire to the main island and make your way to the old town of Oia to catch the famous Santorini sunset, or step into the achingly stylish sanctuary at the Perivolas Wellness Studio with its outdoor Jacuzzi overlooking the caldera. Later, retire to the Vinsanto Restaurant at the Vedema Resort, located in a 400-year-old winery or, for a special occasion, dine in the resort's Privé Dining Room in a secluded area of the wine cellar. Other recommendations for dining ashore include 1800 in Oia for fusion cuisine, or Giorgaros for fresh, local fish. For slightly more complex fish dishes, Koukoumavlos and Feredini are both highly recommended.

A throwback to the island-hopping days of the 1970s, the island of Kithnos is a little remote in comparison to its neighbouring islands. Few tourists call in, but nostalgic Greeks come to sample its rustic charms, most evident at Dryopida, a traditional village, or to visit the attractive spa resort of Loutra. The Katerina Taverna overlooking Loutra's Schinari Beach serves a simple but delectable range of home-grown produce with stunning views.

You can then sail on to Ios, an island adorned with small coves, countless chapels, olive trees and vineyards. The island has 365 churches, most of which are Byzantine, and the cube-shaped houses that crowd the small village squares are all painted white with blue or green doors and windows. For one of the greatest shows on earth, find a

ringside seat in the town of Chora and sip a sundowner while watching the sky towards Sikinos turn to fiery red. The island was once a hub for young hippies, but today attracts a more up-market crowd. Further north, the island of Paros is a superb location for windsurfing. Spend the day enjoying all manner of water sports before retiring to the bustling fishing village of Naoussa on the northern side of the island. A quiet fishing village by day, the bay transforms in the evening with restaurants and bars frequented by visitors and locals.

MAGICAL MYKONOS

The cosmopolitan Greek island of Mykonos is famous for its plethora of hip bars and restaurants. You could sip an ouzo in the cafés that line the colourful harbour of Hora or, to escape the crowds, visit Mykonos Town with its maze of alleyways and impressive churches. The old town has some seriously good restaurants, with cuisine ranging from Japanese fusion to the simple seafood and staples of traditional Greek tavernas.

Located above Psarou Bay, the tranquil Mykonos Blu is a refuge away from the pulsating nightlife of Mykonos Harbour. Begin the evening with a cocktail or ouzo in Delos Lounges bar as the sun sets, then make your way to one of the finest restaurants in Greece: Aegean Poets. The following day, enjoy a languorous lunch at

Above:
Sunset over the magical island of Santorini.

Left:
The 56m 'Selene' is available to charter through CNI from €189,000 per week for 10 guests.

Far Left:
Beach-side dining at Mykonos.

N'Ammos on Psarou Beach, followed by an afternoon at the Royal Myconian Resort & Thalasso Spa. Try the unique programme offering the curative effects of mineral-enriched seawater. After so much down time you should be ready to party, so either head to the island's hippest hotel, the Mykonos Theoxenia, where you can enjoy gourmet Mediterranean cuisine at The Plate restaurant on the waterfront terrace admiring the beautiful sunset; or, for something a little more slick, try Nobu at the Belvedere Hotel. For those really looking to immerse themselves in Mykonos' vibrant nightlife, there is a plethora of lively bars and clubs. Interni is the current favourite, and although you will have missed the sunset, Caprice Bar is set right on the water's edge and great for a pre-club cocktail before moving on to party till the early hours at Sea Satin or the Paradise Beach Club and Cavo Paradiso.

DELOS AND AMORGOS

For those with an interest in antiquity, walk the sacred grounds of Delos. Only a short hop across from Mykonos, the island is reputed to be the birthplace of Apollo and Artemis, and boasts the most important archaeological site in the Cyclades. It was a centre for trade and worship as far back as the ninth century BC and you will still find the remains of temples, houses and a theatre today.

The most easterly island of the Cyclades, Amorgos is a magical place, largely down to the fact that the island has no airport and its nearest airstrip is on Naxos. The beaches, especially by the northern port of Aegiali, are white and relatively untouched, and the sea so blue it was chosen as the location for the Luc Besson film The Big Blue. Dominating Amorgos' 30-kilometre length are towering mountains.

THE DODACANESE

The most distant island chain from mainland Greece is the Dodecanese. Owing to their occupation by the

Turks and then the Italians, the islands share a unique architectural heritage of castles, minarets and art-deco buildings from the Mussolini era. From the cosmopolitan to the arty, these islands alone are worthy of a two-week charter, but en-route to Turkey for disembarkation, a short stop in Rhodes, Kalymnos or Kos will give you a taster of Dodecanese diversity.

Camper & Nicholsons have a wide range of luxury yachts available to charter in the Cyclades islands, including the following:

'Maltese Falcon'   *88m (288'8")*
from €375,000 per week for 12 guests
'Ethereal'   *58m (190'5")*
from €225,000 per week for 10 guests
'Selene'   *56m (183'8")*
from €189,000 per week for 10 guests
'Perseus'   *50m (164')*
from US$175,000 per week for 10 guests
'Parsifal III'   *54m (177')*
€198,000 per week for 12 guests
'Northern Spirit'   *37m (121')*
from €52,000 per week for 7 guests
'Aime Sea'   *35.1m (115')*
from €48,000 per week for 8 guests

Above:
The stunning 88m 'Maltese Falcon' is available to charter through CNI from €375,000 per week for 12 guests.

Left:
The small town of Aegiali on Amorgos island, has sea so blue it was chosen as the location for the film 'The Big Blue'.

Far Left:
Lindos, Rhodes Island is a wonderful anchorage with white beaches and plentiful shore side restaurants.

For Charter
'AMNESIA'

Launched in spring 2008, the 60m 'Amnesia' is the third in the line of successful 'Amnesias'. An evolution in design, her interior and exterior have been conceived by the owner in conjunction with Redman Whiteley Dixon and built by the renowned Benetti shipyard. A yacht of unquestionable pedigree, 'Amnesia' draws on the owner's experience and knowledge of large yachts. Accommodating 12 guests and 16 crew, the facilities on board allow guests to socialise in every way. Various interior lounging and dining spaces offer a host of well-conceived opportunities for formal entertaining and easy relaxation, while an innovative accommodation arrangement ensures superior levels of comfort. From relaxing in the sundeck Jacuzzi or enjoying an afternoon of watersports, to dining in silver service style before dancing in the salon, her spacious deck areas are complemented by her equally inviting interior where you will find all the latest in communications and technology.

SPECIFICATIONS:	'AMNESIA'
Length Overall:	60m (196' 10")
Beam:	10.4m (34' 1")
Draught:	3.2m (10' 5")
Builder:	Benetti
Designer:	Redman Whiteley Dixon
Guests:	12
Crew:	16
Propulsion:	2 x 3512B Caterpillars
Speed:	15 knots
Charter Area:	Summer: Mediterranean
	Winter: Caribbean
Charter Rate:	From €325,000 / week

For Charter
'CLOUD 9'

'Cloud 9' is a magnificent yacht designed equally for charter and the enjoyment of her owners. Her classic blue hull and white superstructure set the scene for a truly nautical and contemporary yacht with four guest cabins, a VIP suite and the owner's suite. Her interior is enriched with warm woods and subtle blue and cream tones, combining natural materials and textures into a formal but relaxing environment. With all modern communication systems and a water toys list to satisfy the most discerning charter clients, 'Cloud 9' is a truly exciting addition to the charter market.

SPECIFICATIONS:	'CLOUD 9'
Length Overall:	60.00m (196' 10")
Beam:	11.2m (36' 9")
Draught:	3.45m (11' 4")
Builder:	CMN Cherbourg
Interior Design:	Andrew Winch
Year:	2009
Guests:	12
Crew:	15
Cruising Speed:	14 knots
Charter Area:	Summer: Mediterranean
	Winter: Caribbean
Charter Rate:	From €315,000 / week

For Charter
'NATORI'

Camper & Nicholsons
International
YACHTING SINCE 1782

London
T: +44 (0)20 7009 1950
E: info@lon.cnyachts.com

Antibes
T: +33 (0)4 92 912 912
E: info@ant.cnyachts.com

Monaco
T: +377 97 97 77 00
E: info@mon.cnyachts.com

Geneva
T: +41 223 47 27 08
E: info@gen.cnyachts.com

Palma
T: +34971403311
E: info@cnipalma.com

Puerto Portals, Spain
T: +34 971 67 92 47
E: info@cnipalma.com

Ft. Lauderdale
T: +1 954 524 4250
E: info@ftl.cnyachts.com

Miami
T: +1 561 655 2121
E: info@mia.cnyachts.com

Palm Beach
T: +1 561 655 2121
E: info@pal.cnyachts.com

New York
T: +1 212 829 5652
E: info@ny.cnyachts.com

www..camperandnicholsons.com

This stunning new Baglietto yacht with her distinctive and avantgarde exterior styling by Francesco Paszowski and interior design by Bannenberg, is available for charter in 2009. 'Natori' provides fantastic accommodation for 10 guests in five cabins, including a full width master suite with its own private en-suite full beam his and hers bathrooms. 'Natori' offers a great variety of spacious indoor and unsurpassed outdoor areas, compared to that normally found on much larger yachts. The large bridge deck area has ample space for sun loungers and a shaded dining area for up to 12 guests. Her sun-deck houses a large Jacuzzi and ample sunbathing areas, along with a bar and sitting areas. Her main deck also boasts plenty of space for shaded dining, whilst the huge windows on both her main deck and bridge deck allow guests to also enjoy relaxing in the light and cool interior or alternatively use the gym.

SPECIFICATIONS:	'NATORI'
Length Overall:	41.80m (137' 2")
Beam:	8.50m (27' 10")
Draught:	2.2m (7' 3")
Builder:	Baglietto
Year:	2009
Guests:	12
Crew:	8
Propulsion:	2 x MTU 2,800HP
Cruising Speed:	16 knots
Charter Area:	Summer: Mediterranean
	Winter: Please enquire
Charter Rate:	From €135,000 per week

For Charter
'ETHEREAL'

**Camper &
Nicholsons**

International

YACHTING SINCE 1782

London
T: +44 (0)20 7009 1950
E: info@lon.cnyachts.com

Antibes
T: +33 (0)4 92 912 912
E: info@ant.cnyachts.com

Monaco
T: +377 97 97 77 00
E: info@mon.cnyachts.com

Geneva
T: +41 223 47 27 08
E: info@gen.cnyachts.com

Palma
T: +34971403311
E: info@cnipalma.com

Puerto Portals, Spain
T: +34 971 67 92 47
E: info@cnipalma.com

Ft. Lauderdale
T: +1 954 524 4250
E: info@ftl.cnyachts.com

Miami
T: +1 561 655 2121
E: info@mia.cnyachts.com

Palm Beach
T: +1 561 655 2121
E: info@pal.cnyachts.com

New York
T: +1 212 829 5652
E: info@ny.cnyachts.com

www..camperandnicholsons.com

Informed commentators are already describing 'Ethereal' as the most technologically advanced and complex superyacht ever built. Created by Ron Holland Design, Pieter Beeldsnijder Yacht Design and Royal Huisman – who also conceived her inspiration, the 43m ketch 'Juliet', back in 1993 - 'Ethereal' is a graceful, 58m world cruising ketch with classic sheer, easy-on-the-eye superstructure and beautifully appointed accommodation. But beneath the surface lies a host of leading-edge design and engineering features that collectively represent a quantum shift in energy efficiency, enabling 'Ethereal' to operate for extended periods under her own resources. Certain to be one of the world's leading charter yachts, she is available through Camper & Nicholsons International.

SPECIFICATIONS: 'ETHEREAL"	
Length Overall:	58.06m (190' 6")
Beam:	11.40m (37' 5")
Draught:	4.9m (16' 1")
Builder:	Royal Huisman
Design:	Ron Holland Design
Interior Design:	Pieter Beeldsnijder Yacht Design
Displacement:	471 ton
Charter Area:	Summer: Mediterranean
	Winter: Caribbean
Charter Rate:	From €225,000 / week

For Charter
'ANJILIS'

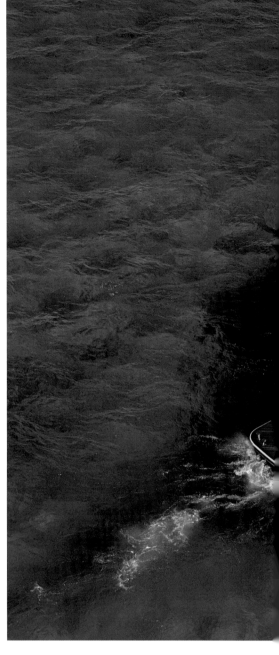

Camper & Nicholsons
International
YACHTING SINCE 1782

London
T: +44 (0)20 7009 1950
E: info@lon.cnyachts.com

Antibes
T: +33 (0)4 92 912 912
E: info@ant.cnyachts.com

Monaco
T: +377 97 97 77 00
E: info@mon.cnyachts.com

Geneva
T: +41 223 47 27 08
E: info@gen.cnyachts.com

Palma
T: +34971403311
E: info@cnipalma.com

Puerto Portals, Spain
T: +34 971 67 92 47
E: info@cnipalma.com

Ft. Lauderdale
T: +1 954 524 4250
E: info@ftl.cnyachts.com

Miami
T: +1 561 655 2121
E: info@mia.cnyachts.com

Palm Beach
T: +1 561 655 2121
E: info@pal.cnyachts.com

New York
T: +1 212 829 5652
E: info@ny.cnyachts.com

www..camperandnicholsons.com

'Anjilis' is a sophisticated Glade Johnson designed yacht built by the prolific Trinity Yachts yard in the USA. Featuring an 'Art Deco' inspired interior with several creative elements, 'Anjilis' exudes style and comfort with her custom marquetry, stone inlays and elegant luxurious furnishings. With state-of-the-art audio visual and surround sound throughout the yacht, a unique main deck bar with electronic organ, spacious outdoor areas for al-fresco dining, and a full array of water toys, she is quite simply the perfect charter yacht.

SPECIFICATIONS:	'ANJILIS'
Length Overall:	49m (161')
Beam:	8.5m (28')
Draught:	2.28m (7' 5")
Builder:	Trinity Yachts
Guests:	11
Crew:	9
Propulsion:	2 x Caterpillar 2,250hp
Speed:	18 knots cruising
Charter Area:	Summer: Mediterranean
	Winter: Caribbean
Charter Rate:	From US$235,000 -
	US$ 280,000/week

For Charter
'XANADU'

Camper & Nicholsons
International
YACHTING SINCE 1782

London
T: +44 (0)20 7009 1950
E: info@lon.cnyachts.com

Antibes
T: +33 (0)4 92 912 912
E: info@ant.cnyachts.com

Monaco
T: +377 97 97 77 00
E: info@mon.cnyachts.com

Geneva
T: +41 223 47 27 08
E: info@gen.cnyachts.com

Palma
T: +34971403311
E: info@cnipalma.com

Puerto Portals, Spain
T: +34 971 67 92 47
E: info@cnipalma.com

Ft. Lauderdale
T: +1 954 524 4250
E: info@ftl.cnyachts.com

Miami
T: +1 561 655 2121
E: info@mia.cnyachts.com

Palm Beach
T: +1 561 655 2121
E: info@pal.cnyachts.com

New York
T: +1 212 829 5652
E: info@ny.cnyachts.com

www..camperandnicholsons.com

If ever a yacht was conceived to fulfill all imaginable desires for a luxury vacation afloat, it is 'Xanadu'. She is unlike any other yacht from the shipyard thanks to her original styling. But beauty is only skin deep: what really sets 'Xanadu' apart is the detail. You won't find a more relaxing sun-deck, a more original selection of water toys or a more entertaining entertainment system anywhere on the water. Innovatively styled both inside and out by Andrew Winch, she is certain to turn heads wherever she goes and will live up to her name as an idyllically beautiful home away from home.

The central, cantilevered floating staircase rises from the lower deck to the upper deck, forming the heart of 'Xanadu' and linking her expansive sun-deck with her dining area, Jacuzzi, bar and barbecue area. The seven stateroom configuration is also truly stunning. All in all, 'Xanadu' provides her guests with an unforgettable experience afloat.

SPECIFICATIONS:	'XANADU'
Length Overall:	60m (196' 8")
Beam:	10.4m (34' 1")
Draught:	3.2m (10' 4")
Builder:	Benetti
Guests:	12
Crew:	15
Propulsion:	2 x 1850hp Caterpillar
Cruising Speed:	12 knots
Charter Area:	Summer: Mediterranean
	Winter: Caribbean
Charter Rate:	From €325,000/week

For Charter
'ODESSA'

Built at the Proteksan-Turquoise shipyard, 'Odessa' is a fine example of subtle yet exceptional style. She is a well planned yacht with perfectly balanced indoor and outdoor spaces. The sun deck is where it's at, with sumptuous sun loungers, a bar, Jacuzzi and a shaded dining area. State-of-the-art entertainment systems include a cinema with surround sound and there is plenty of scope for water sports of all varieties. 'Odessa' combines comfort and style throughout.

SPECIFICATIONS: 'ODESSA'	
Length Overall:	50m (164')
Beam:	9.3m (30' 7")
Draught:	2.95m (9' 7")
Builder:	Proteksan-Turquoise Construction
Guests:	10
Crew:	12
Propulsion:	2 x Caterpillar 820/1100kW
Cruising Speed:	14 knots
Charter Area:	Summer: Mediterranean
	Winter: Caribbean
Charter Rate:	From €245,000/week

For Charter
'KOGO'

Step aboard 'Kogo' and enter a world of pure luxury, your very own floating idyll with all the sensuous delights of an exotic island! With bold exterior styling by Tim Heywood and an exquisite interior designed by Terence Disdale, luxury and elegance are key. Warm neutral tones and clean, modern lines connect each area of 'Kogo' seamlessly, creating a "zen" atmosphere of spacious tranquillity and relaxation.

For the active charterers 'Kogo' boasts a fully equipped gym with adjacent Turkish bath and large Jacuzzi dip pool with jet stream as well as full dive facilities. 'Kogo's' cutting edge GPS-based dynamic positioning system allow her to stop in any location without the need to drop anchor and her electric powered Azipods have the added benefit of reduced noise and vibration. 'Kogo' has truly raised the standards in luxury yacht charter.

SPECIFICATIONS: 'KOGO'

Length Overall:	71.7m (235' 3")
Beam:	13.5m (44' 3")
Builder:	Alstom Marine
Year:	2006
Guests:	12
Crew:	20
Propulsion:	2 x Caterpillar & 2 x MTU generators supplying 2 x 1800kW Azipods
Cruising Speed:	12-14 knots
Charter Area:	Summer: Mediterranean Winter: Please enquire
Charter Rate:	From €476,000/week

BURGESS

London tel +44 20 7766 4300
Monaco tel +377 97 97 81 21
New York tel +1 212 223 0410

www.burgessyachts.com

CHARTER & BROKERAGE

For Charter
'LADY SHERIDAN'

'Lady Sheridan' is a luxurious floating palace boasting exterior and interior styling of the highest pedigree. She is perfectly conceived to provide the ultimate cruising holiday.

The 58m Abeking and Rasmussen motor yacht was designed with the latest in contemporary styling, state-of-the-art luxuries and infinite comforts, all combining to offer a once-in-a-lifetime yachting experience. Splendid finishes, rich architectural detailing and an integrated audio-visual system spread across 'Lady Sheridan's four levels present guests with the absolute in fine yachting.

The first-class crew goes beyond the superficial to deliver a personal and customized experience for all who charter this immaculate, elegant yacht.

SPECIFICATIONS:	'LADY SHERIDAN'
Length Overall:	57.9m (190')
Beam:	10.7m (35' 1")
Builder:	Abeking & Rasmussen
Year:	2007
Guests:	12
Crew:	15
Propulsion:	2 x 1877hp Caterpillar
Cruising Speed:	14 knots
Charter Area:	Summer: Mediterranean
	Winter: Caribbean
Charter Rate:	From €329,000/week

BURGESS

London   tel +44 20 7766 4300
Monaco   tel +377 97 97 81 21
New York   tel +1 212 223 0410

www.burgessyachts.com

For Sale & Charter
'MALTESE FALCON'

Measuring an awe-inspiring 88m (288.7ft) in length 'Maltese Falcon', the largest sailing yacht in the world, is a new class of yacht. Her revolutionary sailing system powers her to remarkable speeds when under full sails.

Her incomparable interior is luxurious with a rich, contemporary décor offering uncompromising comfort for her 12 guests in 6 double cabins. Her three decks are united in the atrium by a circular stairway surrounding the main mast creating a stunning spiralling effect.

Sailing on board 'Maltese Falcon' is both delightful to the eye and soothing to the soul. Offering all the space, grace and luxuries of a large motor yacht, she is ideal for large scale entertaining while meandering between smart anchorages, or for that once in a lifetime blue water ocean passage.

A masterpiece of technology and design, the 'Maltese Falcon' is without equal in the world.

SPECIFICATIONS: 'MALTESE FALCON'	
Length Overall:	88m (289' 1")
Beam:	12.6m (42' 2")
Builder:	Perini Navi SpA
Year:	2006
Guests:	12
Crew:	18
Propulsion:	2 x 1499hp Deutz
Cruising Speed:	16 knots
Charter Area:	Summer: Mediterranean
	Winter: Caribbean
Charter Rate:	From €335,000/week

BURGESS

London   tel +44 20 7766 4300
Monaco   tel +377 97 97 81 21
New York   tel +1 212 223 0410

www.burgessyachts.com

For Sale & Charter
'SIREN'

BURGESS

One of the most significant superyacht launches in recent years, 'Siren's fresh and modern exterior style gives her a distinctive character which is easily recognisable on the water. The yacht is well geared towards an outdoor lifestyle with vast, versatile deck areas which include a cleverly designed indoor/outdoor bar area, Jacuzzi and outdoor cinema.

Her bright, crisp, angular interior is softened by clever detailing and use of lighting and works of art, which create a calm ambience throughout. The guest cabins mix wood panelling with silk-covered bulkheads to great effect.

The fashionable functionality of this yacht is matched by her strong sea keeping qualities and powerful performance underway. 'Siren' is a benchmark for contemporary superyachting.

SPECIFICATIONS:	'SIREN'
Length Overall:	73.5m (241' 2")
Beam:	12m (39' 5")
Builder:	Nobiskrug
Year:	2008
Guests:	12
Crew:	16
Propulsion:	2 x 2360hp MTU
Cruising Speed:	15 knots
Charter Area:	Summer: Mediterranean
	Winter: Please enquire
Charter Rate:	From €440,000/week

London   tel +44 20 7766 4300
Monaco   tel +377 97 97 81 21
New York tel +1 212 223 0410

www.burgessyachts.com

For Sale & Charter
'ELANDESS II'

'Elandess II' is a recent launch of great style and quality from the reputable Heesen yard. Bannenberg has created a unique interior with a pallet of four striking woods, suede wall panels, nickel edging and marbles from Italy. With exquisite detailing and perfect finishing 'Elandess II' is pure aesthetic pleasure and sumptuous comfort.

There are four luxuriously spacious guest suites each featuring a Kaleidescape view-on-demand video system, iPod docking station and hidden speakers. All cabins have a generous en-suite bathroom, built-in vanity unit and a desk. Her excellent, adaptable layout and attractive contemporary interior make her a perfect charter yacht.

The yacht's systems and technologies are equally up-to-the-minute; performance is not at the expense of comfort. All this results in 'Elandess II' being the perfect all-rounder yacht.

SPECIFICATIONS: 'ELANDESS II'	
Length Overall:	47m (154' 3")
Beam:	8.5m (27' 10")
Builder:	Heesen Yachts
Year:	2008
Guests:	10-12
Crew:	10
Propulsion:	2 x 1556hp MTU
Cruising Speed:	14 knots
Charter Area:	Summer: Mediterranean
	Winter: Please enquire
Charter Rate:	From €224,000/week

BURGESS

London   tel +44 20 7766 4300
Monaco   tel +377 97 97 81 21
New York   tel +1 212 223 0410

www.burgessyachts.com

For Charter
'VA BENE'

'Va Bene' is simply one of the most prestigious superyachts in the world. The yacht is brilliantly designed for comfort, recently refitted to the highest standards and crewed by an exceptional team offering the ultimate luxury charter experience.

'Va Bene' accommodates 12 guests in 5 immaculate cabins, all combining comfort and quality furnishings, linens, accessories and service that will make your stay aboard 'Va Bene' truly unforgettable.

The highlight of 'Va Bene's recent redesign is the owner's master suite, with its huge, mini-spa bathroom featuring teak flooring, walk-in rain shower and luxury bath. 'Va Bene' takes outdoor living to another level with water toys galore for guests with energy to burn, while the sun deck provides a balance of sun and shade, as well as a Jacuzzi and relaxed dining space.

SPECIFICATIONS: 'VA BENE'	
Length Overall:	47.5m (156')
Beam:	8.9m (30' 4")
Builder:	Kees Cornelissen
Year:	1992 (refitted 2007/8)
Guests:	12
Crew:	13
Charter Area:	Summer: Mediterranean
	Winter: Caribbean
Charter Rate:	From US$189,000/week

For Sale & Charter
'BOADICEA'

Boadicea' is a true world cruising yacht, designed to voyage far and wide in great style and comfort. Everything from her inherent seaworthiness to her practical operation has been extremely well thought out. Designed by the acclaimed British designer Terence Disdale, she is a yacht of outstanding pedigree.

The interior volume provides an abundance of space and facilities unusual for a 70m motor yacht. On deck there is an array of choice, whether it is for quiet private relaxation or serious entertainment, the stunning and vast sun deck is complete with a large pool and swim jet.

'Boadicea' is the epitome of refined elegance.

BURGESS

SPECIFICATIONS:	'BOADICEA'
Length Overall:	70.5m (231' 4")
Beam:	14m (45' 9")
Builder:	Amels
Year:	1999
Guests:	14
Crew:	26
Propulsion:	2 x 2590hp Caterpillar
Cruising Speed:	14 knots
Charter Area:	Summer: Mediterranean
	Winter: Please enquire
Charter Rate:	From €427,000/week

London   tel +44 20 7766 4300
Monaco   tel +377 97 97 81 21
New York   tel +1 212 223 0410

www.burgessyachts.com

For Sale & Charter
'NERO'

Imagine being able to turn back the clock and experience the elegance and style of 1920's yachting, without sacrificing any of the modern comforts of luxury yachting today. Welcome aboard the astonishing 'Nero'. At 90m, 'Nero' echoes the authentic line and form of the classic steam yacht, while incorporating the speed, comfort, accommodation and quietness of the modern superyacht.

The owner of 'Nero' was utterly involved in every detail of her design and has created an interior that feels cosy and welcoming despite her expansive proportions. The impressive master duplex suite includes a full-width stateroom, his and her bathrooms, dining salon, observation lounge/cinema, study, private sun deck and pool. As for leisure facilities, a deck Jacuzzi and an outdoor cinema are supplemented by two speedboats, five Waverunners and an array of other water toys.

SPECIFICATIONS:	'NERO'
Length Overall:	90.1m (295' 6")
Beam:	12m (39' 4")
Builder:	Corsair Yachts
Year:	2008
Guests:	12
Crew:	20
Propulsion:	2 x 2333hp MAK/Caterpillar
Cruising Speed:	16 knots
Charter Area:	Summer: Mediterranean
	Winter: Caribbean
Charter Rate:	From €350,000/week

For Charter
'INDIAN EMPRESS'

'Indian Empress' incorporates luxurious living and exceptional standards with impressive maximum speeds. Her sheer volume makes her a unique and dominating presence in the water. The yacht is well known for hosting events, from Grand Prix celebrations for up to 500 people to formal, intimate dining parties in the banqueting suite.

Her living spaces are gracious and comfortable in a spirit of relaxed grandeur. Facilities include two extensive principle salons plus several smaller lounges, a conference room, a fully equipped gym with sauna and steam room, shaded outdoor dining, a deck Jacuzzi and plenty of sun loungers.

Accommodation for 12 guests is arranged in 16 cabins including a vast and very private master suite comprised of a full beam double cabin with day lounge and private deck, plus 3 additional cabins.

She is living proof that big really is beautiful.

SPECIFICATIONS: 'INDIAN EMPRESS'	
Length Overall:	95m (311' 8")
Beam:	14.6m (47' 9")
Builder:	Oceanco
Year:	2000
Guests:	12
Crew:	33
Propulsion:	3 x 9130hp MTU
Cruising Speed:	18 knots
Charter Area:	Summer: Mediterranean
	Winter: Unavailable
Charter Rate:	Please enquire

BURGESS

For Charter
'SLIPSTREAM'

BURGESS

Sharing some of her predecessor's finest features, the new build 60m 'Slipstream' sports the same distinctive livery of black hull and silver superstructure, this time applied to a new, racier profile. Andrew Winch has ensured that the interior design work is as dramatic as the exterior, using a neo-art deco style combining dark ebony joinery with red leather panelling. Particularly striking are the vertical windows for the wheelhouse and the panoramic lounge of the owner's suite.

The VIP suite boasts a private foredeck, while four remaining guest cabins on the lower deck offer every conceivable comfort. Al-fresco living areas are equally spacious; the upper deck boasts an indoor/outdoor dining area and the fabulous sun-deck features a host of amenities. 'Slipstream' offers vast interior volume, superb facilities all combined with the latest in superyacht technology.

SPECIFICATIONS:	'SLIPSTREAM'
Length Overall:	60m (196' 9")
Beam:	11.2m (36' 7")
Builder:	CMN
Year:	2009
Guests:	12
Crew:	15
Propulsion:	2 x 2201hp Caterpillar
Cruising Speed:	About 14.5 knots
Charter Area:	Summer: Mediterranean
	Winter: Caribbean
Charter Rate:	From €315,000/week

For Sale & Charter
'MEAMINA'

'Meamina's highly refined floating environment elegantly combines private family living with luxurious features that would satisfy even the most discerning charter client. The stunning Massari designed interior creates an elegant, relaxing, comfortable space by using neutral creams, greens and beige colourings. 'Meamina's sophistication comes through her clever detailing epitomized by her dining room which is exquisitely inlaid with mother-of-pearl, ebony, boxwood, mahogany and ash marquetry. The owner's cabin is especially unique with two adjacent offices, one with the most spectacular panoramic view over the bow. 'Meamina's most dramatic, striking feature is the eel skin and leather encased elevator which runs from the lower deck accommodation up to the well-equipped gym on the sun-deck. Outside living is a key feature of 'Meamina,' as is comfort with vast deck areas for al-fresco dining and her array of tenders.

SPECIFICATIONS:	'MEAMINA'
Length Overall:	59.3m (194' 6")
Beam:	10.4m (34' 2")
Builder:	Benetti
Year:	2008
Guests:	12
Crew:	15
Propulsion:	2 x 2000hp MTU
Cruising Speed:	15 knots
Charter Area:	Summer: Mediterranean
	Winter: Please enquire
Charter Rate:	From €329,000/week

For Sale & Charter
'ABILITY'
MANGUSTA 130

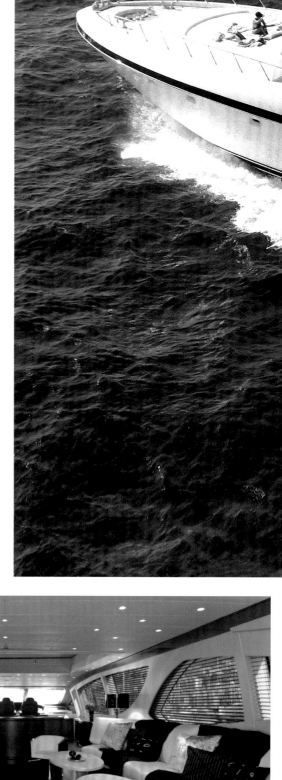

OCEANSTYLE

This magnificent sports yacht provides a thrilling ride, capable of speeds in excess of 35 knots! 'Ability' recently had a complete interior refit including new carpets and exotic furnishings, creating a soft, contemporary interior. The spacious salon and elegant cabins ensure guests can cruise in absolute comfort.

Accommodation is provided for 9 guests and includes a full beam master suite with walk-in wardrobe and large en-suite bathroom, a VIP double cabin with shower room en-suite, a double cabin with shower room en-suite and a twin cabin with extra Pullman berth and shower room.

There are plenty of water toys to play with: a 4.6m tender with 130hp engine; 2 Yamaha Waverunners; waterskis and snorkelling gear to keep guests busy. Further luxuries include satcom & cellular communications, WiFi internet access and audio visual systems throughout the yacht.

SPECIFICATIONS:	'ABILITY'
Length Overall:	39.6m (130')
Beam:	7.8m (25' 6")
Draught:	1.4m (4' 4")
Builder:	Overmarine SpA, Italy
Year:	2004 (refit 2008)
Guests:	9 guests in 4 cabins
Crew:	5
Propulsion:	2 x 3465hp MTU's
Max Speed:	Approx. 35 knots
Charter Area:	Western Mediterranean
Charter Rate:	From €150,000/week
For Sale Price:	Please enquire

London: +44 20 7766 4299
Monaco: +377 9797 8310
Miami: +1 305 672 9400
Athens: +30 6932 408 285
Palma: +34 672 070 005
Mumbai: +34 672 070 006

info@osyachting.com
WWW.OSYACHTING.COM

For Sale
ISA 120
NEW BUILD

The ISA 120 is part of an extremely successful series from the rapidly growing ISA fleet. Striking lines with fabulous outdoor areas, her interior is modern yet rich offering ultimate guest comfort on all three decks.

The ISA 120 model is under constant innovation with all future yachts carrying the new Quantum Zero Speed™ stabilisation system. The interiors can be fully customised, benefiting from the ultimate use of volume. The owner's cabin, laid out on two floors, makes the best possible use of the bow area on the main and lower decks. The 3 engines, each 1,790 kW coupled to two KaMeWa hydrojets and 1 central booster make the yacht extremely agile and manoeuvrable, with quick acceleration, gentle deceleration and turning. Top speeds in excess of 32 knots can be reached. The garage is located between the engine room and crew's quarters and allows for a 5m tender storage with easy accessibility by means of a side door.

SPECIFICATIONS: ISA 120 NEW BUILD

Length Overall:	36.5m (120')
Beam:	7.4m (24' 4")
Draught:	1.5m (5')
Builder:	International Shipyard Ancona
Year:	2009
Guests:	10 Guests in 5 cabins
Crew:	6
Propulsion:	3 x 2,400hp MTU's
Max. Speed:	About 32 knots
For Sale Price:	Please enquire

Sistership photos

For Charter
'LA DEA'
AZIMUT 116

OCEANSTYLE

Built in 2004, 'La Dea' offers all the comforts and amenities for a memorable cruise. Whilst the sheer size of the spaces on board will simply amaze you, what will win you over completely is the way the yacht manages to exude classical elegance at the same time as boasting the ultimate in modern technology and water sports equipment.

Her lay-out contains of a formal dining area in the main salon and additional al-fresco dining can be enjoyed on the aft deck. The generous lay-out of the fly bridge deck also provides the perfect platform for enjoying the outdoor life and includes a breakfast table which converts into a sun pad, additional sun loungers, Jacuzzi tub and bar area.

The accommodation for up to 11 guests in 5 cabins is first-class, with sumptuous standards of comfort and well-appointed en-suite facilities. The lower deck features a full width owner's cabin with king size bed and en-suite bathroom with bath tub and shower. Two double guest cabins and twin cabin with an additional Pullman berth can be found forward of the master cabin and a full beam VIP cabin with queen size bed is located on the main deck forward.

SPECIFICATIONS: 'LA DEA' - AZIMUT 116	
Length Overall:	35.5m (116' 4")
Beam:	7.4m (24' 4")
Draught:	2.1m (6' 9")
Builder:	Azimut SpA, Italy
Year:	2004
Guests:	11 in 5 cabins
Crew:	7
Propulsion:	2 x 2,000hp MTU's
Max. Speed:	About 22 knots
Charter Area:	Western Mediterranean
Charter Rate:	From €72,000/week

London: +44 20 7766 4299
Monaco: +377 9797 8310
Miami: +1 305 672 9400
Athens: +30 6932 408 285
Palma: +34 672 070 005
Mumbai: +34 672 070 006

info@osyachting.com
WWW.OSYACHTING.COM

For Sale & Charter
'MOMENTUM'
NOTIKA 108

OCEANSTYLE

Built in 2006, 'Momentum' offers all the comforts and amenities for a memorable cruise. At 32.8m and with twin MTU 2,000hp engines, the yacht is capable of cruising at 21 knots and has a maximum speed of approximately 25 knots.

Her performance and stylish modern interior make 'Momentum' a great charter yacht for the discerning charter guest. Formal dining is available in the main salon while additional al-fresco dining can be enjoyed on the aft deck and sun-deck. The generous layout of the fly bridge deck also provides the perfect platform for enjoying the outdoor life and includes a sun pad, additional sun loungers, Jacuzzi tub and bar area.

The main deck features a full width owner's suite, while the lower deck includes a full beam VIP cabin with queen size bed, a double guest cabin with queen size bed, both en-suite and a twin guest cabin with two separate berths, a Pullman bed and en-suite shower room.

SPECIFICATIONS:	'MOMENTUM'
Length Overall:	32.8m (108')
Beam:	7.7m (25')
Draught:	1.5m (5')
Builder:	Leight Notika, Turkey
Year:	2006
Guests:	8 guests in 4 cabins
Crew:	7
Propulsion:	2 x 2,000hp MTU engines
Max Speed:	Approx. 25 knots
Charter Area:	Western Mediterranean
Charter Rate:	From €65,000/week
For Sale Price:	Please enquire

London: +44 20 7766 4299
Monaco: +377 9797 8310
Miami: +1 305 672 9400
Athens: +30 6932 408 285
Palma: +34 672 070 005
Mumbai: +34 672 070 006

info@osyachting.com
WWW.OSYACHTING.COM

CHARTER & BROKERAGE

For Charter
'MURCIELAGO'
PREDATOR 100

OCEANSTYLE

This magnificent sports yacht has a sleek black and silver painted hull and superstructure, giving it a true 'wow' factor. 'Murcielago' has had a complete interior refit including new soft furnishings and carpet, creating a pleasantly light and warm interior. The spacious salon and cabins ensure guests can cruise in absolute comfort.

Accommodation is provided for 8 guests and includes a full beam master cabin amidships, a VIP double cabin forward and a twin and bunk bed cabin, all en-suite. There are plenty of water toys to play with. A 200hp tender, 3 Jet-skis, 2 Seadoo GTI underwater toys, 4 sets of water-skis, kneeboard and tows will keep everyone, young and old, occupied. Other luxuries include satellite communications and audio visual systems throughout the yacht. A large opening roof panel above the dining area creates an al-fresco feeling.

SPECIFICATIONS:	'MURCIELAGO' SUNSEEKER PREDATOR 100
Length Overall:	30.5m (100')
Beam:	6.6m (21' 8")
Draught:	0.9m (3' 1")
Builder:	Sunseeker, UK
Year:	2004 (refit in 2008)
Guests:	8 guests in 4 cabins
Crew:	3
Propulsion:	3 x 2,000hp MTU's
Cruising Speed:	Approx. 48 knots
Charter Area:	Western Mediterranean
Charter Rate:	From €65,000/week

London: +44 20 7766 4299
Monaco: +377 9797 8310
Miami: +1 305 672 9400
Athens: +30 6932 408 285
Palma: +34 672 070 005
Mumbai: +34 672 070 006

info@osyachting.com
WWW.OSYACHTING.COM

For Charter
'NAVI'
RIVA VENERE 75

Built in 2009, 'Navi' is a sleek and stylish looking yacht with an informal and understated interior. Your attention is grabbed by the striking exterior with a deep black hull and contrasting Riva crème superstructure. Her windscreen extends aesthetically up to the fly-bridge in such a way that, seen from the front, it gives it a very sporty look.

The exterior provides the ultimate facilities for guests to enjoy the yacht, especially on the spacious sun-deck where a Bimini top is operated by the push of a button, to provide shade when required.

Inside, the spacious and tastefully appointed accommodation is offered for 7 guests in 4 cabins. The owner's cabin is at full beam amidships giving optimum space and stability. A large double bed and living area on the port side with table and two sumptuous chairs make this cabin especially comfortable.

SPECIFICATIONS:	'NAVI'
Length Overall:	23m (75' 5")
Beam:	5.7m (19')
Draught:	1.9m (6')
Builder:	Riva, Italy
Year:	2009
Guests:	7 guests in 4 cabins
Crew:	3
Propulsion:	2 x 1,524hp MTU's
Max Speed:	Approx. 31 knots
Charter Area:	Western Mediterranean
Charter Rate:	From €35,000/week

For Charter
'DREAM'

Equipped with an elevator that has access to all four decks, 'Dream' is outfitted with everything needed for complete comfort. The seven staterooms include the king master suite on the main deck and a VIP king stateroom on the bridge deck. Below deck there are five additional staterooms and a gym. From her toys to a relaxing Jacuzzi and wet bar on her sun-deck, 'Dream' will live up to her name in every sense of the word providing you with a devine charter experience.

FRASER YACHTS

ESTD ★ 1947

T: +1 954 463 0600
E: florida@fraseryachts.com
W: www.fraseryachts.com

SPECIFICATIONS:	'DREAM'
Length Overall:	51.82m (170')
Builder:	Feadship
Year:	2003 (refit 2006)
Guests:	12
Crew:	12
Cruising Speed:	12 knots
Charter Area:	Summer: Bahamas
	Winter: Caribbean
Charter Rate:	From US$240,000/week

For Charter
'PRINCESS MARIANA'

'Princess Mariana', built at the Danyard Aalborg – Royal Denship yard in Denmark, is an exceptionally stylish vessel equipped with innovative and exhilarating features. This outstanding yacht has been built with six luxurious staterooms to accommodate twelve guests in unparalleled comfort.

One of the most impressive areas aboard 'Princess Mariana' is the Beach Club. Both starboard and port hull sections lower to just above sea level, forming a vast, teak decked sun terrace, providing easy access for water sports. For the ultimate in entertaining or relaxing, guests aboard can enjoy the cinema, beauty salon, gymnasium, nightclub, or soak in one of two Jacuzzis. Having recently completed a 12 million dollar refit, 'Princess Mariana' is consistently maintained to the highest standard of a mega yacht.

SPECIFICATIONS:	'PRINCESS MARIANA'
Length Overall:	78.59m (257' 10")
Builder:	Royal Denship
Year:	2003 - refit 2006
Guests:	12 in 6 staterooms
Crew:	26
Cruising Speed:	15 knots
Charter Area:	Summer: Wsetern Mediterranean
	Winter: Caribbean
Charter Rate:	From €610,000/week

FRASER YACHTS

ESTD ✦ 1947

T: +1 954 463 0600
E: florida@fraseryachts.com
W: www.fraseryachts.com

CHARTER & BROKERAGE

For Charter
'LATINOU'

FRASER YACHTS

ESTD • 1947

T: +377 93 101 480
E: monaco@fraseryachts.com
W: www.fraseryachts.com

'Latinou' is one of the latest masterpieces launched by Italian shipyard Benetti. Her art deco interior is masterfully revitalized with contemporary trends in design creating an elegant and modern atmosphere. 'Latinou' boasts a wonderful layout offering several lounge and dining areas including a large interior formal dining room and an al-fresco dining area on the aft deck. An impressive elevator adorns the five decks with natural light. Her fly deck is fully equipped with a range of sun chairs and sunpads to take in the all day Mediterranean sun.

Designed for ultimate pleasure with a full range of facilities and toys, 'Latinou' accommodates twelve charter guests in a spacious master suite and staterooms all equipped with top quality entertainment systems and en-suites.

Built in 2008, the Italian luxury custom yacht builder Benetti has once again displayed its world class excellence in workmanship aboard 'Latinou'.

SPECIFICATIONS:	'LATINOU'
Length Overall:	51.99m (170' 7")
Builder:	Benetti
Year:	2008
Guests:	12
Crew:	12
Cruise Speed:	14 knots
Charter Area:	Summer: Western Mediterranean
	Winter: Western Mediterranean
Charter Rate:	From €203,000/week

For Charter
'SOUTH'

B uilt in 2008, the luxury motor yacht 'South' is a 53m composite yacht constructed by the Italian shipyard, Rossi Navi. With accommodation for up to twelve charter guests in six cabins, 'South' has a modern stylish interior designed by Officina Italiana Design, using a wide selection of exotic woods and luxurious fabrics.

Elegent and sophisticated, 'South' is available for charter in the western Mediterranean both during the summer and winter months.

SPECIFICATIONS:	'SOUTH'
Length Overall:	53.20m (174' 06")
Builder:	Rossi Navi
Year:	2008
Guests:	12
Crew:	12
Cruising Speed:	16 knots
Charter Area:	Summer: Mediterranean
	Winter: Western Mediterranean
Charter Rate:	From €270,000/week

T: +377 93 101 480
E: monaco@fraseryachts.com
W: www.fraseryachts.com

For Charter
'GRACE E'

'Grace E' is a 50m (164') luxury motor yacht built by Codecasa of Italy in 2004. With a stunning interior by Franco and Anna Maria Dellarole, and superb outside areas, this yacht is the ultimate in luxury chartering.

Onboard, a guest elevator provides easy access to all of her four decks, while her expansive on-deck areas are perfect for enjoying the fresh sea breezes, sunbathing on the comfortable loungers or relaxing under the protection of the ample awnings. 'Grace E' accommodates a total of twelve guests in six elegant staterooms. Each guest suite includes a beautiful private bathroom and modern entertainment system with LCD television. A new sun-deck gym and other equipment was added during the refit.

SPECIFICATIONS: 'GRACE E'

Length Overall:	50m (164')
Builder:	Codecasa
Year:	2004 (refit 2009)
Guests:	12
Crew:	11
Cruising Speed:	14 knots
Charter Area:	Summer: Western Mediterranean
	Winter: Caribbean
Charter Rate:	From US$245,000/week

FRASER YACHTS

ESTD ★ 1947

T: +1 954 463 0600
E: florida@fraseryachts.com
W: www.fraseryachts.com

For Charter
'TRIBU'

The motor yacht 'Tribu' is an explorer style 50m motor yacht built in 2007 by Mondomarine of Italy. As a true expedition yacht she is able to cruise the world's oceans in complete safety.

'Tribu' offers a contemporary minimalist interior style designed for simplicity, comfort and functionality. With good deck space and a vast arrangement of toys she has all the systems onboard requisite for extended stays in remote areas and accommodates up to ten guests in luxurious comfort.

FRASER YACHTS

T: +377 93 101 480
E: monaco@fraseryachts.com
W: www.fraseryachts.com

SPECIFICATIONS:	'TRIBU'
Length Overall:	50.50m (165' 8")
Builder:	Mondomarine
Year:	2007
Guests:	10
Crew:	12
Cruising Speed:	12 knots
Charter Area:	Summer: Eastern Mediterranean
	Winter: Pacific
Charter Rate:	From €185,000/week

For Charter
'INEVITABLE'

'Inevitable' is a classic Feadship, originally built in 1990 but rebuilt over 18 months to the exacting standards of the DeVries craftsmen. Her relaunch in 2008 ushered in a new era in classic motor yachting with all the modern comforts and safety built into her gorgeous interior and exterior. She accommodates up to ten yacht charter guests in luxurious comfort and now boasts comfort features such as Zero Speed stabilizers and modern conveniences such as WiFi and Kalidescape A/V.

SPECIFICATIONS:	'INEVITABLE'
Length Overall:	49.99m (164')
Builder:	Feadship
Year:	1990 (rebuilt 2008)
Guests:	10
Crew:	10
Cruising Speed:	12 knots
Charter Area:	Summer: Western Mediterranean
	Winter: Western Mediterranean
Charter Rate:	From US$195,000/week

FRASER YACHTS

T: +1 954 463 0600
E: florida@fraseryachts.com
W: www.fraseryachts.com

For Charter
'CYAN'

'Cyan' was built in Italy by Codecasa Yachts of Italy in 1997 and was recently refitted in 2008. Her timeless shape and deeply angled bow give her a contemporary look and luxurious functionality. Featuring large deck space which provides plenty of sunbathing and relaxation options, either around the Jacuzzi or on the aft sun deck, 'Cyan' accommodates up to twelve guests on yacht charter with six cabins. There is also comfortable dining, inside or outside, under the open sky or under the shade of awnings and umbrellas, while the active guest will find a good complement of water toys for leisure entertainment.

SPECIFICATIONS:	'CYAN'
Length Overall:	48.70m (159' 9")
Builder:	Codecasa
Year:	1997 (refit 2008)
Guests:	12
Crew:	11
Cruising Speed:	12 knots
Charter Area:	Summer: Mediterranean
	Winter: Caribbean
Charter Rate:	From €165,000/week

For Charter
'LET IT BE'

FRASER YACHTS

ESTD · 1947

T: +377 93 101 480
E: monaco@fraseryachts.com
W: www.fraseryachts.com

Luxury motor yacht 'Let It Be' is a semi custom built, 47.7m (156' 6") Heesen yacht launched in 2007. She is a displacement motor yacht with a steel hull. Her 8V4000 engines power her along at up to 16 knots and give her an easy 14 knot cruising speed, so the time taken to get between locations is minimal. Packed with many original features 'Let It Be' represents an ideal charter yacht for a wonderful vacation.

SPECIFICATIONS:	'LET IT BE'
Length Overall:	47.7m (156' 6")
Builder:	Heesen Yachts
Year:	2007
Guests:	12
Crew:	9
Cruising Speed:	14 knots
Charter Area:	Summer: Mediterranean
	Winter: Mediterranean
Charter Rate:	From €160,000/week

For Sale
'LADY ANN MAGEE'

'Lady Ann Magee' is one of the finest yachts ever launched by the distinguished Italian shipyard, Codecasa. Built to the highest custom standards in 2001 she has since been maintained in immaculate condition attaining a reputation as one of the most successful 50m charter yachts over the last 5 years.

She benefits from every possible comfort. Her main deck offers an informal dining area, comfortable lounge and a separate, formal dining area - all designed in a traditional style. A centrally located elevator allows easy access to all decks. The skylounge has comfortable seating with access aft to a spacious exterior dining area, while the top deck is perfectly fitted out for sunbathing, al-fresco dining and relaxing in the Jacuzzi.

'Lady Ann Magee' has had the same owner from when she was first commissioned and is now being sold because he has a 65m yacht launching in 2010. She has been continuously upgraded and has been seriously priced to sell in the current market.

SPECIFICATIONS: 'LADY ANN MAGEE'

Length Overall:	49.9m (163'8")
Beam:	9.5m (31' 2")
Draught:	3.2m (10' 5")
Builder:	Codecasa 2001
Accommodation:	12 guests + 12 crew
Engines:	2x Caterpillar 3516B
Max. Speed:	17.0 knots
Sale Price:	€16,500,000

For Sale
'LEONORA'

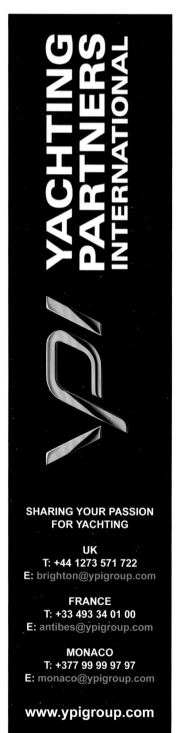

'Leonora' was built by the world's pre-eminent superyacht shipyard, Lürssen, in 1991. She received worldwide recognition when she was launched, winning two of the industry's major awards: The 'Superyacht of the Year Award' from Showboats International and the 'International Superyacht Design Award' from the prominent Superyacht Society.

'Leonora' has recently undergone a major multi-million euro refit in 2007/8 and into 2009 which included bringing the yacht back into Lloyd's class and MCA compliancy. Following this refit she is now in superb cosmetic and technical condition and her wood panelled interior by the celebrated 'Celeste Dell'Anna' is among the finest you will see on any yacht of her size.

In sum, she is undoubtedly one of the finest displacement yachts available for sale on the worldwide market.

SPECIFICATIONS: 'LEONORA'

Length Overall:	40.4m (132')
Beam:	8m (26' 2")
Draught:	2.4m (8')
Builder:	Lürssen, 1991
Accommodation:	8 guests + 8 crew
Engines:	2x Caterpillar 3508
Maximum Speed:	14.0 knots
Classification:	Lloyd's + 100 A1 Yacht, LMC
Sale Price:	€9,900,000

For Sale
AB 116

This AB 116 with a Kevlar-Carbon hull is the ultimate fly bridge boat. Built in 2009, she has enormous power and presence reaching a maximum speed of 40 knots powered by 3 x 2400 HP MTU engines and MJP water jets.

The impressive light interior decor within is the workmanship of Guido De Groot and achieves that impressive, and often evasive, balance between aesthetic beauty and functionality. Her look has won lavish critical praise and it is easy to see why.

Given her speed, high volume (with five cabins with en-suite bathrooms), and raffish good looks this AB 116 is a fantastic opportunity. She will be a brand new yacht with a short waiting time! The specification. is to the highest standards and if purchased quickly, the new owner can change the layout, colours, electronics etc to his desires.

The AB yard has rapidly gained a reputation for building sensational, highly engineered, and fast boats. The AB 116 will only add credence to this view!

SPECIFICATIONS:	AB 116
Length Overall:	36.25m (118' 10")
Beam:	7.5m (24' 6")
Draught:	1.6m (5' 3")
Builder:	AB Yachts 2010
Accommodation:	10 guests + 5 crew
Engines:	3 x 2400 HP MTU3 + MJP Waterjets
Maximum Speed:	40 knots
Construction:	Kevlar-Carbon
Asking Price:	€6,600,000

For Sale
'AVENTURA'

Designed by Ted Fontaine, 'Aventura' was born from a brief to match world-cruising capability and style with the need for safety and comfort for a young family. In this aim she succeeds admirably. Built by Danish Yacht and finished by Holland Jachtbouw in the spring of 2006, 'Aventura' fuses classic beauty with the latest technology to give a spacious and sleek sailing yacht.

Her cutting edge design provides versatility: the centreboard gives access to coastal waters where other sister ships would not dare tread, whilst the push-button rig and fold-down stern allow for a smooth sailing experience. With three entrance/exits, an on-deck and raised salon, plus four staterooms aft for owner and guests, she offers excellent space for a yacht that can be handled by only four crew.

Her interior is rich in teak, timeless in appearance and suffused with natural light. 'Aventura' in all, is a yacht both comfortable, elegant and a pleasure to sail.

SPECIFICATIONS: 'AVENTURA'	
Length Overall:	33.2m (109'1")
Beam:	8m (26'5")
Draught:	2.7m (8'10") - 5.9m (19'3")
Builder:	Danish Yacht & Holland Jachtbouw bv
Accommodation:	8/10 guests + 4 crew
Construction:	Composite
Engines:	Scania 420hp /313kw
Asking Price:	€6,495,000

For Sale & Charter
'GLADIUS'

'Gladius' is a splendid example of the Cantieri di Pisa yard's craftsmanship and attention to detail. Completed in 2007 to the highest custom standards she is both very fast and elegant. With a top speed of 26 knots she offers exhilarating performance, whilst her Carlo Paladini designed interiors give both luxury and refinement.

Her current owner is a very experienced yachtsman who has ensured that she has been maintained to the highest standards and she is only now for sale because he is taking delivery of a new Pisa Akhir 153.

'Gladius' has an enviable charter record with her combination of grande vitesse and extreme comfort proving very popular with guests. Her spacious sundeck with open-air barbecue and bar is the envy of much larger yachts and she provides ample space to eat, rest and play. In sum 'Gladius' is a motor yacht both personal, accessible and luxurious.

SPECIFICATIONS: 'GLADIUS'

Length Overall:	38.7m (125')
Beam:	7.5m (24' 6")
Draught:	1.9m (6')
Builder:	Cantieri di Pisa, 2007
Accommodation:	10 guests + 7 crew
Construction:	GRP
Engines:	2 x MTU 12V 4000
Maximum Speed:	26 knots
Asking Price:	€11,500,000
Charter Region:	Please enquire
Charter Price:	Please enquire

For Sale
'OCEAN SEVEN'

'Ocean Seven' is a spectacular aluminium motor yacht designed by Jon Bannenberg. Following a significant refit in the winter of 2007/08 several improvements were made. The refit included a new deck lounging area forward of the mast with an additional hot tub and refurbishment of the sundeck and bridge deck areas. It also included the addition of zero-speed stabilizers so that comfort at anchor is guaranteed.

'Ocean Seven's sundeck is close to peerless, offering vast expanses of teak floors, two spa dip pools and a refreshing deck shower and mister. The living accommodation exudes style. The owner's suite, with its own private lounge, occupies the full beam on the main deck and has his and hers marble lined bathrooms, whilst the main salon has a superb bar area and is masterfully designed for soirees and fetes.

'Ocean Seven' exudes the class and aesthetic style that one has come to expect from Bannenberg. She is an iconic boat, is in turn-key condition and represents the ideal platform for launching one's 2010 season!

SPECIFICATIONS: 'OCEAN SEVEN'	
Length Overall:	53.5m (175' 6")
Beam:	10m (32' 9")
Draught:	2.7m (8' 10")
Builder:	Oceanfast, 1994
Accommodation:	12 guests + 11 crew
Engines:	2 x 2445hp
Maximum Speed:	18.5 knots
Asking Price:	Please enquire

For Charter
'KOKOMO'

'Kokomo' is a striking, high performance sloop with spacious interiors and extensive accommodation. This is complemented with a Redman Whiteley Dixon designed interior that includes a large salon and formal dining area for up to ten guests. The timberwork throughout the yacht is in walnut and wengé.

Accommodation onboard 'Kokomo' includes an owner's suite and four guest suites. The owner's suite spans the full beam of the yacht, making for a very spacious arrangement. All guest suites have expansive portholes, electric blinds, climate control, mood lighting and music systems. Forward, the crew's quarters contain five cabins all with en-suite facilities for up to ten crew. The comprehensive fly bridge is accessed from the aft cockpit.

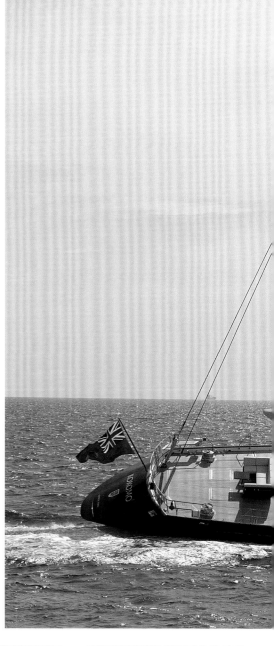

SPECIFICATIONS: 'KOKOMO'	
Length Overall:	52m (170' 6")
Beam:	10.2m (33' 5")
Draught:	4.9m (16' 1")
Builder:	Alloy Yachts, 2006
Guests:	10
Crew:	10
Engines:	Caterpillar Diesel 3412E
Cruising Speed:	12 knots
Charter Price:	€200,000/week

Dubois Yachts Ltd.
Beck Farm
Sowley
Lymington
Hampshire SO41 5SR
UK

T: +44 (0)1590 626688
F: +44 (0)1590 626696
E: yachts@duboisyachts.com

www.duboisyachts.com

For Charter
'MARGARET ANN'

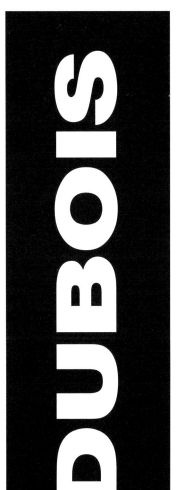

Launched from Pendennis Shipyard, this fast cruising sloop with her pretty lines, spacious accommodation and high performance is a highly sought after charter yacht.

'Margaret Ann's calm and contemporary Redman Whiteley Dixon interior offers state of the art entertainment and can accommodate six to eight guests. The full width master stateroom has two 4' beds, an en-suite bathroom and en-suite shower room. Her two twin cabins each have an additional Pullman berth which makes her an ideal yacht for family charters.

SPECIFICATIONS: 'MARGARET ANN'	
Length Overall:	29.13m (95' 6")
Beam:	7.35m (24' 1")
Draught:	3.85m (12' 7")
Builder:	Pendennis Shipyard, 2004
Guests:	6/8
Crew:	4
Engines:	Scania DL9 44M
Cruising Speed:	10.5 knots
Charter Price:	Please enquire

Dubois Yachts Ltd.
Beck Farm
Sowley
Lymington
Hampshire SO41 5SR
UK

T: +44 (0)1590 626688
F: +44 (0)1590 626696
E: yachts@duboisyachts.com

www.duboisyachts.com

For Charter
'NELSON'

DUBOIS

Built to an exceptionally high standard by Vitters Shipyard in Holland in 2003, 'Nelson' is available for charter in Australia. This is a unique opportunity as she is the only yacht of this size and calibre with five staterooms. She has an owner's suite, two double cabins and two twin cabins, all with en-suite facilities.

'Nelson' has an interior detailed by Dick Young Designs. The ambience is calm and restful using minimal detailing in birchwood, brushed stainless steel and oiled teak. The bathrooms have floating teak counter tops with stone basins and hidden back lighting.

SPECIFICATIONS: 'NELSON'	
Length Overall:	42.9m (140' 8")
Beam:	9m (29' 6")
Draught:	4.2m (13' 9")
Builder:	Vitters Shipyard bv, 2004
Guests:	10
Crew:	6
Engines:	MTU 183TE72
Cruising Speed:	12 knots
Charter Price:	US$100,000/week

Dubois Yachts Ltd.
Beck Farm
Sowley
Lymington
Hampshire SO41 5SR
UK

T: +44 (0)1590 626688
F: +44 (0)1590 626696
E: yachts@duboisyachts.com

www.duboisyachts.com

For Charter
'RED DRAGON'

The distinctive and unique 'Red Dragon' is one of the most beautiful large sailing yachts in the world. The stylish Dubois lines and the modern and light interior by Wilmotte & Associates makes this a unique sailing vessel.

Built by Alloy Yachts in New Zealand to their normal exacting standards, the crew of 'Red Dragon' have worked together as a team for many years on the owner's previous yachts. Ben Marshall, the captain, runs a very professional and happy ship and is highly regarded in the superyacht industry.

DUBOIS

SPECIFICATIONS: 'RED DRAGON'	
Length Overall:	51.7m (169' 6")
Beam:	10.2m (33' 5")
Draught:	4.9m (16' 1")
Builder:	Alloy Yachts, 2008
Guests:	10
Crew:	9
Engines:	Caterpillar Diesel C32
Cruising Speed:	12 knots
Charter Price:	€200,000/week

Dubois Yachts Ltd.
Beck Farm
Sowley
Lymington
Hampshire SO41 5SR
UK

T: +44 (0)1590 626688
F: +44 (0)1590 626696
E: yachts@duboisyachts.com

www.duboisyachts.com

For Charter
'GANESHA'

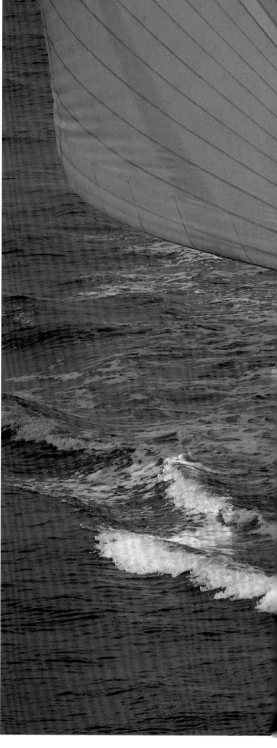

This fast yet comfortable Dubois design boasts a graceful Redman Whitely Dixon interior finished in walnut with wengé detailing and complemented by pale fabrics.

Her stylish and generous accommodation includes a full width master stateroom, a double cabin and two further twin cabins sleeping eight guests in great comfort. Additionally she has Pullman berths in both twin cabins increasing her guest complement to ten if required.

Winner of the Dubois Cup 2009, she is fast and exciting to sail. Her superb crew has established her as one of the most sought after yachts available for charter.

SPECIFICATIONS: 'GANESHA'	
Length Overall:	38.9m (127' 7")
Beam:	8.25m (27' 1")
Draught:	4m (13' 2")
Builder:	Fitzroy Yachts, 2006
Guests:	10
Crew:	5
Engines:	Caterpillar Diesel 3406D
Cruising Speed:	12 knots
Charter Price:	€80,000/week

Dubois Yachts Ltd.
Beck Farm
Sowley
Lymington
Hampshire SO41 5SR
UK

T: +44 (0)1590 626688
F: +44 (0)1590 626696
E: yachts@duboisyachts.com

www.duboisyachts.com

CHARTER & BROKERAGE

For Charter
'LUDYNOSA G'

Built by Fitzroy Yachts in 2005, 'Ludynosa G' accommodates eight guests in four luxuriously appointed double cabins, including her full-width master suite. Three double en-suite crew cabins accommodate up to six crew.

Her interior is finished to an extremely high standard, enhanced by perfectly placed large portholes for great visibility and additional light. All furniture has been designed to offer maximum flexibility of use and is of the highest quality.

SPECIFICATIONS: 'LUDYNOSA G'	
Length Overall:	37.5m (123')
Beam:	8.2m (26' 11")
Draught:	4m (13' 2")
Builder:	Fitzroy Yachts, 2005
Guests:	8
Crew:	6
Engines:	Caterpillar 3406E 'D'
Cruising Speed:	12 knots
Charter Price:	€72,000/week (High Season)
	€65,000/week (Low Season)

DUBOIS

Dubois Yachts Ltd.
Beck Farm
Sowley
Lymington
Hampshire SO41 5SR
UK

T: +44 (0)1590 626688
F: +44 (0)1590 626696
E: yachts@duboisyachts.com

www.duboisyachts.com

CHARTER & BROKERAGE

For Charter
'MOONBIRD'

DUBOIS

The stunning 'Moonbird' is an impressive sailing yacht. Fast and luxurious, her fantastic crew provide a charter experience second to none.

Built by Fitzroy yachts in 2006, she was re-fitted in 2008 and is in excellent condition. She is available in the Mediterranean during the summer and spends most winters in the Caribbean.

On 'Moonbird' particular attention has been given to the deck layout including two expansive cushioned seating areas, one on the aft deck and the other forward of the Jacuzzi spa, which also includes the additional benefit of a luxurious sun pad.

She has excellent capacity for both formal and informal entertaining in the pilothouse bar and the comfortable and stylish lower salon and dining room.

SPECIFICATIONS: 'MOONBIRD'

Length Overall:	37.15m (121' 10")
Beam:	8.38m (33' 5")
Draught:	4.9m (16' 1")
Builder:	Fitzroy Yachts, 2006
Guests:	10
Crew:	9
Engines:	Caterpillar Diesel 3196E
Cruising Speed:	12 knots
Charter Price:	€70,000/week (High Season)
	€65,000/week (Low Season)

For Charter
'NOSTROMO'

DUBOIS

Launched from Pendennis Shipyard in 2009, this stunning 100 foot yacht is ideal for charter due to her four cabin layout which is unique in a yacht of her size. 'Nostromo' is the latest in a line of superyachts with the winning Dubois/ Pendennis formula. Her deck layout, superstructure and hull lines follow the best Dubois concepts to combine fantastic sailing performance with practical, all-weather comfort and usability.

Externally, a spacious aft deck offers magnificent opportunities for sunbathing, while the large and comfortable bimini-sheltered cockpit is designed for al-fresco dining.

Below decks, the living space is split over two levels, taking full advantage of light through the 180^0 panoramic windows and providing the owner with an elegant salon for dining and general relaxation, together with a spacious and practical pilothouse and deck-level lounge. The accommodation is spread out over four beautifully appointed en-suite cabins complete with the latest audio visual equipment.

SPECIFICATIONS: 'NOSTROMO'	
Length Overall:	30m (98' 5")
Beam:	7.37m (24' 2")
Draught:	3.85m (12' 7")
Builder:	Pendennis Shipyards, 2009
Guests:	8
Crew:	4
Engines:	Scania D112
Cruising Speed:	12 knots
Charter Price:	€50,000/week (High Season)
	€45,000/week (Low Season)

Dubois Yachts Ltd.
Beck Farm
Sowley
Lymington
Hampshire SO41 5SR
UK

T: +44 (0)1590 626688
F: +44 (0)1590 626696
E: yachts@duboisyachts.com

www.duboisyachts.com

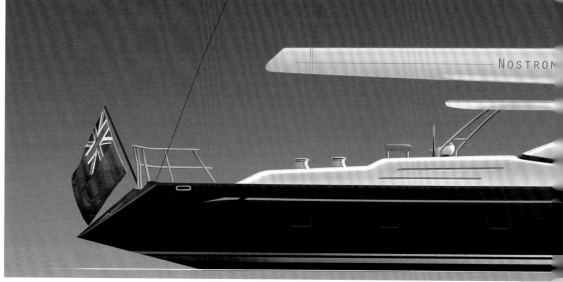

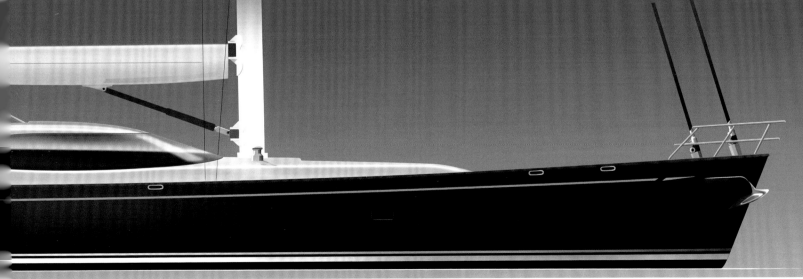

For Sale & Charter
'ONE MORE TOY'

The luxury yacht 'One More Toy' is a fine example of a boat with classic beauty, exquisite style and impeccable taste. Decorated in fine fabrics with black walnut throughout, she is fully equipped with a range of excellent entertainment systems and areas, ideal for keeping guests entertained at all times. The main salon is cool and comfortable with an entrance lobby forward of amidships. Large panoramic windows illuminate the salon and provide great views of the beautiful Caribbean or Mediterranean. The main salon is also equipped with a complete entertainment centre including a 42" plasma TV and DirecTV satellite. 'One More Toy' provides luxurious accommodation for twelve charter guests in six glorious staterooms. The master stateroom has an owner's office and study, a king sized four-poster bed and his & hers en-suite bathrooms with marble flooring. A VIP stateroom and four further comfortable guests staterooms all with their own en-suite bathrooms, mean this yacht can cater for twelve guests in consummate luxury.

SPECIFICATIONS:	'ONE MORE TOY'
Length Overall:	47.24 m m (155')
Beam:	8.53m (28')
Builder:	Christensen
Guests:	12 guests in 6 staterooms
Charter Area:	Please enquire
Charter Price:	From $252,400 / week
Sale Price:	Please enquire
Central Agents:	**Mark Elliott**
	mark@iyc.com / +1 305 794 1167

For Sale & Charter
'KATHARINE'

INTERNATIONAL YACHT COLLECTION
FORT LAUDERDALE
1850 SE 17th Street - Suite 301
Fort Lauderdale, FL 33316. USA
T: +1 954 522 2323
F: +1 954 522 2333

INTERNATIONAL YACHT COLLECTION
NEWPORT
Casey's Marina, Spring Wharf
Newport, RI 02840. USA
T: +1 401 849 0834
F: +1 401 849 0835

INTERNATIONAL YACHT COLLECTION
PALM BEACH
4200 North Flagler Drive
West Palm Beach, FL 33407
T: +1 561 844 4141
F: +1 561 845 8774

INTERNATIONAL YACHT COLLECTION
SINT MAARTEN, W.I.
Isle de Sol Marina, Airport Road
Sint Maarten, Netherlands Antilles
T: +1 599 544 2515
F: +1 599 544 2833

INTERNATIONAL YACHT COLLECTION
SINT MAARTEN, W.I.
Port de Plaisance Marina
Union Road, Cole Bay, Phillipsburg
Sint Maarten, Netherlands Antilles
T: +1 599 544 3780
F: +1 599 544 3779

INTERNATIONAL YACHT COLLECTION
NASSAU, BAHAMAS
Atlantis
P.O. Box C R 56766 #401
Nassau, Bahamas
T: +1 954 6814644 or
T: +1 242 363 4458
F: +1 242 363 4481

INTERNATIONAL YACHT COLLECTION
MONACO
Palais Majestic, 23 Albert 1er
MC 98000, Monaco
T: +377 97 98 24 24
F: +377 97 98 10 13

www.iyc.com

The 177' motor yacht 'Katharine' was originally built as 'Seahawk' in 2001 and at the time was Trinity's flagship yacht. When her current owner purchased the vessel, she went through an interior refit designed by Marie Meiko. It is evident that the owner spared no expense to ensure that the vessel now embodies the finest taste and refinement. With a recent refit in 2006, 'Katharine' has accommodation for twelve guests in six stylish staterooms, all with en-suite facilities. The main saloon is amply furnished with three large sofas, French antique chairs, a game table and two cocktail tables that offer many unique conversation and entertainment areas.

SPECIFICATIONS:	'KATHARINE'
Length Overall:	53.9m (177')
Beam:	9.4m (31')
Draught:	2.3m (7'5")
Builder:	Trinity Yachts
Guests:	12 guests in 6 staterooms
Crew:	12
Sale Price:	Please enquire
Charter Price:	US$245,000 / week
Central Agent:	**Mark Elliott**
	mark@iyc.com / +1 305 794 1167

For Sale
'STARSHIP'

**INTERNATIONAL YACHT COLLECTION
FORT LAUDERDALE**
1850 SE 17th Street - Suite 301
Fort Lauderdale, FL 33316. USA
T: +1 954 522 2323
F: +1 954 522 2333

**INTERNATIONAL YACHT COLLECTION
NEWPORT**
Casey's Marina, Spring Wharf
Newport, RI 02840. USA
T: +1 401 849 0834
F: +1 401 849 0835

**INTERNATIONAL YACHT COLLECTION
PALM BEACH**
4200 North Flagler Drive
West Palm Beach, FL 33407
T: +1 561 844 4141
F: +1 561 845 8774

**INTERNATIONAL YACHT COLLECTION
SINT MAARTEN, W.I.**
Isle de Sol Marina, Airport Road
Sint Maarten, Netherlands Antilles
T: +1 599 544 2515
F: +1 599 544 2833

**INTERNATIONAL YACHT COLLECTION
SINT MAARTEN, W.I.**
Port de Plaisance Marina
Union Road, Cole Bay, Phillipsburg
Sint Maarten, Netherlands Antilles
T: +1 599 544 3780
F: +1 599 544 3779

**INTERNATIONAL YACHT COLLECTION
NASSAU, BAHAMAS**
Atlantis
P.O. Box C R 56766 #401
Nassau, Bahamas
T: +1 954 6814644 or
T: +1 242 363 4458
F: +1 242 363 4481

**INTERNATIONAL YACHT COLLECTION
MONACO**
Palais Majestic, 23 Albert 1er
MC 98000, Monaco
T: +377 97 98 24 24
F: +377 97 98 10 13

www.iyc.com

'Starship' is a stunning and classic cruising yacht with vast areas for either entertainment or relaxation. The yacht offers three casual dining areas, including one formal dining area and a bar area, so makes an ideal charter boat for entertaining. Guests can enjoy the superior views from the sun-deck whilst relaxing on the sun pads or enjoying the Jacuzzi. 'Starship' can comfortably accommodate ten guests in five spacious staterooms, all with en-suite facilities and full entertainment facilities. Her main master stateroom has a king size bed, a walk-in closet, an en-suite bathroom with shower, a 30" flat screen TV and a comfortable sitting area. She also has four further guest staterooms, two with king sized double beds, one with a queen bed and Pullman and the last with twin beds. All the guest cabins have full electronic entertainment, including 22" flat screens. 'Starship' also has Quantum stabilizers and a large array of watersports equipment for the energetic.

SPECIFICATIONS: 'STARSHIP'	
Length Overall:	43.6m (143')
Beam:	7.25m (23' 10")
Accommodation:	10 guests + 10 crew
Engines:	Caterpillar 3512B
Maximum Speed:	17 knots
Cruising Speed:	12 knots
Sale Price:	Please enquire
Central Agent:	**Mark Elliott**
	mark@iyc.com / +1 305 794 1167

For Sale
'DOMANI'

Launched in August 2004, 'Domani' is the third Benetti Vision with an elegant interior by the highly acclaimed interior designer Francois Zuretti.

The master cabin is situated forward on the main deck with a king sized bed positioned in the centre of the room. There is an adjoining study with a small pullout bed. On the lower deck are two double staterooms with queen sized beds. Located amidship on the same deck are two twin bedded cabins with additional Pullman bunks. The yacht sleeps ten guests comfortably.

The sun deck is fantastic with a cocktail bar, barbecue, Jacuzzi, plenty of space for sunbathing and a relaxing panoramic sitting area.

SPECIFICATIONS:	'DOMANI'
Length Overall:	45m (147' 6")
Beam:	9.26m (30' 5")
Draught:	2.72m (8' 11")
Builder:	Benetti
Guests:	10 guests in 5 staterooms
Sale Price:	Please enquire
Central Agents:	**Mark Elliott**
	mark@iyc.com / +1 305 794 1167
	Frank Grzeszczak
	fg@iyc.com / +1 954 494 7096

For Charter
'HOKULANI'

**INTERNATIONAL YACHT COLLECTION
FORT LAUDERDALE**
1850 SE 17th Street - Suite 301
Fort Lauderdale, FL 33316. USA
T: +1 954 522 2323
F: +1 954 522 2333

**INTERNATIONAL YACHT COLLECTION
NEWPORT**
Casey's Marina, Spring Wharf
Newport, RI 02840. USA
T: +1 401 849 0834
F: +1 401 849 0835

**INTERNATIONAL YACHT COLLECTION
PALM BEACH**
4200 North Flagler Drive
West Palm Beach, FL 33407
T: +1 561 844 4141
F: +1 561 845 8774

**INTERNATIONAL YACHT COLLECTION
SINT MAARTEN, W.I.**
Isle de Sol Marina, Airport Road
Sint Maarten, Netherlands Antilles
T: +1 599 544 2515
F: +1 599 544 2833

**INTERNATIONAL YACHT COLLECTION
SINT MAARTEN, W.I.**
Port de Plaisance Marina
Union Road, Cole Bay, Phillipsburg
Sint Maarten, Netherlands Antilles
T: +1 599 544 3780
F: +1 599 544 3779

**INTERNATIONAL YACHT COLLECTION
NASSAU, BAHAMAS**
Atlantis
P.O. Box C R 56766 #401
Nassau, Bahamas
T: +1 954 6814644 or
T: +1 242 363 4458
F: +1 242 363 4481

**INTERNATIONAL YACHT COLLECTION
MONACO**
Palais Majestic, 23 Albert 1er
MC 98000, Monaco
T: +377 97 98 24 24
F: +377 97 98 10 13

www.iyc.com

'Hokulani' is a beautiful and functional new Palmer Johnson 150' performance motor yacht, designed by Nuvolari & Lenard. This superb superyacht provides luxury accommodation for up to twelve guests in five cabins and she has a fantastic crew for select charter vacations.

This luxury motor yacht offers a sleek raised pilot house which has masterfully fused fashion and function. 'Hokulani' has some revolutionary new ideas too, such as a fly bridge which features a glass atrium roof panel that slides fore and aft so guests can choose whether to cruise either in the sun or in the shade. Further clever uses of space include a custom swim platform with a self-deploying ladder and a hydraulically powered tender garage.

SPECIFICATIONS: 'HOKULANI'

Length Overall:	45.72m (150')
Beam:	8.36m (27' 6")
Accommodation:	12 guests + 7 crew
Builder:	Palmer Johnson
Charter Area:	Please enquire
Charter Price:	Please enquire
	charter@iyc.com

For Sale & Charter
'BIG CITY'

INTERNATIONAL YACHT COLLECTION
FORT LAUDERDALE
1850 SE 17th Street - Suite 301
Fort Lauderdale, FL 33316. USA
T: +1 954 522 2323
F: +1 954 522 2333

INTERNATIONAL YACHT COLLECTION
NEWPORT
Casey's Marina, Spring Wharf
Newport, RI 02840. USA
T: +1 401 849 0834
F: +1 401 849 0835

INTERNATIONAL YACHT COLLECTION
PALM BEACH
4200 North Flagler Drive
West Palm Beach, FL 33407
T: +1 561 844 4141
F: +1 561 845 8774

INTERNATIONAL YACHT COLLECTION
SINT MAARTEN, W.I.
Isle de Sol Marina, Airport Road
Sint Maarten, Netherlands Antilles
T: +1 599 544 2515
F: +1 599 544 2833

INTERNATIONAL YACHT COLLECTION
SINT MAARTEN, W.I.
Port de Plaisance Marina
Union Road, Cole Bay, Phillipsburg
Sint Maarten, Netherlands Antilles
T: +1 599 544 3780
F: +1 599 544 3779

INTERNATIONAL YACHT COLLECTION
NASSAU, BAHAMAS
Atlantis
P.O. Box C R 56766 #401
Nassau, Bahamas
T: +1 954 6814644 or
T: +1 242 363 4458
F: +1 242 363 4481

INTERNATIONAL YACHT COLLECTION
MONACO
Palais Majestic, 23 Albert 1er
MC 98000, Monaco
T: +377 97 98 24 24
F: +377 97 98 10 13

www.iyc.com

'Big City' is a 42.97m (140' 11") semi-displacement, aluminium hulled yacht built by Trinity Yachts with an interior designed by Patrick Knowles. Launched in 2009 she offers everything expected of a contemporary luxury motor yacht.

On board she features great outdoor space, including a wonderful Jacuzzi on the sun-deck. There is luxurious accommodation for ten guests in five suites including a very spacious en-suite master stateroom positioned on the main deck. Built for entertainment, 'Big City' has the latest audio-visual equipment onboard including a Kaleidescape central movie/music server with universal touch screen remote control throughout, remote lighting control by Crestron touch screen throughout and iPod docking stations in all cabins.

SPECIFICATIONS: 'BIG CITY'	
Length Overall:	42.97m (140' 11")
Beam:	8.51m (27' 11")
Builder:	Trinity Yachts
Accommodation:	10 guests + 9 crew
Sale Price:	Please enquire
Charter Price:	Please enquire
	charter@iyc.com
Joint Central Agent:	**Kevin Bonnie** - kbonnie@iyc.com
	+33 616 39 1959

For Sale & Charter
'VICTORIA DEL MAR'

Built by Moonen Shipyards in 2001, the 36.9m 'Victoria Del Mar's elegant decor accentuates her European ancestry. Boasting luxurious accommodation for ten guests in five staterooms as well as seven crew in four cabins, the spacious master stateroom is located on the main deck and features a full complement of entertainment electronics, as well as his and her en-suite baths which are joined by a shower for two.

Rich dark stained cherry wood and contemporary fabrics set the mood of the beautiful salon and dining area. The yacht's main salon is separated from the dining salon by a centre column and is complete with a bar with stools and a hidden state-of-the-art 42" plasma television/video system.

'Victoria Del Mar' is now offered for sale and charter by International Yacht Collection.

SPECIFICATIONS: 'VICTORIA DEL MAR'	
Length Overall:	36.9m (121')
Beam:	8.2m (26' 11")
Draught:	2.4m (8')
Accommodation:	10 guests + 7 crew
Builder:	Moonen
Charter Area:	Please enquire
Charter Price:	Please enquire
Sale Price:	Please enquire
Central Agent:	**Jim Eden**
	E: jeden@iyc.com
	T: +1 954 258 3434

For Sale
NEWCASTLE 5500

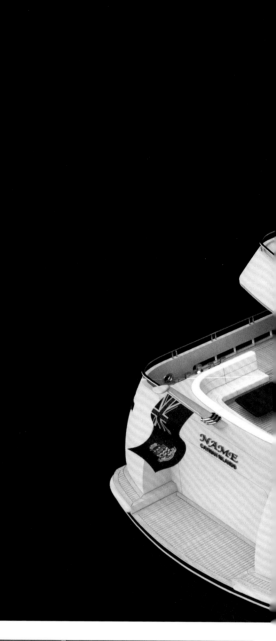

INTERNATIONAL YACHT COLLECTION
FORT LAUDERDALE
1850 SE 17th Street - Suite 301
Fort Lauderdale, FL 33316. USA
T: +1 954 522 2323
F: +1 954 522 2333

INTERNATIONAL YACHT COLLECTION
NEWPORT
Casey's Marina, Spring Wharf
Newport, RI 02840. USA
T: +1 401 849 0834
F: +1 401 849 0835

INTERNATIONAL YACHT COLLECTION
PALM BEACH
4200 North Flagler Drive
West Palm Beach, FL 33407
T: +1 561 844 4141
F: +1 561 845 8774

INTERNATIONAL YACHT COLLECTION
SINT MAARTEN, W.I.
Isle de Sol Marina, Airport Road
Sint Maarten, Netherlands Antilles
T: +1 599 544 2515
F: +1 599 544 2833

INTERNATIONAL YACHT COLLECTION
SINT MAARTEN, W.I.
Port de Plaisance Marina
Union Road, Cole Bay, Phillipsburg
Sint Maarten, Netherlands Antilles
T: +1 599 544 3780
F: +1 599 544 3779

INTERNATIONAL YACHT COLLECTION
NASSAU, BAHAMAS
Atlantis
P.O. Box C R 56766 #401
Nassau, Bahamas
T: +1 954 6814644 or
T: +1 242 363 4458
F: +1 242 363 4481

INTERNATIONAL YACHT COLLECTION
MONACO
Palais Majestic, 23 Albert 1er
MC 98000, Monaco
T: +377 97 98 24 24
F: +377 97 98 10 13

www.iyc.com

Due to be launched in 2010, the Newvastle 5500 has been designed to carry an owner's party of twelve in six stylish staterooms. These consist of two master staterooms, one on the upper deck with a 270 degree exterior view and the other on the main deck featuring eight oval windows almost 2 metres tall, for spectacular ocean views. The main deck will feature an expansive main salon and dining area, while the upper deck will feature a panoramic sky lounge area, as well as the captain's cabin and one of the master staterooms. Once completed, the Newcastle 5500 will provide the highest level of comfort for her guests in all sea conditions and will be capable of navigating the globe safely, with her twin Caterpillar engines offering trans-atlantic range.

SPECIFICATIONS:	NEWCASTLE 5500
Length Overall:	54.97m (180' 5")
Beam:	10.25m (33' 1")
Draught:	2.93m (9' 1")
Builder:	Newcastle Shipyards
Guests:	12 guests in 6 staterooms
Sale Price:	Please enquire
Central Agent:	**Jim Eden** - jeden@iyc.com
	T: +1 954 258 3434
	Thom Conboy - tconboy@iyc.com
	+1 561 441 6131

ADVERTISER INDEX

53	Abeking & Rasmussen	123	Marina Barcelona 92
136	Aegean Yacht	34	Moonen Shipyards
480	Antibes Shipservices	15	Oceanco
124	Antibes Yacht Show	8	Oceanstyle
120	Arredamenti Porto	32	Oyster Marine
141	Burger Boat Company	20	Palmer Johnson
3/6	Burgess Yachts	118/126	Pantaenius Insurance
4	Camper & Nicholsons International	30	Peri Yachts
41	CMN Yachts	39	Perini Navi
131	CRN	122	Philippe Briand
24	Curvelle	38	Picchiotti-Vitruvius Explorer Series
130	Cyrus Yachts	44	Platinum Yachts
14/52/137	Drettmann	128	Princess Yachts
117/119/121	Dubois Yachts	112	Quantum Marine
16	Fairline	36	Rolls-Royce Motor Cars
138	FIPA	134	Sanlorenzo
482	Fraser Yachts	50	Soraya Yachts
22	Hakvoort Shipyard	48/142	Sunboats
12	Hargrave Custom Yachts	18	Sunseeker
132	Horizon Yachts	26	Trinity Yachts
46	IAG Yachts	42	Ulysse Nardin
484	International Yacht Collection	40	Vitters Shipyard
140	ISA Yachts	54	Wally Yachts
116	Jotun Yacht Paints	114	Watkins Superyachts
28/37	Lürssen Yachts	10	Yachting Partners International

PHOTOGRAPHERS

All photographs copyright of the contibuting company, except as stated below:

Page	Feature	Photographer
104 - 105	MB92 (Sedation Images)	Thierry Ameller
238-239	'Cyrus One'	Ed Holt
358 - 367	Vitters	Ed Holt (exterior), Albert Brunsting (interior)
432 - 439	CMN 'Slipstream'	Guillaume Plisson (exteriors) and Simon McBride (interiors)
450 - 459	Lurssen Yachts	Klaus Jordan
510 - 511	'Amnesia'	Ed Holt
512 - 513	'Cloud 9'	Yvann Zedda
514 - 515	'Natori'	Jerome Kelagopian (profile) and David Churchill (interiors)
516 - 517	'Ethereal'	Jeff Brown
518 - 519	'Anjilis'	Dana Jinkins
520 - 521	'Xanadu'	Thierry Amelier
530 - 531	'Siren'	Klaus Jordan
606 - 607	'Katharine'	Jim Raycroft
614-615	'Big City'	Jim Raycroft
616-617	'Victoria Del Mar'	Jim Raycroft